Gay Priori

Gay Priori

A Queer Critical Legal Studies Approach to Law Reform

LIBBY ADLER

Duke University Press / Durham and London / 2018

© 2018 DUKE UNIVERSITY PRESS / All rights reserved
Printed in the United States of America on acid-free paper ∞
Text designed by Courtney Leigh Baker.
Cover design and illustration by Julienne Alexander.
Typeset in Garamond Premier Pro by
Westchester Publishing Services

Library of Congress Cataloging-in-Publication Data
Names: Adler, Libby S., [date] author.
Title: Gay priori : a queer critical legal studies approach to law
    reform / Libby Adler.
Description: Durham : Duke University Press, 2018. | Includes
    bibliographical references and index.
Identifiers: LCCN 2017043523 (print)
LCCN 2017047661 (ebook)
ISBN 9780822371663 (ebook)
ISBN 9780822371182 (hardcover : alk. paper)
ISBN 9780822371496 (pbk. : alk. paper)
Subjects: LCSH: Gays—Legal status, laws, etc.—United States. |
    Homosexuality—Law and legislation—United States. | Law
    reform—United States. | Sexual minorities—United States—
    Social conditions. | Marginality, Social—Economic aspects—
    United States.
Classification: LCC KF4754.5 (ebook) | LCC KF4754.5 .A35 2018
    (print) | DDC 342.7308/7—dc23
LC record available at https://lccn.loc.gov/2017043523

For José and Natalie

Contents

Acknowledgments

I wish I knew a word that encompassed the meanings "beloved friend," "indispensable colleague," and "intellectual and political ally." If such a term does exist, it describes three people in my life to whom—and for whom—I am endlessly grateful. Janet Halley has been providing wisdom, comradeship, and unbelievable food for many years. She advanced this project in one thousand ways, from inception to fruition. It is impossible to overstate the value of her support to me personally or to the academic scene in which I do most of my learning. Aziza Ahmed was a find-and-a-half. Time and again, she nonchalantly and (it often seems) unintentionally teaches me something crucially important while going about the business of her smart, gutsy, and politically engaged work and conducting herself in a generous fashion that comes so naturally to her you could almost not notice it. Rashmi Dyal-Chand is my sister-from-another-mister. Every facet of my job is more gratifying because we are on the same team. She always can be counted on to have more confidence in me than I have in myself and her loyalty is more stalwart than anyone is entitled to expect. The constant dialogue I have enjoyed with these cherished friends enriches my work and my life.

Karl Klare was generous with me far beyond the call of duty, providing careful notes and talking over ideas literally for hours. Karl was my Torts professor in 1991. I thought at the time that he was the best teacher I had ever had, inspiring my deep pleasure in the study of law. More than twenty-five years later, it remains true.

Margaret Burnham, Daniel Medwed, Lucy Williams, Gabriel Arkles, and Michael Boucai all gave me helpful comments and led me to important sources. Suzanna Walters and Jyoti Puri read drafts, provided enormously helpful feedback, and aided me greatly in addressing my audience.

I presented portions of the manuscript and received important comments at the Northeastern University School of Law faculty colloquium, especially from a particularly astute discussant, Rachel Rosenbloom. I delivered portions at a proseminar on Queer Critical Legal Theory (sponsored by the Institute for Global Law and Policy at Harvard Law School) and thank my cohorts in that ongoing conversation for terrific insights, especially Adrienne Davis and Prabha Kotiswaran. I also received feedback on portions of the work at the Queer Theory Workshop at Columbia University organized by Katherine Franke and Beth Povinelli, and at the Boston area Graduate Consortium in Women's Studies organized by Jyoti Puri, Lisa Lowe, and Kimberly Juanita Brown. I am grateful for the help I received from my colleagues and comrades across these events.

My dean, Jeremy Paul, enthusiastically supported this project from the outset, as he does the scholarly endeavors of all Northeastern law faculty, even in lean times. He also read carefully and provided terrific feedback. I benefited from lunchtime conversations with Duncan Kennedy, who always advances my thinking by a long jump. I was fortunate to work closely with Chase Strangio of the ACLU LGBT and HIV Project, and Jim Rowan, Director of Clinical Programming at Northeastern University School of Law. I gained genuine insight from their work with low-income LGBTQ people and from getting the opportunity to join them in some small portion of that work. BostonGLASS has been a friend to this project through its own work with low-income LGBTQ youth and through our collaborative efforts on legal issues that the youth face. Darby Hickey led me to stories and sources regarding the legal issues facing trans sex workers.

Jackie LaCorte provided administrative support and law librarians Alfreda Russell and Catherine Biondo lent research support. Over the course of several years, research assistants, mostly now graduated, contributed to the research and analysis that eventually found its way into this book, including kt crossman, Margaret Laffan, Emily Miller, Amanda Montel, and Sarah Petrie. Ken Wissoker, Jade Brooks, and Olivia Polk of Duke University Press have been patient and supportive editors.

I am, as always, grateful for the friendship of Wendy Zazik, Rebecca Dowling, and Betsy Hinden. I thank my brother, David Adler, who kindly read random installments. I am fortunate to have had the support of my father, George Adler, who died as the manuscript neared completion, and to carry the memory of my mother, Elaine Adler.

My two children, José and Natalie Adler, are good, soulful, and strong. Everything is more meaningful to me because they inhabit this world. I dedicate this book and all of life's work to them, with love.

Chapters 1, 2, and 5 include arguments I made in earlier forms. I revised and recontextualized the arguments for this book. See "Just the Facts: The Perils of Expert Testimony and Findings of Fact in Gay Rights Litigation," in *Unbound: Harvard Journal of the Legal Left* 7 (2011): 1–38, http://www.legalleft .org/category/2011-issue/; "Gay Rights and Lefts: Rights Critique and Distributive Analysis for Real Law Reform," in *Harvard Civil Rights-Civil Liberties Law Review* (Amicus) 46 (2011): 1–19, http://harvardcrcl.org/cr-cl-presents-a -colloquium-gay-rights-and-lefts-rights-critique-and-the-distributive-analysis /; "T: Appending Transgender Equal Rights to Gay, Lesbian and Bisexual Equal Rights," in *Columbia Journal of Gender and Law* 19, no. 3 (2010): 595–15; "The Gay Agenda," in *Michigan Journal of Gender and Law* 16, no. 1 (2009): 147–216; and "An Essay on the Production of Youth Prostitution," in *Maine Law Review* 55, no. 1 (2003): 191–210.

Priorities

In 2004, Hastings College of Law, part of California's public university system, rejected the application of the Christian Legal Society to become a "recognized student organization." That status would have entitled the Christian Legal Society to receive law school funding, use the law school's logo, and take advantage of its publicity venues to promote its events. Hastings's policy requires recognized student organizations to be open to any enrolled student, but the Christian Legal Society explicitly excludes from membership people who engage in "unrepentant homosexual activities." The Christian Legal Society requested an exemption from the school's policy but was turned down, giving rise to a lawsuit that traveled all the way up to the U.S. Supreme Court.

Hastings was joined in the defense of its policy by the National Center for Lesbian Rights (NCLR), a major lesbian, gay, bisexual, and transgender (LGBT) law reform organization with offices in the Bay Area, and Jenner and Block, a large national law firm with an office in Washington, DC, that maintains a specialty in Supreme Court litigation. The powerful alliance proved successful. In 2010, in *Christian Legal Society v. Martinez*, Justice Ruth Bader Ginsburg found on behalf of five justices that Hastings's nondiscrimination requirement was "viewpoint-neutral" under the First Amendment and that the Christian Legal Society was not entitled to an exemption under the Constitution.[1]

Meanwhile, also in 2010, at the very same time that Hastings awaited the Supreme Court's ruling, another controversy was brewing just outside its campus gates. San Francisco was debating a proposed ordinance known as "sit-lie." The substance of the ordinance, which was ultimately passed by referendum, is a prohibition against sitting or lying down on a city sidewalk between 7 AM and 11 PM on penalty of arrest and possible fines, community service, or jail time, depending on whether it is a first or subsequent offense.[2] The law was proposed by Mayor Gavin Newsom, who gained national attention in 2004 for defiantly ordering the issuance of marriage licenses to same-sex couples prior to the cascade of state and federal lawsuits sorting out the legality of same-sex marriage in California. Newsom's ordinance was intended to deter loitering and panhandling by the city's homeless population.

An estimated four thousand youth are among the homeless in San Francisco, and surveys suggest that up to 40 percent of them identify as lesbian, gay, bisexual, or transgender.[3] They are disproportionately black and Latino/a.[4] In spite of the well-known overrepresentation of LGBT youth among the homeless—in San Francisco and in many of our nation's major cities—I was unable to find any trace of an organized LGBT presence in the fight to stop sit-lie. The homelessness organizations campaigned against the ordinance alone and to no avail.

Thousands of gay and trans young people face arrest under sit-lie, but no throng of gay law students ever sought admittance to the Christian Legal Society. So why did all of those LGBT law reform resources go into the battle over the latter rather than the former? Why did these major players in the movement for LGBT advancement dedicate themselves to defending a student organization policy that affects nearly (or perhaps precisely) no one and is effectively a matter of principle rather than to a fight happening simultaneously, on the same city block, that affects so many of the most vulnerable in the LGBT community?

Gay Priori begins with the premise that this juxtaposition—of the full-throttle Christian Legal Society litigation against the absence of an organized LGBT presence in the fight over sit-lie—reflects distorted priorities on the part of the leading LGBT advocacy organizations. Access to marriage, as any observer knows, was at the forefront of the battle for LGBT advancement for more than a decade, along with antidiscrimination protection, hate crimes legislation, and the repeal of Don't Ask, Don't Tell. Even now that same-sex marriage is a constitutional right in the United States, whether religious exemptions will come to swallow up that right has become the most embattled terrain. These priorities have garnered the most resources and attention, and they have brought significant benefits to the LGBT community.

They also neglect pressing needs in the most marginalized sectors of that community. LGBT people are overrepresented among foster children, the homeless, the poor, and the food-insecure. They are disproportionately vulnerable to police abuse, incarceration, HIV, insufficient access to health care, and unwanted pregnancy (yes, pregnancy). While antidiscrimination reform and marriage may make some small incursion into these conditions, they are hardly the way to effectuate real redistribution for the benefit of the most vulnerable members of the LGBT community. Why, when the mainstream LGBT movement is experiencing a pinnacle of its success and influence, do its law reform priorities continue to neglect those most in need?

One possible explanation for the priorities of the mainstream LGBT advocacy organizations is that the donors, executive directors, general counsels, and board members of those organizations are drawn predominantly from an adequately housed and well-nourished class. Their experience of being gay may well involve discrimination, but for most of them it probably does not involve homelessness. The resulting class bias is certainly plausible as a partial explanation, but this relative privilege of gay elites does not explain the movement's priorities adequately. On the contrary, several of the major LGBT organizations have devoted resources to studying LGBT youth. They are acutely aware that the streets of our cities are populated by LGBT kids selling sex, shoplifting, and panhandling to survive. They know very well that LGBT kids run away and are kicked out by their parents at a higher rate than the general population of youth.

Professionals in the LGBT human services sector have responded to the phenomenon, contending with the usual obstacle of insufficient resources to serve everyone as well as they would surely like, and some LGBT legal advocates have represented these kids in juvenile or child welfare proceedings. LGBT law reformers, however, who have spent years splashing the front page with news of their latest triumph, have been of little help to homeless LGBT kids. Proposals to devote more resources to serving vulnerable LGBT youth abound, but law reform targeting the basic conditions of their daily lives is scant. Why, despite keen awareness in the organized, professional LGBT world, does the LGBT law reform agenda appear not to be designed with these kids' lives in mind? Why does sit-lie not appear on the LGBT law reform radar while so many resources go into fighting a matter of principle?

LGBT Equal Rights Discourse

Gay Priori proposes that a crucial factor in explaining the priorities of the mainstream LGBT law reform movement is the power of LGBT equal rights discourse. As I use the term, *LGBT equal rights discourse* refers to a host of narrative practices evident in contemporary U.S. LGBT equal rights advocacy, including legal advocacy, lay advocacy, and public relations, as well as academic and empirical work that supports advocacy efforts. The discourse comprises a cluster of constituent strands that depict, characterize, and represent LGBT people—recognizable tropes that tell us about our virtues, our vulnerabilities, and our relationships. It also encompasses strands that appease the requirements of American constitutional and antidiscrimination law, the American civil rights progress narrative, and the neoliberal emphasis on personal responsibility. The term refers neither to equality nor to rights in general, both of which cover a vast conceptual territory, much of which is totally unaddressed by the argument in this book. Instead, LGBT *equal rights discourse* is meant to summon to mind a collection of practices that fuse into a current and recognizable pattern—one in which LGBT law reform is deeply immersed.

The well-intentioned leaders of the LGBT law reform movement are participants in a culture war, the terms of which are familiar to all. The struggle is feverish, and its exigencies play a powerful role in driving the political agenda and sidelining nonconforming alternatives. Gay rights advocates have hotly pursued the dream of formal equality, prioritizing antidiscrimination reforms and imagining the zenith of gay emancipation to be access to marriage. The discourse of LGBT equal rights that advances these objectives, however, produces myopia, so that access to marriage, antidiscrimination protection, hate crime legislation, and international human rights reforms that mimic American conceptions of equal protection come easily into view, while a broader array of law reform possibilities is eclipsed. Understandably, the discriminatory logic of cultural conservatism provokes habitual insistence on formal equality by LGBT advocates, but that constant call and response unnecessarily entrenches conceptual boundaries around what it means to make progress on behalf of LGBT people. As we fight, we stifle our own imaginations. Consequently, the largely symbolic *Christian Legal Society* case is readily intelligible as an LGBT legal issue while sit-lie and scores of other legal issues that have far more impact on the daily lives of our most marginalized community members go unnoticed—even by those who care deeply and want to help.

In 2012, Chad Griffin, the new president of the Human Rights Campaign (HRC), visited a shelter for homeless youth in Utah. HRC is the national gay lobby and the largest LGBT civil rights organization in the country, claiming more than 1.5 million members and supporters. In conjunction with his trip, Griffin issued this statement: "We can and must continue to push for federal advances like workplace protections and marriage equality, but we must simultaneously work to better the lives of LGBT youth. That means many things—it means making schools safer; it means calling out and eradicating homophobia and transphobia in popular culture; it means settling for nothing less than full equality."[5] Griffin gave a few subsequent media interviews, including one to the *Washington Blade* (an LGBT newspaper), in which he named homelessness among LGBT youth as an issue that garners too little attention. He cited the need for more public funds to provide direct services to LGBT youth and lamented the rejection (by parents, teachers, and churches) that results in their disproportionate homelessness, noting that LGBT kids represent as much as 40 percent of the homeless youth in Salt Lake City.[6]

This was Griffin's first trip as HRC president, and he made it to a youth shelter. He cannot be faulted for failing to care about homelessness among LGBT youth. But once he got there, he did not know what to do other than call for equality and condemn homo- and transphobia. It did not seem to occur to Griffin, on the occasion of visiting a homeless shelter, to urge that the LGBT organizations join the fight against homelessness. The mind-set that hid that reformist course from him is precisely the same mind-set that endows Newsom with a reputation for allegiance to the gay community. Newsom's brash and premature order that marriage licenses be issued to same-sex couples in San Francisco notwithstanding, he is also the man responsible for subjecting homeless youth, not unlike those Griffin visited in Utah, to arrest for sitting down.

That mind-set is a consequence of LGBT equal rights discourse, and it has played an important role in occluding reform alternatives that are oriented toward redistribution rather than formal equality, though to be sure these two goals often overlap. A purpose of the book is nonetheless to illustrate how the discourse has steered LGBT law reform objectives toward formal equality, neglecting and even impeding law reform that would foreground redistributive goals. *Gay Priori* proposes an alternative that would reverse these priorities.

The vocabulary in this book draws a sharp distinction between formal equality, equal rights, and antidiscrimination, on the one hand, and redistribution, on the other. This is not a total giving up on equality (or an embrace of discrimination); nor is it an insistence that a redistribution of resources cannot be properly conceived as an equality project. It is fully compatible with the message of the book to read it as a reimagining of the equality objective. The discourse of LGBT equal rights has been so powerful, though, that using a different vocabulary represents an effort to disengage it and to make a shift to a different set of priorities and objectives.

To focus on the discursive aspect of LGBT equal rights means that if we make a deliberate effort at critical examination, we can discern tropes and patterns in the arguments, factual assertions, and narrative tales that compose the overall endeavor. From the critical position I propose, we are not assessing arguments for their force, claims for their truth, or facts for their accuracy; rather, we are looking for evidence of these tropes and patterns and then assessing them for their productive power. LGBT equal rights discourse, including professional legal argument as well as less technical versions offered by and for non-lawyers, plays a powerful role in producing LGBT identities, as well as what looks to be innate desire for specific law reforms.

What is tricky about a discourse is that we both deploy it and subject our-selves to it. We are its instruments as well as its subjects,[7] so that even as we par-ticipate in it, it exerts power to orient our perceptions. A discourse can make some ideas seem natural and others inconceivable, depending on whether the ideas make sense according to the terms of the discourse—whether they sound in its key. A discourse should be understood not as the sole determina-tive factor controlling one's every thought but, rather, as a network of deep cultural understandings, shared and also perpetually under construction, that establishes conceptual boundaries.

This book, like many others that have gone before, assumes a critical pos-ture toward LGBT identities. It does not, however, propose jettisoning these identities altogether as a path to liberation; nor does it propose abandoning the whole project of a movement to advance the interests of LGBT people in favor of a strict antipoverty movement. Whether those things would be desirable is beside the point because they are implausible. While we who take seriously the insights of critical theory regard LGBT and other identity categories as histori-cally contingent, an aspect of the knowledge that we produce rather than a part of nature, we ought also to appreciate that liberating ourselves entirely from the discourses that are constantly producing our social and conceptual world is not realistic. For this reason, complete repudiation of LGBT identity or LGBT equal rights would be an artificial gesture. That does not mean we cannot push in the direction of resignification, but we cannot escape entirely the knowledge we inhabit.[8]

It is important to acknowledge that LGBT equal rights have brought many benefits to the LGBT community. Those benefits have been widely heralded in books, speeches, news articles, and judicial decisions. LGBT equal rights as a discursive practice, however, comes with costs that have been less thoroughly discussed. *Gay Priori* is an effort to shine a light on some of those costs and to offer an alternative way to think about law that could widen the expanse of reformist possibilities that are imaginable to us. The argument in *Gay Priori* extends its consideration beyond the winning of cases and the acquisition of formal rights, to the production of LGBT people and the distribution of re-sources. This is not to claim that a redistributive alternative is divorced from the discursive conditions in which it is generated. Its virtues instead lie in being the product of critical methods that shine a new light on LGBT reformist agenda setting and in being based on an explicit normative preference for redistribut-ing access to safety, health, housing, nutrition, jobs, and income. *Gay Priori* employs a suite of critical methods drawn from queer and critical legal theory to illustrate some of the costs of LGBT equal rights discourse and to make the case that there are other ways to advance the interests of LGBT people.

Among the costs of LGBT equal rights discourse is the obscuring of the discourse's tendency to entrench identities, as well as distributions of power and resources, within the LGBT community, favoring the community's most privileged members on axes of race, class, age, and region. Those distributions, we will find, circle back and contribute again to our ideas about LGBT people and what we want from law, forming a highly productive discursive cycle that disadvantages marginalized constituencies and nonconforming policy proposals. Nothing here is a charge of nefarious intent to harm or exclude; it is, rather, a description of a circuit that, through conscious deliberation, can be critiqued and interrupted.

As many before me have complained, the advances made by the mainstream movement for LGBT people have disproportionately benefited the most privileged members of the LGBT community. We should not be leaving poverty issues such as homelessness to the poverty organizations and legal aid lawyers. The priorities of the LGBT movement, however, have been set within the terms of a powerful discourse, the bounds of which make it difficult to imagine another set of primary objectives that would benefit a different subset of LGBT people. To shift the focus to those most in need, LGBT advocates would have to apply a specific kind of intersectionality that not only takes into account race, class, age, region, and other factors, but also attunes itself to highly localized legal and economic conditions facing LGBT subconstituencies.

Gay Priori is about our law reform priorities. It is an argument about a discourse that plays an under-recognized role in shaping our priorities and in shaping us. LGBT people and our longing for equality do not preexist the discourse of LGBT equal rights. This is not a historical claim. It is a claim, rather, about the operation of a dynamic. LGBT people and our desire to be treated equally with straight people do not exist prior to LGBT equal rights discourse in a linear, temporal progression.[9] By our participation in the discourse, we are constantly producing ourselves and the breadth of changes we are capable of imagining. LGBT equal rights discourse has a hand in forming our ideas about ourselves and influencing what we want from the law.

In this respect, the analysis offered in *Gay Priori* is queer. Queer theory developed methods drawn from antecedent traditions in critical social thought, honing those methods with particular attention to gender and sexuality. Over the past three decades, queer theory has become quite rich and varied and means different things to different people. I have approached queer theory as lawyers notoriously do history, economics, psychology, and other fields: to pillage. The question animating my visit to queer theory has been: *What here could be of utility to those interested in social, economic, and racial justice on behalf of people marginalized by virtue of their gender or sexuality?* The argument therefore takes up only a fraction of what queer theory has to offer. The primary current of queer theory that runs through *Gay Priori* concerns the power of discourse to produce identity and desire.

Throughout *Gay Priori*, I consider LGBT equal rights arguments and claims not on their own terms and merits but from one step removed. How do those arguments and claims, and the empirical facts and narrative depictions marshaled in their support, reflect and mold what it means to be LGBT, giving LGBT identity a race, a class, a lifestyle, and a demeanor? How does that meaning engender in us desire for specific law reforms? And how do those law reforms, and the distributions that they effectuate, feed back into LGBT identity? In other words, how does our participation in LGBT equal rights discourse shape us and our law reform agenda? Critical methods can give us insight into these questions and prepare us to modify how we conceive of LGBT law reform so that alternatives in pursuit of redistributive objectives become more visible. Dwelling uncritically in LGBT equal rights discourse is not our only option. Rigorous law reform alternatives become visible once we tear our gaze away from its captivating and deceptively simple promise.

Left Politics

The dominant narrative of the past several years has been one of LGBT triumphalism. Commentators endlessly tout the victorious march of LGBT equal rights, pointing especially to achievements such as same-sex marriage and military inclusion. Many on the left, however, have felt riven over the priorities of LGBT law reform, vaguely distressed by its "mainstreaming" or "cooptation." Dissident voices have long been audible from the margins of sexuality and gender to those who have been willing to listen. Self-identified radicals and queers have criticized the mainstream LGBT advocacy organizations for neglecting the most marginalized constituencies, including the poor, people of color, trans people, sex workers, undocumented immigrants, prison inmates, HIV-positive people, the polyamorous, and practitioners of BDSM. Many of the existing critiques bemoan the corporatism of the major organizations, collusion with the bourgeois family ideal, and incompatibility of state regulation with genuine freedom. What happened, some leftist critics have queried, to the more radical politics of days gone by? The sexual liberation? The lesbian feminism? The race and class consciousness? The refusal to yield to all of capitalism's demands, including commercialism, militarism, and environmental degradation? How did our politics come to be all about the marital exemption from the estate tax and booking the highest-ranking White House official for the HRC gala?

While *Gay Priori* is not a polemic against anything that tends toward the mainstream, I nonetheless hope it will clarify and vindicate at least some of this hazy unease and disappointment on the left. For LGBT and LGBT-friendly readers who have felt internally split over whether to support same-sex marriage or the Don't Ask, Don't Tell repeal, not wanting to side with the homophobic right but unable to shake the nagging disquiet that there is something retrograde about the mainstream LGBT agenda, *Gay Priori* will speak into that dissonance with an explanation. I want us to see how we argued ourselves into this corner.

Left and queer critiques of the mainstream gay agenda abound, many of which have been profoundly influential in my thinking. *Gay Priori* nonetheless distinguishes itself from those that have gone before in at least two respects. First, it brings together assets from queer and left legal theory, extracting insights from each in what I hope will read as an unusually clear, concrete, and integrated explanation of the costs of LGBT equal rights discourse from a queer/left perspective. Second, *Gay Priori* expresses no antipathy toward the state or toward law. It engages law, making a granular-level inquiry into the possibilities for regulatory change. Law has real effects—not all of which are equally visible—on the daily life of every individual. We can use critical legal analysis to identify some of the levers that allocate resources and locate opportunities for change.

These opportunities, it will become clear, emerge on a small scale rather than in the form of wholesale emancipation. While the absence of a revolutionary vision may be dispiriting to some, the purpose is optimistic; it is to leave readers emboldened that alternatives to the current LGBT agenda are possible so that we can demand it of our leaders when they come to us seeking contributions and other forms of solidarity.

The goal of the book is to make conceivable a cognitive shift. For academic readers, whether oriented to the social sciences, the humanities, or law, I hope to instill some optimism that the field of law contains possibilities for critique and that strands of queer and critical legal theory can be put to practical reformist use. For legal advocates and activists willing to consider alternative strategies, I hope that *Gay Priori* helps to unlock the reformist imagination, showing how an adjustment in perspective opens up new possibilities for real change.

I hope, finally, to convey deep respect for decision and action, along with acceptance that none of us can know for sure what will be all of the consequences of our choices. The best we can do is to cast an ever broader net of thoughtfulness and responsibility.

What Follows

Part I describes and analyzes LGBT equal rights discourse. It is divided into three chapters, each of which isolates distinct strands of the discourse and draws attention to the underappreciated costs they impose.

Chapter 1 discusses some of the unique requirements of American judicial reasoning and the discursive elements that these requirements elicit from LGBT advocates. The chapter introduces the ideal of judicial neutrality and explores the charge of *judicial activism*, or politically motivated deviation from constitutional fidelity and deductive reasoning—a charge that has been a culture war mainstay. Deductive reasoning in the judicial context cannot, as leftist legal critics have argued for decades, live up to its pretense to political neutrality, and yet the maintenance of the pretense remains a preoccupation of American law. The result is a distinct set of discursive requirements designed to affirm judicial neutrality. In the context of courtroom battles, LGBT advocates have had no choice but to embroil themselves in this entwined discourse. Operating within the American constitutional structure, advocates must argue in terms that legitimate the system. The need for judicial legitimation is heightened by a stubborn indeterminacy of meaning that plagues concepts such as "equality." Chapter 1 argues that the problem of indeterminacy, the anxiety over judicial legitimacy that it inflames, and the resulting discourse of apolitical deductive reasoning, impose an under-recognized cost. As advocates strive to legitimate the logic of the legal regime in which they work, they simultaneously create the impression that inequalities that are left unaddressed are fair, or the result of natural, rather than legally constructed, hierarchies, rendering some inequities especially intransigent.

Chapter 2 is about the tremendous power of LGBT equal rights discourse to generate identities. The discourse produces its own archetypes—LGBT equal rights-bearing subjects. *Knowledge* about gay and trans people is a constant byproduct of LGBT advocacy. The chapter illustrates the process by which we become healthy and ill, ordinary and flamboyant, patriotic and traitorous, and domestic and perverse, as we march toward equality.

As Michel Foucault used the term and as it is now commonly used in queer theory,[10] *knowledge* is different from, say, *information*. Information is readily available for our reference or examination. In the case of knowledge, however, one must assume a deliberately critical posture to do more than merely *inhabit* it, rendering it an artifact available for study.[11] For example, much of the time we might uncritically inhabit the knowledge that the human population is divided into male and female when we carelessly ask, "Is it a boy or a girl?" With a little deliberate effort, however, we know that the duality of gender can be critiqued. We can contemplate (perhaps live in) transitivities, liminal gender identities, and intersexed bodies. The dichotomized gender system is a discourse; it organizes our perceptions, producing the knowledge that there are two. We may never rid ourselves entirely of the discourse of gender duality, but we can position ourselves to critically assess it and the knowledge that it produces.

Among the most prolific contemporary producers of knowledge about LGBT people is the Williams Institute, a gay rights think tank housed at the University of California, Los Angeles, and the major legal academic center for the support of LGBT advocacy. The Williams Institute fulfills its role by churning out a stream of facts about gay and trans people, same-sex couples, the effects of same-sex marriage on children, the benefits of same-sex marriage for state economies, and so on. An email missive from the Williams Institute to its supporters in 2013 read, "Children Reared by Female Couples Score Higher on Good Citizenship than Children Reared by Heterosexual Parents."[12] This conclusion was based on a study of Dutch children age eleven to thirteen raised in lesbian households, who apparently, on average, manage conflict and difference more productively than others in their peer group. So many studies now suggest spectacular outcomes for children raised in lesbian households that lesbian parents could be forgiven for expecting their kids to sprout capes and start fighting crime.

The Williams Institute and supportive social scientists have generated sufficient data on the equivalency or superiority of outcomes for children raised by same-sex parents that it has become irrational for a court to decide against gay parenting or same-sex marriage based on child welfare concerns. This has been an obvious rejoinder to cultural conservatives' assertions that children do not fare as well when raised by gay parents—an assertion that became increasingly difficult to maintain as such studies accumulated.

All of this fact generation contributes to the creation of archetypes, such as the civic-minded lesbian soccer mom, that are becoming increasingly recognizable to the popular eye. And empiricism is not the only vehicle for producing these archetypes. Gay rights advocates carefully select plaintiffs for high-profile courtroom battles, while outside the courtroom they make deft use of public relations (PR) campaigns and closely monitor depictions of gay characters on television and throughout popular culture, all in pursuit of strategically crafted ideal figures.

As advocates display LGBT virtues in the production of ideal archetypes, what must we do with our embarrassing relatives? If we are domestic, what of our sex workers? If we are bourgeois, what of our homeless? If we are the girl next door, what of our six-foot girls with extra-long lashes?

The archetypes, moreover, can be dizzyingly contradictory. In the battle against bullying, for example, advocates turn to data that illustrate the terrible consequences of stigma and rejection endured by LGBT youth. Rather than the cheerful, impossibly wholesome, civically engaged parent, LGBT advocates display her younger self by perhaps twenty years: the depressed, substance-abusing adolescent contemplating suicide. The contradiction represented by these two discursive types is unruly. What if our injured, suicidal selves show up while we are trying to establish our stolid well-being? What if our healthy capacity for social engagement materializes while we attempt to demonstrate how injured we are by stigma? Like the mad scientist who releases his greatest creation into the world, LGBT advocates cannot prevent the havoc that might be wrought when hostile forces deploy our archetypes against us. Drawing on the work of Foucault and Eve Kosofsky Sedgwick, chapter 2 illustrates the perils of uncritically generating volatile LGBT identities and their potential to generate unintended meanings, as well as an arsenal of weapons for those who seek to halt LGBT advancement.

Chapter 3 argues that LGBT equal rights discourse produces an unnecessarily constricted range of law reform objectives—notably, access to marriage, antidiscrimination protection, heightened constitutional scrutiny, hate crimes legislation, and international human rights protections that mimic American conceptions of equal protection. The discourse curbs the imagination we need to generate alternatives to the mainstream equal rights agenda. It does this in part by proliferating a teleological narrative about equality that contemplates a singular reformist path that concludes with access to marriage.

The chapter also addresses the related element of LGBT equal rights discourse that stresses love and interdependence. These tropes align far too easily with the neoliberal discourse of personal and family responsibility. The emphasis that the mainstream LGBT movement placed on same-sex marriage could not help but collaborate with the valorization of so-called family values to the disadvantage of those living on the wrong side of that norm. The prioritization of same-sex marriage for the past two decades (and perhaps the next two, as culture warriors battle over religious exemptions) has collaborated with the neoliberal trend that favors privatization of family obligation, the concomitant diminution of the welfare state, and the rise of criminalization and other anti-welfarist policies that broaden the divide between the haves and the have-nots. In effect, the major organizations have doggedly pursued law reforms that do not always help, and sometimes harm, some of the most marginalized among us. Our own discourse, even as it furthers the reformist goals that have predominated, impedes the advancement and even survival of our most vulnerable community members.

As the mainstream LGBT agenda bears fruit, it creates a new world—one in which antigay discrimination is increasingly forbidden on the terms set forth by LGBT equal rights discourse. This kind of progress rewards versions of gay identity that benefit from the improved system, resulting in further shaping of identity and reformist goals in the image of the rewarded constituencies. The successes of LGBT law reform should not be expected to "trickle down" to the most marginalized LGBT constituencies—to the contrary: They should be expected to entrench themselves as producers of what it means to be LGBT and what LGBT people want.

While marching along the well-laid path to equality, a nagging question surfaces and resurfaces: Am I equal? Certain longings stir: Is my group included in that antidiscrimination law? That hate crimes bill? Are people like me protected against discrimination in that other country? What questions do not come to mind? What reform options are not on the table? That brings us to part II.

Part II switches out the narrow LGBT equal rights discursive lens for one that enables a broader scope. The central purpose of this part is to reconceptualize sexuality and gender as axes of distribution rather than as fixed identity categories that suffer discrimination and require an equal rights solution.

Chapter 4 begins this undertaking by situating the argument of *Gay Priori* in a longer conversation about progressive strategies on behalf of marginalized constituencies. It reviews antecedent and contemporary debates about how to understand the injury to a marginalized group and what kinds of reformist interventions would address the core problems it faces. In the vocabulary of law, the question is whether to accord primacy to symbolic and formal equality or to substantive and economic justice. This dichotomy has shown tremendous resilience across movements and time. The question before the LGBT movement now echoes one that has persisted throughout the history of black civil rights in America. A vast literature explores the intersections of race and economic disparity, but LGBT equal rights discourse has had such a hold on the reformist imagination that an analysis of sexual and gender identities as involving distributive facets, particularly at racial and economic intersections, has not been as thoroughly developed.

The chapter digs into a debate between Nancy Fraser and Judith Butler over the nature of the legal injury to sexuality and gender constituencies—that is, is it one of recognition or one of distribution?—and the appropriate framing of remedial efforts. It concludes by offering a revised understanding of the place of sexual and gender identities in political economy. Law is a dynamic presence, constantly reproducing itself in slight variations that adjust both resource distribution and knowledge. As a consequence, political economy is pliable in myriad small ways. The first task for progressive law reformers ought to be to discern how law conditions distributions of resources and knowledge and what variations are possible.

Chapter 5 introduces a methodological turn to what lawyers call *background rules*. The idea of a background rule is drawn from the American legal realists, a group of late nineteenth century–early twentieth century legal thinkers with intellectual connections to the pragmatism of William James and Charles Peirce.[13] The Columbia University economist Robert Hale was a central figure. Hale explained conceptual shortcomings plaguing the ideal of contractual freedom, observing that individual choices are—to a greater or lesser extent—constrained by the alternatives available to a decision maker.[14] In a contract negotiation, both parties experience some constraint, although one may have more and better alternatives to the terms offered by the other— and that party can be regarded as having superior bargaining power. A constitutive element of each party's range of alternatives is law. Legal conditions operate *in the background*, not directly governing the contract but shaping the alternatives to the contract that are available to the bargaining parties. This insight can be extended to social negotiations more generally. Shifting analytic focus to background legal conditions can enable reformers to intervene in a given inequity by improving the range of choices available to a relevant constituency.

The "crits," a leftist group of legal scholars that came together in the 1980s under the rubric of critical legal studies (CLS), drew crucial lessons from the realists, paying attention to background rules in an effort to open up questions of law's role in the distribution of resources.[15] Distributive analysis is informed by the details of a given population's legal, economic, and other conditions as it negotiates with other bargain seekers.

Examples in chapter 5 illustrate how sexuality and gender, often intersecting with race, class, region, and age, create a complex scheme for allocating resources. Once reconceived in this way, a new dimension of potential legal reforms reveals itself to intervene in the distribution of health, safety, housing, nutrition, jobs, and income. The purpose is to generate fresh possibilities for law reform that, while illegible within the familiar terms of the culture war, might effect some positive redistribution at a tolerable cost level.

Nothing in the chapter has the majestic quality of an emancipatory destination—it makes scarce mention of equality, dignity, liberty, self-determination, or any other lofty goal. It is designed to tear the reader's gaze away from grand aspiration and principled vindication and redirect it downward, toward the gritty, low-profile rules, doctrines, and practices that condition daily life on the margins. The analysis uncovers potential targets for law reform, accepting that any change we make is likely to impose some cost even as it brings some relief. Child support regulations, contract doctrine, shelter rules, credit practices, mandatory arrest policies, labor laws, food stamp application forms, and a host of other low-profile legal conditions will take center stage, while titanic clashes between morality and equality, tradition and progress, red and blue will take a back seat. Chapter 5 does not offer a prescription for all social justice movements at all times. Indeed, a key point is that the work of setting a law reform agenda must be done on location, where one can observe closely the legal, economic, and ethnographic detail.

The conclusion brings the argument around to the role of lawyers in social movements. It confronts the complaint that law reformers often distort grassroots priorities, arguing that this is not a necessary feature of law or lawyers' participation. Lawyers should take their direction from a careful assessment of background legal conditions that affect the daily lives of their constituencies, particularly the most vulnerable. They have more tools at their disposal than has been widely recognized. A shift in perspective opens up a new world of reform possibilities.

I Have Met the Enemy and It Is "Us"

In 2012, during his bid for reelection, President Barack Obama publicly declared his support for same-sex marriage. This was a watershed moment for the same-sex marriage campaign. In previous election cycles it had been an untouchable position for a serious presidential contender. By 2012, however, it was to the president's advantage; it turned out to be a fundraising boon. According to one report, one in six of his large, individual donors was gay.[16] The week of the announcement, the president attended a Hollywood fundraiser at the home of George Clooney that brought in more than any single event in the history of U.S. presidential campaigns ($15 million), and some of that donor enthusiasm was thought to be due to the president's newfound willingness to embrace same-sex marriage openly.

Commentary followed. Conservative opponents of the president charged him with pandering to a wealthy and powerful interest group. Admiring onlookers marveled at the astonishingly rapid progress of gay rights. Leftist cynics observed that gay rights advocates were enjoying an easier road than immigrant rights groups or environmentalists because their agenda posed no obvious threat to corporate power.

That commentary is reactive, but it is also productive. It produces an archetypal subject of gay rights who is wealthy, politically connected, in control of popular culture, typically white, and (notwithstanding the "T" in "LGBT") probably not transgender.

That archetypal gay rights subject, in turn, has consequences for who is "us" when we conceptualize law reform on "our" behalf. An amply fed, well-housed archetype is not likely to give rise to a reform agenda focused on hunger and homelessness. President Obama's endorsement and the comments that followed obscured not only the contest over whether marriage ought to be our chief concern but also the contestants.

Uncritical participation in a discourse that attempts to stabilize LGBT subjects comes with hazards, and those hazards are not imposed only by the homophobe and the transphobe. We impose those hazards on ourselves, often while making LGBT equal rights claims. The specific plea here is for cognizance of the power of LGBT equal rights discourse to produce "us" and "what we want."

Reconsidering Our Priorities

Gay Priori does not argue that equal rights strategies should never be used. It offers instead a call to awareness that the discourse in which LGBT equal rights has been pursued has impeded our thinking. While LGBT equal rights discourse has opened some doors to be sure, it has sealed off others from our sight, often to the detriment of people living far out on the margins. This book is a deliberate effort to gain some insight into our own limitations and—in some necessarily limited way—to try to exceed them.

I write for those who have been plagued by the sense that while some of us are getting the fair treatment we should never have been denied, others of us are being left behind. The unfolding of LGBT progress in this way is not happenstance, and we should not wait for the gains we have seen to flow to those least well positioned to benefit from them. We should take responsibility for the adverse as well as the beneficial impact of our actions. We should change how we think about law and we have the tools to do it.

PART I

LGBT Equal Rights Discourse

1

THE INDETERMINACY TRAP

The Unexceptional Case

In 1993, a decade before Massachusetts became the first jurisdiction in the United States to treat same-sex marriage as a constitutional right, Christine Huff, a faculty member at the Chapel Hill–Chauncy Hall boarding school in Waltham, sued her employer under state law for discrimination based on sexual orientation. After Huff's successful year as a teacher, coach, and "dorm parent," the headmaster of the school expressed his wish to renew her contract. Huff had been living on campus, and the renewal of her contract would have meant the continuation of that arrangement. In the course of her contract renewal discussions, Huff asked her headmaster whether she could be permitted to live in a dorm with her same-sex life partner. According to Chapel Hill–Chauncy Hall policy, married teachers were permitted to live in dormitories with their spouses, but unmarried teachers who lived on campus were required to live alone. The headmaster refused Huff's request, thereby placing her in a cruel dilemma: scale back on her employment responsibilities or continue to live separately from her partner. Huff left her position and filed a lawsuit.[1]

Under Massachusetts law, employment discrimination claims begin in front of an administrative agency called the Massachusetts Commission Against Discrimination (MCAD).[2] The governor of the commonwealth at the time was William F. Weld, a socially liberal, fiscally conservative Republican who had received support from a gay organization known as the Log Cabin Republicans. Unsurprisingly, Log Cabin members could be found throughout state government in important positions during the Weld administration. One such person was Michael T. Duffy, whom Governor Weld appointed to the chairmanship of MCAD. As an out gay official at the helm of a state agency, and one who would later campaign for statewide office seeking the support of the gay community, Duffy found himself in a tight spot when Huff's case landed on his desk.

The Massachusetts statute that protects against discrimination on the basis of sexual orientation had been in place for just a few years at the time.[3] Under the law, an aggrieved person could make out a claim even if the discrimination was not intentional or explicit but was the result of *disparate impact*, or discrimination that results from a neutral policy that has the *effect* of disproportionately disadvantaging members of a protected class. That was Huff's principal claim: that gays and lesbians as a group were harmed by the school's attaching on-campus living to certain employment opportunities while permitting only married couples to reside on campus at a time that only heterosexual couples could marry. The availability of a disparate impact claim combined with explicit statutory protection against discrimination in employment might have led Huff to a victory.

Duffy felt constrained, however, by language that the Massachusetts legislature had included in the law: "Nothing in this act shall be construed so as to legitimize or validate a 'homosexual marriage,' so called."[4] According to Duffy's reading, this language served as an express prohibition against a claim such as Huff's. If MCAD were to apply the antidiscrimination statute to require Chapel Hill–Chauncy Hall to treat Huff's partnership the same way it treated a marriage, it would risk offending the legislature's intent. In an era in which even the most progressive localities were just beginning to trot out limited laws recognizing domestic partnerships, that was just what somebody anxious about gay people, gay rights, and the advent of gay marriage would expect a gay political appointee to do. Duffy decided that Huff's claim amounted to a request that her relationship be "legitimize[d] or validate[d]" as a marriage and that the statute forbade such an outcome.

Huff also made a *disparate treatment* claim, which, according to Duffy, entailed a contention that the school discriminated against her based on her sexual orientation and that this was intentional. This claim was weaker, in part because the headmaster had known Huff to be a lesbian when he hired her, gave her excellent performance reviews, and indicated his intention to renew her contract. Moreover, to succeed on a disparate treatment claim, Duffy explained, a plaintiff had to show that "similarly situated co-workers not in the protected class" received more favorable treatment.

But who were these similarly situated co-workers? Were they the married co-workers—similar to Huff because they, too, were in committed partnerships? If so, Huff should have been permitted to reside with her partner just as the married employees were. Duffy, without explanation, went the other way. He characterized "unmarried heterosexuals who wanted to live with a partner" as the similarly situated group. Plainly, a teacher in a heterosexual, nonmarital relationship would not have been permitted to cohabit with a partner on campus. Duffy believed that comparison compelled him to rule in favor of the school on the disparate treatment claim, as well.

Huff's case against Chapel Hill–Chauncy Hall raises a number of questions that surface and resurface in LGBT equal rights advocacy. First, what did it mean to prohibit discrimination against Huff in employment based on her sexual orientation? A widely accepted theory of justice credited to Aristotle holds that "like cases" ought to be treated alike. Was Huff's same-sex committed life partnership, under a legal regime that did not permit her to marry, "like" a marital partnership or "like" an unmarried heterosexual one? Put slightly differently, to avoid discriminating, should the school have treated Huff's nonmarital same-sex relationship the same way it treated nonmarital heterosexual relationships, or should it have accommodated the different circumstances of committed lesbian and gay partnerships—that is, the unavailability of marriage?

Further, what would it mean for Duffy to "legitimize or validate a homosexual marriage"—something the legislature said he could not do? Duffy had to choose between construing that language broadly (so that requiring the school to accommodate Huff would contravene the law) or narrowly (so that only an actual attempt to confer the status of marriage on a same-sex couple would contravene the law). Both readings are defensible within prevailing norms of equality argumentation, and different decision makers operating under different political conditions might reach different conclusions.

Next, if Huff had appealed the MCAD ruling and taken Chapel Hill–Chauncy Hall to court, could the school not have argued that it, too, had rights? Perhaps the law protects the school's freedom to operate according to its own values and speak in its own voice about such moral issues as nonmarital cohabitation, especially in close proximity to the impressionable students who are its charges. Might competing rights of association or expression be implicated?

Finally, one can detect in Duffy's written decision some angst. It might have been the politics, which had to have created something of a predicament for him, but maybe it was the genuine anguish of one who is entrusted with the responsibility for neutral decision-making and who feels he must assure others (and perhaps himself) that he will not be swayed by tribal loyalties. Duffy wrote, "I am not unaware of, nor unsympathetic to, the difficulties and hardships that the law imposes upon gay men and lesbians and their partners. [Read, *I am gay*!] Nonetheless, these inequities, as in the instant case, currently have no remedy under law. . . . This Commission may not accomplish by "quasi-judicial" fiat that which the Legislature has expressly chosen not to countenance and, indeed, has forbidden by statute. It is clear that such an end may be accomplished only by appeal to the [Legislature]."[5] Duffy laments the limits on his own power. He would like to help Huff; he appreciates the injustice being done to her, but he claims to be bound by the text of the statute and his own institutional role—a "quasi-judicial" one. Whatever injustice might result is being done not by him but by the legislature. Still, might a different reading of the statute have unbound him?

The issues that the Huff case raises and the tools that Duffy used to navigate them and to justify his decisions are features of an analytical problem known in legal theory as the *indeterminacy of law*. Huff's right against discrimination under the Massachusetts statute is not sufficient to determine the outcome of her case, even when combined with a process of deductive reasoning. Intermediate choices arise in the course of the decision maker's analysis—for example, how to construe the terms of the governing statute and what kind of heterosexual couple Huff and her partner were more "like." To answer those questions, Duffy had to make decisions that were enabled but not required by the legal materials or by logic.

This is not to suggest that his choices were random or based entirely on idiosyncratic opinion. It is to suggest merely that he did in fact make unacknowledged choices. Those choices may have been shaped by political, moral, or aesthetic influences or by the operating assumptions of his bureaucratic agency. That is inevitable and not to be condemned, but those influences were not openly explained. Duffy read from governing legal materials and used deductive reasoning, to be sure, but he did not state forthrightly what his interpretive choices were or why he made them. He declined to acknowledge the limits of what deductive logic could do for him and to what values he turned to complete the journey to his conclusion. The *criticism* in the indeterminacy *critique* is of the failure of decision makers to elaborate their decisions fully and honestly; it is of the pretense to chaste deductive reasoning from a cold and static legal starting point and the occluding of unmentioned values and conditions that inevitably help to shape decisions. [6]

But *indeterminacy* refers to more than the idea that legal materials combined with a deductive reasoning process are not always sufficient to determine a conclusion—although that is part of it, to be sure. The indeterminacy of law is bound up with a deep, dogged, and institutionalized need to preserve a safe distance between objective, neutral correctness and subjective, political desire. The maintenance of that space requires engagement in discursive practices meant to justify case outcomes by reference to a process of neutral deduction.

Those practices pervade American law, and quite understandably, LGBT legal advocates—like advocates in other fields—have used the tools that American law makes available to them to pursue their goals. But our advocates have often operated uncritically within conventional justificatory discourse, formulating their desired legal objectives as "required" by law and reason. This has had untold costs. By their uncritical participation in conventional American legal discursive practices, LGBT legal advocates have been complicit (along with judges and legal advocates of all stripes) in the denial of reason's limits; they have lent their endorsement and prestige to the elision of choice available to legal decision makers; and—even as they strive toward progressive change—they have contributed to the sense that existing social arrangements are as law and reason require them to be. Even as they change the world in some respects, they also promote apparent limits on legal possibility.

This chapter begins exploring the costs of LGBT equal rights discourse—costs that occur in registers other than litigation victory and defeat. Huff lost her case, and one could attribute her defeat to the vagaries of indeterminacy, but this chapter does not argue that we should expect LGBT litigants to lose all—or even most—of the time. To the contrary, *Obergefell v. Hodges*, in which the U.S. Supreme Court found a constitutional right for same-sex couples to marry, makes evident that gay equality is on a winning streak.[7] The argument here, however, is that winning and losing within the terms of LGBT equal rights discourse have more in common than you might think.

Institutional Competence

Duffy's plea of "It's not me; it's the legislature" is what legal thinkers call an *institutional competence* rationale. Judicial (or quasi-judicial) decision makers routinely decline to vindicate rights claims and then attribute their decisions to their adherence to the limits on their own power and respect for the proper role of their institution in the larger system of government. Institutional competence rationales tie the outcome of a specific case to preservation of the integrity of the system. It is important to observe, however, that when a judicial (or quasi-judicial) body refuses to vindicate a rights claim for reasons of institutional competence, gallantly deferring to the legislature, it typically does so while taking full advantage of its power to construe the texts that are relevant to whether the claimant will prevail. Duffy's institutional limit is self-imposed; it rests on his interpretive decisions to frame Huff's committed partnership as "similarly situated" to nonmarital heterosexual relationships and to accord the prohibition against "legitimiz[ing] or validat[ing] a 'homosexual marriage'" its broadest possible meaning. Those interpretive moves must accompany his humility in relation to the legislative prerogative. If Duffy had construed the relevant terms in Huff's favor, then it would have fallen entirely within his institutional mandate to award her a legal remedy; he had to construe them against her to throw up his hands, powerless to help. Indeed, Duffy might have felt just a bit more compulsion toward institutional competence apologia precisely because he *was* sympathetic to Huff's claim.

Not all equal rights claims are made in a judicial (or quasi-judicial) forum. An equal rights-seeking constituency might go to Congress and push for a voting rights act or to a state legislature for protection against discrimination in housing. When a legislature acts, it is also bound by institutional limits. In the federal system, for example, Congress may not reverse by statute the Supreme Court's interpretation of a constitutional provision. All three branches have purviews and boundaries around those purviews, although those boundaries are constantly contested. Concerns about the limits on the institutional competence of federal courts are unremarkable in this respect, but read enough constitutional law, especially equal protection and due process decisions, and you cannot help but be impressed that the boundaries around the power of the Third Branch are uniquely fraught.[8] This becomes evident quickly to any practiced reader, who will become familiar with a pool of tropes habitually embedded in arguments justifying or, alternatively, attacking decisions to strike down an act of the majority's will in favor of an individual right. When an equal rights-seeking claimant comes before a *counter-majoritarian* body—that is, a body that is not accountable to the electorate but is nonetheless empowered to negate legislative or executive pronouncements—*it activates a specific discourse of institutional competence designed to affirm the legitimacy of unelected officials' making important decisions in a democracy.*

When *Bowers v. Hardwick* came before the U.S. Supreme Court in 1986,[9] gay rights advocates asked the Court to strike down Georgia's sodomy prohibition on "right to privacy" grounds. Michael Hardwick was arrested in his own bedroom for engaging in oral sex with another man. The American Civil Liberties Union (ACLU) had been waiting for the chance to challenge a state's sodomy prohibition in a case involving consenting adults who had violated the law in a private setting. The arrest occurred because an unusually determined antigay police officer went to Hardwick's home to deliver a warrant for non-payment of a fine for an open-container violation (in error—the fine had been paid), and a houseguest (foolishly) invited the officer in. Snooping around the apartment, the officer spied Hardwick and his partner engaged in the forbidden act. Hardwick's arrest provided the ACLU the opportunity it had been waiting for to bring a state sodomy law before the Supreme Court.

At the ostensible outset of his analysis, Justice White wrote for the majority that the case did "not require a judgment on whether laws against sodomy . . . are wise or desirable."[10] The decision, White was assuring readers, would not be based on his policy preference or personal opinion. He was perfectly cognizant of "the limits of the Court's role in carrying out its constitutional mandate," characterizing the question before him as strictly "whether the Federal Constitution confers a fundamental right upon homosexuals to engage in sodomy."[11]

Hardwick, of course, did not frame his claim that way. He claimed that his conduct was protected by the general constitutional right to privacy. Previous victories for the right to privacy had made it easy to hope that he was headed for a constitutional slam dunk. Advocates were able to present the *Bowers* Court with a line of cases litigated under the right to privacy contained within the due process clause, protecting a range of activities associated with marriage, child rearing, sex, and reproductive control. Justice White, however, found that the claim made in *Bowers* bore no resemblance to the claims in those other cases. Sodomy, he thought, was utterly unlike any of the activities covered by the privacy right. The very reframing of the question by White, from the broad "right to privacy" to the narrow "fundamental right [of] homosexuals to engage in sodomy," reflected White's conclusion.

Further, White expressed his commitment to construing the constitutional terms cautiously, lest he be guilty of deciding the case based on his own opinion, without proper regard for the state legislature. "Nor are we inclined to take a more expansive view of our authority to discover new fundamental rights imbedded in the Due Process Clause. The Court is most vulnerable and comes nearest to illegitimacy when it deals with judge-made constitutional law."[12] The Court was limited, White reasoned, by its institutional role. A victory for Hardwick, he intimates, could threaten the entire system.

To signal his institutional concerns, White dropped references to the *Lochner* era and President Franklin D. Roosevelt's Court Packing Plan. The *Lochner* era took place in the early twentieth century (it is usually dated from 1897 until 1937) and is now regarded by most legal thinkers across the ideological spectrum as a bleak period in American legal history,[13] when a politically conservative Supreme Court reflexively struck down legislative attempts to recover from increasingly dire economic conditions. To assert some control over the still nascent industrial economy, state legislatures of the time were enacting minimum wage and maximum hour laws. The New Deal president and Congress were passing ambitious regulatory packages, including labor laws, price controls, and social insurance programs. The Supreme Court, however, remained enthralled with laissez-faire and embraced a vision of the U.S. Constitution that seemed to require the striking down of any law that impinged on contractual freedom.

In the case from which the era takes its name, *Lochner v. New York*, the Court struck down a unanimously passed state law setting a maximum of sixty hours of labor per week for bakers. The Court held that a state law limiting the number of hours that a baker could work interfered with the freedom of the employer and employee to make a contract for whatever number of hours they wished.[14] Over the next few decades, the Court struck down laws regulating wages, hours, and prices, often on the grounds that the laws violated liberty of contract, which it deemed a feature of the due process clause and therefore under judicial protection.

During this same period, the Court was also suspicious of any expansion of congressional power under the commerce clause. The commerce clause grants Congress one of its key sources of authority to enact legislation. It was the principal mechanism by which Congress would be able to regulate activities affecting the increasingly complex and interstate economy. At the time, business interests were growing larger than they had ever been. The free market no longer comprised small businesses competing for local customers. The country was beginning to see the emergence of large, powerful "trusts" that exerted control over wages and prices, to the disadvantage of labor and consumers and to the detriment of the national economy. New federal regulatory mechanisms arose in response. For a while, the Court was striking down congressional efforts to regulate the economy, construing the commerce clause narrowly and reasoning that the clause did not grant Congress the authority to pass much of the legislation that the New Dealers thought the country needed. If the meaning of the Constitution's commerce clause could not keep up—could not expand as the power of private enterprise was expanding—then Congress could not keep up, either, and these new business interests would go unregulated. There would be no New Deal.

Frustrated by defeats in the Supreme Court, President Roosevelt proposed his Court Packing Plan, which would have added six pro–New Deal justices to the nine justices who were already sitting on the Supreme Court, assuring a pro–New Deal majority. Nothing in the Constitution explicitly forbade it, but the Plan was so brazen in its political manipulation of the Court that even senators who favored Roosevelt's legislative efforts refused to support him. The conflict subsided when Justice Owen Roberts, who had been voting to strike down economic reforms, began voting to uphold them (the famous "switch in time that saved nine"). Soon thereafter, Roosevelt was able to replace enough retiring justices to secure a New Deal majority, and a constitutional crisis was averted.

Since the demise of the *Lochner* era, the dominant view has held that the *Lochner* majority failed to appreciate the limits on its own role in our system of government, running roughshod over majority preferences. For decades, progressives in particular valorized majority preference and judicial restraint, perhaps overconfident that such a jurisprudence would maximize progressive outcomes. The Warren Court era, however, chastened adherents to that position, when civil rights demonstrators and antiwar demonstrators turned to the Supreme Court to protect their First Amendment rights to protest and associate, when African Americans accused of crimes benefited from expanding interpretations of provisions within the Fourth, Fifth, and Sixth Amendments (including the right against unreasonable searches and seizures, the right against being put in jeopardy twice for the same offense, the right to counsel, and so on), and perhaps most pointedly, when the right against state-imposed racial segregation under the equal protection clause of the Fourteenth Amendment was announced in *Brown v. Board of Education*.[15]

As the legal historian Morton Horwitz observed in 1979, "For a half century until the decision in *Brown*, the notion that courts should ordinarily defer to the policies of the legislature became [an] article of faith of liberal jurisprudence. All of that changed with *Brown*, which forced liberal opinion to begin the gradual abandonment of the dogma of judicial restraint."[16] Since that time, *Brown* has garnered nearly universal fealty in American legal culture and mainstream American culture generally, creating a conceptual dilemma against the history of *Lochner*. "In some sense, all of American constitutional law for the past twenty-five years [plus another forty since publication of Horwitz's article] has revolved around trying to justify the judicial role in *Brown* while trying simultaneously to show that such a course will not lead to another *Lochner* era."[17] The challenge for contemporary rights claimants is to persuade courts not only that they should be granted the outcome they seek, but that recognition of their asserted right will not lead the country down the path to judicial usurpation of the legislative prerogative.

When a contemporary justice invokes the *Lochner* era and the constitutional crisis it nearly provoked—and any student of constitutional law quickly learns that the justices do so habitually—it is intended to serve as a warning, a shorthand for why Courts must remain mindful of the limits on their institutional competence: *Let us not overstep our bounds and start striking down legislative enactments based on phantom rights that are not firmly grounded in the Constitution. We do not want to damage the Court's credibility the way the* Lochner *Court did. We do not want to foment another crisis or provoke drastic measures to manipulate the power of a Court that comes to be seen as just another political branch.* Indeed, the early twentieth century is a period of disrepute for the Supreme Court that offers cautionary tales worth heeding. Legal thinkers of liberal as well as conservative inclination now disclaim any right to free contract under the due process clause. Contemporary consensus holds that the *Lochner* Court attributed too much meaning to that clause and thereby overly empowered *itself* to strike down legislation of which it did not approve.[18]

When, however, a justice trots out *Lochner* and the Court Packing Plan to tell you that *your right* could instigate the next constitutional calamity, you are entitled to some skepticism. That the Court may only interpret and apply the law and may not usurp the legislative role is a matter of universal assent in American legal culture and is therefore offered as a premise. That it would have overstepped the judicial role to strike down Georgia's sodomy law on right-to-privacy grounds, however, does not inexorably follow.

Justice White examined the privacy line of cases (granting constitutional protection to, among other things, married people's use of contraception, unmarried people's access to contraception, a woman's choice to terminate a pregnancy, and interracial marriage) and had to decide whether sodomy fell into that set. Is sodomy "like" these other activities, or "not like" them? The answer to that question cannot be found in the Constitution; logical deduction cannot get you there, either. Justice White made a choice,[19] notwithstanding his assurances to the contrary. This is to posit not that Justice White was entirely unguided but that the relevant constitutional language (guaranteeing due process), combined with chaste deduction, does not adequately explain his decision. There were "reasons" to which he might have appealed, including religious morality, sexual ethics, and political and social distaste for homosexuality, but he did not do so explicitly.

White's multidetermined position on the "unlikeness" of sodomy to constitutionally protected activities such as the use of contraception is embedded in his contention of institutional competence. The system is in jeopardy of entering another *Lochner* era only if the Court oversteps its role, and it is only overstepping if the Court extends privacy protection to an activity that is unlike the already protected activities. If sodomy were "like" contraception, abortion, and interracial marriage, then it would merit privacy protection, and striking down the Georgia law would fall neatly within the judicial purview.

In other words, White told us that he established the limits on his role *first*, then conducted his analysis, focusing on a limited question that had nothing to do with his policy preferences. The determination that a contrary conclusion would place him outside of the judicial purview, however, could not have been a genuine starting point. Only a wrong decision jeopardizes the system.

To state the matter with a bit more nuance, the decision in *Bowers* does not follow a neat, linear path. White's choice to frame the constitutional question as narrowly as he did and to reject analogies from prior privacy cases were tangled up with—rather than subsequent to—his ostensibly initial assertion regarding the proper scope of his power. It may even be the case that his ideological commitments, acknowledged as well as unacknowledged, bore just as indeterminate a relationship to his ultimate decision as the constitutional provision did. After all, while Justice White was a dyed-in-the-wool homophobe, Michael Duffy was an outspoken gay community leader. Both men made their actual decisions in a kind of middle space, between reason and its death.[20] That space is filled with culture, ethics, political leanings, professional norms, and other accumulated learning.

Chief Justice Burger joined the majority opinion in *Bowers*, but he also submitted a brief concurrence. The chief justice's opinion exuded contempt for Hardwick's claim, invoking the eighteenth-century British jurist Sir William Blackstone, author of *Commentaries on the Laws of England* (also known as *Blackstone's Commentaries*),[21] to brand sodomy "the infamous crime against nature," "an offense of 'deeper malignity' than rape," and "a heinous act 'the very mention of which is a disgrace to human nature.'" It would, Burger fumed, "cast aside millennia of moral teaching" to grant constitutional protection to such depravity.[22]

Chief Justice Burger was having some feelings, and those feelings are evident in the first two paragraphs of his three-paragraph opinion. Yet in his final paragraph, the tone takes a peculiar turn, from overtly hostile to oddly technocratic. In it, Burger sounds almost as if he himself did not hold an opinion on the subject of sodomy: "This is essentially not a question of personal 'preferences' but rather of the legislative authority of the State. I find nothing in the Constitution depriving a State of the power to enact the statute challenged here."[23] No matter how transparent after his opening invective, the chief justice was bound to disclaim that his "preferences" had anything to do with it: He acted only in deference to the proper legislative authority.

Why did these men attribute their votes in *Bowers* to the limits on their own power, and respect for the legislative prerogative, ostentatiously distancing themselves from their own politics or morality? Why does the ghost of *Lochner* haunt the judicial enterprise so relentlessly?

The justices were performing what in legal theory is referred to as a *legitimating* function. The majority, through its elected representatives, is expected to govern in a republican democracy. In the American system, however, federal judges are appointed rather than elected, and they have life tenure. The design of the federal judgeship is to insulate judges from public opinion—precisely the opposite design of the House of Representatives, which is theoretically highly responsive and accountable to its constituents through the mechanism of biannual elections. (The framers of the Constitution apparently did not anticipate the degree of entrenchment that would result from gerrymandering.)

The federal courts' counter-majoritarianism and the relative immunity to public opinion that it affords enables them to serve as a check on the majoritarian branches, which might otherwise pass and enforce laws that violate the Constitution. As Alexander Hamilton explained in *Federalist No. 78*, "This independence of the judges is equally requisite to guard the Constitution and the rights of individuals from the effects of those ill humors, which the arts of designing men, or the influence of particular conjunctures, sometimes disseminate among the people themselves, and which, though they speedily give place to better information, and more deliberate reflection, have a tendency, in the meantime, to occasion dangerous innovations in the government, and serious oppressions of the minor party in the community."[24] This theory of the design and role of the federal judiciary was crystalized in *Marbury v. Madison* (1803),[25] which established the principle of judicial review—that is, it is the federal court's role to interpret the nation's Constitution and laws and to strike down those laws that (according to a judicial reading) violate the Constitution, which is our highest law.

It is also our most enduring. The Constitution contains within it a process for its own amendment (in Article V), and that process is arduous. The first ten amendments were ratified in 1791, just two years after the original Constitution. There have been only seventeen more since, and one of those repeals another one. The relative stability of the Constitution,[26] as compared with any old law, makes it an appropriate document in which to set forth the basic structure of government, as well as the bedrock values that garnered sufficient consensus to survive ratification. For those values to endure, the theory goes, even when the tide of public opinion rushes in a contrary direction, a body that is *unresponsive* to the majority must be responsible for their preservation. That is the federal judiciary.

But the federal courts' unaccountability is also why the limits on their power are so crucial. In a republic, we are free to vote for representatives who share our values and policy preferences, and they must account to us at the next election cycle. We cannot, however, vote a federal judge out of office. That is why when a federal judge makes a controversial decision, the judge does not say, as a politician might, "I am a family values conservative, so that is how I decided." Instead, the decision reads "the Constitution and our structure of government *require* this outcome."

Require is an important word here. Counter-majoritarian decision makers strive to convey the *necessity* of the outcomes they reach. Generations of American jurists and constitutional scholars have devoted themselves to debating what method of decision-making most closely preserves the judicial role, excluding judges' personal political views from their decision-making processes. Justice Thomas believes in cleaving to the original intent of the framers when interpreting the Constitution, while Justice Scalia believed that *intent* does not matter but original *meaning*—that is, how a text would have been widely understood when it was adopted—should guide interpretation. Justice Breyer and retired Justice Stevens believe that the practical effects of a decision are permissible considerations—long a hotly debated question—along with such considerations as original meaning and intent. Some scholars believe that the Constitution makes little provision for case *outcomes* but exists mainly to provide us with fair *processes* for making decisions (including speech protections so that we might have vigorous public debates, fully representative legislative procedures, jury trials, and so on), while others believe that a judge can discern the purposes of the framers of the Constitution at a general level and determine how best to serve those general purposes when deliberating on specific problems that the framers never anticipated.

These are but a few vulgarized summaries of some of the well-known approaches to constitutional interpretation. Jurists and scholars work out their theories with mind-numbing levels of nuance and illustrate the intricacies exhaustively, using real cases as well as hypotheticals. When they do so, they are chasing the same elusive aim: solace that an unelected body can make decisions in a democracy in a way that is maximally neutral and constrained rather than political and better left to elected representatives. We live every day with a potential outrage: Unelected officials with life tenure make major and sometimes highly controversial decisions in a democracy. It takes a lot of singing to keep that beast asleep.

Bowers v. Hardwick was reversed seventeen years after it was decided, in *Lawrence v. Texas* (2003).[27] Again, the facts of the case involved grown men enjoying consensual sodomy (anal sex this time) in the privacy of one man's home (although subsequent investigation revealed that the sex probably never took place).[28] It is not easy to find cases with "facts" such as these to mount a challenge to the sodomy laws, for the practical reason that when consenting adults engage in sex at home, the police rarely intrude. Arrests for sodomy are typically associated with sexual assaults or indecent exposure charges resulting from sex acts in public parks or restrooms. In the *Lawrence* case, the police entered the premises based on a false report of a weapons disturbance. When John Lawrence and Tyron Garner were arrested on a "clean" case, the opportunity for a mulligan on constitutional protection for sodomy was too good for gay rights advocates to pass up.

Justice Kennedy wrote the main opinion in *Lawrence*, and while he did not make it entirely clear in his opinion that sodomy is now protected by the right to privacy, what the case does hold is that states may no longer prohibit noncommercial sodomy between consenting adults in private. *Consent* and *private* are highly contested concepts, as subsequent lower court cases have illustrated, but at least in a clear-cut situation involving two grown men engaging in oral or anal sex at home, where there is no allegation of prostitution or coercion, no injury and no per se hierarchy in the relationship (e.g., teacher-student or differential military rank), the sheer fact that their brand of sex offends the state's moral sensibilities is not sufficient to result in their criminal punishment. Kennedy found this much to be entailed in the liberty protected by the due process clause.

In the *Huff* and *Bowers* cases, the authors declared their deference to the legislatures, pleading no authority to vindicate the right asserted by the gay claimant. *Lawrence* went the other way: The Court identified a right and exerted some judicial power to protect it. In such instances, it falls to the dissent to protest the institutional excesses of the majority.

Predictably, Justice Scalia, joined by Chief Justice Rehnquist and Justice Thomas, wrote a lengthy and bitter dissent covering institutional competence territory and then some.[29] All that is de rigueur. Despite signing on to Scalia's more than thorough dissenting opinion, though, Justice Thomas apparently felt that something was missing, because he submitted a two-paragraph dissent of his own, in which no one joined:

> I write separately to note that the law before the Court today "is . . . uncommonly silly." If I were a member of the Texas Legislature, I would vote to repeal it. . . .

Notwithstanding this, I recognize that as a Member of this Court I am not empowered to help petitioners and others similarly situated. My duty, rather, is to "decide cases 'agreeably to the Constitution and laws of the United States.'"[30]

In contrast to Chief Justice Burger of seventeen years before, who seemed bent on distinguishing himself as more rabidly homophobic than his brethren, Thomas went out on his own in an apparent effort to soften the tone. The sodomy laws, he effectively conceded, are ridiculous. Still, he is "not empowered" as a judge to address the situation. Only a legislator would be positioned to do so. He attributed his dissenting vote in *Lawrence* to institutional competence considerations rather than to any personal judgment regarding the inherent moral value of sodomy.

But again, institutional competence is not a premise, as it so often purports to be. Thomas famously disbelieves in the existence of any right to privacy and construes the due process clause narrowly in purported accordance with his originalist method. Other substantive rights fall short of the due process bar for him, as well, not only sodomy. Despite Justice Thomas's preferable tone, his institutional competence rationale suffers from the same weakness as Justice White's in *Bowers*. If the right were real in Thomas's mind, he would have the institutional authority to enforce it.

The Commonwealth of Massachusetts shares an important attribute with the federal system: Its judges are appointed, and while those judges do not have life tenure, they do have tenure until age seventy. Unlike the judges of many states, therefore, who must run for office and serve a limited term before having to seek reelection, Massachusetts judges are genuinely counter-majoritarian. The federal system was in fact modeled on the Massachusetts system, which was installed first.

This may have something to do with Massachusetts's being the first jurisdiction in the United States to declare same-sex marriage a right under its state constitution. In 2003, the same year that the U.S. Supreme Court decided *Lawrence*, the Massachusetts Supreme Judicial Court (SJC) decided *Goodridge v. Department of Public Health* by a vote of 4–3.[31]

As anyone located in the Massachusetts legal culture will attest, even in 2003 it would have been unthinkable for a justice of the SJC to denigrate homosexuality with Scalia-style vitriol or Blackstonian epithet. All three dissenters were firmly disposed to the Justice Thomas tonality; the bulk of their dissenting opinions perseverated on the institutional excesses of the majority's decision.

Justice Sosman, for example, wrote in a regretful tone reminiscent of Duffy's in the Huff case.[32] Responding to the majority's rejection of arguments that heterosexual marriage was optimal for childrearing, Sosman lamented:

> Based on our own philosophy of child rearing, and on our observations of the children being raised by same-sex couples to whom we are personally close, we may be of the view that what matters to children is not the gender, or sexual orientation, or even the number of the adults who raise them, but rather whether those adults provide the children with a nurturing, stable, safe, consistent and supportive environment in which to mature. . . . It is therefore understandable that the court might view the traditional definition of marriage as an unnecessary anachronism, rooted in historical prejudices. . . . It is not, however, our assessment that matters.[33]

Sosman went on to reason that the legislature should be given the leeway to wait out longitudinal studies on the comparative well-being of children raised in households with same-sex parents before being held to fail minimum constitutional standards. She did not express any *personal* skepticism about gay parenting—in fact, she seemed at pains to avoid affront, as if she feared the cold shoulder her gay friends were probably going to give her after reading her opinion. *I think you're a great parent*, she seemed to be pleading, *but the legislature is entitled to see some data. It's not up to me.*

Another dissenter, Justice Spina, began: "What is at stake in this case is not the unequal treatment of individuals or whether individual rights have been impermissibly burdened, but the power of the Legislature to effectuate social change without interference from the courts. . . . The power to regulate marriage lies with the Legislature, not with the judiciary. . . . Today the court has transformed its role as protector of individual rights into the role of creator of rights, and I respectfully dissent."[34] Spina, too, drove directly to the institutional competence rationale. To get there, however, he had to take an analytical route through the question at the heart of the case: *Were the plaintiffs, by seeking the right to marry their same-sex partners, asking to be treated equally or asking for something new?*

To answer this question, one has to have a view of whether heterosexuality is essential to the definition of marriage. If you believe that marriage is inherently a heterosexual union, then it would follow that all of the constitutional requirements were already satisfied by permitting the plaintiffs to enter into heterosexual marriages, which they were perfectly free to do. The request to enter into same-sex marriages would be "new" and not entailed in either the due process right to marry or the right to be treated equally. If, however, you believe that marriage need not be heterosexual and that homosexual unions are morally equivalent to heterosexual ones, then it would follow that homosexual and heterosexual couples are "alike" for purposes of marriage and, as a constitutional matter, should be treated alike by the law.

Spina was of the former mind. "Using the rubric of due process," he wrote, the court "has redefined marriage."[35] In one sense, that is exactly what happened. In response to an argument by the plaintiffs that the Massachusetts statute could be read to permit same-sex marriage, the *Goodridge* majority determined that the legislature had in mind the "ordinary" (read, "heterosexual") meaning of marriage in enacting the marriage licensing law.[36] The SJC did not, however, end its inquiry with statutory construction. It went on to address the constitutional question—that is, whether the statute, so construed, impermissibly denied same-sex couples access to marriage. To answer that question, one must go beyond construction of the term *marriage* as it is used legislatively to its absolute meaning. To reach a conclusion on the constitutional issue, Spina had to hold the belief that not only the legislative definition but the *inherent* definition of marriage was heterosexual. The majority's holding, therefore, amounted to the generation of an invented right to enter into a new institution rather than equal access to an existing one, a patent usurpation of the legislative prerogative. This view led Spina to his opening sentence, asserting that the very question was properly legislative rather than judicial.

Twelve years later, when the U.S. Supreme Court decided *Obergefell v. Hodges*,[37] making same-sex marriage a right under the *federal* Constitution, a few things had changed. Opponents of same-sex marriage could no longer point to an absence of data on child outcomes. By the time of *Obergefell*, not only had any concern about the impact of same-sex parenting on children been put to rest in study after study, but Justice Kennedy, in his majority opinion, could confidently flip the issue of child well-being on its head: One "basis for protecting the right [of same-sex couples] to marry is that it safeguards children and families and thus draws meaning from related rights of childrearing, procreation, and education."[38] For Kennedy, discriminatory marriage laws "harm and humiliate the children of same-sex couples" while marriage "allows children 'to understand the integrity and closeness of their own family and its concord with other families in their community'" and "also affords the permanency and stability important to children's best interests."[39] Judicial deference to the legislature to enable further study, therefore, did not figure in *Obergefell* as it did in *Goodridge*.

Moreover, in stark contrast to the *Bowers* Court's refusal to observe any similarities between heterosexuals' privacy interests (in contraception, abortion, childrearing, and interracial marriage) and "homosexual sodomy," Justice Kennedy traces the right he recognizes in *Obergefell* directly back to this line of case law. He argues further that "identification and protection of fundamental rights is an enduring part of the judicial duty," and while "history and tradition guide and discipline [his] inquiry," they "do not set its outer boundaries."[40] Far from binding himself to any version of originalism, Kennedy believes that rights "rise . . . from a better informed understanding of how constitutional imperatives define a liberty that remains urgent in our own era."[41] By the time of *Obergefell*, the common understanding of same-sex intimacy had leapt forward. While majorities in several red states remained opposed to same-sex marriage, the national majority favored its legalization. For a judge who believes that the meaning of "liberty" in the due process clause evolves with social progress, it would be unconstitutional to deny same-sex couples the chance to share in a basic civic institution.

What had *not* changed in the twelve years since *Goodridge* was the salience of institutional competence argument. Even though child outcome studies deprived dissenters of the "we should leave open empirical questions to the legislature" argument, even though public opinion had shifted rapidly and dramatically on the meaning of liberty and equality for gay and lesbian people, and even though eleven states plus the District of Columbia had legalized same-sex marriage using a legislative or referendum process rather than a judicial one (in addition to the five state court decisions finding a state constitutional right), usurpation of the majoritarian prerogative remained a danger with which pro-gay advocates were forced to reckon.

The brief submitted in *Obergefell* by the director of the Ohio agency responsible for administering marriage licenses argued that the law "Leaves Marriage Recognition to Federalism's Active Democratic Processes," asserting an institutional preference both for states (rather than the federal government) and legislatures (rather than courts) to decide the requirements for marriage. A subsection entitled "The Constitution delegates most sensitive policy choices to democratic debates, not judicial mandates" reads in part: "Article III's limits on judicial review highlight the courts' *limited* role in social change. . . . 'Great constitutional provisions,' like the Fourteenth Amendment, 'must be administered with caution' . . . because they are 'made for people of fundamentally differing views.' . . . Courts must avoid inserting into the amendment's capacious language a single generation's answers to 'the intractable economic, social, and even philosophical problems of the day.' "[42] Plaintiffs seeking marriage recognition offered this entirely predictable, even formulaic, rejoinder in their reply brief: "Nothing in [the relevant precedent] supports relegating the fates of [same-sex couples] and their children exclusively to Ohio's political arena. If federalism required public consensus as a prerequisite to invoking constitutional rights, then many of this Court's landmark decisions . . . would not exist."[43] Neither argument is extricable from the substantive question: whether gay people were being denied an existing right or asking for a change in social policy. Although the tones of advocates and judges differ considerably, the basic dialectic on judicial competence that takes place between litigants mirrors that which occurs between majority and dissenting justices. This makes sense; the arguments available are perpetual rivals within American constitutional rights discourse.

Chief Justice Roberts wrote a lengthy dissent making essentially the same point as the Ohio respondent, if more elaborately and passionately. He began with the premise that marriage *is* a heterosexual institution. That, explained the chief justice, has been the "singular understanding of marriage . . . throughout our history,"[44] and it is rooted in neither politics nor religion but in the biological reality of procreation. It follows, therefore, that the plaintiffs seek something *new*, a constitutionally mandated *change* in the definition as a matter of right. Other changes in the history of marriage (interracial marriage, the replacement of an arranged economic exchange with a companionate and legally egalitarian version of marriage) were not changes to marriage's essential definition, but this is. The change effectuated by the majority's decision, Roberts believes, will trouble "those who believe in a government of laws, not of men."[45] "Five lawyers have closed the debate [over same-sex marriage] and enacted their own vision of marriage as a matter of constitutional law . . . stealing this issue from the people."[46] Roberts did not rule out the possibility that if he were a state legislator he might be persuaded by policy arguments as to the wisdom of changing the meaning of marriage to encompass same-sex relationships, but—he pointed out—he is not a legislator. His conclusion, therefore, is that the majority's decision lacks "humility and restraint" and thereby jeopardizes the legitimacy of the Court.[47]

The chief justice invoked *Lochner* no fewer than thirteen times, as if repetition might persuade readers that "the majority's approach has no basis in principle or tradition, except for the unprincipled tradition of judicial policymaking that characterized discredited decisions such as *Lochner v. New York*,"[48] and that "only one precedent offers any support for the majority's methodology."[49] Guess which? *Lochner v. New York*. (Roberts also tossed in a couple of references to *Dred Scott* for good measure.[50])

Justice Scalia also dissented, echoing the chief justice but "writ[ing] separately to call attention to this Court's threat to American democracy."[51] He castigated the majority, writing, "This practice of constitutional revision by an unelected committee of nine, always accompanied (as it is today) by extravagant praise of liberty, robs the People of the most important liberty they asserted in the Declaration of Independence and won in the Revolution of 1776: the freedom to govern themselves."[52] For Scalia, who adhered to an interpretive method that valued above all else the common understanding of constitutional terms at the time of their ratification, the meaning of marriage in 1868, when the Fourteenth Amendment was added to the Constitution, "resolves these cases."[53] Further debate rightfully belongs to the majoritarian process, but "to allow the policy question of same-sex marriage to be considered and resolved by a select, patrician, highly unrepresentative panel of nine is to violate a principle even more fundamental than no taxation without representation: no social transformation without representation."[54]

Justice Thomas and Justice Samuel Alito each wrote a separate dissent, as well. Even as the interpretive methodologies differed among the four dissenters, the central theme remained constant: Justice Kennedy had usurped the majoritarian prerogative and jeopardized the legitimacy of counter-majoritarian decision-making. Justice Thomas admonished against attributing *any* substantive rights to the due process clause, tracing his narrow reading of the terms back to the Magna Carta and cautioning that a more expansive reading "invites judges to do exactly what the majority has done here—'roa[m] at large in the constitutional field' guided only by their personal views."[55] Justice Alito wrapped up the case with a concise treatise on judicial restraint.

The *Bowers* and *Lawrence* courts conducted their analyses under the due process clause rather than the equal protection clause, although the issue of gay equality looms large in both. In the latter, Justice O'Connor submitted a concurrence expressing a preference for the equal protection clause as the vehicle for protecting the sodomy right (perhaps because this would avoid overruling *Bowers*, in which she joined). The *Goodridge* court did not specify which of the two clauses in the state constitution guaranteed same-sex marriage in Massachusetts. The primary analysis in *Obergefell* was conducted under the due process clause but held that the rights of same-sex couples to both due process and equal protection had been abridged. Indeed, Justice Kennedy stated explicitly that the "interrelation of the two principles furthers our understanding of what freedom is and must become," going on to explore their mutually reinforcing natures in past cases concerning marriage.

Romer v. Evans, by contrast, squarely raised a question of equal protection.[56] In *Romer*, the U.S. Supreme Court reviewed Amendment 2 to Colorado's state constitution to determine whether it conflicted with the U.S. Constitution.

Amendment 2, which was passed by statewide referendum, rendered it a violation of the state constitution for Colorado or any of its cities or towns to extend antidiscrimination coverage to protect people on the basis of their sexual orientation. Justice Kennedy determined this to be inconsistent with the federal equal protection guarantee because, he found, it was based on nothing more than animus against gay people.

Justice Scalia began his dissent with this brief but potent sentence: "The Court has mistaken a Kulturkampf for a fit of spite."[57] The literal translation of the German term is *culture struggle*, but the reference is to Otto von Bismarck's nineteenth-century effort in Prussia to strip back the influence of what he viewed as an overly powerful Catholic Church by enacting hostile legislation and exiling church officials. Both the literal translation and the historical reference help to divine Scalia's meaning.

What Scalia saw happening in Colorado was a culture struggle—or, in more familiar parlance, a *culture war*. It recalls that which ensued between Bismarck and the papacy—a brawl between two powerful political foes over social policy. To hammer home the point, Scalia cited data that purported to establish the disproportionate wealth concentrated in gay urban communities and the success gays have had in capturing the thinking of the aristocracy, including elite sectors of the legal profession. Gays were not the victims of the majority's tyranny in this story; they were mighty warriors doing battle against well-matched adversaries.

The court, Scalia argued, has mistakenly perceived a "fit of spite." Of course, Kennedy did not use the term "spite"—he called it "animus." Where Scalia saw "tolerant Coloradans [trying] to preserve traditional sexual mores against the efforts of a politically powerful minority to revise those mores,"[58] Kennedy saw a bullying majority that pulled the lever to deny antidiscrimination protections to a vulnerable minority.

What majority and dissent agreed on in *Romer* was the tenet of the American system that the Court serves as guarantor of individual rights against what can be a tyrannical majority; that is the purpose of having a counter-majoritarian institution. If gays and lesbians were a formidable political opponent, however, rather than a weak minority oppressed by a prejudiced majority, then why was the counter-majoritarian branch stepping in on their behalf? If this was a *Kulturkampf,* a political struggle between fairly matched opponents, then the proper institutional venue for that fight was majoritarian, not counter-majoritarian, and the Court ought to have declined the invitation to intervene.

The dispute between Kennedy and Scalia presents an epistemological problem—that is, a problem with the foundation of knowledge on which they conduct their analyses. Did Colorado's voters approve Amendment 2 for reasons of *morality* or *animus*? If you view homosexuality as immoral, then you are likely to see efforts to attain antidiscrimination protections as waging political battle over social policy. If you instead begin with the premise that homosexuality is morally good or morally neutral, then you are likely instead to view the same battles as efforts to secure equal rights for a minority group and Amendment 2 as discriminatory. Your view, in turn, will suggest a position on the institutional competence question—that is, whether counter-majoritarian assistance in the form of striking down Amendment 2 was justified.

For Scalia to assert that Kennedy had "mistaken" a culture war over morality for "a fit of spite" was no more or less rooted in personal belief than Kennedy's certainty that Amendment 2 was based on animus. Both men began on a foundation composed of unacknowledged values. It is not inherently problematic for an ordinary person to do that, but when a judge does it, it presents a problem for our system. That is why judges constantly rehearse that they are deciding neutrally and deductively, not politically; that they are adhering faithfully to their judicial role, not exceeding it. It is also why advocates frame their arguments in those same terms.

The critique of feigned neutrality can be levied at judges on both sides of a case such as *Romer*. The real burden, however, is on the judge who is trying to justify a decision to strike down a majoritarian act to vindicate a right. In other words, if—as in *Bowers, Lawrence, Goodridge, Obergefell*, or *Romer*—there is a judge who would strike down a sodomy law or a marriage law or a state constitutional amendment, it is *that judge*, and *not* the one who wishes to defer to the majority, who bears the burden of providing an adequate rationale for doing so.

Again, the *Lochner* decision, striking down the maximum hour law for bakers on the grounds of due process, is a lynchpin. That case came down with two dissents. One was written by Justice John Marshall Harlan,[59] a turn-of-the-(twentieth-)century liberal who is best known for dissenting from *Plessy v. Ferguson* and other decisions that set back black civil rights.[60] Harlan thought that the State of New York was acting properly to protect the health and safety of its citizens when it sought to regulate the hours that people could toil in hot, industrial bakeries and inhale airborne flour dust. Two other justices joined his dissent.

Justice Oliver Wendell Holmes Jr. was not one of them. He dissented separately.[61] No other justice joined his opinion, perhaps because none of them quite understood his point. It probably read as rather opaque at the time. The opinion has, however, become one of most revered in American jurisprudence, studied carefully every year by scholars and students of constitutional law and legal history.

Holmes's *Lochner* dissent is brief but rich. In it, he attacks the majority for overstepping the judicial role. Justice Peckham, who wrote the main opinion, had begun by declaring his fidelity to his role. This, as we have seen, is a standard trope in constitutional opinion writing. Recall that the sine qua non of the *Lochner* Court was an interpretation of the due process clause that included a fundamental right to contract and an apparent judicial warrant, therefore, to strike down laws that infringed on that right. But Holmes pointed out that the Court had *not* used the due process clause to strike down Sunday laws (prohibiting business operations on Sundays) or usury laws (prohibiting exorbitant rates of interest). These laws fettered free contract. Why, Holmes was inviting the reader to wonder, were those laws permitted to stand, while the New York labor law was being struck down?

Holmes offered an explanation with this famous sentence: "General propositions do not decide concrete cases."[62] This might read as bland to the uninitiated, but I promise you, it is not. It is a frontal assault on the possibility of deduction from first principles and, ultimately, therefore on the legitimacy of counter-majoritarian decision-making. The right to contract, Holmes was alleging, did not really determine the outcome of this case—or any case. He first accused the majority of deciding the case "upon an economic theory which a large part of the country does not entertain" (i.e., laissez-faire), adding "the Fourteenth Amendment does not enact Mr. Herbert Spencer's Social Statics" (referring to a foundational tract of social Darwinism).[63]

But Holmes went even further than charging his adversaries on the Court with overstepping the bounds of their role in this specific case, asserting that in "concrete cases" generally, "the decision will depend on a judgment or intuition more subtle than any articulate major premise."[64] So it gets worse. How are judges making decisions? *Intuition*. WHAT?!? That cannot be allowed, can it? No—which is why he added this: "I think that the word liberty in the Fourteenth Amendment [the language in the due process clause that the majority thought entailed freedom of contract] is perverted when it is held to prevent the natural outcome of a dominant opinion, unless it can be said that a fair and rational man necessarily would admit that the statute proposed would infringe fundamental principles as they have been understood by the traditions of our people and our law."[65]

In other words, the *Lochner* majority over-interpreted the due process clause and thereby overly empowered itself at the expense of the majority will. New

York wanted this labor law. The elected representatives of that state passed it unanimously. *You are not supposed to make "liberty" mean anything you want it to mean so that you can strike down laws that do not comport with your preferred economic policy. Your intuitions are guiding you,* Holmes was chiding, *not deduction from a first principle. And that is not entirely legit, because there is a voting public out there, and they did not elect us. We pervert the language of the Constitution when we use it to interfere with the majority's will.*

Unless . . . there is an *unless* after the comma. Holmes did not advocate that the justices hang up their robes and call it quits. He did not conclude his opinion by admonishing judges to leave every law standing as long as the majority favored it. Some laws have to go; some laws *are unconstitutional.* Judges are still charged with preserving the fundamental principles. Holmes gives us precious little guidance regarding how to determine the nature and extent of those principles (what a "fair and rational man would admit") and thus circles us back into some of the same analytical problems he brings to light. But he can be forgiven; he was among the earliest and clearest voices to elucidate conundrums that have consumed legal thinkers for more than a century. And we can still take from among the many insights packed into his *Lochner* dissent this crucial lesson: If the neutrality of judicial deduction from first principles is suspect, and something more like intuition is driving the outcome of cases, that presents a threat to our democratic expectations, thus counseling in favor of deference to the majority. The burden is therefore heavy on those who would ask the counter-majoritarian branch to undo the majority's work.[66]

It may be that Scalia and Kennedy were equally without foundation regarding whether morality or animus was behind Colorado's Amendment 2—that both were guided by "intuition" or perhaps by unacknowledged values. Only Kennedy, however, needed to justify striking down a law passed by the majority of voters in Colorado. In a country where the majority is supposed to make the laws, Kennedy's burden was to show why he was not "perverting" the Constitution and overstepping the judicial role—or, in contemporary popular parlance, why he was not being an "activist" judge. Why was Kennedy's assertion of the majority's animus, as against Scalia's assertion of Colorado's tolerant morality, not merely reflective of his personal political preferences?

The epistemological difficulty evident in *Romer* is a feature of the indeterminacy of rights. Some legal questions have answers that would garner a broad consensus in the legal community, irrespective of any individual judge or lawyer's political leaning. Sometimes we get unanimous decisions from politically divided tribunals, and sometimes cases do not arise in the first instance because a lawyer counsels a client that the consensus legal answer is so thoroughly arrayed against the client that it would be folly to bring a suit. This is so not necessarily because the interpretive questions that arise in those cases have intrinsic answers, but because at any given moment in history, forces of knowledge and culture make some answers to legal questions seem obvious. At another moment, the consensus could shift, and the obvious answer could change. This has happened in many areas of law, including with regard to questions specific to LGBT people.

The conclusion to be drawn is not that legal reasoning is nothing in the end but judges' political preferences. Legal reasoning does admit some real constraints. As the critical legal scholar Karl Klare has explained, "No serious participant in this debate claims that legal and political reasoning are identical or that they collapse into one another or that law is 'nothing but politics.' . . . Legal argument permissibly appeals to a narrower range of relevant norms and considerations than political decision-making. Legal practices are structured and inflected by distinct intellectual traditions and argumentative techniques inculcated by professional training and socialization."[67]

In law schools, we refer to this distinction by using the phrase *learning to think like a lawyer*. Central to legal education is the disciplining of law students' argument into the range that is acceptable and useful in legal culture. As Klare writes, "Critical theory doubts that we can identify foundational, self-applying, politically neutral principles but fully embraces dialogue based on good-faith reason-giving and attempts to persuade by appeal to social experience, empathy, solidarity, and sensitivity to difference with a goal (among others) of distinguishing between good/persuasive legal arguments and bad/unconvincing legal arguments."[68] It is not always easy, however, to identify the determinants of a decision, even where political leanings or cultural norms are forthrightly identified. Critical examination may reveal that somewhere in the course of applying the law to the facts of a case, an unacknowledged facet of a judge's accumulated learning steered the reasoning process toward its outcome.

Indeterminacy provokes what a Freudian might call a *reaction-formation*: insistent tropes of political chastity in which lawyers and judges on both sides of controversial disputes collaborate, whether by insisting on the logical correctness of their own position or by indignantly charging their opponents with deviation from the apolitical ideal. Counter-majoritarianism—as imagined by the Federalists, made the official theory of the judicial department in *Marbury v. Madison*, and brought to the brink of disaster by the *Lochner* Court and a president who determined that institutional pieties were not worth the price to a country fighting its way out of economic despair—demands each day that lawyers and judges participate in a discourse that feeds an insatiable need for judicial legitimation.

A school of leftist legal scholars (of which Klare is a prominent member) collectively known as critical legal studies (CLS) advanced the indeterminacy critique in the 1980s and 1990s. Writers of the CLS school viewed Holmes as a key progenitor due in part to the flaws he observed in the process of judicial deduction, and they proceeded to develop the critique. Duncan Kennedy, another leading CLS scholar, explained how rights arguments are vital to the legitimation enterprise:

> Rights play a central role in the American mode of political discourse. . . .
> It is a presupposition of the discourse that there is a crucial distinction
> between "value judgments," which are a matter of preference, subjectiv-
> ity, the arbitrary . . . and "factual judgments," or scientific, objective, or
> empirical judgments. . . . Claims that . . . a rule will "promote the general
> welfare" [a.k.a. policy preferences] are conventionally understood to
> be on the subjective side . . . and are best settled by majority vote. . . . The
> point of an appeal to a right, the reason for making it, is that it can't be
> reduced to a mere "value judgment."[69]

In American legal discourse, rights have "two crucial properties" that place them in a mediating position between the domains of fact and value: "First, they are 'universal' in the sense that they derive from . . . values" that are widely shared.[70] "Second, they are 'factoid,' in the sense that 'once you acknowledge the existence of the right, then you have to agree that its observance requires x, y, and z.'"[71]

When advocates assert a rights claim, they might begin with a universal precept—for example, we all have a right to equality or against discrimination. They must also assert a *necessary* link between equality and the sought-after outcome. The broad consensus and constitutional validity undergirding the initial value, plus the "factoid" necessity of the consequences that are alleged to follow logically, combine to lend the claim the discursive suggestion of neutrality and objectivity. The claim is not "This is a good policy." A judge would push a litigant making that claim to the legislature. A rights claim is framed *as a right* precisely to distinguish it from mere policy preference and to strip it of any sign of political desire. Why? Because if rights claims are wishes—even wishes based on sound policy analysis—then an unelected, life-tenured court's granting them is profoundly antidemocratic. Rights claims must exceed our desires. They must be *correct*.[72]

Advocates for LGBT equal rights are always engaged in two interconnected tasks: arguing for the substantive outcome they seek *and* affirming the court's neutrality should they prevail. Judicial opinions mirror that structure when they explain the bases for their decisions. The legal culture requires this. To pursue LGBT equal rights objectives in a judicial setting is necessarily to acquiesce to the demand that the system's logic and legitimacy be constantly reaffirmed.

Formal versus Substantive Equality and Other Interpretive Conundrums

Most people in modern legal cultures agree that equality is a right to which we are all entitled. (Privacy is quite a bit more controversial.) We expect belief in natural hierarchy and aristocratic entitlement to decline with the progress of history. Despite widespread accord that equality is desirable, however, its meaning remains unsettled. A number of interpretive dilemmas associated with equality claims generally and LGBT equality claims in particular also contribute to the indeterminacy of LGBT equal rights argument.

One recurring controversy is whether equality requires that everyone be treated "blindly"—that is, *identically* (as if certain features of our identities or circumstances were irrelevant or even invisible)—or whether it would be more "equal" to take into consideration our differences. If we should be treated identically, then affirmative action based on race would violate the equality guarantee, as would any accommodation for disabled people or taking into consideration child-care obligations when deciding whether a female employee should receive a bonus. The contrary view is that it is not "equal" to require exactly the same credentials of college applicants no matter their race, given the history of discrimination and educational deprivation inflicted on people of color; provision of a ramp or a computer program that reads aloud to a disabled employee provides equal opportunity to that person; and if leaving the office in time to cook supper disqualifies employees from earning bonuses, the workplace is effectively rigged against women. According to this view, treating people who are differently situated as if they were the same violates, rather than furthers, the equality guarantee. In legal jargon, the contrast is denoted by the terms *formal equality* (which mandates the same treatment for all) and *substantive* or *functional equality* (which allows for differences in treatment that reflect traits or circumstances distinguishing categories of people).[73]

Any minimally competent lawyer in the United States appreciates the range of meanings encompassed in a word such as *equality*. (Those who do not may be so righteously certain that they "know" what *equality* is that it hampers their interpretive capacities.) When a decision maker is faced with a choice such as the one Duffy faced in the Huff case, the mere command of equality, alas, is no guide. The same command contains contradictory possibilities.

Other terms relevant to antidiscrimination efforts contain interpretive conundrums, as well. Title VII of the Civil Rights Act of 1964 prohibits discrimination in employment because of, among other things, sex.[74] But what exactly does the term *sex* entail? With no independent statutory category for gender identity under federal law, the question became one of critical significance to transgender plaintiffs seeking remedies for employment discrimination as early as the 1980s. In *Ulane v. Eastern Airlines*,[75] a pilot, Kenneth Ulane, transitioned medically and socially to become Karen and was consequently discharged by her employer. Ulane sued for sex discrimination under Title VII, prevailing in the trial court, but the U.S. Court of Appeals for the Seventh Circuit held that discrimination on the basis of *sex*, on a plain reading, referred only to discrimination against men because they were men or against women because they were women and that Congress had not contemplated transsexuals in enacting the statute. According to the court, antidiscrimination protection for Ulane would have required additional statutory language. A few other courts construed Title VII in this narrow fashion around the same time.[76]

In 1989, the Supreme Court decided *Price-Waterhouse v. Hopkins*,[77] a case in which an accounting firm passed over a high-performing female employee for partnership. The record contained evidence that one partner had described the employee as "macho" and another had suggested that she dress and walk more femininely, wear makeup, and so on. The Court found that the Title VII prohibition against sex discrimination barred *sex stereotyping*—that is, discrimination on the basis of nonconformity with expectations of manhood or womanhood. This decision did not open the door right away for transgender plaintiffs, but eventually there were some discernible benefits, initially outside the Title VII context. In a First Circuit case, *Rosa v. Park West Bank and Trust Company*, which arose under the Equal Credit Opportunity Act,[78] Rosa, a transwoman, claimed she was discriminated against by her bank due to her gender presentation and feminine attire. Her case was permitted to proceed on a sex-stereotyping theory in 2000. In 2004, the Sixth Circuit embraced the sex-stereotyping theory in a Title VII case involving an Ohio transgender firefighter whom the city attempted to badger into resigning with mandated psychiatric evaluations.[79] Since that time, a number of federal courts have followed suit.

In the much ballyhooed case *Schroer v. Billington* in 2008, Diane Schroer, a former U.S. Army Colonel in Special Ops, applied to be a terrorism analyst with the Library of Congress.[80] She was still David Schroer at the time, and

David was offered the position. Once she informed her employer of her intent to transition, however, the offer was rescinded. The District Court for the District of Columbia invoked the sex-stereotyping theory but also reasoned that discrimination on the basis of transgender status was sex discrimination under Title VII even if the employer held no particular stereotypes of men or women, just as it would be religious discrimination to discriminate against someone for converting regardless of whether the employer held stereotypes of any particular religious group.

The *Schroer* decision issued from a lower court and is therefore of limited precedential value outside DC, but President Barack Obama's recess appointment of Chai Feldblum to the Equal Employment Opportunity Commission (EEOC) may have assisted in ushering in the shift that *Schroer* represents. Long a scholar of and advocate for LGBT rights (as well as disability rights), Feldblum likely contributed to the agency's revised construction of *sex* to encompass discrimination on the basis of gender identity and gender nonconformity, which it announced in 2012 in its decision in *Macy v. Holder*.[81] Mia Macy was a transgender applicant for a position in a crime lab affiliated with the U.S. Bureau of Alcohol, Tobacco, Firearms and Explosives (ATF). She revealed her transgender status in the course of the hiring process and, suddenly, what looked to be a new job pending only the background check fell through. Suspicious, Macy launched a process that began in the Equal Employment Opportunity office within ATF, but eventually led to her appeal to the EEOC.

In the course of her appeal, and in response to the ATF's rejection of Macy's discrimination claim, the EEOC stated that it "hereby clarifies that claims of discrimination based on transgender status, also referred to as claims of discrimination based on gender identity, are cognizable under Title VII's sex discrimination prohibition."[82] The EEOC floated a couple of theories: that, under *Price-Waterhouse*, discrimination on the basis of transgender status constituted sex-stereotyping, and, as in *Schroer*, that discriminating against a person for making a transition from one gender identity to another constituted sex discrimination.

The EEOC's rulings do not bind the federal courts, but they are entitled to a degree of deference on the grounds that the EEOC is the expert federal agency on employment discrimination. It remains to be seen whether the *Macy* jumble of theories will carry. In 2014, President Obama's Department of Labor announced that discrimination against transgender employees working for federal contractors was prohibited under an existing federal law that proscribes discrimination based on sex, with no mention of the *Schroer* rationale. Later that year, the EEOC brought a funeral home in Michigan and an eye and ear clinic in Florida to federal district court for discriminating against transgender employees in violation of Title VII, raising both gender stereotyping and *Schroer*-style "transition" theories. Such a dramatic potential increase in antidiscrimination coverage may portend a complete reversal of the *Ulane*-era trend.

Even accepting that gender identity is encompassed in the term *sex*, however, what will it mean to *discriminate* on that basis? Refusing to hire someone because the person is transgender would be an easy case. But if an employee who transitions from male to female wishes to use the women's restroom in her workplace, and her employer refuses her admittance, will courts consider that discrimination?

In *Goins v. West Group*, a trans woman named Julienne Goins was denied access to the women's restroom nearest her workstation at the publishing company where she was employed in Minnesota.[83] The Supreme Court of Minnesota did not view this as discriminatory:

> Goins does not argue that an employer engages in impermissible discrimination by designating the use of restrooms according to gender. Rather, her claim is that the [Minnesota Human Rights Act (MHRA)] prohibits West's policy of designating restroom use according to biological gender, and requires instead that such designation be based on self-image of gender.... We do not believe the MHRA can be read so broadly.... We believe ... that the MHRA neither requires nor prohibits restroom designation according to self-image of gender or according to biological gender.... Bearing in mind that the obligation of the judiciary in construing legislation is to give meaning to words accorded by common experience and understanding, to go beyond the parameters of a legislative enactment would amount to an intrusion upon the policy-making function of the legislature. Accordingly, absent more express guidance from the legislature, we conclude that an employer's designation of employee restroom use based on biological gender is not ... discrimination in violation of the MHRA.[84]

To view West's exclusion of Goins from the women's restroom as discriminatory, one must first hold the view that Goins was properly classified as a woman. This was not the Minnesota court's view; it accepted West's use of a biological basis for classification. A concurring justice emphasized the point: "I concur in the result reached by the court. I write separately to clarify one point with respect to the court's conclusion that Goins has failed to establish that 'she is eligible to use the restrooms designated for her biological gender.' ... To satisfy this element, Goins must establish that she is biologically female.

Because she has failed to do so, her disparate treatment discrimination claim fails as a matter of law."[85]

This case was an early defeat for advocates of trans equality, but since then results have been more promising. A transgender patron of a Denny's restaurant in Maine survived a motion to dismiss on a similar claim in 2010 (but under a public accommodations law), prompting Denny's to change its policy and permit transgender people access to restrooms consistent with their gender identities.[86] A transgender Verizon employee repairing the phone lines in Grand Central Terminal was harassed (by police and others) while attempting to use the women's restroom. The resulting action eventually yielded a settlement that included adoption of a "self-identification" policy regarding bathroom usage in New York City transportation terminals.[87] New York City, which subsequently made ID cards available on which residents may list the gender with which they identify, was among the first few locales with such a progressive policy.

The victory for six-year-old Coy Mathis against her school district in Colorado was an especially happy one.[88] Coy was assigned the male sex at birth, but even before she could speak Coy began expressing a female gender identity. She had been using the girls' restroom at her elementary school apparently without incident, and with the knowledge of her teacher and principal, until a school psychologist learned of it and informed the superintendent, who put the kibosh on it, insisting that Coy be diverted to a single-sex staff restroom or the restroom in the nurse's office. Coy's parents brought the school district before Colorado's Division of Civil Rights (DCR), the state agency responsible for hearing claims of discrimination. The DCR determined that, notwithstanding indication to the contrary on her birth certificate, Coy was in fact a girl and therefore entitled to use the girls' bathroom. Citing research in the field, the DCR reasoned that "sex assignment at birth ... is merely ... based on observable anatomy, and does not take into consideration ... psychological and biological variations."[89] Subsequent documentation identified Coy as a girl, and the DCR held accordingly.

Soon after the Colorado DCR issued its decision, the Supreme Court of Maine became the first state supreme court to award a victory to a transgender student in these circumstances.[90] Nicole Maines, a teenager by the time of the decision, was prevented in fifth grade from using the girls' room in her elementary school. She was sent instead to a unisex staff restroom. The Maine Supreme Court construed transgender antidiscrimination protections in the Maine Human Rights Act to permit access to school bathrooms consistent with gender identity.[91]

The school bathroom issue has gone federal. The U.S. Department of Education's Office for Civil Rights (DOE-OCR) is responsible for enforcing the provisions of Title IX, which prohibits sex discrimination in any federally funded educational program.[92] In response to a growing number of cases involving trans schoolchildren, the DOE-OCR issued an "opinion letter" in 2015 construing Title IX to require that schools "treat transgender students consistent with their gender identity" in providing access to bathrooms and locker rooms. Not all jurisdictions agreed. North Carolina infamously enacted HB2, which (among other provisions) prohibits people in public agencies, schools, and universities from using bathrooms inconsistent with their assigned sex at birth.[93] The Department of Justice (DOJ) sued the state to enjoin enforcement of the law on the grounds that it violates Title VII and Title IX.

In 2016, a transboy, Gavin Grimm (G.G. in the court documents), sued his school district in Virginia for discriminating against him in violation of Title IX. G.G. initially used the boys' room with his school's approval, but a group of hostile parents and school board members succeeded in enacting a policy that prohibited him from continuing to do so. The federal district court dismissed the boy's lawsuit, but the Court of Appeals for the Fourth Circuit, once thought to be quite conservative, surprised a lot of people by reinstating the suit, reasoning that the district court had not accorded proper deference to the DOE-OCR's interpretation of how sex is determined for purposes of Title IX. President Obama's DOE-OCR and DOJ had jointly issued a "Dear Colleague" letter explaining school districts' obligation to treat transgender students in accordance with their gender identities and reminding readers "how [federal enforcement agencies] evaluate a school's compliance." That letter, which contained the implicit threat of loss of federal funds for recalcitrant schools, immediately prompted eleven states to sue the federal government, claiming that the executive branch had exceeded its powers and imbued the statutory law with more meaning than the language warrants.[94] A few months later, ten more states filed a similar lawsuit in another federal court.

Soon after President Donald Trump took office, however, his administration revoked the letter, rendering the issue of administrative deference moot. The Supreme Court had been poised to hear the case, but after the letter was revoked the case was instead remanded back to the Fourth Circuit to address the question of what Title IX requires, irrespective of the letter. It would be a tremendous advance for trans equality if Title IX itself were deemed to protect trans students' right to have access to facilities consistent with their gender identity, particularly if affirmed by the Supreme Court.

Combatants on this latest culture war terrain are working toward an authoritative decision that will resolve these cases. In the meantime, expectations for bathrooms, along with locker rooms, dormitories, prisons, and other sex-segregated facilities, remain unsettled, and transgender people face barriers to gaining access to facilities that accommodate the most basic needs. The politics of the anti-trans position is undoubtedly phobic, but the controversy nonetheless winds us back to the Aristotelian question: Who is the transgender individual "like"? Is a transgender woman "like" other women or "like" others who were assigned the male sex at birth? Sometimes the cases raise the question of what it takes (hormones? surgery? a therapist's letter?) to establish that one has become more "like" the gender with which one identifies. In any event, a transgender woman is both like and unlike a ciswoman or a cisman,[95] depending on the aspects compared, creating a decision point in an antidiscrimination analysis that is likely informed by one's politics.

Same-sex marriage as an equal rights claim was beset with similar analytic difficulties. One must, for example, decide whether to frame the question at the level of couples or individuals. In the case of the former, are same-sex couples "like" heterosexual couples? It depends again on the points of comparison. Certainly same-sex partners can love each other and pool their finances just as heterosexual partners do, but for opponents of same-sex marriage the fact that same-sex couples cannot produce offspring without involving a third party is more important.

Suppose one believes that formal equality ought to govern at the level of the individual—that is, gay and lesbian individuals ought to be treated exactly the same as heterosexual individuals, regardless of any differences. Does that mean that it is sufficient that an individual lesbian be legally permitted to marry a man? That is one possible conclusion within formal equality argumentation. It is certainly not, however, what William N. Eskridge Jr., a leading American academic proponent of same-sex marriage, had in mind when he maintained that "the principle of formal equality requires the state to recognize same-sex unions on the same terms as which it recognizes different-sex unions."[96]

Formal Equality and Indeterminacy

In his book *The Case for Same-Sex Marriage* (1996), written well in advance of any real progress on the issue, Eskridge made an early case for same-sex marriage, spurred by a wish for the extinction of what he viewed as a libertine and immature gay lifestyle in favor of what the subtitle of the book labels "Civilized

Commitment."[97] Not all of the arguments in the book are constitutional; he takes up historical, cultural, and philosophical debates, as well. On the issue of constitutional entitlement, though, Eskridge turned to *Loving v. Virginia*, the 1967 case in which Chief Justice Earl Warren, writing for a unanimous U.S. Supreme Court, struck down a state ban on marriage between white and nonwhite people.[98] A tight analogy between interracial and same-sex marriage, according to Eskridge's thinking, would suggest that the same fate was consti- tutionally required for heterosexual-only marriage laws.

Before *Obergefell*, every year that I taught *Loving* in Constitutional Law, a student would ask why it did not settle the question of same-sex marriage. Why, if it is race discrimination for a state to limit one's choice of marital partner by race, is it not sex discrimination for a state to limit one's choice of marital part- ner by sex? Eskridge explains how the two issues were typically distinguished. The statute in *Loving* classified people based on race; Chief Justice Warren found that the underlying ideology was white supremacy and that the statute effectively created a "caste system" that disadvantaged nonwhite people. In the case of a challenge to the heterosexual-only marriage laws, however, the statutes categorize people by sex (not by sexual orientation); the ideology that sustains this arrangement is heterosexism (rather than sexism); and the disadvantage is allocated to gays and lesbians (rather than to women). In the interracial mar- riage context, therefore, there is continuity among the statutory classification, the particular form of bigotry that animates it, and the group that suffers as a result—it is race all the way down. The same-sex marriage claim, however, jumps from the statutory classification (sex) to the ideology and injured group (heterosexism and gays).

Eskridge set out to revive the *Loving* analogy in an effort to prove that the same formal equality principle vindicated in *Loving* mandated recognition of same-sex marriage. He did so by making deft use of the flexibility on the same-sex marriage side of the analogy. First, citing the work of Sylvia Law and An- drew Koppelman,[99] he proposed that heterosexism is, at its core, sexism, and that women—confined historically to a subordinate role in the marital relation— are disadvantaged by the traditional marriage definition. This reading produces continuity across the three poles (sex/sexism/women) so that the *Loving* anal- ogy holds.

But Eskridge was not really convinced by the Law-Koppelman argument that heterosexism is, at its base, sexism, so he moved on to propose an analogue to *Loving* that put the gay issue (not the women issue) at the center. Rather than bringing the sexual orientation poles (ideology, injured group) into line with the statutory classification, Eskridge brought the statutory classification into line with the sexual orientation poles. Marriage statutes may *appear* to classify people on the basis of sex (i.e., by defining marriage as the union of one man and one woman), but there is case law to suggest that when a statute has heavily "lopsided effect[s]," those effects are relevant to apprehending the classification.

The Supreme Court had said as much in *Washington v. Davis*, in which it rejected a challenge to a standardized test that disproportionately excluded black applicants from the District of Columbia's police force.[100] The effects in the case were not lopsided enough to sustain the challenge—that is, too many black applicants scored well on the test. The Court suggested, however, that if the test resulted in no or nearly no black police officers, the outcome might have been different. The standardized test that was the subject of the lawsuit was *facially neutral* as to race—that is, it employed no explicit racial classification. It did not, for example, allocate an automatic ten-point disadvantage to black test takers.[101] Even in an instance of facial neutrality, however, an extreme racial imbalance, the Court seemed to be saying, could set up a viable equal protection challenge for an affected racial group.

Relying on this message from the Court, Eskridge proposed that the *real* classification in a same-sex marriage case was sexual orientation, because the sex-specific marriage laws allocated radically lopsided adverse effects to the class of gays and lesbians. This wrapped the third pole back into the first— the classification (regardless of what the statute says) is effectively determined by the injured group if the injury is disproportionate enough. Now we have continuity across the three poles: Sexual orientation is the true classification; heterosexism sustains the classification; and gays and lesbians are the injured group. The *Loving* analogy holds.[102]

The elasticity between sex and sexual orientation makes it possible to rework the relationships among the poles to overcome the distinction that is usually offered between interracial and same-sex marriage. Whether using the Law-Koppelman "heterosexism is really sexism" approach or Eskridge's "the effect of sex as a facial classification is extreme lopsidedness as to sexual orientation," one can effectively massage the same-sex marriage side of the analogy into shape. To complete his argument, however, Eskridge required one more step, and that step is over a much broader chasm than he acknowledges.

Ultimately, what Eskridge was trying to prove was not just that *Loving* and a same-sex marriage case were analogous, but that "the principle of formal equality requires the state to recognize same-sex unions on the same terms as which it recognizes different-sex unions." Let us bracket, for the time being, the question of whether formal equality is necessarily the correct goal—that question is the subject of the next section. The issue for the moment is whether formal equality *requires* recognition of same-sex marriages. Eskridge worked the analogy for thirty pages on the apparent assumption that the principle of formal equality logically and inexorably determined the outcome of *Loving*. But just as Eskridge labored and maneuvered to achieve continuity among the three conceptual poles in the same-sex marriage context to serve his political purposes, Chief Justice Warren made deliberate and motivated choices in the interracial marriage context.

The Virginia statute in *Loving* classified marital partners by race, but Virginia denied that its purpose was to maintain a racial hierarchy. That might seem absurd, but an earlier and much more conservative Supreme Court accepted the same contention in *Pace v. Alabama* when it upheld an antimiscegenation statute addressed to "adultery and fornication."[103] The notion that legal separation and inequality were inherently entwined was not the governing assumption in American law until 1954 with the decision in *Brown v. Board of Education*, and for the same idea to take root in the contexts of sex (*McLaughlin v. Florida* [1964]) and marriage (*Loving* [1967]), the country had to wait until the 1960s—a Supreme Court era both condemned and celebrated for its "judicial activism."[104]

In *Loving*, Virginia denied that its law was racially discriminatory because all offenders regardless of race were equally subject to punishment. The state offered instead a eugenic rationale. Warren saw this as a distinction without a difference. The ideology that animated the statute, in Warren's view, was obviously white supremacy.

That settles two poles: The Virginia statute classified marital partners by race, and the animating ideology was white supremacy. One pole remains: Who was the injured group? Eskridge reads Warren's opinion to find that Virginia created a "caste system" in which nonwhite people were subordinate. The Virginia statute did permit nonwhite people of whatever races to intermarry among themselves. It was only the purity of the white race with which the statute was preoccupied. (And even then, the statute made a bizarre exception for people who were less than one-sixteenth Native American, who were free to marry whites to honor the descendants of John Rolfe and Pocahontas.) But the two defendant spouses—Mildred Loving, a black woman, and Richard Loving, a white man—were equally subject to criminal punishment under the Virginia law.

As Eskridge acknowledges, it is therefore entirely plausible to conceptualize the third pole, the injured group, not as subordinates in the racial hierarchy but, rather, as "people who fall in love with a person of another race" (across the white-nonwhite divide).[105] This group does not have a label in common parlance, like *gay* or *homosexual*, although it could. Some people experience relatively consistent cross-racial desire, just as some experience relatively consistent same-sex desire. If Warren had found in *Loving* that the injured group was "people characterized by consistent cross-racial desire," it would have introduced discontinuity among the three poles. He chose not to do that.

Moreover, Warren did not have to conceptualize either of the first two poles as he did. He could have wrapped the "lopsided effects" back around the way that Eskridge did when he read the classification in the marriage laws as based on sexual orientation rather than sex.[106] Then the classification would have been "people characterized by consistent cross-racial desire." And if Warren had been a much more conservative justice, inclined to apologia for Virginia's racism, he might have accepted—as his predecessors on the Court had done in the Alabama case—that the state's eugenic explanation was distinct from white supremacy, changing the ideology pole. Each of the three poles was as malleable in the interracial marriage context as it was in the same-sex marriage context.

Hitching the same-sex marriage wagon to *Loving* does not mean that same-sex marriage is *required* by formal equality any more than interracial marriage was. Both outcomes are the product of political choices made at crucial decision points in the course of the analysis. Chief Justice Warren made good choices in *Loving*, but they were *choices*. They were not required by formal logic.

When Warren went to the grocery store and saw apples in one bin and oranges in another, do you think he suspected the grocer of an apple-supremacist ideology? In that context, separation does not suggest hierarchy. But because we live in a world in which we have a pretty good idea what Virginia was up to, white supremacy seems like the obvious explanation for its antimiscegenation statute. As Oliver Wendell Holmes famously wrote, "The life of the law has not been logic: it has been experience."[107] It is easy to think that Warren's conclusion was logically determined, but formal logic did not tell him the difference between his grocer and Virginia's statute; experience did.

The problem of *indeterminacy* encompasses this failure of logical deduction alone to carry a decision maker from a first principle (in this case, formal equality) to the outcome of a specific case. To reach the conclusion he reached in *Loving*, Chief Justice Warren needed to consult more than logic. He needed to consult his experience and intuition to tell him something that seems so plain that we might easily mistake it for logic: that the separation in the statute was driven by white supremacy.

Formal equality is equally dependent on experience in the same-sex marriage context. Judges have to make decisions that cannot be made using a chaste deductive process from the formal equality principle. Experience, values, intuition, and politics enter the chain of reasoning as the judge makes choices about whether to conceptualize equality around an individual or couple, whether same-sex couples are "like" heterosexual couples, whether the right being sought is a "new" right, and whether protecting marriage as a heterosexual institution is done out of morality or animus. This is not a wholesale indictment of reasoning; it is, rather, an acknowledgment of reasoning's gaps and a call to attend to what seeps into those gaps.

Formal Equality as an Impediment to Other Versions of Equality

While formal equality has its virtues, it is hardly agreed on as the singular goal toward which law reformers ought to be driving at all times. Indeed, formal and substantive equality goals can conflict, as is evident in the controversy over affirmative action, in which language such as "color-blindness" or "the content of [one's] character"[108]—initially offered by progressives to advance the cause of formal equality—is now routinely deployed by conservatives to impede the substantive equality goal of affirmative action. In the struggle over workplace accommodation for working mothers, women have found that they have divergent interests and that those interests are served by contrasting conceptions of equality. Many women who are mothers of young children would welcome workplace accommodations such as family leaves and flextime. Those women are best served by a substantive version of equality in which their special circumstances are accorded consideration. Women who are not mothers, however, may be served better by a requirement that everyone be treated the same.[109] Those women might find themselves passed over for the most competitive opportunities because they are mistakenly presumed likely candidates for the "mommy track," or they could end up performing uncompensated extra labor while their coworkers leave at 3 PM to attend to childcare responsibilities.[110]

LGBT constituencies were never unified about whether same-sex marriage was good for "us." Even if we concede for purposes of argument that formal equality requires it, why should we not instead have pursued a substantive version of equality in which the law customizes itself to the idiosyncrasies of LGBT subcultures, such as gay men's proclivity toward non-monogamy, transgender people of colors' ball houses, or extended lesbian families of former lovers? Lesbian feminists and sex radicals of various stripes have made such arguments for years.[111] They are typically met with the rejoinder, "Sure, live that life if you want, but give me the choice to marry." I will take that up in chapter 2 in the discussion of norm production, but for now observe only that the insistence that LGBT people be treated as formally *the same* can work against recognition of, and treatment in accord with, LGBT *differences*. The pursuit of equality contains *at least* two contradictory possibilities, and—given the ways in which we have seen formal and substantive equality objectives vie against one another in numerous contexts—it is not self-evident whether formal equality is desirable for everyone all the time.

This is not to insist that the mainstream movement for LGBT equal rights has consistently pursued formal equality objectives to the exclusion of all else. In the *Huff* case, for example, the pro-gay position was to ask for accommodation of Huff's difference from her heterosexual colleagues; this could be understood as a substantive equality objective. We may at times seek to be understood as the same and at other times wish to be recognized for our differences. Marriage has so dominated the agenda in recent years, however, that particularly in public discourse (it is a bit more complicated in the legal discourse, as chapter 2 explains) our advocates have emphasized sameness over difference.

Finally, the attainment of formal equality carries with it an underappreciated danger. The formal equality argument, understood as insistence on sameness of treatment, always carries the potential to legitimate inequities that remain after formal equality has been achieved,[112] setting up a painful impasse. We would not want to be without *Brown v. Board of Education*, but, of course, our nation's public schools remain thoroughly segregated. Because we have *Brown*, which is predominantly understood as a formal equality ruling,[113] it is much harder to explain today's segregation as a legal problem. When opportunity is formally equalized and antidiscrimination law pervades spheres of education and employment, it enables those who are reticent about progressive law reform on behalf of racial minorities to locate inequality (in unemployment rates, poverty rates, incarceration rates, university admissions, etc.) in the people whose advancement is stalled. This dynamic has long been appreciated in the context of race,[114] but it has gone woefully under-recognized in the context of sexuality and gender identity.

Imagine a future in which LGBT people have absolute formal equality, constitutionally and in every antidiscrimination law at federal, state, and municipal levels, plus access to same-sex marriage in every jurisdiction. Will our troubles be over? Will whatever inequalities remain be due to our own moral inferiority? What will we say when we have formal equality but our youth are still disproportionately homeless, in foster care, and suicidal? What will we say when we have formal equality but we are still injecting street-quality silicone and hormones and subjecting ourselves to police and prison violence for engaging in survival sex? What will we say when we have formal equality but we still find ourselves especially vulnerable to allegations of obscenity, lewdness, sexual impropriety, or predation? What will we say when we have formal equality and HIV, or some as yet unforeseen successor, ravages our communities? The LGBT movement's preoccupation with formal equality has prevented it from looking down the road and asking these kinds of questions.

It is no answer that these battles will come next. That answer ignores the costs of proceeding as we have. Formal equality *competes* with other equality strategies. We have seen time and again that efforts to achieve formal equality can *impede* other kinds of progress and affirm the fairness of the inequities that remain after formal equality has been gained. Once you have been treated the same, just as you asked, what do you have left to complain about?

Conclusion

If we take a step back from the merits of LGBT arguments and from the winning and losing of cases, we can observe some initial features of LGBT equal rights discourse. That discourse is entwined with the discourse of judicial neutrality. Part of what an equal rights argument is meant to do when it is levied in a judicial forum is to pacify a professionally endemic anxiety about institutional fidelity. Advocates urging a counter-majoritarian body to undo the will of a majoritarian one must argue in terms of logical deduction from first principles; judges who grant that wish must elaborate a justification that sounds in that same key; and opponents can be expected to launch a *j'accuse* of institutional excess.

Legal questions regarding LGBT equality are steeped in indeterminacies. Terms such as "equality" contain within them directly contradictory meanings. Decision makers make unacknowledged choices in their analyses about what marriage "is" or what two things are "alike."

The apprehension brought on by the indeterminacy problem elicits from judges as well as advocates a discourse that is designed to reassure. That effort is characterized by a pretense to logical necessity. The arguments that advocates have to offer legitimate the logic of the legal regime and collaborate in the myth of neutral deductive correctness. The consequence of constant reaffirmation of the pretense is that as one vision of equality is achieved yet rampant lived inequalities remain, the problems of the most marginalized become more entrenched and harder to crack. That is one of the under-recognized costs of LGBT equal rights discourse.

It is worth noting that arguments made in a legislative environment are by no means immune to similar critique. Even in the context of the "political branches," a parallel discourse distinguishes "policy" (which is professional, scientific, and informed by hard data) from "politics" (which is dirty, partisan, and debased).[115] Many of our biggest LGBT equal rights victories, however, have been won in courts. Moreover, our tripartite system of government and the ideal of being governed by laws and not men rely especially on perpetuation of the myth of judicial neutrality because of the unelected, life-tenure structure of the Third Branch. This has lent the discourse of judicial neutrality tremendous potency.

One might ask: Why, despite manifest indeterminacy, do concepts such as formal equality nonetheless exert such power? The power of discourse is that *we* are its instruments. Formal equality is not powerful merely by virtue of its logical force; formal equality is powerful because of its hold on us, because of its key place in a larger discursive system in which we think, reason, and argue. It operates within a larger cultural apparatus of common understandings—not static but circulating—as we simultaneously deploy it and are subject to its deep influence.

LGBT advocacy occurs predominantly within the terms of this discursive structure. As a consequence, even when we win, we also lose.

2

THE LGBT RIGHTS-BEARING SUBJECT

Aristotle's Revenge

This chapter examines a handful of cases, as well as public relations and legislative campaigns, conducted in LGBT equal rights discursive terms, and discusses their role in the production of knowledge. LGBT identities, and sometimes other identities, are products of the discourse in which LGBT advancement occurs. Those productive repercussions become evident once one tunes in to the knowledge production channel.

The case *Perry v. Schwarzenegger* was an especially fecund source of knowledge production.[1] The legal team representing same-sex couples in this case introduced a mountain of evidence on everything from the nature of gay identity to the efficiency of gay versus straight households to gay electoral power.

When David Boies and Theodore Olsen, famously opponents in *Bush v. Gore*,[2] agreed to join forces on behalf of two same-sex couples in California suing in federal court for the right to marry, a buzz of anticipation issued forth. A showdown seemed to be at hand. The two lawyers did what they could to foment the excitement, lending themselves to any news outlet that would have them, inviting questions about their unity on the issue and especially on the participation of Olsen, a Republican who had served as counsel to President Ronald Reagan during the Iran-Contra investigation and as solicitor general under President George W. Bush.

California's same-sex marriage story is a winding one. The most populous state in the country had a pretty robust domestic partnership statute, providing same-sex couples all of the rights available to heterosexual couples under state law excepting only the term "marriage" (and therefore the best chance at portability of their status outside the jurisdiction). Still, the remaining disparity prompted a lawsuit. In 2008, the California Supreme Court held that same-sex marriage was a state constitutional right, temporarily making California the second American jurisdiction to confer the status of marriage on same-sex couples.[3] The victory, however, was short-lived. Almost immediately after the decision issued, Proposition 8, a referendum to amend the state's constitution and restrict the definition of marriage to its heterosexual version, was certified for the November ballot. Prop 8 was passed the same night that Barack Obama was elected to his first term as president, and while millions across the country rejoiced, thousands of gay and lesbian Californians grieved.

Advocates for LGBT equal rights sued again, this time to invalidate Prop 8 under an arcane procedural feature of California constitutional law. Their argument was not as strong this time around, however, and in 2009 they lost by a vote of six to one in the California Supreme Court, reaching the end of the road under the state constitution.[4] They could have undertaken the arduous grassroots task of trying to reverse Prop 8 at the polls, but they had failed to defeat the proposition that way the year before, even with Obama at the top of the ticket. Prospects in the near-term for California's gays and lesbians and their intendeds looked bleak.

The strategy of the same-sex marriage campaign was a state-by-state one. This strategy yielded tremendous progress in the course of little more than a decade, initially in courts, beginning with the first major victory in Massachusetts, followed by Connecticut and Iowa, and later in legislatures (in New York, Rhode Island, and Illinois) and even by referendum (in Washington State, Maryland, and Maine). It also, however, dealt advocates some brutal blows along the way. Prop 8 in California was one. Maine also saw a repeal by referendum. Advocates in New York endured a judicial defeat, and advocates in New Jersey could not get legislation past Governor Chris Christie. These states all eventually came around by one path or another. Finally, challenges in federal court began chipping away at the intransigence of the deep red jurisdictions, culminating in *Obergefell v. Hodges*.[5] Along the way, however, the strategy of those hold-out jurisdictions was to pile up statutes and state constitutional amendments declaring the eternal heterosexuality of marriage and drive a wedge even further into the nation's cultural divide.[6]

The setbacks were too much for some to bear. In 2009, supported by a handful of wealthy Californians impatient with the state-by-state strategy and with the apparent intractability of their own state's electorate, Boies and Olsen filed

Perry in federal court in San Francisco, challenging Prop 8 under the U.S. Constitution and launching speculation that they were on course to the final battle over same-sex marriage in the United States.

Seasoned LGBT rights advocates at organizations such as Lambda, the National Center for Lesbian Rights, and the American Civil Liberties Union (ACLU) were cautious—reticent even. As a group, they tend toward gradualism, and they were more familiar than Boies and Olsen—neither of whom has dedicated his career to LGBT advocacy—with the realities of homophobia. The liberal outsider "simple fairness" perspective that Boies and Olsen brought to the issue, while sweet, might have turned out to be painfully naïve in the face of the disgust and moralism that LGBT advocates knew all too well in the eyes of some of the judges who regularly decided their fates. Eventually, the professional LGBT advocacy community had no choice but to lend its wary support, as Boies and Olsen went to trial in the Northern District of California. The major organizations crossed their fingers behind their backs, however, hoping that *Perry* would not make it to the U.S. Supreme Court before one of the carefully constructed challenges to the Defense of Marriage Act (DOMA) that they were ushering up the pipelines of several federal circuits.[7] They submitted a supportive *amicus* brief in *Perry*, but one that offered narrow grounds on which the judge might strike down Prop 8, with the apparent wish for the decision to be limited in its effect to California rather than serve as the last word for the entire country.

Meanwhile, the State of California, then under Governor Arnold Schwarzenegger and Attorney General Jerry Brown, both supporters of same-sex marriage, declined to defend Prop 8 in federal court. As a result, antigay activists, referred to in *Perry* as the *proponents* of Prop 8, defended the state constitutional amendment they had worked to pass. The lack of willingness on the part of California to stand up for the law would eventually prevent *Perry* from materializing into the final showdown that many had anticipated it would be. The Supreme Court would eventually find that the case ended when the trial court struck down Prop 8 because the proponents lacked standing to appeal that initial ruling. This effectively limited *Perry*'s impact to Prop 8 itself, and therefore to California.[8]

Unlike all of the same-sex marriage litigations from the preceding decade, *Perry* went to trial. State court cases in jurisdictions such as Massachusetts, New York, and Iowa had been argued on a procedural motion, without the apparent need for a trial. None of the important facts in those cases were deemed to be in dispute: A same-sex couple went to the appropriate clerk's office asking for a marriage license and was refused based on sex alone; on that much, all parties agreed. The lawyers and judge were therefore focused on the legal question—that is, whether the constitution required that the couple be granted a marriage license notwithstanding the fact that the two people were of the same sex. *Perry*, however, was a full-scale theatrical production, and central to that production was the testimony of expert witnesses.

One of the experts was Professor Nancy Cott of Harvard University, who is among the nation's leading historians of marriage. Cott testified about the trajectory of marriage in the United States. Marriage, she said, originated in the common law, "and the common law included a doctrine that was called 'coverture' that described what the marital roles and duties were."[9] Cott explained that the husband's "obligation was to support his wife, provide her with the basic material goods of life, and to do so for their dependents. And [the wife's] part of the bargain was to serve and obey him, and to lend him all of her property, and also enable him to take all of her earnings, and represent her in court or in any sort of legal or economic transaction."[10]

Asked about the reason for coverture, Cott stated, "Assumptions were at the time, that men were suited to be providers ... whereas women, the weaker sex, were suited to be dependent. ... The sexual division of labor underlay the formation of the marital household, and the reason that a man and a woman were seen to be necessary to form the marital household. So that their complementary tasks and duties and talents would be put in synch and would enable the household to survive."[11]

Cott proceeded to delineate the factors that were significant in the transformation of marriage as it was understood in early American history to its contemporary incarnation. She discussed industrialization and the shift "away from agrarian society," changes in values about what kinds of behavior are appropriate to the sexes, and, of course, legal developments. Cott described the demise of coverture and the capturing by women of their legal personalities, the advent of Title VII of the Civil Rights Act of 1964, and a series of equal protection decisions by the U.S. Supreme Court in the 1970s invalidating rules that treated men and women differently, all of which together produced something approaching formal equality between husbands and wives.[12]

What was the importance of this history to the issue of same-sex marriage? Cott testified, "Well, in the many years when the sexual division of labor and this assumption that the marital couple was ... an asymmetrical couple with a provider and a dependent, that was quite consistent with marriage between a man and a woman. However, the more symmetrical and gender-neutral spousal roles have become in fact, I would say, in the social world and certainly in the law, the more that the marriage between couples of the same sex seems perfectly capable of fulfilling the purpose of marriage."[13]

Judge Vaughn Walker, presiding in the federal district court, drew from Cott's testimony that marriage had grown into a "union of equals" and that "gender no longer forms an essential part of" the institution.[14] The roles of spouses, once legally specified to be economically complementary, are now the same, just as two people of the same sex are the same. Under coverture, same-sex marriage would not have made sense, but marriage has evolved to accommodate the homosexual union.

Plaintiffs also called to the witness stand Professor Lee Badgett, an economist at the University of Massachusetts, Amherst. Badgett's testimony was offered in part to establish the economic harm that exclusion from marriage inflicts on same-sex couples. She described, in particular, the benefits of *specialization* in marriage.[15] This concept is perhaps most closely associated with the Nobel Prize–winning economist Gary Becker, who famously elaborated the idea that households operate most efficiently when men specialize in market labor where they hold a "comparative advantage" while women specialize in domestic labor, where they hold a different advantage. A gender-based division of labor will therefore continue to predominate, Becker argued, as couples rationally seek to allocate their labor most efficiently.[16]

In her book *Money, Myths and Change*, Badgett disentangles specialization from these essentialized gender-based roles but maintains a definition of the concept that entails one partner in a couple devoting himself or herself to market labor more than the other.[17] For heterosexuals, socialized expectations regarding breadwinner and homemaker roles are one possible explanation for how a couple might allocate its labor, but efficiency considerations such as differing opportunities for wage employment may also play a role. The rational pursuit of efficiency should also be expected to drive the decisions of same-sex couples, but according to the data cited by Badgett, specialization is substantially more pronounced in married heterosexual households than in unmarried same-sex households, whether measured from the angle of domestic responsibilities or time devoted to labor market participation. Cultural expectations regarding gender may, therefore, make a determinative difference.[18]

Badgett also observes in her book, however, that rational efficiency concerns that typically weigh in favor of specialization for married heterosexual couples may actually prevent same-sex couples from specializing—or, at least, from the extreme version in which one partner exits the paid labor market entirely, let us say, to stay home with a baby. If the paid worker cannot share his or her employer-based health insurance with the rest of the family, for example, it may make better economic sense for both partners to remain in the wage labor market. A married couple would not be faced with this particular choice. Moreover, marriage—or, more precisely, *divorce*—comes with some protections (e.g., equitable distribution of property and the possibility of alimony, depending on the law of the jurisdiction) that enable one spouse to diminish his or her value as a wage laborer to specialize in domestic labor. Married couples are therefore freer to rely on the protections of marriage and take the risks associated with specialization.[19] The availability of marriage means fewer constraints in deciding how to allocate labor within a couple and provides efficiency-maximizing opportunities to a household.

Badgett testified in *Perry* that barring same-sex couples from marriage deprives them of the efficiency benefits of specialization. Her testimony strains to avoid the deeply gendered associations found in the work of Becker and others. On the stand, Badgett explained the concept using vague and genderless examples ("certain types of labor, whether that's labor—getting training to enhance your job possibilities or other sorts of training that would make you more productive in other ways").[20] This is the least clear moment in Badgett's testimony, which is otherwise forceful and articulate. Her trouble illustrating her point without resorting to heavily gendered imagery suggests the difficulty of extricating specialization from its heteronormative moorings. Despite the suppression of "his and her" language, however, the gendered associations persist, and even if involuntarily, the specialization argument conjures the image of the butch lesbian suited up for marketplace participation while the femme stays home to feed the baby and vacuum.[21] In Badgett's testimony, people living in homosexual relationships may be of the same sex but in economic terms they are complementary, or hetero. Marriage does not have to "evolve" for these couples.

Judge Walker cited lack of access to specialization among the negative economic consequences of the state's discriminatory marriage law.[22] He did so apparently without noticing any contradiction between this conclusion and the conclusion that he drew from Cott's testimony. This is not to say that as between Cott and Badgett, only one can be right. They are both highly respected for good reason, and they spoke from different disciplines in answer to different questions. I juxtapose them to draw attention to the knowledge of gay people that their testimony produced, particularly once Judge Walker "found facts" based on the opinions the experts offered in service of Boies and Olsen's carefully conceived legal purposes.

Cott's account of the trajectory of American marriage highlights the elimination of legally specified economic complementarity. By offering a historical narrative designed to suggest that marriage has become amenable to same-sex couples because it has become amenable to *sameness* within marriage, her expert testimony evokes an image of homosexuality that really emphasizes the *homo*. Gay couples do not resemble straight couples, but it no longer matters, because the contemporary law of marriage renders heterosexual difference legally insignificant. Badgett, by contrast, produces an image of a same-sex couple characterized by complementarity. Her testimony suggests similarity *between* heterosexual and homosexual couples, both of which—if permitted to marry—might make rational decisions that result in specialization. The contradiction between the two experts is one not of fact but of representation. A careful reading reveals the *economically homo* same-sex couple, suited to labor non-differentiation, contrasted with the *economically hetero* same-sex couple, deprived of the opportunity for maximal efficiency. Each expert sketched contours around her subjects, especially with regard to the "likeness" of homosexuals to heterosexuals—a reference point to which the pursuit of equal rights bound her. The judge ratified contradictory conceptions when he accepted the opinions of both experts.

This kind of contradiction is a regular feature of *knowledge* in its Foucauldian sense. Knowledge is less a matter of empirical fact or sensual perception than of conceptual ordering. We inhabit knowledge, assume it in a deep and cultural sense. Cott and Badgett testified explicitly about history and economics, but knowledge of gay couples as like and unlike straight couples emerged as a byproduct of their testimony. As knowledge, this sameness/difference conundrum is absorbed into the common cultural understanding and is available to help or to hurt. We cannot escape discourse or knowledge production altogether, but we can deliberately assume a critical posture that enables us to take better stock of the costs and risks associated with the knowledge regime within which we advocate for progress.

Judge Walker also explicitly found that same-sex couples and different-sex couples were alike with respect to love, commitment, and "standardized measures of relationship satisfaction."[23] He relied heavily on the expert testimony of the psychologist Letitia Anne Peplau of the University of California, Los Angeles (UCLA), who specializes in the study of human relationships, sexual orientation, and gender. Peplau testified that research showed "great similarity" between heterosexual and homosexual couples with regard to relationship quality.[24] On cross-examination, Peplau was confronted with evidence of a statistical difference between gay male and other (both heterosexual and lesbian) couples with respect to the value and practice of monogamy. She had to concede that a higher percentage of gay male couples "may have an agreement that their relationship does not need to be sexually exclusive" but hastened to add that "if a couple has an agreement . . . then acting on that agreement is not a breach of trust" and does not affect relationship satisfaction.[25] This statistical difference did not appear in Judge Walker's factual findings; nor did it shake his confidence in his conclusion that gay and straight couples are, in all relevant respects, the same.

At other moments of the trial, however, Boies and Olsen needed to establish the fact of homosexual distinction. To accomplish that objective, they turned to another expert witness, Gregory Herek, a psychologist at the University of California, Davis, who "regularly teaches a course on sexual orientation and prejudice."[26] Herek testified, "Sexual orientation is a term that we use to describe an enduring sexual, romantic or intensely affectional attraction to men, to women, or to both men and women. It's also used to refer to an identity or a sense of self that is based on one's enduring patterns of attraction. And it's also sometimes used to describe an enduring pattern of behavior."[27] Herek's emphasis is on the thrice-used term *enduring*. He stressed in his testimony that "the vast majority of people are consistent in their behavior, their identity, and their attractions."[28]

How does Herek know? He asked them. Herek conducted studies in which he asked people whether they were "heterosexual, straight, gay, lesbian or bisexual" and found that people were "generally able to answer" his question.[29] He also asked 2,200 people, all of whom self-identified as gay, lesbian, or bisexual, about the degree of choice they had about their sexual orientation. According to his testimony, "Among gay men, eighty seven percent said they experienced no or little choice . . . [and a]mong lesbians seventy percent said that had no or very little choice."[30] What about the other 13 and 30 percent? Not much is said in the trial transcript about them.

Herek was asked about those who exhibit some "inconsistency" in their attractions or behavior. Heterosexual acts in the trajectories of gay people's lives are, Herek testified, easily explained by the burden of heterosexual expectations with which most gay people grow up. Some gay people, therefore, engage in heterosexual sex in error, but "it's not part of who they are."[31]

This obviously does little to explain inconsistency running in the other direction—that is, when an otherwise straight person engages in same-sex sex. As Professor Aaron Belkin, a political scientist at San Francisco State University and executive director of the Palm Center, an independent institute that conducts research on gender and sexuality issues in the military, testified in one of the legal challenges to Don't Ask, Don't Tell, the military has long been cognizant that many of its heterosexual service members engage in homosexual sex. This is why the so-called *queen for a day* exception was included in the now-repealed policy, allowing service members to claim that, despite participation in a homosexual act, they are in fact heterosexual and should not be discharged.[32] Belkin also testified that male veterans of military service are more likely than lifelong civilian men to have had homosexual encounters.[33]

This is not to locate the phenomenon solely in the military. A well-known doctoral dissertation from 1970 (that has been severely criticized on ethics grounds for its improper treatment of its study subjects but is still regarded as having generated valid findings) showed that many of the straight men who engage in the so-called tearoom trade (anonymous sex in men's restrooms) live otherwise flawlessly respectable middle-class existences, complete with wives and children. The dissertation, written by Laud Humphreys, a doctoral candidate at Washington University, found that many of the men having sex in public restrooms were conservative and religious.[34] Perhaps all of these men are "closet cases," as some gay commentators have rushed to assume, but perhaps some take pleasure in both their heterosexual marriages and their anonymous homosexual encounters.

Similarly, some black men who are living otherwise heterosexual lifestyles enjoy same-sex sexual encounters on the "down low." According to the typical account, men on the down low, or DL, do not generally identify as gay, a label they may associate with whiteness, effeminacy, or just infringement on their sexual autonomy.[35] In the past few years, the DL has been subjected to abundant critique by black queer scholars. C. Riley Snorton described it "as one in myriad discursive practices that link black sexuality with duplicity."[36] Indeed, the phenomenon has been blamed in the popular media for HIV infection rates among unsuspecting black women. Critics do not seem to dispute the assertion that such encounters occur—and obviously not only among black men—but rather direct attention to how the down low, as a "discursive concept," "connect[s] race and sex together in a way that fortifie[s] long-standing racist and heterosexist views."[37] "Black men are depicted as disease carriers, now not just of moral diseases (degeneracy, feeblemindedness, etc.) but of AIDS."[38]

Brad Elliott Stone proposes, however, to reinterpret the down low so "that there is a way for [it] to exist without black men entering into what appears to be monogamous heterosexual relationships with non-suspecting women."[39] Deceiving a female partner need not be an inherent feature of life on the DL. Stone argues "The Down Low transgresses white supremacy in both its racist and heterosexist forms. It complicates the clean categories of sexual orientation by resisting the dominant discourse of the closet in exchange for a highly nuanced network of black bodies and pleasures. . . . It is tempting to make the

Down Low fit the model of resistance already at work in the LGBT community. It might be more interesting, however, to not do so, and allow the Down Low to be its own form of critique . . . divorcing the question of sexual act and sexual partner from the question of (external) gender and race roles."[40] Such a critique deals a terrific blow to the world-view offered by Herek, according to which identity and acts line up neatly and consistently.

The secret homosexual rendezvous is, of course, about as newsworthy as gambling at Rick's American Cafe ("I'm shocked, *shocked*"). According to a study by Gary Gates, Distinguished Scholar at the Williams Institute at UCLA, "only 1/3rd of adults who have had same-sex sexual experiences identify as lesbian, gay, or bisexual."[41] Where are all of these people in Herek's study? Well, only those who first identified themselves as gay, lesbian, or bisexual were invited to answer the rest of Herek's survey questions. When specifically confronted on cross-examination about heterosexual-identified men who have sex with other men, Herek grudgingly replied, "This is a phenomenon that has been observed, yes."[42]

To maintain his unshakable position that sexual orientation is "enduring," Herek found himself having to explain away the scholarly work of his fellow witness for the plaintiffs, Peplau. In one article, Peplau included a table distinguishing "Old Perspectives" on women's sexual orientation from "New Perspectives." One "Old Perspective" was the idea that "sexual identity, attractions and behavior form discrete categories, i.e., heterosexual, homosexual, bisexual."[43] On the "New Perspectives" side, it read "sexual identity, attractions and behavior can be varied, complex and inconsistent."[44] Apparently unwilling to disagree with Peplau outright when questioned about her characterization of the latest thinking on women's sexuality, Herek surmised on the witness stand that Peplau was probably referring to a "relative minority of individuals."[45] Peplau is also the co-author of a study characterizing women's sexuality as "fluid, malleable, shaped by life experiences, and capable of change over time."[46] Confronted with this scholarly paper, Herek conceded the possibility of change but insisted that, for "most people, it doesn't seem to happen."[47]

Citing Herek's testimony and data, Judge Walker made this finding: "Sexual orientation is fundamental to a person's identity and is a distinguishing characteristic that defines gays and lesbians as a discrete group."[48] Why would Boies and Olsen decide it was important to establish this fact, and why would a sympathetic judge oblige? Why not embrace the "fluidity" and "inconsistency" of sexual practice and concede the imprecision of gay identity? While cross-examining Herek, the proponents of Prop 8 raised the possibility that—given all of the variability that occurs under the banners of "gay" and "straight"—sexual orientation might be a "social construction." Herek shot them down, of course, but why not concede that much? As Suzanne Goldberg, a longtime gay rights advocate and clinical professor at Columbia Law School, explains (reflecting on another case), "The argument that sexual orientation was a social construct rather than a biological or otherwise deeply rooted, 'natural' trait seemed ... dangerous. . . . I feared the Court might seize on the social construction argument and find the category of 'gays and lesbians' too diffuse to amount to a cognizable class. After all, a court needs to understand who has been harmed before deciding whether and how to order relief from an injurious classification."[49] Goldberg argues that gay rights are best served by a solid idea about the class of gay people. Boies and Olsen apparently concurred. They made a deliberate choice to call Herek as their expert on the definition of sexual orientation and the contours around the class of gay and lesbian people. They did not examine Peplau in this area, despite her obvious qualification. She was called to the witness stand to testify to the benefits of same-sex marriage, the similarities between same- and different-sex couples, and the unlikelihood that same-sex marriage would harm heterosexual marriage.

Boies and Olsen also had the plaintiffs' witness George Chauncy on hand. A highly regarded historian at Yale University, Chauncy is perhaps best known for his meticulous book *Gay New York: Gender, Urban Culture, and the Making of the Gay Male World, 1890–1940*.[50] In it, he brilliantly illustrates how economic conditions, race and class biases, police practices, morality campaigns, and other historical forces forged the sexual identities that emerged in twentieth-century New York City. Chauncy easily could have testified to the historical contingency of modern gay identity, but Boies and Olsen examined him only on the history of antigay discrimination and the historical resonance of the stereotypes relied on by the campaign to pass Prop 8.

By calling Herek to the witness stand and leaving Peplau and Chauncy on the sidelines when it came to addressing the topic of sexual orientation as a classification, Boies and Olsen were carrying out a strategic decision to depict the most static and essentialized possible version of homosexuality: one that stabilizes gay identity and its correlation with homosexual desire and practice while minimizing or explaining away exceptions. This is surely the best gay rights strategy . . . sometimes.

The Williams Institute is the leading pro-gay think tank in the United States. It provides expert opinions (such as Lee Badgett's) and submits *amicus* briefs in gay rights cases, in addition to funding research, sponsoring fellows, and hosting events. One of its leading scholars, the respected and prolific demographer Gary Gates, produced the study finding that just a third of the people who have had homosexual sex maintain a gay, lesbian, or bisexual identity. He argued that his findings were good for gay rights. "These provocative findings demonstrate the challenge in understanding the complex relationship between sexual orientation identity and behavior. Given that nearly half of Americans still believe that homosexual relationships are morally wrong, it is not surprising to find ambiguity between how people behave sexually and how they identify their sexual orientation."[51] The suggestion that homosexuality is diffuse and ambiguously related to gay identity rather than concentrated in a small segment of the population is a long way from Herek's consistency refrain. Why would the Williams Institute, a savvy pro-gay participant in the culture war, undermine the discreteness of gay identity with such a missive? Well, sometimes the best strategy is a consolidated idea about who is gay, and sometimes the best strategy is to implicate as many people as possible. Gates's findings provide an empirical basis for arguing that homophobia has artificially reduced the number of people willing to claim a gay identity and that more people are implicated in the gay rights cause than gay population numbers would indicate.

The contrast represented by Herek and Gates calls to mind Eve Kosofsky Sedgwick's analytical frame of *minoritizing* versus *universalizing* conceptions of homosexuality.[52] For Herek, gay people simply *are* a discrete minority, and he is dismissive of any inconsistent evidence with which he might be confronted. Gates's data, however, suggest that conduct and identity do not line up quite so neatly, and he uses that evidence in an attempt to disperse political investment in gay equality. Both portrayals can be useful to the gay rights cause, but Sedgwick warned that both are available for antigay purposes, as well. The minoritizing conception, while consolidating a class for remediation in court, also risks minimizing the political significance of gay concerns or focusing attention on some distinguishing feature that renders gays ill-suited to be treated as "the same." The universalizing conception, while suggesting that a lot more folks have skin in the game of homosexual emancipation, simultaneously poses the danger described by Goldberg of depriving courts of a discrete subject to which a legal remedy might be addressed. Sedgwick called this structure a "double-bind," and the trouble with it is that pro- and antigay rights advocates can draw from the same arsenals. Gay rights advocates could be blindsided if they let themselves believe that either the "fact" of gay people being distinctive and discrete or the "fact" of homosexuality pervading a broad swath of the population is logically tethered to advancement of the gay cause.

In *Perry*, the deployment of experts to establish the fundamental likeness of gay and straight people and then, also, their fundamental distinctness took place inside the terms of gay equal rights discourse and the pressures of the counter-majoritarian setting, but it may be the case that the double-bind is a recurring side-effect of that discourse, regardless of forum. Just as the counter-majoritarian setting demands a discourse of judicial neutrality and logical correctness, gay equal rights in general demands a stable rights-bearing subject, and just as indeterminacy in judicial reasoning prompts reassurances regarding institutional fidelity, so the chronic instability of the gay subject requires constant efforts at stabilization. As advocates strive to satisfy competing mandates (i.e., that gay people be enough like straight people to be entitled to the same treatment but distinct enough to substantiate a class), however, they entrench the representational difficulties that they face.

The "true" subject of gay rights is, of course, elusive. It exists as a product of expert testimony, findings of fact, public-relations campaigns and other generative techniques—that is, the gay subject exists as *knowledge*. That knowledge can be wildly conflicting, unwieldy, and, as Sedgwick advised, "densely charged with lasting potentials for powerful manipulation" not only by friend, but by foe.[53] Equal rights as a strategy for change, insofar as it demands the constant production of a subject who can bear those rights, is always doing more than it purports to do. An equal rights claim is never "just" a legal claim on behalf of an identity group; it is always also a *making* of that group, sometimes with under-recognized contradictions, which may also turn out to be vulnerabilities.

The Kids Are Alright

We are *made*, for example, in conflicting ways in the process of establishing our fitness to parent. In the case law granting or denying same-sex couples access to marriage, the marriage right is tightly bound up with the question of gay parenting. The *Perry* team had no choice but to address this issue and in so doing fell into a recognizable knowledge-producing pattern.

In general, the legality of gay parenting is managed under a state's custody and adoption regimes, not under its marriage law. The gays and lesbians of California enjoy broad parenting rights that would not have been directly affected by the outcome of the *Perry* case. Still, the suitability of gays and lesbians to the parenting task emerged as central to the case. A number of states and sympathetic *amici* defended discriminatory marriage laws by maintaining that the heterosexual, marital household is the optimal setting for children and that the rearing of children is the central purpose of marriage.

The proponents of Prop 8 called David Blankenhorn to the witness stand to attest to the unique importance of the traditional family form. Blankenhorn is the author of several books, including his best known, *Fatherless America*.[54] He is also the founder of a think tank called the Institute for American Values. For a quarter-century, Blankenhorn opposed same-sex marriage—before making a very public one-eighty in 2013 (more on that in chapter 3).

Blankenhorn's testimony in the *Perry* trial consisted of trite and unsubstantiated assertions of the supremacy of married, heterosexual, biological households for producing favorable outcomes for children, many of which he repudiated under the rigors of cross-examination. The judge described Blankenhorn's demeanor on the witness stand as "defensive" and gave his testimony zero credence, verging on mockery of Blankenhorn's low academic standards. ("His study of the effects of same-sex marriage involved 'read[ing] articles and hav[ing] conversations with people, and try[ing] to be an informed person about it.' "[55])

In contrast, Michael Lamb, a psychologist who testified for the plaintiffs, took the stand armed with elite credentials and peer-reviewed studies. He made it easy for Judge Walker to rely on his opinion and find that, as a factual matter, "children raised by gays and lesbians are just as likely to be well-adjusted as children raised by heterosexual parents" and that "studies have demonstrated [this] 'very conclusively.' "[56]

Boies and Olsen worked hard to ensure that this point would be driven home effectively because they knew that the fate of same-sex marriage was intricately bound up with the issue of gay parenting. They also must have been cognizant that findings about the adequacy of gay parents made by a federal judge, especially if eventually incorporated into a U.S. Supreme Court opinion, might have implications for cases that explicitly address the legal status of gay parenting. Gay adoption or custody cases could raise many of the same issues, review the same data, and even involve some of the same experts.

Florida, for example, saw a protracted battle over its total ban on gay adoption, including litigation in federal and state courts. After a couple of failed challenges by gay rights advocates, the thirty-three-year-old ban finally fell in 2010, when a mid-level state appellate court affirmed the decision of a juvenile court to approve the adoption of two brothers, ages eight and four, by a gay man who had been their foster father for four years. Gay foster parenting was already legal in Florida, but before the decision in 2010, *Florida Department of Children and Families v. Adoption of X.X.G. and N.R.G.* (hereafter *X.X.G.*), adoption by a gay individual or same-sex couple was banned by statute.[57] In *X.X.G.*, a state appellate court struck down that statute as a violation of Florida's constitution.

Lamb and Peplau, both of whom would later testify for the plaintiffs in *Perry*, testified during the *X.X.G.* trial in 2008 in favor of the adoption of the two boys by their foster father, Martin Gill. The trial and appellate courts agreed that the testimony of Lamb, Peplau, and the other experts for the petitioning father established a professional consensus that "there are no differences in parenting of homosexuals or the adjustment of their children . . . [and] the issue is so far beyond dispute that it would be irrational to hold otherwise."[58] The state called two experts who interpreted the available data on gay parenting differently, but both trial and appellate courts discounted the state's experts' testimony, insinuating that their work was methodologically flawed and beneath the standards of their profession.[59]

The impression of a consensus among mainstream experts that children reared by gay or lesbian parents are equally likely to be well adjusted is imperative to law-reform goals in this domain. Opponents of gay parenting or same-sex marriage need not establish that gay parenting is calamitous to prevail; even an absence of certainty is enough of a reason for judicial deference to the legislature. In her *Goodridge* dissent, Justice Sosman observed back in 2003 that "stud[ies] of the ramifications of raising children in same-sex couple households are themselves in their infancy and have so far produced inconclusive and conflicting results."[60] She argued that this should have deterred the court from stepping into a properly legislative arena. When established facts cannot be said to render a legislative preference irrational, then—applying the usual constitutional analysis—a court is expected to defer. In the years between *Goodridge* and *Perry*, however, studies establishing that children of same-sex parents were equally well adjusted accumulated, and the question was effectively closed.

Just one study was a thorn in gay rights advocates' side: the infamous and abhorred Regnerus study, published in 2012.[61] Mark Regnerus is a sociologist at the University of Texas, Austin. In his study, which concludes that gay parents produce inferior outcomes for children, he made some peculiar methodological choices, such as asking young adult children of divorce whether their parents had ever engaged in a same-sex relationship, then classifying those who had as gay and comparing outcomes for children of those parents with outcomes for the children of parents who were married for the duration of their children's upbringings. The Regnerus study came out too late for the *Perry* trial, but Regnerus testified about his findings in the federal trial on Michigan's same-sex marriage ban, which accompanied the *Obergefell* case to the Supreme Court. The study was denounced as flawed by Regnerus's own university and the American Sociological Association, and the major LGBT advocacy organizations debunked the thing into a deep pit and buried it under a ton of empirical gravel. It was vital for advocates to eliminate even the slightest whiff of a difference between the outcomes for children with heterosexual and homosexual parents. Happily, with a few easily discredited exceptions, the empirical work generated during the ensuing decade obliged.

Moments arise, however, when advocates for gay equal rights employ a discursive vehicle that collides with the parental equivalency contention. Boies and Olsen, for example, apparently wanted to demonstrate in *Perry* that discrimination is not a trifle; it imposes appreciable harm. To illustrate the point, they called to the witness stand the epidemiologist Ilan Meyer of Columbia University, who testified that Prop 8 inflicted "minority stress," a psychological burden resulting from the stigma associated with being a member of a minority group.[62] Asked about the mental health consequences of minority stress on gays and lesbians, Meyer testified, "There ha[ve] been pretty consistent findings that show excess disorder or higher level of disorder in gay and lesbian populations as compared to heterosexuals."[63] Judge Walker relied on Meyer's testimony to support his finding that Prop 8 places the force of law behind antigay stigma. He did not, however, dwell in his opinion on the adverse psychological consequences to which Meyer attested. Why not? Well, if gays and lesbians are suffering an elevated incidence of mental health disorders as a consequence of the stress associated with antigay stigma, then would we not be impaired in our ability to maintain healthy relationships and raise well-adjusted children? Perhaps Judge Walker sensed the double-edged sword of "minority stress."

In *X.X.G.*, one of the state's experts testified that "homosexual adults have a higher lifetime prevalence of major depression, affective disorders, anxiety disorders and substance abuse."[64] The statement easily could have been uttered by Meyer to substantiate the ill effects of antigay stigma, but the expert in *X.X.G.* was deployed to help make the case that gay people are often psychologically ill-equipped to parent. The Florida juvenile court looked for a way to manage this information. It concluded, "Taken as a whole, the research shows that sexual orientation alone is not a proxy for psychiatric disorders, mental health conditions, substance abuse or smoking.... [W]hile the average rates [for these problems] are generally slightly higher for homosexuals than heterosexuals, the rates ... are also higher for American-Indians as compared to other races.... [I]f every demographic group with elevated rates ... were excluded from adopting, the only group eligible to adopt ... would be Asian American men."[65] The Florida court did not dispute the data but did make an effort to minimize their significance.

In response to the negative data on mental health, advocates for gay equal rights *could* take the tack they took with child outcome studies: They could begin the arduous process of developing empirical work to refute the allegation that gays and lesbians are psychologically impaired, perhaps leading to eventual wholesale dismissal of assertions of gay mental ill health in cases such as *X.X.G.* One problem with that strategy, however, is that sometimes equal rights advocates need gay people to be impaired. Meyer (who is now a senior scholar at the Williams Institute) is generating data about minority stress in service of the idea that items on the LGBT equal rights agenda are needed to diminish stigma. The work is strategically useful because some items on the agenda rely heavily on the notion of psychological injury. The anti-bullying campaign, for example, requires the depressed, substance-abusing, suicidal adolescent. Antigay harassment in schools or on social media cannot be a small matter of hurt teenage feelings if advocates are to garner the attention of policy makers and battle effectively against antigay forces claiming that the bullies are being deprived of the right to free speech. For this particular equality campaign to be effective, bullying has to result in a psychologically injured young person.

That injured young person, however, may grow up and want to marry or adopt a child. At that point, the injured gay or lesbian suffering the stigma of discrimination and driven to depression, substance abuse, or suicidality could present some difficulties for the argument regarding his or her equivalency of fitness to parent. The juvenile court judge in *X.X.G.* seemed intuitively to appreciate this problem as she attempted to minimize and disperse the mental health consequences of discrimination.

Judge Walker in *Perry* also veered away from Meyer's "minority stress" thesis, perhaps to protect his findings regarding the psychological fitness of gays to marry and parent. The proponents of Prop 8, however, sniffed out an opportunity and raised the issue in their cross-examinations of Meyer and Lamb. First, they tried to cast doubt on the contention that gays were psychologically injured, asking Meyer to agree to characterize a well-known study of homosexuals conducted in the 1950s by Evelyn Hooker as "classic" and "methodologically rigorous."[66] Meyer did agree. Proponents' counsel then asked him to agree that the study found that "heterosexual and homosexual groups did not differ significantly in their overall psychological adjustment."[67] Again Meyer agreed, enabling proponents to put on display the psychologically healthy—or, at least, ordinary—homosexual and disrupt Meyer's narrative of injury. Later on cross-examination, however, proponents' counsel asked Meyer, "If one of the members of [a] partnership or … marriage … if … one member suffered from minority stress, it would increase general stress on the relationship and would have a negative impact on their satisfaction, correct?"[68] Meyer had to agree, of course, that stress takes a toll on a relationship. Proponents later asked Lamb whether he "would agree that lots of researchers have shown that being a depressed parent changes the way you behave and interact with your child, and that can indirectly affect the child's adjustment." Lamb concurred, saying, "That's correct."[69] Homosexuals are psychologically as healthy as their straight peers at one moment and suffering the psychological consequences of antigay stigma the next. Both sides of the *Perry* litigation wanted it both ways.

It is not impossible to reconcile the finding that discrimination causes stress, which in turn has adverse psychological consequences, with the finding that gay and lesbian parents are just as likely as heterosexual parents to raise well-adjusted children. According to Meyer, one possible explanation is that a "selection" process occurs in which gays and lesbians who emerge from childhood with the least injurious consequences of minority stress are the most likely to form families. Perhaps. I am not arguing in this section that the "injured gay" and the "psychologically fit gay" are irreconcilable *in fact* but, rather, that they contradict one another at the level of *discourse*. Discourse produces knowledge about gay and lesbian people, giving us conceptions, images, and archetypes. The two archetypes are conflicting, produced at different moments to meet different demands of equal rights work. Reading the transcripts and cases, one can tell when a pro-gay judge senses the contradiction, when the judge knows that the imaginary gay subject for whom he or she is adjudicating is becoming unmanageable, at odds with itself. Precisely as Sedgwick warned, the contradictions render the discourse pliable and amenable to both good and ill purposes.

Moreover, the *injured gay/fit gay* contradiction creates particular peril in a judicial setting because of how it entwines with the relevant legal doctrine. When a group makes an equality claim in a counter-majoritarian forum, the court might consider whether the history of discrimination against that group and the group's general political powerlessness warrant a little extra judicial attention. This is a species of what is known among constitutional scholars as "representation-reinforcement."[70] The idea is that courts are generally expected to defer to the branches that are accountable to the voters, but courts might sometimes be justified in throwing their weight around if it is necessary to protect minority rights that otherwise could be trampled by the majority. The way that courts signal their treatment of a claim as deserving of this extra judicial solicitude is with an elevated *level of review*.

Generally, courts reviewing the work of legislatures for constitutional defect apply a level of review known as *rational basis*, meaning that they ask (1) whether the legislature was pursuing a legitimate governmental interest; and (2) whether the law under review is rationally related to that interest. If the answer to those two questions is yes, then the work of the legislature or other majoritarian body will be upheld. This is ordinary judicial deference; the court requires of the legislature only that it behave rationally. Sometimes, however, that gentle inquiry is insufficiently probing to protect the right at stake or the group making the claim. One way to get the court to ask tougher questions, to assume a less deferential posture, is to invoke a representation-reinforcement argument—that is, that the right-claiming group's history of discrimination and systematic exclusion from majoritarian politics justifies it. If a claimant group can effectively make that case, then it may convince the court to apply a higher level of review, known as *strict scrutiny*. If the court agrees to strictly scrutinize the work of the majority, it will ask not whether the majority's purposes were merely legitimate, but whether they were compelling. Furthermore, it will ask not whether the challenged law rationally furthers the government's interest, but whether the law is narrowly tailored to furthering that interest. This is a much more exacting standard and signals a court's increased willingness to invalidate the work of the majority. A minority group asking a court to strike down a discriminatory law, therefore, would generally prefer that its claim be reviewed using strict scrutiny, because it means the group begins with the benefit of judicial skepticism toward the law rather than with the usual posture of judicial deference to the majority.

The multitiered review structure (there is also an intermediate level, and there are a few variations on the three primary tiers) provides incentives for equality-seeking groups to depict themselves as chronically marginalized and powerless. Connecticut's same-sex marriage case, *Kerrigan v. Commissioner of Public Health*,[71] provides one of the most demoralizing examples of this. Advocates persuaded the majority to elevate the level of scrutiny (to the intermediate tier) by depicting gay and lesbian people as weak, frightened, and despised. During the long history of antigay discrimination, the court recounted in its ruling, "gay persons were widely deemed to be mentally ill," and "the conduct that defines the class [was] criminal." It went on, "Homosexuality is contrary to the teachings of more than a few religions"; many people "experience revulsion toward gay persons and the intimate sexual conduct with which they are associated," and "large numbers of hate crimes . . . are perpetrated against gay persons." Moreover, gay people "are ridiculed, ostracized, despised, demonized and condemned merely for being who they are . . . perhaps even more severe[ly] than [other] groups that have been accorded heightened judicial protection." Gay people are radically underrepresented in places of power, including Congress, the Cabinet, the federal appeals court, and "the highest levels of business, industry, and academia." Of course, "many gay . . . officials hide their sexual orientation." This goes on (and on), but you likely have absorbed the court's point. Despite some gains, "the pervasive and invidious discrimination to which [gay people] have historically been subjected" warrants an elevated level of judicial review.[72]

Majority rule with an exception built in for minorities that cannot possibly succeed using majoritarian means is the way our system is structured—and I am not complaining about that. It is not an irrational system. It is important to appreciate, however, that the structure creates incentives to serve oneself up to the counter-majoritarian branch as abject. The structure invites participation in a specific discursive practice of inscribing and reinscribing an injured identity on a group as it pursues equal rights. As a result, an equality-seeking constituency that accesses counter-majoritarian avenues—that is, makes constitutional claims to equality in court—is always working against itself in at least one respect. As Wendy Brown has asked, is there a point at which "legal 'protection' for a certain injury-forming identity discursively entrenches the injury-identity connection it denounces . . . codify[ing] within the law the very powerlessness it aims to redress?"[73] Can law designed to protect an identity group also inhibit the process of transforming what we "know" about the group?

In the judicial arena, representation-reinforcement and the tiered structure of review press equal rights-seeking constituencies into this problem.[74] In *Perry*, political scientists sparred over the question of gay political power in California. Prop 8's proponents called Kenneth Miller, a political scientist at Claremont McKenna College, to testify that gays wielded real power in California politics. The judge deemed his testimony to be of limited value; it was obviously not Miller's area of expertise. Plaintiffs called Stanford University's Gary Segura to establish that the gays of California *lacked* political power. In the end, the issue was not crucial to the outcome. Judge Walker applied rational basis-level review—that is, he assumed a deferential posture toward the majority—and he *still* struck down Prop 8. He found the ban on same-sex marriage to fail even the minimal test of rationality.

But the *Perry* court could have determined that the standard of review was the critical question. Maybe the state had a legitimate interest, but not a compelling interest, undergirding Prop 8. If that had been the judge's thinking, then it would have been crucial to persuade him that the claim should be reviewed using strict scrutiny. The political power or powerlessness of gay people would have featured prominently in that assessment.

If that moment had arrived (and it still could in another context—for example, in a case in which religious rights vie against same-sex marriage), an unimpaired, healthy gay population that parents fabulously well-adjusted children would have been the wrong "fact" to have on display—at least in that section of the brief. It would have been better to exhibit the injured gay, suffering from minority stress, vulnerable to hate crimes, provoking revulsion and religious condemnation, and unlikely to be found in the highest echelons of business or government. That would have been the best course for persuading a court to adopt skepticism toward the majority's rule.

But the next step in the analytical progression, after determining what level of review the court should apply, is to *apply it.* In *Obergefell*, the brief for the couples first argued that "homosexuals are among the most stigmatized, misunderstood, and discriminated-against minorities in the history of the world."[75] The brief on behalf of eighteen leading constitutional scholars bolstered that position, adding that the long history of discrimination, ostracization, and humiliation caused gay people to "feel inferior and reviled," noting that many "attempted, often desperately, to hide their secret shame."[76] But then the section of the couples' brief addressing the merits of the ban against recognizing same-sex marriages characterizes a "broad scientific consensus" as concluding "there is no scientific evidence that parenting effectiveness is related to parental sexual orientation."[77] On that point, the couples were aided by the brief of the American Psychological Association and a number of other professional organizations in related fields (social work, pediatrics, and so on) that stated, "Same-sex couples form deep emotional attachments and commitments, with levels of relationship satisfaction similar to or higher than those of heterosexual couples."[78]

If a court had agreed to apply strict scrutiny on the grounds of gay powerlessness and the history of discrimination, the court would have next asked: Is the state's interest (e.g., in protecting children) compelling? Is the ban on same-sex marriage narrowly tailored to that interest? If the state asserted an interest in children's well-being based on parents' mental health, the court would have had to consider how well the policy of excluding same-sex couples from marriage served that objective. At that point, the injured gay, suffering from depression and abusing substances, would have had to hide under the bed in favor of the psychologically fit-as-a-fiddle gay.

Section I of the gay rights brief presents the stigmatized and despised homosexual, but in Section II, we meet his twin sister, the picture of health, happiness, and success. Both were summoned into existence by the demands of equal rights advocacy. We could accept this as strategic necessity, but Sedgwick's insight holds: Knowledge produced in each section can be turned around to undermine the purposes of the other section. The dynamic is by no means exclusive to the judicial setting, but the specifics of judicial review methodology render the problem especially acute.

The Business Side of a Norm

Knowledge in this sense is closely connected to *norm production*, or *normalization*. As Janet Halley explained Michel Foucault's concept, normalization "is not the generation and imposition of some consolidated idea of good behavior or good values, the coercive herding of more and more people into normalcy. . . . [Instead,] it is the ever-shifting, provisional ordering of a social, conceptual, and ethical field around a distinction—say, married/unmarried; or a range of distinctions—say, wife/mistress/girlfriend; or a standard—say, 'room temperature' or 'illness' or 'reasonableness.'"[79] Legal advocacy and opinion-writing, as it characterizes LGBT people in the service of LGBT advancement, can result in such conceptual ordering, sometimes to the detriment of vulnerable populations.

Take the example of Diane Schroer. Schroer is a transgender woman who sued the Library of Congress under Title VII after the offer to her of a position as a specialist in terrorism and international crime with the Congressional Research Service (CRS) was withdrawn. The clarity of the facts of Schroer's case boded well for her claim. When presenting as a man, Schroer was the clear first choice for the position. She had been offered the job and had accepted it before disclosing her plans to transition to a female gender presentation. Only then was the offer withdrawn.

Schroer's résumé also made her case a good one from the perspective of an impact litigator:

> She is a graduate of both the National War College and the Army Command and General Staff College, and she holds masters degrees in history and international relations. During Schroer's twenty-five years of service in the U.S. Armed Forces, she held important command and staff positions in the Armored Calvary, Airborne, Special Forces and Special Operations Units, and in combat operations in Haiti and Rwanda. . . . Before her retirement from the military in January 2004, Schroer was a Colonel assigned to the U.S. Special Operations Command, serving as the director of a 120-person classified organization that tracked and targeted high-threat international terrorist organizations. In this position, Colonel Schroer analyzed sensitive intelligence reports, planned a range of classified and conventional operations, and regularly briefed senior military and government officials, including the Vice President, the Secretary of Defense, and the Chairman of the Joint Chiefs of Staff. . . . At the time of her military retirement, Schroer held a Top Secret, Sensitive

Compartmented Information security clearance, and had done so on a continuous basis since 1987.... After her retirement, Schroer joined a private consulting firm, Benchmark International, where, when she applied for the CRS position, she was working as a program manager on an infrastructure security project for the National Guard.[80]

But Schroer's anti-terror bona fides had the additional and paradoxical effect of rendering her peculiarly vulnerable to discrimination. One of the library's rationales for rescinding the job offer was concern about possible delays in completing the necessary security clearance under Schroer's soon-to-be new first name. The federal court did not take this rationale seriously, but administrative difficulties associated with gender transition, especially in our era of perpetual war, are hardly unknown, as law professor Dean Spade has shown.[81] In government alone, administrative agencies at every level maintain varying policies or tacitly permit discretionary practices regulating gender reclassification. A person who has transitioned might, for example, be able to satisfy the State Department standard for gender reclassification on his or her passport but fail the standard applied in his or her state's Department of Motor Vehicles, resulting in conflicting forms of identification. Moreover, someone who has been identified by a government agency under an original name, and then by a different agency under a new name (with the Social Security number remaining constant) might, through a computerized process called "batch checking," find himself or herself turned away from a job or government benefit.[82] The library may well have raised the possibility of delays in Schroer's security clearance as a pretext for discrimination, but it was not at all implausible to suggest that a change in name and gender identity could result in administrative confusion. Schroer's pre- and post-transition records, in all of the bureaucratic entities with which she had been associated, might easily have come into conflict, resulting in administrative snags.

Another rationale offered by the Library of Congress for rescinding the job offer was that Schroer's credibility before Congress would be undercut because no woman could possibly have built her résumé. Her transgender status would therefore always make itself evident. It can be said, therefore, that Schroer's exceptional record of service rendered her peculiarly vulnerable to discrimination.

Still, when the Library of Congress discriminated against Schroer, it discriminated against a patriot. This must have bolstered her claim. As our nation learned after World War II in the context of black civil rights, the argument against discrimination is stronger when it is made on behalf of those who keep

America safe. Schroer's case transmogrifies the transwoman archetype from lurking danger in the ladies' room to keeper of our national secrets, guardian of innocents—at least for a moment.

In *Terrorist Assemblages*, Jasbir Puar traced a similar transformation in the gay archetype. Gays were once "figures of death (i.e., the AIDS epidemic)" but are now "tied to ideas of life and productivity (i.e., gay marriage and families)"; they were once "fixtures of espionage and double agents, associated with communists during the McCarthy era,"[83] but are rapidly being incorporated into American imperialist projects by serving as objects of liberal toleration that help to justify military and other aggressions into foreign national cultures. Puar coined the term *homonationalism* to capture a dynamic of gay inclusion that strongly tends to correlate with, and perhaps requires, the *exclusion* of Muslims and others associated with terrorism and threats to the nation: "Homonationalism ... is fundamentally a deep critique of lesbian and gay liberal rights discourses and how those rights discourses produce narratives of progress and modernity that continue to accord some populations access to citizenship—cultural and legal—at the expense of the delimitation and expulsion of other populations. The narrative of progress for gay rights is thus built on the back of racialized others."[84] After a Muslim man from New York shot up a gay nightclub in Orlando in the summer of 2016, killing forty-nine patrons and injuring fifty-three more, Senator Marco Rubio (R-FL), who—suffice it to say—does not have a history of supporting gay equality initiatives, had the chutzpah to comment, "I think common sense tells you that he targeted the gay community because of the views that exist in the radical Islamic community about the gay community."[85] It certainly would not have done for Rubio to say, "I agree with the shooter that homosexuality is immoral. We just can't shoot them." No, at this tragic juncture, Rubio put himself on the side of tolerance and against homophobia, in contrast to the unenlightened radical Muslim other whose views—he implies—trail his own.

Puar's insight suggests that Rubio's framing was hardly innovative. It was effectively readied by the gay progress narrative—a narrative that comes "at the expense" of Muslim others. Gay equal rights *externalizes* some of its costs. The Foucauldian concept of norm production is a useful mechanism for understanding the process by which the Western progress narrative of gay rights imposes costs on groups that are out of step with that narrative.

In *Beyond Gay Marriage*, which has become a classic in queer theory, Michael Warner illustrates the utility of the concept for marriage: "Marriage sanctifies some couples at the expense of others. It is selective legitimacy. This is a necessary implication of the institution. ... To a couple that gets married, marriage just looks ennobling. . . . Stand outside it for a second and you see the implication: if you don't have it, you and your relations are less worthy. Without this corollary effect, marriage would not be able to endow anybody's life with significance. The ennobling and the demeaning go together."[86] In this context, the unmarried find themselves on the devalued side of the norm.

Same-sex marriage was always controversial within the LGBT community, with some queer and otherwise radical segments opposed to what the gay mainstream sought so fervently. Proponents of same-sex marriage maintained that the issue should be understood as being about choice or the simple right of gay and lesbian people to choose legal recognition for their lifetime, loving commitments. Part of what makes Warner's essay compelling is his confrontation with this discursive fragment of *choice* and the accompanying suggestion that marriage "has nothing to do with" those who "choose" to remain unmarried.[87] But *choice* is not all that marriage has brought to the gay community. Access to this form of state recognition has normalizing power. The advent of same-sex marriage (not entirely unlike straight marriage, just at a different juncture) means that each gay-identified individual is located in relation to a new governing norm: married/unmarried. Why does this matter?

One set of consequences is regulatory. Marriage as a legal institution involves rules governing how title to property is held, which contracts are valid, and what testimony can be compelled in court, as well as administrative matters under regimes that range from Social Security and taxation to immigration and prison visitation. Many of these regulatory distinctions (not all) favor married over unmarried couples. As Chief Justice Marshall of Massachusetts wrote in *Goodridge*, "Individuals who have the choice to marry each other and nevertheless choose not to may properly be denied the legal benefits of marriage."[88]

But consequences also occur at the level of social meaning. As same-sex marriage advocates rhetorically imbued marriage with more and more sentimentality, wholesomeness, and sanctity, they further endowed the marital norm with the power to distinguish the "Good Gay" from the "Bad Queer."[89] As advocates legitimated the lives of some gay people, they simultaneously delegitimized the lives of others.

Puar's observation is related but attends to the effects of the norm of liberal toleration of gays as an American value: There is no patriot without the terrorist and no progressive civilization without a backward, barbarous one. Her argument is that inclusion of gay and lesbian rights bearers in full American citizenship has come *at the expense of* the racialized and religiously identified others who occupy the underside of the norm. The progress narrative of gay rights in the West spins out effects for our conception of Islam so that Rubio's line practically writes itself.

This is not limited to the right wing. Recall how the Muslim men tortured at Abu Ghraib were cast as *particularly* humiliated by coerced homosexuality and nakedness before a female tormenter. That narrative was ostensibly relativistic and compassionate but as Aziza Ahmed has argued it also suggested that Arabs and Muslims were *especially* homophobic and sexist while (non-Muslim) Americans were sexually cool.[90] Attitudes toward homosexuality and women have emerged as key markers distinguishing advanced and developed civilizations from retrograde and customary cultures. The march toward gay equality in the West, conceptualized as a norm, puts the East in the Dark Ages.[91]

As the case for trans equal rights accumulates, it will be worth observing what norms the case installs and, further, who find themselves on the undersides of those norms. Concepts such as patriotism, productivity, wholesomeness, and safety analytically rely on threats to the nation, decay, pollution, and danger. The concepts from the second set (and others like them) land somewhere—*on* someone. Sometimes LGBT equal rights discourse produces costs for Muslims and additional "others," and sometimes the costs are borne within the LGBT community.

The latter situation occurred in 2005 in Lexington, Massachusetts, where a kindergartner arrived home from school one day carrying a "diversity book bag." Inside was a children's book entitled *Who's in a Family?* The book depicted a single-parent family, a biracial family, a family in which the parents had divorced, and a family with same-sex parents. When the child's father, David Parker, saw that same-sex parenting was being presented as a legitimate familial arrangement, he became outraged. He went to his son's elementary school and refused to leave until administrators excused the boy from further instruction conveying that message. The principal called the police, and Parker was arrested for trespassing. He refused bail and spent the night in jail, making himself a cause célèbre for the antigay right.[92] Fred Phelps's notorious Westboro Baptist Church (an independent church, the slogan of which is "God Hates Fags") came to Lexington to demonstrate; Governor Mitt Romney made a public statement in support of parental rights; and MassResistance, the commonwealth's premier antigay marriage organization, came to Parker's aid and supported his unsuccessful federal lawsuit against the town of Lexington.

Among Parker's claims was that Lexington had violated a state statute that provides that "every . . . school district implementing . . . curriculum which primarily involves human sexual education or human sexuality issues shall adopt a policy ensuring parental/guardian notification. Such policy shall afford parents or guardians the flexibility to exempt their children from any portion of said curriculum through written notification to the school principal. No child so exempted shall be penalized by reason of such exemption."[93] Parker claimed that this law entitled him to notice of the lesson in his son's kindergarten class and the opportunity to have him excused. The position of the school district, however, joined by the ACLU and other gay rights organizations, was that the statute did not apply to the lesson. As one of the briefs siding with the school district argued,

> None of the books objected to by the plaintiffs here are part of a curriculum "primarily["] about "sexual education" or "human sexuality issues" for purposes of the statute and thus fall outside of its scope. [They] simply ... contain gay characters. ... The argument that depictions of gay characters constitute ... "sexual" content would mean that depictions of families with a husband and wife as parents are also about sexuality education, a plainly absurd notion. The promotion of tolerance, acknowledgement of diversity, and discussion of equal treatment and rights of gay people in society is [*sic*] not "sex education."[94]

School officials summarized the district's position succinctly in the *Boston Globe*: "the material was about families, not sexuality."[95]

This argument holds undeniable appeal. The implication of Parker's claim, after all, is that the mere appearance of a gay couple makes the lesson sexual. The defendant school district and its allies understandably were trying to de-stigmatize same-sex relationships and convey that they are not importantly different from heterosexual relationships or inappropriate content for young children. Moreover, Parker's claim that the lesson fell under the sex education statute rests on the pretense that one cannot distinguish the "Who's in a Family?" lesson delivered to that kindergarten class from the kind of instruction one might find in a high school health class about, say, how to use a condom.

Still, the specific rebuttal offered by the school district and its allies invoked a very familiar opposition between "families" and "human sexuality." It is a trope that echoes throughout the culture war. That sharp dichotomy has *normalizing* power. To borrow from an old feminist critique, the argument recalls the virgin-whore dichotomy: The gays who have children are somehow not quite the same gays as those who have sexuality.

Insisting that gay couples are familial rather than sexual is a tried-and-true advocacy practice. Advocates for gay rights work overtime to depict the gay family as a morally upstanding and legitimate fragment in the multicultural mosaic. Nowhere has this strategy been more in evidence than it was in the campaign for same-sex marriage.

As the battle over same-sex marriage ensued in New Jersey, *Newsweek* explained:

> Lambda is trying to soften up public opinion with town-hall meetings designed to show that gay families are good for the community. "The town halls we're doing tell people, 'Hey, we're just like anyone else—a middle-class, hometown suburban couple that's been called boring,'" says Cindy Meneghin, 45, who with her partner, Maureen Kilian, also 45, and their two children, Joshua, 10, and Sarah, 8, are suing to be recognized as a legal family in New Jersey. "You can't look at our beautiful charming kids and not notice that we're a family, and the myths start tumbling down. What we've found is that people get to know us as people with families and kids, that I coach soccer and take pictures, and Maureen is the best dessert maker in town, and oh yes, Maureen and Cindy are a gay couple.[96]

With no disrespect whatsoever toward suburban parenting, soccer, or dessert, it is hard to remain sanguine about the images in this paragraph once one approaches them as examples of normalization or as the production of a distinction that organizes the social world and (in this case) proposes to allocate equal rights accordingly. Why should gay people be accorded equal rights? Because we are middle class? Because we are suburban? Because we have children? Who is on the other side of that coin?

Wholesome images such as these do a lot of work. First, they are decidedly *chaste*. Depiction of the bourgeois gay couple subtly depends on expulsion of the *sex* from *sexual orientation*. Examples from gay rights litigation abound. In a precursor to *Obergefell, United States v. Windsor*,[97] the Supreme Court struck down Section 3 of DOMA, which denied federal recognition to marriages even when those marriages were valid in the couples' states. After the case came down, a revealing article in the *New Yorker* magazine profiling the plaintiff, Edith Windsor, was flawlessly entitled "The Perfect Wife."[98] Edith's battle to avoid the $363,000 federal tax bill on the estate left to her by her lawful spouse and love of her life, Thea Spyer, led her to become a national gay rights heroine.

According to the *New Yorker*'s account, Edith was eighty-four years old by the time the decision issued. She had spent forty years with Thea, many of them caring for her through chronic progressive multiple sclerosis that rendered her increasingly disabled. Ariel Levy, who wrote the article, described Edith as "platinum blonde" with a "blow-dried bob," lipstick, painted nails, and pearls. Edith's lawyer, Roberta Kaplan, a partner at a prestigious corporate law firm in New York, saw in Edith an ideal plaintiff, a "non-threatening little old lady." Americans would sympathize with her, Levy wrote, because "they could imagine that [she] had aged out of carnality."

Far from it. Once freed from the constraints of litigation, Edith shared with Levy heartwarming details of her life with Thea, such as, "I never wanted anybody inside me till Thea. And then I wanted her inside me all the time." The couple installed a mechanism in their bedroom to lift the increasingly disabled Thea into bed; for these two it served as a sexual aid, as well. And because they adhered strictly to a butch-femme aesthetic, it enraged them when anyone referred to Thea as Edith's "wife." Feminizing terms were reserved for Edith; for Thea such terms were an affront. To the end, Edith made clear, these women were lovers, even as Thea required more and more care. "Keep it hot!" was their secret to longevity, Edith told Levy.

But "Kaplan [had] instructed Windsor not to talk publicly about sex" while the case was pending. "All I needed was Antonin Scalia reading about Edie and Thea's butch-femme escapades," Kaplan said. This view appears to be consistent with the collective judgment of the gay rights professionals that the mention of gay sex is bad for gay equality. When pro-gay advocates defending the diversity book bag in Lexington drew a sharp distinction between sex and family and insisted that the gays in the children's book fell to the family side of the line, they were working inside a convention, reproducing a norm that gay rights advocates are very much in the habit of affirming. It might often "work" in the sense that the pro-gay side won both the Lexington case and the *Windsor* case, but it also degrades homosexual sex and makes gay equality dependent on its suppression.

Moreover, the selection and depiction of Edith Windsor and the suburban New Jersey soccer moms has obvious class dimensions. Kaplan, Windsor's lawyer, specifically resonated to the idea of a plaintiff with an unfair tax bill, Levy reported. Some of the movement lawyers apparently had a bankruptcy case in mind to challenge Section 3 of DOMA, but Kaplan's response was, "I don't want to be disrespectful or classist, but do you really think that people who couldn't pay their personal debts are the best people to bring this claim?" In *Goodridge*, Chief Justice Marshall observed that the gay and lesbian plaintiffs included "business executives, lawyers, an investment banker, educators, therapists, and a computer engineer"[99]—a perfect list of middle-class next-door neighbors. Gay rights advocates and sympathetic judges surely believe that go-go dancers and female impersonators deserve equal rights, too, and may feel content with the idea that the rights earned by the respectable gays will be equally available to us all. And, in fact, some poor people may well benefit from the rights won by their more privileged counterparts. The law will not read "middle class, white, suburban same-sex couples may marry while low-income drag queens of color may not." As a formal matter, such a result is entirely implausible. The winning or losing of formal rights is not, however, the only effect of equal rights strategies. The pursuit of equal rights seems to demand, from the vantage point of our chief strategists, that LGBT subjects be patriotic, bourgeois, and domestic. But just as married will have its unmarried, civilized its barbarous, and patriotic its terrorist, so bourgeois will have its marginalized and domestic its perverse.

Members of the LGBT "community" differ from one another in every demographic dimension (age, race, religion, education, class, and income), as well as in our sexual practices, lifestyles, and politics. Cindy and Maureen, the "boring" suburban soccer coach and dessert chef, do not represent everyone equally well. It is not lost on those who find themselves on the degraded side of norms governing sex, class, or civic inclusion that Cindy and Maureen bring themselves into the civic fold at the expense of the more marginalized among us, and it should therefore come as no surprise when resentment results. By gaining admittance to equal rights on grounds of their desexed, bourgeois acceptability, Cindy and Maureen and the advocates who carefully selected and portrayed them, provoke alienation in the people living on the other side of the norms that they helped to install and entrench.

Advocates support arguments for LGBT equal rights with depictions of virtuous rights bearers who are deserving of equality: patriotic, bourgeois, and familial. Those archetypes do not, however, stand on their own; they depend on degraded others hidden in the subtext of the discourse.

Competing Rights

In the culture war over the status of LGBT people, it once seemed that the discourse consisted of assertions of equal rights and privacy on the pro-LGBT side vying against vituperative moralism emanating from the cultural right. More and more, however, the conflict has come to conform to the terms in which scholars of critical legal studies have described rights battles: Rights assertions compete with, and even *provoke*, competing rights assertions.

In *Goins*, the trans antidiscrimination case litigated under Minnesota state law back in 2001 (see chapter 1), Goins's employer, West Publishing, defended its expulsion of Goins from the women's restroom partly by arguing that other female employees had complained that her presence created a "hostile work environment" for them.[100] *Hostile work environment* is a term of art in Title VII jurisprudence. It means that the other occupants of the women's room felt that they were being subjected to sexual harassment and that the employer might be vulnerable to a Title VII lawsuit if it permitted Goins continued access. When Goins's co-workers made this complaint, they were claiming not that Goins actually engaged in harassing behavior but that Goins effectively harassed them *just by being there.*

Emboldened perhaps by Goins's defeat, a Minnesota teacher brought a federal lawsuit to expel a transgender co-worker from the women's bathroom in her school. In *Cruzan v. Special School District No. 1*,[101] the teacher sued her school district claiming hostile work environment as well as religious discrimination. (She lost.)

In Colorado, the culturally conservative Pacific Justice Institute alleged that a trans teenage girl was harassing other girls in the school bathroom but upon further inquiry explained, "It is our position that the intrusion of a biological male into a restroom for teenage girls is inherently intimidating and harassing."[102] Any implication that the trans girl's *behavior* was harassing, the group contended, was not misleading, because her mere presence was sufficient to justify the charge.

Coy Mathis (see chapter 1) faced a similar argument from her school district but framed in prospective terms. *She may be six now, but eventually she will develop adolescent male characteristics, stealthily emerging as a threat to the bathroom safety of the very girls with whom she now innocently skips down the elementary school hallways.*

String a few stories like this together and it begins to seem as if transgender people are a menace to girls' and women's safety. Maybe the equality interests of transgender people and the anti-harassment interests of women and girls are inherently in conflict. Maybe if you are *for* transgender people, then you are *against* safety for women and girls.

In fact, that is precisely what the Women's Liberation Front (WoLF) asserted in its lawsuit challenging the U.S. Department of Education's interpretation of Title IX that, for purposes of access to bathrooms and lockers, schools must treat trans students in accordance with their gender identity. Characterizing the department's position as a mandate that "every public school and university in the United States unconditionally admit men to women's bathrooms, locker rooms, changing rooms and other facilities," the complaint, filed in the District of New Mexico, raised the specter of increased risk of sexual assault or indecent exposure by "men" who have "unfettered" access to women's spaces.[103]

Arranging transgender and women's interests antipodally has become standard practice among opponents of trans rights. In the early 2000s, it was not uncommon for opponents to give any antidiscrimination bill that would protect on the basis of gender identity the name "the bathroom bill" in the press,[104] fixing attention on the (apparently terrifying) prospect of transgressions of gender-segregated bathrooms. Now the term seems to refer to both antidiscrimination and anti-trans bills. To minimize confrontation on the bathroom point, many of the early antidiscrimination laws did not guarantee access to one's bathroom of choice, leaving the question to be answered differently in different settings. North Carolina definitionally excluded trans people from the bathrooms that comport with their gender identities in 2016. Even though that landed North Carolina in litigation with the federal government and subjected its businesses to boycotts, a half-dozen more states introduced similar legislation in early 2017.

California bucked the early trend of avoiding the bathroom issue with a law that specifically permits transgender students to have access to bathrooms, locker rooms, and sports teams that are consistent with their identities.[105] Anti-trans activists who tried to reverse the California law by referendum described it as "allowing students who self-identify as the opposite sex to walk into bathrooms and locker rooms and have their rights trump everybody else's privacy rights."[106] They organized into the "Privacy for All Students coalition."

The Massachusetts statute, in contrast, was initially enacted with a glaring concession: the omission of protections for public accommodations altogether.[107] This concession, while very possibly necessary to obtain passage of the other protections (in employment, housing, education, and lending), worked a bit of mischief by accepting the image of the predatory transgender bathroom interloper. Happily, however, advocates in Massachusetts have since succeeded in appending protections for public accommodations.[108]

Fear of the transgender menace can also seep outside the bathroom. In New Hampshire, a legislator argued against antidiscrimination legislation for transgender people in employment by urging that if such protections were adopted, a private school would be unable to rid itself of a transgender bus driver who was confusing the children. Another fretted about the potential demise of the state's summer camp industry. Not only might women's sacred restroom space be intruded on, but the fragile minds of children, riding the bus to school or enjoying a carefree summer on Squam Lake, could be robbed of their innocent clarity if antidiscrimination provisions were to take effect.

The antidiscrimination right asserted in Goins and other disputes over trans people's access to bathrooms provoked the assertion of a counter-right framed in feminist, anti-harassment terms. The factual vacuity of the counter-right—no case of a transgender person harassing someone in the rest-room has been documented—does not seem to hamper its rhetorical efficacy. The depiction of transwomen as threats to the privacy and safety of ciswomen shows up in both courtroom and legislative battles. In the judicial setting, the problem of conflicting rights is a feature of indeterminacy, as discussed in chapter 1. But more broadly, once competing rights are asserted, they are outside the rhetorical control of the LGBT community. And those competing rights, like equality rights asserted in the first instance, have the capacity to attach meaning to LGBT identity.

In the popular imagination, a right—once recognized as such—is a kind of trump card. *People may not like it when I burn a flag, but it is my right to do so.*[109] The structure is perceived as a democratic majoritarian preference versus a constitutionally guaranteed individual right. Often, however, a right is met with a counter-right, and the trump card loses its trump. The substantive equality right of people of color in the context of affirmative action vies against the formal equality right of white people. The privacy right of an abortion-seeking woman clashes with the "right to life" of the fetus.[110] Even in criminal cases, where the adversaries are the public at large (in the form of the prosecutor) against a rights-bearing accused individual (as in *State v. Smith*), criminal defendants now contend with "victims' rights."

Sometimes the counter-rights exist mainly in the popular imagination, at the level of rhetoric, and do not benefit from the same legal pedigree as the originally asserted right. "Victims' rights," for example, are not constitutional rights and therefore do not benefit from the same degree of judicial recognition as the rights of criminal defendants. Even in the flag-burning scenario, some counter-right (against violent provocation, say) may be asserted, but realistically it is too weak in its constitutional pedigree or in its legal-cultural context to compete. In the domain of abortion, while the Supreme Court has not (so far) recognized a "right to life" for fetuses under the due process clause, over time one can detect a subtle shift in how the Supreme Court refers to the state's interest in protecting a fetus (from the tentative "potential life" to the attribution of "fetal life").[111] As law in a given arena evolves, one can often see advantages accrue as a result of reframing opposition to a right as a counter-right. Specifically, it alters the conception of the initial right-asserting party; that party is no longer a victim of tyranny but is itself a tyrant, proposing to trammel the rights of others.

The Supreme Court's relatively recent establishment of a personal right to bear arms under the Second Amendment provoked this: "In evaluating an asserted right to be free from particular gun-control regulations, liberty is on both sides of the equation. . . . *Your* interest in keeping and bearing a certain firearm may diminish *my* interest in being and feeling safe from armed violence."[112] That is Justice Stevens attempting (in his dissent from one of the two key cases establishing the fundamental right to bear arms) to attach the due process clause to gun *control*, not just gun possession. He is reframing gun control as an individual right rather than leaving it to be understood as a majoritarian policy preference. Justice Stevens picked up a tool that was lying around in legal discourse, ready to serve his purposes. The opposition between freedom and security surfaces in numerous legal contexts, from wiretapping to child abuse.[113] And the inclination to generate a counter-right when faced with a right one opposes evidences itself across the political spectrum; it is not just a tactic of conservatives.

Gay rights against discrimination have invited a host of competing rights, once framed largely as moral preferences. During the fight to repeal Don't Ask, Don't Tell, the military's now defunct antigay policy, opponents of repeal asserted not only a rationale of military cohesion for maintaining the policy but also a counter-right of straight soldiers to privacy—that is, a right not to be forced to shower surrounded by the leering eyes of gays and lesbians.[114] The repeal effort was successful in the end, but the dispute left a residue. The counter-right against gay leering contains at least two suggestions that may have more adhesive power than the counter-right itself. First, the counter-right depicts gay and lesbian people as letches. Everyone else is there to do their job, but gay people are despoiling the military by behaving as if they were in a bathhouse.

Second, and more powerful because it is subtler, the counter-right contains and furthers the assumption that gay and straight soldiers are to be sharply distinguished and that gay identity travels neatly with homosexual conduct and desire, while straight identity travels neatly without those things. In the military context in particular, this is a wildly unjustified assumption. The architects of the Don't Ask, Don't Tell policy understood this very well. As Professor Aaron Belkin, who testified in one of the pre-repeal challenges to Don't Ask, Don't Tell, explained, even if the military were to expel all of the gay and lesbian service members, including those who were out and those who were closeted, "It's very clear that there would still be sexual activity among same sex service members. The reason is that many of the people who have same-sex sex in the military are not gay. This is why Congress has put a Queen For A Day exception in the law [permitting people to prove that even though they have engaged in homosexual sex, they are nonetheless heterosexual]. The military knows quite well that there are straight service members who engage in same sex sexual activity in military spaces."[115] If, under the Don't Ask, Don't Tell regime, heterosexual service members were engaging in homosexual sex and then subsequently establishing their heterosexuality, one must conclude that homosexual desire cannot be excised from the military setting simply by banishing the gay people. Furthermore, if there is leering going on in the showers, it is not at all clear that it is the gay people who are doing it.

Assertion of the privacy counter-right, even while it ultimately failed to prevent the repeal of Don't Ask, Don't Tell, cultivated an idea in the public imagination. This is not to hold the privacy counter-right entirely responsible for the rigidity of sexual orientation categories. It is merely to identify its contribution to the ongoing production of the relevant identities.

Gay rights have clashed with the First Amendment's expressive provisions in two classically framed cases: *Hurley v. Irish-American Gay, Lesbian and Bisexual Group of Boston* and *Boy Scouts of America v. Dale*.[116] In *Hurley*, a gay group hoped to march in the St. Patrick's Day Parade in Boston, but the organizers would not permit it.[117] The gay group sought protection under the state's antidiscrimination law and won at the state level, but the U.S. Supreme Court reversed, on the grounds that the parade organizers had a right under the First Amendment to express a "pro-family" message and that this expressive right superseded the gay group's antidiscrimination right. Dale's dispute with the Boy Scouts was similarly structured. Dale was an out gay scoutmaster who was expelled from the Boy Scouts pursuant to their long-standing discriminatory policy.[118] He won in state court under New Jersey's antidiscrimination law, but the U.S. Supreme Court reversed, holding that the First Amendment guaranteed the Boy Scouts a right to *expressive association* and therefore a right *not* to associate with Dale, who, by being openly gay, undermined their message of "moral . . . straight[ness]."[119]

Gay rights advocates lost those cases, but they do not always lose cases in which expressive rights conflict with gay equality. They won in Rhode Island, where two Catholic firefighters sued the city of Providence for requiring them to drive a fire truck in the 2001 gay pride parade; the court deemed the assignment an ordinary work duty and not an expression of support for the parade.[120] Gay rights advocates also won in *Romer*.[121] In that case, defenders of Amendment 2 in Colorado made much of the prospect of a religious landlord forced by an antidiscrimination provision to rent to gay couples doing God knows what right upstairs from where the landlord and his family eat, sleep, and pray. Voters bought it, but the Supreme Court did not. Sometimes the LGBT right will prevail over the counter-right, and sometimes the LGBT right will be defeated. Either way, though, the assertion of the initial right raises a ghoul that has been biding its time, waiting only to be summoned into service.

Opponents of same-sex marriage, endeavoring to stave off some of its effects, now routinely tap religious freedom as a counter-right belonging to private business owners who do not wish to serve gays and lesbians. In Arizona, the legislature adopted a bill vetoed by Governor Jan Brewer (R) that would have enabled businesses such as florists and bakeries to refuse services for same-sex weddings based on the owner's beliefs.[122] Those beliefs, according to the bill, did not have to be a part of any religious system. (This, I suppose, was designed to circumvent the obvious line of questioning on cross-examination: *Which part of baking the cake, exactly, violates your religion? Measuring the flour? Beating the eggs? Adding the sugar? Is it male-on-male anal intercourse that violates your religion? Do you have to do that to bake a cake?*) If one's mere *belief* is sufficient justification for refusing service, without regard to whether that belief is integral to a religious system, then one can simply *not believe* in making cakes for people who do those sorts of things. Even states and counties are attempting to circumvent the requirements of *Obergefell* by permitting exemptions based on individual "conscience" for clerks and judges who do not wish to participate in licensing or performing same-sex marriages. Gay rights litigators (like advocates for access to contraception and abortion[123]) see clearly that religiously framed claims designed to exempt private actors from complying with antidiscrimination and health care access laws are proliferating. Opponents of gay rights seem to be operating on the (sound) assumption that framing the conflict as one in which their own sacred freedom is in jeopardy will go over better (in courtrooms as well as in public opinion) than accepting the frame in which gay equal rights vie against majoritarian moral preferences.

LGBT equal rights is really only one side of a discourse, the other side of which is put into service by cultural conservatives who have reshaped their moral argument into a cluster of counter-rights (against harassment, to privacy, to expressive association, and to freedom of religion). The two sides of the discourse relate dynamically, each provoking the other, so that neither side can expect to bring the argument to a single right-determined conclusion. This occurs in judicial and nonjudicial environments. Any one cultural conservative counter-right may or may not have substantial factual or legal grounding, but even when it is largely rhetorical, it can inflict damage. At the very least, counter-rights stoke the culture war, as religious exemptions continue to illustrate.

Worse, the unique rhetorical force of rights in our system means that when pro-LGBT advocates assert rights claims that encroach on cherished prerogatives (e.g., gender-segregated bathrooms, not baking a "gay" wedding cake) the people who cherish those prerogatives are likely to retaliate with their own claim of an objectively good right in relation to which LGBT people and our demands pose an unholy threat. We become the rights trammelers. Counter-rights to be free of LGBT incursions into privacy, safety, free expression, and religious conscience do more than they appear to do. Even when anti-LGBT counter-rights fail to achieve their immediate purposes, they nonetheless spawn fears of terrifying figures that ogle heterosexuals in the showers, befoul morally pure environments such as the Boy Scouts, disorient innocent children, or threaten ladies in the powder room. They drop into the public imagination subtle ideas about LGBT people and our relationship to prized values such as freedom of expression and religion. *And they put us on the side of power*—an uncomfortable position for any rights claimant. The right–counter-right dynamic is one (just one) avenue by which equal rights as a discourse produces knowledge about LGBT rights bearers. As opponents of LGBT equality spar with LGBT advocates, they might succeed or fail in any one effort to keep us out of the bathrooms, the Boy Scouts, the barracks showers, or the clerk's office, but along the way they are subtly shaping social conceptions of gay and trans identity.

Progressives have been caught off-guard by counter-rights in the past.[124] After the *Goodridge* decision declaring same-sex marriage to be a constitutional right in Massachusetts, cultural conservatives made repeated (failed) efforts to reverse the decision by amending the state constitution. Constitutional amendment is a long process in Massachusetts, requiring legislative action as well as a voter referendum. Anti-gay activists and Governor Mitt Romney argued that "the people" had a "right to vote" on the matter. Aghast at the flipping of the rights rhetoric, proponents of gay rights protested that it was basic American civics that rights belong to the equality-seeking minority, not to those who would deny the minority its equality.

The political scientist Jonathan Goldberg-Hiller conducted a detailed analysis of the controversy that resulted in Colorado's Amendment 2 (the antigay law struck down in *Romer v. Evans*). He described the cultural right's "religious landlord" strategy as "dominant majority political interests . . . viewed through a minoritarian lens."[125] I take him to mean that the gay equality right was the *real* right, while the landlord's right was a distortion.

But however morally superior the gay right may be, it is not necessarily *analytically* superior. Advocates for progressive change may sometimes have difficulty taking conservative counter-rights seriously because they do not believe that cultural conservatives have any claims that are legitimately made from a position of marginalization, exclusion, or powerlessness.[126] *We know who the oppressed are, and rights belong to the oppressed.* In a counter-majoritarian setting, this is so because an equal rights claim contains the implicit assertion that the claimant is the real victim, the one who needs a hero—in the form of counter-majoritarian vindication. This, again, is a species of *representation-reinforcement theory*[127]—the idea that the counter-majoritarian branch has a warrant to protect marginalized and powerless minorities.

Representation-reinforcement is, in strict terms, a creature of counter-majoritarianism: It is a rationale for an unelected body to aggressively review the work of the majority. While in general the counter-majoritarian branch is expected to defer to the elected branches, an exception is warranted where a minority is unable to vindicate its interests using traditional majoritarian means (e.g., voting, petition drives, letters to the editor, and so on) due to the minority group's history of discrimination and systematic political exclusion. In that exceptional circumstance, the federal court may provide representation-reinforcement for the group that is systematically deprived of a fair shot of winning elections or legislative drives. Each assertion of a right, therefore, entails a claim of vulnerability for its constituency and power for its opponent.

But the idea that rights belong to the vulnerable spills outside of the formal precincts of the courtroom. When a constituency comes before a legislature seeking antidiscrimination protection, it emphasizes its vulnerability. Then that constituency's opponents may try to steal some of that victim mojo for themselves. This is why opponents of antidiscrimination legislation to protect transgender people routinely invoke women's safety or the specter of the innocent child who might be "confused" by a transgender person. There is no "right not to be confused" by another person's gender presentation, but the proffering of the confused child is nonetheless of a piece with the right–counter-right dynamic and the implicit claim to superior vulnerability. The "real victim," it suggests, is not the trans person who may be denied a job, a home, or access to the facilities, but the vulnerable woman or helpless child. This is why it is far less common to encounter right-wing depictions of transmen as "threatening"; when transmen use men's restrooms, it is they who appear most vulnerable to sexual violence.

Cognizance of this dynamic is what prompted Justice Scalia to depict gays as rich. If gay people are, as Scalia ritually proclaimed, teeming with disposable income and wielding outsized influence in the political arena, then we are not a disempowered minority in need of representation-reinforcement. Power and powerlessness are intricately bound up with the right–counter-right dynamic. The credibility of an equal rights claim—in a counter-majoritarian forum or a majoritarian one—depends on demonstrating a justification for helping out a vulnerable group.

This presents—in Sedgwick's terms—another double-bind. On the one hand, LGBT equal rights claims rely on plaintiff selection and public relations to promote a bourgeois, suburban, patriotic, professional archetype. Edith Windsor's attorney thought DOMA would be more effectively challenged by a plaintiff with a huge estate tax bill than by a plaintiff in personal bankruptcy;

the *Goodridge* court gratuitously listed the professions of the people suing for the right to marry; the New Jersey soccer coach and dessert chef ostentatiously display their middle-class ordinariness. To gain public as well as judicial sympathy seems to require presenting oneself as a middle-class next-door neighbor.

This presentation, however, comes with a risk. The picture of a respectable, taxpaying, professional gay couple can easily bend into an image of overly empowered, wealthy, invulnerable, gay people; this presents an obstacle to gay advancement. The bourgeois archetype enables the argument that the gay minority is too privileged and powerful to require representation-reinforcement. This is a matter of constitutional theory, but it also plays to a widespread intuition in the lay consciousness about rights.

To refute the image of the rich, white, privileged gay community, several of the major LGBT organizations have published data on the realities of LGBT poverty. The Williams Institute has sponsored numerous studies documenting poverty in the LGBT community. According to one report, "Post recession, LBG Americans are more likely to be poor than heterosexual Americans. Gender, race, education and geography all influence poverty rates among LBG populations, and children of same-sex couples are particularly vulnerable to poverty."[128] Data released by the Williams Institute in 2014 demonstrate that LGBT Americans were disproportionately likely to be food-insecure in 2013 and to rely on the Supplemental Nutrition Assistance Program (SNAP, a.k.a. food stamps).[129] Scholars such as Lee Badgett and Gary Gates have provided an abundance of data establishing the reality of economic disadvantage associated with LGBT populations. The data revealed in these studies enable equal rights advocates to showcase LGBT vulnerability and combat the archetype that undermines our claim to protection.

We must be bourgeois to engender the identification of courts and the public, but we must be poor and vulnerable to warrant protection. If we are privileged and powerful, we do not need any protection; in fact, it is the religious landlords and women in the restroom who need protection from us.

Both depictions are crucial to effective participation in rights claiming. We need it both ways. This is part of the price we pay for participating in the right–counter-right dynamic.

Conclusion

"Representation," Leo Bersani urged, "implies the active work of selecting and presenting, of structuring and shaping; not merely the transmitting of already existing meaning, but the more active labour of making things mean."[130] Equal rights advocacy on behalf of LGBT constituencies *represents* us in this full sense, not merely speaking for us, but shaping our identities. This activity takes place not on a wide-open field but inside preexisting discursive constraints, including American rights-consciousness and the virtue of being oppressed. Rights play a special role in protecting vulnerable minorities from what Alexis de Tocqueville dubbed the "tyranny of the majority,"[131] but to attain those rights a constituency must accommodate itself to certain discursive conditions. These conditions establish terms with which pursuers of equal rights must comply. As our representatives (lawyers, public relations professionals, and so on)—savvy players who are deeply familiar with the demands of equal rights advocacy—*represent* us, they have a hand in producing our identities accordingly.

Knowledge of LGBT people is a constant byproduct of LGBT equal rights advocacy. The enormous power of knowledge production lies in its taking place largely beyond notice, yet close examination of these examples drawn from across LGBT advocacy illustrate the capacity of LGBT equal rights discourse to generate identity, making us what we are as it speaks on our behalf.

An analytical conundrum lies at the heart of LGBT equality claims: Are we the same or different? Of course, just about any two categories of people or things are endlessly alike and different; the bread and butter of legal analysis, as any first-year law student knows, is analogy and distinction. Moreover, at different moments in the course of an equal rights effort, a constituency may have to be both so that LGBT people must be enough like heterosexuals to warrant similar treatment but sufficiently distinct to be awarded a remedy. Both representations, however, harbor the potential to defeat LGBT purposes in an inhospitable moment.

Moreover, to warrant the protections of equal rights, we have had to be injured—marginalized, stigmatized, and despised—while to defeat attacks on our merit as parents, spouses, or citizens, we have had to be healthy, successful, and civically engaged. To be deserving of equal rights, LGBT people also must be virtuous on axes of patriotism, chastity, and bourgeois respectability. In the course of generating these archetypes, however, we generate others—of traitorousness, profligacy, and outsiderness—and collaborate in the marginalization of other vulnerable populations. As we have asserted our equal rights, we have provoked assertions of counter-rights by conservative culture warriors to privacy, security, expressive association, and the free exercise of religion. We have become not only threats to those widely shared values but enemies of the rights of others.

3

REFORMIST DESIRE

Victory?

After her triumph in *Windsor*, the case in which the U.S. Supreme Court struck down Section 3 of the Defense of Marriage Act (DOMA), attorney Roberta Kaplan took a well-earned victory lap.[1] At Harvard Law School, in October 2013, Kaplan addressed a friendly audience convened by the LGBT student organization and Harvard's *Journal of Law and Gender*. At the conclusion of the colloquium, which included several highly placed and respected gay rights litigators, Kaplan—now freshly minted as a gay rights luminary—declared, "It's really all over but the shouting. The battle for gay and lesbian rights has been won."[2]

Even on its own terms, the statement was premature. As Kaplan spoke, same-sex marriage remained illegal in most U.S. jurisdictions; Section 2 of DOMA (which permitted each state to refuse to recognize same-sex marriages performed in another state) remained valid law; and we were three years from knowing who would succeed Barack Obama to the U.S. presidency while Justice Ruth Bader Ginsburg—a decidedly liberal member of the precariously balanced Supreme Court—was the sitting justice whose retirement looked most imminent. In addition, congressional sponsors remained unable to secure the passage of the Employment Non-Discrimination Act (ENDA), which would prohibit employment discrimination on the basis of sexual orientation and gender identity, and LGBT people were unprotected against discrimination under federal law and many states' laws in myriad other contexts (e.g., housing, education, lending, and so on).

More striking than Kaplan's hastiness in hoisting the "mission accomplished" banner, however, was her conception of the mission itself. To have the idea that "it's . . . over," one must have a very narrow conception of what *it* is, according to which *it* consists of an obvious set of equal rights measures, of which same-sex marriage is the capstone. Kaplan is hardly alone in conceiving of *it* in this way.

Anyone who was sentient during or before the 1980s had to have been astonished by President Obama's Second Inaugural Address when these words emitted from his mouth: "We, the people, declare today that the most evident of truths—that all of us are created equal—is the star that guides us still; just as it guided our forebears through Seneca Falls, and Selma, and Stonewall."[3] *Dayenu*—it would have been enough—to hear the President of the United States refer to an uprising of drag queens, fairies, and bull dykes throwing bottles at police as "our forebears," likening them to the women whose bold declarations instigated the lumbering course to suffrage and to the civil rights demonstrators who braved billy clubs and tear gas marching toward Montgomery.

But President Obama was not done. "It is now our generation's task to carry on what those pioneers began. For our journey is not complete . . . until our gay brothers and sisters are treated like anyone else under the law—for if we are truly created equal, then surely the love we commit to one another must be equal as well."[4] It was a stunning moment. Having come of age during the Reagan administration—when jokes, revulsion, and moral condemnation predominated; when the president's spokesman claimed never to have heard of the disease that was killing gay men by the thousands in America's cities; and when mere presidential acknowledgment of gay people's existence was considered seminal—I sat before the television in tears. It took time to regain my bearings and begin to contemplate the historical thread that the president had spun.

In spelling out "our generation's task," President Obama extended the Seneca Falls reference by calling for equal pay for equal work, and he extended the Selma reference by declaring that no one should wait in line for hours to cast a ballot. How did he extend the Stonewall reference? To continue the work of those pioneers, gay people must be treated the same as others under the law, and this means we must have equal access to marriage ("the love we commit to one another must be equal"). Marriage represents the completion ("our journey is not complete . . . until") of the task begun at Stonewall. That is our emancipatory destination.[5] Like Kaplan, President Obama framed same-sex marriage as a capstone—a crowning achievement. For the president, this may have been impressionistic, or lyrical, but it is also part of a fully elaborated theory of gay rights that has guided LGBT law reform in recent years.

Professor Kees Waaldijk of the University of Leiden in the Netherlands is a scholar of comparative sexual orientation law. The Netherlands was the first national jurisdiction in the world to confer marital status on same-sex couples, and Waaldijk, a leading academic proponent of gay equal rights in Europe, wrote an influential paper providing a roadmap for other countries to follow to this destination. He wrote, "If you look at the legislative history of the recognition of homosexuality in European countries, it seems that this process is governed by certain trends that can tentatively be formulated as if they were 'laws of nature.' At the very least, there is a clear pattern of *steady progress* according to *standard sequences*."[6] Waaldijk gleans from the European experience that the standard sequence begins with decriminalization of sex acts accompanied by equalization of the age of consent for hetero- and homosexual acts. The next phase in the process is the passage of antidiscrimination legislation, and the final phase involves partnership and parenting rights. Each of the three major phases consists of constituent "small steps"—"a sequence in itself."[7]

Waaldijk's small steps theory is not modest. "Tentatively . . . formulated as . . . 'laws of nature,' "[8] the theory purports to be more than a strategy proposal; it offers itself as empirical description that, while discerned from the European experience, is transnational, if not universal. In fact, Waaldijk has enjoyed broad influence. His work appears in more than a half-dozen languages, including English and his native Dutch, but also Italian, Czech, and Chinese. In the United States, a receptive audience awaited Waaldijk's small steps theory, especially William N. Eskridge Jr., an American legal scholar and the leading academic proponent of same-sex marriage. As early as 2000, Eskridge advocated a sequential and incremental process identical to the one Waaldijk described, citing Waaldijk and the European experience.[9]

The American gay rights movement has been carefully gradual, initiating marriage litigations in jurisdictions in which a foundation of antidiscrimination reforms had already been laid and attacking sodomy laws early. Even after the terrible defeat in 1986 in *Bowers v. Hardwick*,[10] in which the U.S. Supreme Court upheld a state sodomy prohibition against a right-to-privacy challenge, advocates took the issue up at the state level in both courts and legislatures. By the time the U.S. Supreme Court revisited the matter, reversing *Bowers* in *Lawrence v. Texas*, twelve of the twenty-five states that had sodomy prohibitions at the time of *Bowers* had eliminated them.[11]

The theory seems to work. In *Goodridge*, for example, Chief Justice Marshall was able to dispose of the argument that the prohibition against same-sex marriage "reflects community consensus that homosexual conduct is immoral" by referring to the (by then) substantial legislative record of protecting against discrimination on the basis of sexual orientation in employment, housing, credit, public accommodations, and education, as well as case law that de-criminalized private, consensual sodomy and declaring sexual orientation no obstacle to child custody.[12] Same-sex marriage may in fact be attainable only after an attitude of fairness toward gay and lesbian people has been cultivated through the gradual introduction of pro-gay reforms, each leaving the sense of a task unfinished. According to this conception, same-sex marriage is a pinnacle built atop privacy protections and antidiscrimination laws and representing—finally—the equality of gay people.

This decidedly teleological approach is portrayed methodically in Waaldijk's small steps theory, movingly in President Obama's Inaugural Address, and cava-lierly in Kaplan's remarks at Harvard. It also has appeared in historical accounts that have enabled the narrative to proliferate with authority. Linda Hirshman's widely reviewed *Victory: The Triumphant Gay Revolution* tells the history of the gay rights movement in the United States.[13] The story begins around the turn of the twentieth century and culminates in the repeal of Don't Ask/Don't Tell and the legalization of same-sex marriage in New York. Hirshman is a lawyer, philosopher, and political writer for popular news outlets. Her account bursts with detail, compellingly delivered, on everything from the communist Harry Hay and his Mattachine Society of the 1950s to the confrontational activism of the AIDS Coalition to Unleash Power (ACT UP) in the 1980s. The tale is a thrilling one, full of counterculture and radicalism of multiple stripes. Yet somehow, everything in Hirshman's story was leading to marriage and military inclusion, the dual achievements that warrant the appearance of both "victory" and "triumph" in her title.

One might easily have expected that conclusion from Andrew Sullivan, the gay conservative former editor of the *New Republic* who in 1995 published *Virtually Normal*,[14] a political discussion of homosexuals and homosexuality, including a survey of existing positions on the subject and a prescription for legal reform. Sullivan's book, like Hirshman's, was reviewed everywhere, enjoy-ing a wide readership and sparking controversy across the political spectrum, not least because a highly placed conservative made a—as the reviews ritually described it—"sober," "reasoned" case for same-sex marriage. (Predecessors had apparently made hysterical, incoherent cases up until that point.) Moreover, Sullivan's book appeared on the heels of *Baehr v. Lewin*,[15] a case that might have led Hawaii to become the first state in the Union to permit same-sex couples to marry but for a state constitutional amendment that halted the sudden and surprising momentum for eliminating the "one man, one woman" requirement.

Sullivan's path to gay emancipation differs from Waaldijk's in that Sullivan is a conservative who leans libertarian; he is therefore not interested in the law attempting to advance his standing by prohibiting private discriminatory conduct through such mechanisms as housing and employment protections. His prescription contemplates only the most formal legal equality, devoid of intrusion into the mythical domain of exclusively private conscience and conduct, and would require equal treatment only by public institutions, highlighting especially the importance of marriage and the military.

Hirshman's history distinguishes itself from the work of both Sullivan and Waaldijk, concerned as she is with the characters and narrative detail and not merely a skeletal progression of legal steps. She is enamored of the people who have fought the battles for gay rights: their bravery, their modalities, and their learning curves. She admires, even adores, them as they proceed through their communism and their militancy, but in the end the left-leaning Hirshman winds up embracing a position nearly identical to the right-leaning Sullivan's: that marriage and the military were the key institutions into which gays needed to gain entry to attain full citizenship.

Waaldijk's "tentative . . . laws of nature," Kaplan's pronouncement that "the battle . . . has been won," Sullivan's formal equality under the law, and Hirshman's "Victory" narrative are all ostensibly descriptive, purporting to reflect on history and characterize empirical reality. In the vocabulary of queer theory, however, they are also *performative*. As Eve Kosofsky Sedgwick explained, "Performativity is about how language constructs or affects reality rather than merely describing it. This . . . productive aspect of language is most telling . . . when the utterances in question are closest to claiming a simply descriptive relation to some freestanding, ostensibly extradiscursive reality."[16] The teleological narratives of President Obama, Waaldijk, Kaplan, and Hirshman not only report on reality; they produce it. By instilling the sense of a march down a clear path toward a well-lit destination, the speakers tell us what progress is. This in turn produces gays' desire for progress within the terms of the discourse. The small steps theory describes reality accurately because it is making reality. Discursive strands emanating from lawyers, academics, politicians, and chroniclers of history converge to give a narrow range of law reform objectives the appearance of being natural, obvious, and desirable. As a consequence, all eyes turn toward marriage not because it is the only wish that the law can grant, but because runway lights point in that direction.

A fight like the one against the Christian Legal Society (see the introduction) fits like a smooth stone neatly into the path toward equality because of its straightforward antidiscrimination cast. Where might a fight more like the one against San Francisco's punitive sit-lie ordinance fit into the small steps theory? The answer is *nowhere*. It is not a "step" toward same-sex marriage or any other equal rights goal. If "it's really all over but the shouting," if "Victory" is upon us, then sit-lie was never part of the fight.

Teleology is a key feature of LGBT equal rights discourse. Its effect is to channel reformist desire and induce myopia so that law reform objectives off the path are rendered virtually invisible.[17] Reform objectives on the path become the manifest priorities of contemporary, mainstream LGBT equal rights advocacy: antidiscrimination law (legislative and constitutional), hate crimes protection, international human rights reforms that mimic modern egalitarian constitutionalism, and, of course, same-sex marriage. Exceptions can be found (some will be discussed later)—notably, in the context of trans advocacy—but equal rights objectives crowd the field. We who are the subjects of LGBT equal rights advocacy may experience desire for the reforms that predominate in our current moment, but that desire is neither innate nor natural; it is the product of discursive influence. The discourse of equal rights points us to a narrow range of goals and curbs the imagination we would need to generate a wider array of advocacy options.

This chapter explores the relationship between LGBT equal rights discourse and LGBT reformist desire and reveals another underappreciated cost of the discursive constraints within which we labor. The teleology of LGBT equal rights discourse, as well as additional discursive strands emphasizing privacy, love, and interdependence, have influenced the priorities of the mainstream LGBT movement in ways that disadvantage our most vulnerable community members. Moreover, a synchronicity between threads within LGBT equal rights discourse and the discourse of neoliberalism have resulted in a troubling political alignment that should be of grave concern to leftists.

As LGBT reformers succeed in attaining an artificially constricted field of equal rights objectives, they exacerbate—not just neglect but *exacerbate*—the hardship facing some of the most marginalized sectors of the LGBT community. Powerful threads within LGBT equal rights discourse narrate a teleological march that excludes nonconforming reform possibilities. Moreover, threads that stress the moral equivalency of hetero- and homosexual commitment and love are carried out in a vocabulary of *responsibility* and *interdependence*, privatized within the marital couple or family. The ennobling of privatized responsibility and dependence lend support to a neoliberal political agenda that disadvantages low-income people who rely on public programs. Further, the insular, private family that manages its dependence internally because of its shared love and commitment demands protection by the law, sometimes the criminal law, the expansion of which can also be to the detriment of low-income people, especially of color. Meanwhile, the progress we make (call it "Victory") and the increasing prohibition against anti-LGBT discrimination means that the interests of those bearing the identities that benefit from equal rights protections are advanced, entrenching the role of LGBT equal rights as a producer of identity and reformist desire.

Gay Family Values

Evan Wolfson, president and founder of Freedom to Marry and former director of Lambda Legal's Marriage Project, has been one of the country's leading and most persistent voices advocating same-sex marriage.[18] In his book *Why Marriage Matters* (2007), Wolfson recalled historical wrongs associated with the institution of marriage in the United States, including the total exclusion of African Americans from marriage during chattel slavery, the disappearance of women's legal personalities under coverture, and antimiscegenation laws—which were constitutionally permissible as late as 1967.[19] He also, however, recounted the demise of each injustice, concluding, "The general story of our country is movement toward inclusion and equality. The majority of Americans are fair. They realize that exclusionary conceptions of marriage fly in the face of our national commitment to freedom as well as the personal commitment made by loving couples."[20] The national commitment is to "freedom," but the exclusions also offend "personal commitments" made out of love. Wolfson continued, "Americans have been ready again and again to make the changes needed to ensure that the institution of marriage reflects the values of love, inclusion, interdependence, and support."[21] The themes framed and linked together here by Wolfson emerged as crucial in the battle for same-sex marriage. For Wolfson, they are part of a triumphalist narrative in which one injustice after another is vanquished.

One of the events that Wolfson highlighted in this uniquely American story occurred in 1987 in *Turner v. Safley*. In that case, a group that Wolfson does not immediately identify sued for the right to marry and was heard by the Supreme Court. The court, per Justice O'Connor, set forth what it saw as some of the vital aspects of marriage: "First, ... marriages ... are expressions of emotional support and public commitment. These elements are an important and significant aspect of the marital relationship. In addition, many religions recognize marriage as having spiritual significance. . . . Finally, marital status often is a precondition to the receipt of government benefits (e.g., Social Security benefits), property rights (e.g., tenancy by the entirety, inheritance rights), and other, less tangible benefits (e.g., legitimation of children born out of wedlock)."[22] The Court concluded that marriage was too important to be denied without a good reason. Finding none in this case, it awarded the group a unanimous victory, securing the constitutional right to marry for another previously unprotected sector of the population. Announcing the triumph, Wolfson ended the paragraph, hit the return key, and—in an isolated line on the page—dropped the stunner: "That group of Americans was prisoners."[23] That's right, those of you who have never taken a course in constitutional law and were primed for the full impact of Wolfson's delivery: Since 1987, *felons* have had the right to marry under the U.S. Constitution.

Turner v. Safley arose out of a Missouri prison regulation that required inmates to obtain special permission before marrying—permission that was generally denied except to legitimize a child. Prison administrators often enjoy a high degree of deference from judges to pursue penal objectives using their correctional expertise, but the right in this case was deemed so significant, and the rationales offered in defense of its abrogation so paltry, that the Court struck down the regulation. Prison inmates—convicts—therefore had the constitutional right to marry, but gay people, Wolfson put into the starkest possible relief, did not have that right, "no matter how committed and loving their relationship[s]."[24]

The argument from *Turner v. Safley* has special rhetorical force. Wolfson set the "that group . . . was prisoners" revelation apart from the preceding paragraph because he knew that bomb was loaded with deservedness shrapnel. Surely gay people *deserved* to have as many rights as *criminals*.

This would have been a tougher argument to make when gay people effectively *were* criminals, in the days that gave us the Stonewall Uprising in 1969, for example, when police routinely raided gay bars and arrested patrons for public displays of homosexuality or for failing to wear at least three items of gender-appropriate clothing; when the presence of known "perverts" posed a threat to an establishment's liquor license, effectively leaving the gay bar business to the mob; or when it was far more common than it is today for the police to entrap men in subway bathrooms, charge them with solicitation, and ruin their careers and reputations. It would have been more difficult to generate a contrast with *Turner v. Safley* until as recently as 2003, prior to which it was still constitutionally permissible for states to criminalize consensual sodomy, even in the home. Safely on the *post* side of *Lawrence v. Texas*, however, and with a conveniently short memory, at least some gays and lesbians can understand themselves to be decent, law-abiding folks.[25]

Remember Maureen and Cindy from chapter 2, the self-described "boring" New Jersey couple who coach soccer and make dessert? They are Wolfson's Exhibit A of gay moral uprightness:

> Maureen Kilian and Cindy Meneghin of Butler, New Jersey [have been] a committed couple ever since they met more than thirty years ago during their junior year in high school. Maureen works part-time as a parish administrator for Christ Church in nearby Pompton Lakes, where her job includes entering the names of married couples into the church registry. Cindy, meanwhile, is the director of Web services at Montclair State University. The women wish that one of them could stay home full-time to help care for their two children, Josh and Sarah. But because they aren't married, neither of them is eligible for family health insurance through her employer, so both of them have to leave the kids in order to stay insured.[26]

Additional examples of gay virtue follow. Chris Lodewyks and Craig Hutchinson met as college freshmen. Over the course of a thirty-year partnership, they cared for each other's parents through illness and old age. Craig even took a leave from work to care for Chris's mother. Moreover, they were good citizens, organizing town cleanup days and donating their time and money to local causes. According to Wolfson, however, they felt as though "the government treats [their] accomplishments together as worthless" because they were not permitted to marry.[27]

And *worth* is the issue. The longevity of the relationship of the high school sweethearts Maureen and Cindy; the thirty committed years of Chris and Craig; the women's shared responsibility for children and wish that one of them could be home to care for them full time rather than be forced to "leave" them; the care for elderly parents by the two men; and, let us not forget, Maureen's work as a church administrator, in which she must endure the perverse humiliation of entering other people's names into the marriage registry—all were offered in service of gay worthiness to enter the institution of marriage. If prison inmates were permitted to marry, how could it be that these loving, committed, responsible, God-fearing citizens were prohibited?

Same-sex love and commitment had to be portrayed as the moral equivalent of heterosexual love and commitment for the same-sex marriage campaign to succeed. That might seem too obvious a point. Deservedness is part of many civil rights campaigns, and it would be naïve to imagine it otherwise. Recall, however, that gay equality *could have* taken the form of a demand for relativistic accommodation to unique forms of LGBT normativity. Equality might be accorded its formal, or sameness, definition, or it might alternatively be accorded a substantive definition requiring accommodative treatment (see chapter 1). These two definitions take us in diametrically opposite directions on any number of legal questions.

In the *Perry* trial (see chapter 2), when a plaintiff's expert witness was confronted on cross-examination about gay men's propensity for non-monogamy, the question was designed to undermine the gay equality claim, but it could just as easily have been offered by LGBT advocates in another setting as a mark of distinction justifying an accommodation. The dream of equality could lead us to a wish for sameness *or* to a wish for accommodation of difference. The equality train has engines on both ends, and equality discourse contains contradictory possibilities for which engine will do the driving and which will end up as the caboose. Instead of same-sex marriage, framed as a formal equality objective—indeed, as the zenith of formal equality—we might have sought accommodations for variable familial arrangements not unheard of in LGBT subcultures. Nancy Polikoff illustrates the point vividly in *Beyond (Straight and Gay) Marriage*,[28] in which she calls for the law to recognize a much wider array of family forms (not all of them gay or lesbian or even organized around the intimate couple) and urges a change of direction for gay rights advocacy when it comes to formulating a vision of family.

The point is that other courses were possible, even under the rubric of equality, but marriage drove the train. As a result, LGBT equal rights advocates relied on a cluster of specific discursive practices that were the most effective *for purposes of obtaining the marriage goal.* One of those discursive practices is the habitual affirmation of *moral non-differentiation* between homo- and heterosexual love. That theme involves a narrative about our commitment to and responsibilities for one another and for any associated children or elders. I highlight this discursive practice not to quarrel with the *truth* of that moral equivalency; truth is not the issue. The critical question raised here regards the nature of the discourse and what it produces. Moral equivalency and especially the discursive elements of same-sex partners' "interdependence," "mutual support," and "responsibility" have had underappreciated implications for the role that gay advocacy plays in the larger political climate in which it takes place.

The responsibility theme features prominently in *Goodridge*, the first real victory for the same-sex marriage campaign. Chief Justice Marshall of Massachusetts identified the plaintiffs in that case by name and age, stated the longevity of each couple's relationship, and, where relevant, indicated the age of each couple's children. Two of the couples cared for elderly parents, and that information, too, found its way into her introduction.[29] It was pertinent because, as she explained, "Civil marriage enhances the 'welfare of the community.' " . . . [It] provides for the orderly distribution of property [and] ensures that children and adults are cared for and supported whenever possible from private rather than public funds."[30] Decisions favoring same-sex marriage typically stress the *benefits* of marriage to the spouses, but to her credit Marshall did not neglect to mention the many *obligations* spouses incur upon entering the marital union. "Marriage provides an abundance of legal, financial, and social benefits," she wrote, and "in return it imposes weighty legal, financial and social obligations."[31]

The obligations are myriad. During the life of a marriage, spouses are liable for the costs of each other's necessities under the so-called *necessaries doctrine*;[32] on divorce, there will be a division of property (even solely owned property in some jurisdictions) and possibly the extension of support obligations through the mechanism of alimony; Medicaid combines spousal assets to determine eligibility for some kinds of medical assistance so that a low- or middle-income couple may have to "spend down" to qualify for one spouse's care, leaving the other with radically reduced assets;[33] under some circumstances, certain benefits programs such as Supplemental Security Income (SSI, a need-based disability benefit) and SNAP (food stamps) combine a couple's income and assets, which may reduce or eliminate the benefits for which they would have been eligible separately;[34] and on death, state law typically imposes a "forced share" on an estate, preserving some fraction for a surviving spouse regardless of the will of the decedent.[35] These are some of the "responsibilities" of marriage—or, another way to conceptualize them is as legal rules that *contain support obligations within the marital dyad*. That is, these rules ensure that the burden of support is laid on the spouse, or even the ex-spouse or deceased spouse, sparing the public fisc.

The benefits of marriage are, of course, also quite extensive. Some critics of the same-sex marriage campaign from the left have argued that only middle class and wealthy people like Edith Windsor (see chapter 2) benefit from marriage. It is true that only a large estate raises concerns about the estate tax, but the argument that marriage benefits only the rich is nonetheless folly. Same-sex marriage offers benefits to every economic stratum of the LGBT community. When Attorney-General Eric Holder directed his Justice Department, in the aftermath of *Windsor*, to begin treating same-sex married couples the same as heterosexual married couples, federal prison inmates began receiving identical visitation and furlough privileges; benefits programs such as the Radiation Exposure Compensation Fund started treating same-sex spouses the same as different-sex spouses; and the Justice Department adopted the position that same-sex spouses should receive all the protections that different-sex spouses receive in bankruptcy proceedings. Benefits of marriage accrue across class and station.

The responsibilities and benefits sampled here emerge from the details of the *numerous* regulatory regimes that together compose an almost inconceivably elaborate legal web that governs the marital relation (and, by exclusion, nonmarital relations, as well). Careful analysis of any one regulatory regime might turn up an income-based disadvantage, but another regime could easily turn up a comparable advantage. There are simply too many variables to justify such a sweeping conclusion. The leftist critical instinct that same-sex marriage is, on the whole, damaging to the interests of low-income people is a good one, but not because of its multitudinous regulatory features.

It is the *discourse* in which the same-sex marriage agenda is *pursued* that imposes unseen costs on the poor. In particular, the discursive element of moral equivalency and mutual responsibility hurts the poor because, as critics of same-sex marriage from the left have argued, it operates in tandem with the neoliberal trend favoring privatized family obligation.

In *Twilight of Equality*, a concise and handy discussion of neoliberalism, Lisa Duggan enumerates some of neoliberalism's manifestations: "a leaner, meaner government (fewer social services, more 'law and order'), a state-supported but 'privatized' economy, an invigorated and socially responsible civil society, and a moralized family with gendered marriage at its center."[36] In the United States, these political projects are bipartisan, as demonstrated by neoliberal advances under both President Ronald Reagan and President Bill Clinton. Wendy Brown adds that the term *neoliberalism*

> is most commonly understood as enacting an ensemble of economic policies in accord with its root principle of affirming free markets. These include deregulation of industries and capital flows; radical reduction in welfare state provisions and protections for the vulnerable; privatized and outsourced public goods, ranging from education, parks, postal services, roads, and social welfare to prisons and militaries; replacement of progressive with regressive tax and tariff schemes; the end of wealth redistribution as an economic or social-political policy; conversion of every human need or desire into a profitable enterprise ... and ... the increasing dominance of finance capital over productive capital.[37]

Apart from its programmatic aspects, Brown also views neoliberalism "as a governing rationality extending a specific formulation of economic values, practices and metrics to every dimension of human life.... Disseminat[ing] the *model of the market* to all domains and activities ... and configur[ing] human beings exhaustively as market actors."[38]

Whether conceived as a constellation of programs or a governing logic, same-sex marriage and the arguments deployed to advance it sync neatly with neoliberalism. In particular, the argument that gay people deserve marriage because we perform mutual responsibility so well and are eager to acquire the obligations of legal union subtly erases the role of the public sector in providing support and points in the direction of exclusive economic reliance on the condition of coupledom. The more that dependence can be corralled into the private family setting, in which spouses, ex-spouses, and deceased spouses are bound to provide for their spouse's welfare, the more diminished is the rationale for the welfare state. Advocacy for gay equal rights thereby contributes to a political climate that favors defunding social programs on which our most vulnerable community members depend.

Among the earliest observers to notice an overlap between the objective of neoliberal privatization and legal recognition of same-sex couples was the Canadian law professor Brenda Cossman.[39] She watched with interest a rift develop between two distinct conservative constituencies over a Canadian case in 1999, *M. v. H.*, that preceded the advent of same-sex marriage in Canada by six years.[40] M. sought spousal support from her former same-sex partner of twelve years under a statute that defined *spouse* to include someone to whom the petitioner had been legally married *or* a person of the *opposite sex* with whom the petitioner had cohabited for a minimum of three years. To obtain support from her former partner, M. launched a constitutional challenge to the *opposite sex* requirement and won. The Canadian Supreme Court found that the requirement discriminated on the basis of sexual orientation in violation of Section 15 of the Canadian Charter of Rights and Freedoms, which guarantees equal protection and prohibits discrimination.[41] As the case wound its way up to the Canadian Supreme Court, conservative political constituencies that Cossman labels "neo-conservative" and "neo-liberal" diverged. "Neo-conservatives" were committed to "traditional family values" and stood adamant against any accommodation of the law to same-sex couples on moral grounds. A fiscally conservative approach, however, consistent with neoliberal privatization tendencies, was what prevailed. In its decision, the Canadian Court specifically noted that attributing support obligations to same-sex former partners would reduce the "burden on the public purse" that might be imposed by needy people who have former "spouses" able to support them.[42]

If *M. v. H.* had involved a challenge to a discriminatory public benefits program—something like a Social Security survivor's benefit, say—rather than a challenge to a private support obligation like alimony, the neoliberal inclination might well have run in the contrary direction, as Cossman notes,[43] because recognition of the couple as spouses would have increased rather than reduced the burden on the public purse. Does marriage on identical terms for same- and different-sex couples, when one accounts for both sides of the equation (the savings to the state by privatizing dependence on able spouses, as well as the cost to the state of extending public benefits to a new batch of dependents), save or cost the state more in the end? Presumably, an economic answer would settle the quandary for a person to whom *only* the fiscal issue mattered—someone who truly had no commitments on the morality/equality question. But alas, as regulatory regimes change, unemployment and divorce rates rise and fall, and alimony awards vary with ideology and historical circumstance, it is difficult to imagine arriving at a once-and-for-all answer.

Hard-nosed cultural conservatives, of course, deeply antagonistic toward homosexuality on "family values" grounds, cannot be expected to sell out their mores for a fiscal benefit or cede an inch on the moral issue. They do not need any budgetary information to know where they stand because morality tropes provide them with all of the data they require. But morality tropes are not what they used to be. Once the hammer with which the cultural right confidently bludgeoned its adversaries, family values have been increasingly commandeered in service of a pro-gay agenda. The same-sex marriage campaign has by now done nearly as much as the cultural right to promote the virtues of traditional family, arguing for but a single modification—and its essential moral irrelevance.

In Maine, after the sting of a voter-approved referendum in 2009 to preserve the "one man, one woman" definition of marriage, advocates for same-sex marriage came back with a revised playbook. In the campaign of 2012 to bring same-sex marriage to the state, voters would come to appreciate that same-sex unions were familial, based on love and commitment, and morally indistinguishable from heterosexual unions. Regular, straight Mainers would make the point so that other regular, straight Mainers would get it. In one thirty-second television spot, Dan and Pat Lawson, a heterosexual couple in late middle age, explained that they had twin sons—one gay and one straight. "Marriage is a commitment that comes from your heart," Dan said. "If that person wasn't there, you're not going to be complete. If my son finds someone that he's in love with and wants to create a bond that's going to last a lifetime, that's marriage in my mind."[44] Another ad features four generations of the Gardner family, gathered around the kitchen table. The patriarch, white-bearded and wearing suspenders, holds hands with his wife of fifty-nine years, Dottie. He recalls his service as a military pilot during World War II but attributes courage to his granddaughter and her partner for being lesbians. "Marriage is too precious a thing not to share," he says, and after his wife expresses her hope to see Katie and Alex marry legally during her lifetime, he concludes, "This isn't about politics; it's about family and how we as people treat one another."[45] Mainers adopted same-sex marriage by referendum in November 2012.[46]

The winning campaign for same-sex marriage in the state of Washington deployed a similar strategy that year. A Lutheran pastor, John, and his wife of seventy years, Dorothy, star in one compelling ad.[47] Two of John and Dorothy's nine grandchildren are gay. John served on a cargo ship in the Atlantic during World War II. He managed to marry Dorothy during a brief shore leave. She recalled the telegram ("married Thursday?") she received barely in time to get everyone to the church for the wedding. As a pastor, John teaches that Jesus is about love and wants all nine of his grandchildren to have what he and Dorothy have. The couple is warm, loving, and obviously happy, and when their gay grandson indicates his wish for a life that emulates that of his grandparents, it is easy to want that for him, too.

The discourse of family values has demonstrated more elasticity than I suspect its traditional proprietors anticipated. A gay-inclusive instantiation of family values, once perceived to be an oxymoron, is becoming increasingly intelligible to a broad swath of the population. Strategically, this has been monumentally effective. It provides some folks a way out of the morality/equality quandary in which the prior discursive arrangement seemed to put them: They can be for both! And for those few fiscal conservatives who remain agnostic on the morality/equality issue, while they might have no final answer to the question of cost to the public purse, the new gay family values entwine readily with, and advance, privatization discourse. As a result, those fiscal conservatives (or neoliberals) do not require an answer to that impossible question. Same-sex marriage may be a numerical benefit or a detriment to the public purse at any given moment, but in its *pursuit* it is decidedly a discursive boon for adherents of privatized responsibility. As Duggan has argued, upward distribution of wealth, in part through fiscal austerity, is bolstered by a values discourse.[48] If a fiscally conservative, neoliberal argument in favor of privatized family support obligations and a moral argument in favor of responsible, monogamous same-sex coupling can be marshaled on the same side of the issue, we may have a winner. Gay family values and the pitch for moral non-differentiation between homo- and heterosexual love, commitment, and, importantly, *interdependence, mutual support, and responsibility* have emerged from—and, in turn, bolster— the synchronicity of gay equal rights and neoliberalism.

Consider, for example, the role of advocates for same-sex marriage in our nation's conversation about health insurance before the election of President Obama and the passage of the Affordable Care Act. In August 2007, Democratic candidates for president appeared on *Logo*, an LGBT-themed cable network, for an unprecedented televised forum on gay issues.[49] Each of the three frontrunners for the nomination—Senator Barack Obama (D-IL), Senator Hillary Clinton (D-NY), and former Senator John Edwards (D-NC)—*in seriatim*, indicated support for legal benefits for same-sex couples under the label "civil union," and each met with the panel's dissatisfaction with that woefully inadequate position. The lesbian pop star Melissa Etheridge, a longtime supporter of the Human Rights Campaign (HRC), which sponsored the forum, was one of the panelists. In her questioning of Edwards, Etheridge observed that both she and Edwards's wife, Elizabeth, had suffered from cancer. Recalling the exorbitant cost of her treatment, Etheridge asked Edwards, "Do you understand the special needs of people in gay and lesbian couples who cannot depend on their partner's insurance for protection because they are not a legal spouse or have to pay extra on the benefit? What would you do about this?" Edwards launched into a rap about his health care plan. It was a universal plan, closer to single-payer than what either Obama or Clinton was offering, but Etheridge and her co-panelists seemed neither impressed by nor interested in it. Did it not occur to them that some sick people do not have partners? That some sick people have partners who work without health insurance? Did they think that same-sex marriage would solve the nation's health care crisis?

Advocates for gay equal rights have laid claim to resources that same-sex couples have been denied due to formal inequalities, such as shared private health insurance plans. That is what sounds in LGBT equal rights discourse. But in so doing, they have buttressed rather than questioned the apparent naturalness of the market governing those resources, subtly helping to shape the public conversation in the direction of neoliberal assumptions. Does the battle seem "won" because same-sex couples have accrued the right to privately contain their medical dependence? Does it look like "victory" when low-income people, LGBT and otherwise, fall through the crack between private health insurance and declined Medicaid expansion? Did our advocates at the *Logo* forum ask the right questions?

While trans rights advocates are undoubtedly focused on an array of issues that extends far beyond marriage, they are not immune to the romance of mutual responsibility and private support. The Transgender Legal Defense and Education Fund (TLDEF) announced in April 2014 its success in the case of Michael and Nancy, a married couple in which the husband, a transman, had died of cancer after working for four decades for an unidentified major car manufacturer in the Midwest. The terms of Michael's pension should have permitted his widow to receive an income and health insurance for the remainder of her life, but the employer initially refused to comply, claiming that the marriage was a same-sex marriage and therefore invalid in its state at that time. In the immediate aftermath of her husband's death, Nancy was left to rely on food stamps and Medicaid. However, TLDEF intervened to persuade the company's general counsel that, "while Michael had spent his personal life in love with Nancy, he had spent his professional life in service to the company." The appeal for "equal treatment" succeeded. The benefits under the pension were restored.[50] Michael's many years of labor paid off in the support of his widow, and her dependence was returned from her own and the state's shoulders to the marital dyad.

The new traditional family advanced by equal rights advocates not only contains its own dependence but participates in the market as valued consumers, earning powerful allies. When former Governor Jan Brewer of Arizona vetoed SB 1062, the bill that would have permitted business owners to refuse service to gay people based on religious objections,[51] she did so under pressure from Marriott Hotels, Intel, PetSmart, Apple, and Delta Airlines, as well as the National Football League (NFL, which is technically—and laughably—a nonprofit), which planned to hold the Super Bowl in Phoenix the following season but suggested it might change its plans if the discriminatory bill became law.[52] Chad Griffin of HRC wrote an op-ed celebrating the role that private companies played in Brewer's decision, hailing Corporate America as a "beacon of progress,"[53] and the National LGBT Bar Association sent an email to its constituents entitled "Thanking Corporate America: You Can Help."[54] Corporate pressure was likely behind the defeat of similar bills in other states.

The synergy between fiscal conservatism and the new gay family values is evident in American national politics, where it should come as no surprise that support for same-sex marriage has gained tremendous traction on the right. To be sure, a vociferous cultural conservative coterie remains steadfastly in opposition, but high-profile conservatives and Republicans with real conservative bona fides have popped out all over the place to lend their support to the cause. More than a hundred of them, including former top officials in the George W.

Bush administration, Republican former governors and members of Congress, a former chair of the Republican National Committee, and well-known political operatives and commentators signed onto an *amicus* brief in *Perry* on the side of the same-sex couples.[55] More than three hundred leading conservatives signed a similar brief in *Obergefell*.[56] *Amici* identified themselves as supporters of "traditional conservative values, including the commitment to limited government, the protection of individual freedom, and the belief in the importance of stable families."[57] To summarize and introduce their argument, they exhorted that, when government acts on families, "it should promote family-supportive values like responsibility, fidelity, commitment, and stability."[58] Among the headings in the conservative brief was "Marriage Promotes the Conservative Values of Stability, Mutual Support, and Mutual Obligation."[59] The brief urged, "If the government believes that marriage has positive benefits for society, some or all of those benefits may attach to same-sex marriages as well," citing a supportive law review article for the argument that "stable relationships may produce more personal income and less demands on welfare and unemployment programs."[60] The briefs repeatedly remind the justices that marriage diminishes the need for dependence on the state (in old age, in crisis, and so on) and that it reduces the size and role of government.

A few conservatives, including some signatories to the briefs, have ostentatiously proclaimed the reversal of their previous opposition to same-sex marriage. In an effort to make the case that permitting same-sex couples to marry would diminish the stature and dignity of the institution, David Frum, a conservative intellectual and former adviser and speechwriter to President George W. Bush, once famously predicted that "gay marriage will look to the rest of society as . . . a campy parody of the central institution in their lives."[61] Less than a decade later, apparently suffering a bout of human decency (at least toward gay people), he announced his change of heart in multiple media outlets. Frum officially withdrew his concern that same-sex marriage would drag down marriage's prestige and redirected his fretfulness toward the demise of marital commitment among Hispanics.[62]

David Blankenhorn self-identifies as a liberal but has been promoting cultural conservatism for years through his books and the Institute for American Values, which he founded in 1988 and continues to lead. Blankenhorn performed a spectacular reversal on same-sex marriage in June 2012 with an announcement on the *New York Times* editorial page.[63] The op-ed enumerated the reasons for Blankenhorn's change of heart, including his belief in "basic fairness," a preference for "acceptance" and "conciliation" over engagement in the culture war, and "respect for an emerging consensus."[64] (He did not list his humiliating cross-examination by David Boies during the *Perry* trial, revealing most of his contentions regarding the well-being of children to be groundless; nor did he mention experiencing any mortification at the trial judge's conclusion that he offered nothing of value to deliberations.)

Blankenhorn was never vituperatively homophobic in his opposition to same-sex marriage. Before his conversion he always maintained that if he thought same-sex marriage would strengthen the institution, he would be for it, and he gave same-sex marriage advocates such as Evan Wolfson and Jonathan Rauch a fair hearing on the matter, but he found their arguments to be insufficiently concerned with the issue he viewed as central: the well-being of children. Blankenhorn had elaborated on the primacy of both biological relationship and the distinctly gendered roles of mothers and fathers in *Fatherless America* (1995).[65] This book rehearses dozens of benefits that allegedly accrue to the traditional, marital, biological family and attributes numerous social ills to the deterioration of same. Unsatisfied that same-sex couples could fulfill what he understood to be the fundamental purpose of marriage, he opposed same-sex marriage for years.

Blankenhorn's long-standing normative family vision also has an economics. In *The Future of Marriage* (2007), Blankenhorn argued that a decline in the marriage rate (as opposed to the erosion of the social safety net, globalization of labor, a decreasing minimum wage in real dollars, or a crisis in public education) is the principal cause of increasing poverty among children in the United States.[66] More marriage, he deduces, would therefore reduce child poverty. "This effect is not simply because there may be two earners, but also because there is something specifically about *marriage* that tends to boost earnings and reduce poverty."[67] His conclusion is apparently based on correlation rather than causation. There is "something about" the absence of evidence that leaves that impression.

Much of Blankenhorn's position remained intact in 2012 when he proclaimed his reversal on same-sex marriage in the *New York Times*. He did not announce a simple switching of teams; he has, after all, "no stomach for" culture war. He proposed, he claimed, "something new." His new project would be to "bring . . . together gays who want to strengthen marriage with straight people who want to do the same."[68] This new coalition would then contemplate questions Blankenhorn wants discussed, including whether we can all agree that marriage should precede parenthood; whether marriage is not in fact superior to cohabitation; and whether children produced through whatever means ought to know their biological parents. This shift made tactical sense. As Richard Kim of *The Nation* observed, Blankenhorn apparently made the calculation that "gays are more valuable now as recruits than as scapegoats" for the same old political program,[69] one that—however "liberal" he declares himself to be—provides an elaborate values-based rationale for the continuing diminution of the welfare state.

While the moral accommodation by many conservatives of families headed by same-sex partners is of relatively recent vintage, the underlying philosophy that fuses "family values" to fiscal conservatism has a lineage. A key antecedent can be found in *The Negro Family: The Case for National Action* (1965), also known as the Moynihan Report,[70] written by Daniel Patrick Moynihan, who served as an assistant secretary in President Lyndon B. Johnson's Labor Department. The report attributed the "pathology" of African American culture to the displacement of men's authority in favor of a "matriarchal" structure. As Cathy J. Cohen has argued, Moynihan's study made a key contribution to the history of "stigmatization and demonization of single mothers, teen mothers, and, primarily, poor women of color dependent on state assistance."[71] Both welfare dependence and the "perceived nonnormative sexual behavior and family structures of these individuals" were prominent themes.[72] The same themes could be discerned during the Reagan era, a highlight of which was the publication and wide dissemination of the conservative political scientist Charles Murray's influential book *Losing Ground* (1984).[73] Murray endorsed the reinvigoration of the stigma attached to nonmarital reproduction as a means to reduce welfare dependence. The research behind Murray's proposals was supported by a network of conservative organizations bent on promoting the link between undesirable family values and burdens on the public fisc.[74] Numerous welfare policies were implemented or expanded based on that ideological link over the next fifteen years—most importantly, in the federal welfare reform package signed by President Clinton in 1996[75]—including incentives for marriage, requirements for cooperation in child support, and family caps. Advocates for these "reforms" stressed "personal responsibility"—in both its moral and its economic dimensions—and decried dependence (read, dependence on the state as opposed to dependence on one's family). Moreover, these advocates often relied on racist and sexist stereotypes that were largely unsubstantiated by the data of sociologists or political scientists (other than Murray), and they neglected to contend with the lack of educational and job opportunities for both men and women hailing from poor communities.

The coalescence of family values and fiscal conservatism, with an eye toward advancing privatization of responsibility and the withering of the welfare state, has gone on for decades. The new gay family values have done more to buttress than to undermine the connection.

Feeling Insecure

In the United States, the deterioration of the welfare state has correlated with a steep escalation in rates of incarceration. Beginning in the early 1970s, according to the Pew Center on the States, the state prison population began a sharp incline, no longer tracking population growth but, instead, increasing by a multiple of seven over fewer than forty years. Ronald Reagan's vilification of the poor, as well as his "War on Drugs," coincided with skyrocketing rates of incarceration, especially of people of color. As Michelle Alexander points out in *The New Jim Crow*, "There are more people in prisons and jails today just for drug offenses than were incarcerated for *all* reasons in 1980. Nothing has contributed more to the systematic mass incarceration of people of color in the United States than the War on Drugs."[76]

The upward trajectory in incarceration rates held through the 1990s, when crime rates began to fall. When President Clinton signed a major welfare reform package in 1996, eliminating Aid for Families with Dependent Children (AFDC) and replacing it with the block grant system known as Temporary Assistance to Needy Families (TANF), the idea was to reduce dependence on the government through work requirements, increased collection of child support from fathers to reimburse the state for welfare expenditures on mothers and children, and stripped-back benefits through the imposition of time limits and family caps. Alexander explains that at the same time the new, theoretically austere welfare law was enacted, "The penal budget doubled the amount that had been allocated to AFDC or food stamps [and] funding that had once been used for public housing was being redirected to prison construction."[77]

Again according to Pew, the United States was incarcerating one in every one hundred adults in 2008, the highest rate in the world.[78] Accounting for the full criminal justice apparatus, by the end of 2007, more than seven million Americans—or one in every thirty-one adults—were behind bars, on probation, or on parole."[79] In the past few years, some states' inmate populations have declined, possibly as a result of budget constraints, although other states and the federal prison system continue on an upward trend, making for an overall national increase.

The timing of diminished social supports and increased incarceration could be coincidental, but Bernard Harcourt does not think so. Politicians of the past half-century have campaigned on an odd combination of decreasing the size of government while getting "tough on crime."[80] How can we reconcile these seemingly contradictory policies? "The logic of neoliberal penality has made possible our contemporary punishment practices by fueling the belief that the legitimate and competent space for government intervention is the penal sphere."[81] If government should not meddle in the market, what is its proper place? The answer is: outside the market, in what economists sometimes call "market-bypassing" behavior—that is, crime.[82] Harcourt argues not that free market ideology *causes* law-and-order policies or *necessarily* travels with them but, rather, that the ideology of the free market permits the rationalization of harsh penality by allocating a specific role to government—that is, curbing behavior that occurs outside of the market's legitimate precincts.

Some reformers have thrown in their lots with the neoliberal penal trend. In her critique of *carceral feminism*, sociologist Elizabeth Bernstein provides one compelling example. Bernstein argues that a powerful element within feminist advocacy has participated in and furthered a punitive law-and-order agenda that secures the private family using criminal law and incarceration, especially of poor people of color, to address sexual and gendered violence.[83] Relying on sex trafficking to illustrate her point, Bernstein shows that a policy emphasis on law enforcement has unified evangelical Christian conservatives with a subset of feminists, sometimes referred to as *structuralist feminists*, who are closely associated with the thinking of Catharine MacKinnon and Andrea Dworkin. The alliance echoes that which sought to ban pornography in the 1970s and '80s (famously dividing feminists during the "Sex Wars"). The two political constituencies (evangelicals and their structuralist feminist allies) have collaborated to represent women and children as perpetually vulnerable to threats of violence emanating from men who occupy positions outside the safety of the family. This configures the family as a "safe haven" under police protection. The structuralist feminist and evangelical conceptions overlap in the domestication of sexuality and the quest for middle-class security. In the hands of these allied groups, criminal law and family values converge to advance policies that address social problems through incarceration and securitization of the private family domain.

And what about gay rights advocates? In 2009, President Obama signed what Joe Solmonese, then the president of HRC, called "our nation's first major piece of civil rights legislation for lesbian, gay, bisexual and transgender people."[84] The Matthew Shepard and James Byrd, Jr., Hate Crimes Prevention Act provides support to states and localities to enable more effective prosecution of hate crimes and adds protected categories, including sexual orientation and gender identity, to an existing federal criminal provision.[85] Under this law, if a defendant willfully causes a victim bodily injury because of the victim's actual or perceived sexual orientation or gender identity (and if a technical jurisdictional requirement is met so that the crime can be deemed federal), that defendant can be convicted under the statute. Once convicted, a defendant could pay a fine and serve up to ten years in prison; if death resulted from the crime, or if kidnapping or aggravated sexual abuse was involved, a convicted person could be sentenced to life.[86] Willfully causing bodily injury to another person is already a crime in every American jurisdiction. Hate crimes legislation effectively enhances penalties for acts that were already criminal if the prosecutor can prove that bias against a protected identity category motivated the crime. Conviction under a hate crimes statute piles on an additional count and potentially prolongs the term of incarceration.

Most of the major LGBT organizations favored the federal act, and most favor adding sexual orientation and gender identity to hate crimes statutes generally. Even the American Civil Liberties Union (ACLU) got on board for the Shepard-Byrd legislation after years of principled opposition to hate crimes laws, saying it was reassured that the bill was drafted carefully enough to avoid infringing on freedom of speech or belief.[87] Grassroots organizations that sit further to the left, however, and that have directed their advocacy efforts more specifically to low-income LGBT people of color, such as the Sylvia Rivera Law Project and the (now defunct) Queers for Economic Justice, have not been big fans of hate crimes laws.[88] Among their objections is one based on distrust of granting increased authority to law enforcement, specifically the worry that people of color (LGBT and otherwise) may find themselves disproportionately charged under the statutes as the range of protected categories grows.[89] (The moral contrast pressed by Evan Wolfson between gay people and prison inmates is not perceived so starkly in all quarters.)

Hate crimes statutes have not been proven effective as a deterrent. Some critics of hate crimes legislation have suggested that, in the absence of sound evidence of deterrent effect, their obvious purpose is punishment, which may seem tantamount to revenge—although there is a substantial literature on the distinction.[90] Criminologists also contemplate public safety ("incapacitation") and rehabilitation as possible reasons to imprison violent convicts, but you do not often hear proponents of hate crimes legislation argue that the justification for the laws is that sentences for previously existing violent criminal offenses were insufficiently lengthy to protect the public or rehabilitate the offender. For advocates of LGBT equal rights, hate crimes protections are important *symbolically*.

Adding the categories of sexual orientation and gender identity to the hate crimes laws conveys the message that it is unacceptable to commit violence against people because they are (or appear to be) gay or transgender. That admonition carries out a crucial culture war task. Hate crimes statutes are key sites at which legitimate minority groups are designated. Inclusion of sexual orientation and gender identity in those statutes implies that LGBT people are among those legitimate minorities, validated by legally protected status. Hate crimes laws therefore serve a recognition function for gay and trans-identified people, a rationale that is not typically included in the litany of justifications that criminologists contemplate for locking people up.[91] Because hate crimes legislation is a site at which minority status is legitimated, the site is contested. Cultural conservatives, even those who would neither resort to nor countenance physical violence, oppose inclusion of sexual orientation and gender identity in the laws, probably because any legal imprimatur of minority status for LGBT people undermines the cultural conservative position. Cultural conservatives argue that the laws infringe their right to express their opinions on moral issues. It is an absurd argument, of course, unless they intend to express their opinion on moral issues while beating someone up, but the pretense is more palatable than the reality: They do not want to see the classifications included because inclusion certifies LGBT minority group status, authoritatively rendering antagonism toward the group "prejudice" or "animus." The argument over the inclusion of gay and trans in the hate crimes statutes forms a perfect homology to the animus/morality feud between Justice Kennedy and Justice Scalia in *Romer v. Evans* (see chapter 1).[92]

Cultural conservatives make the identical argument in opposition to recently proliferating legislation against bullying—and proponents of anti-bullying legislation are equally hungry for the recognition that such laws can provide. Massachusetts, for example, has had an anti-bullying statute in place since 2010.[93] It requires every school to develop a plan to prevent and address bullying, including disciplinary provisions that balance "accountability" and "teach[ing] appropriate behavior."[94] The statute contemplates the possibility of law enforcement officials becoming involved and criminal charges being pursued, requiring parental notification in such instances.[95] Provisions regarding the involvement of the criminal justice system have put the ACLU in particular in a difficult position as it attempts to locate the sweet spot in which it can be for legislation to address bullying but against punitive consequences that would betray its efforts to interrupt the "school-to-prison pipeline." It has tried to situate itself in favor of a preventive approach that includes tolerance training for students and staff, along with remedies such as counseling and pedagogy.

Under the Massachusetts law, all school personnel, from teachers and coaches to custodians and cafeteria workers, are required to report bullying and therefore must receive training in how to identify it. That training must cover the "specific categories of students who have been shown to be particularly at risk for bullying."[96] It is easy to find out which kids are "particularly at risk." Among other sources, the U.S. Department of Education Office for Civil Rights has a website, Stopbullying.gov, that authoritatively affirms LGBT vulnerability.[97] Still, the law was amended a few years later in part to shore up its recognition function by adding a requirement that school plans explicitly enumerate categories of students who are especially susceptible to bullying. The law now specifies sexual orientation and gender identity on a long list of classifications, not to detail an exclusive list of protected categories but merely to recognize the group and stress the fact of its vulnerability.[98]

The anti-bullying campaign shares two interrelated features with its adult analogue. First, both hate crimes and bullying laws satisfy a paradoxical desire for recognition—paradoxical because that desire coexists with the desire for formal equality and the sameness that formal equality entails. The wish for recognition from the law in the form of explicit legal protection travels uncomfortably with formal equality; recognition is a much more coherent feature of a demand for special treatment. Every time a group bounded by an identity trait, however, seeks explicit mention in protective legislation (whether it is hate crimes legislation or antidiscrimination legislation) or when it seeks elevated scrutiny for its equal protection claims, it effectively asks for official recognition of its difference, both as an a priori matter and in the sense of the group's status as subordinated.

The second shared feature of anti-bullying and hate crimes legislation is their punitive character. Both types of law put the machinery of the state on the side of LGBT identity, cautioning potential foes. Offenders under these regimes can serve time or otherwise suffer public retribution for their infractions. The laws place LGBT people on the protected side of a spreading security apparatus. Legal recognition by way of hate crimes and anti-bullying laws makes meaning for LGBT identity. It produces the knowledge that we *are to be protected* rather than that we *constitute a threat*. For many, this is a welcome advance from old stereotypes of gay pedophiles and turncoats, but not all sectors of the LGBT community experience the effects of the new security divide identically.

Location, Location, Location

In a sense, hate crimes and anti-bullying laws mean that gays can now count themselves among the private individuals, couples, and families who are protected by corrective justice against threats that loom out there on the mean streets. These laws, however, make up only a small subset of legal tools that constitute the security divide. Some gay people have benefited in recent years from a set of legal protections that do not announce themselves as operating on the basis of sexual orientation or gender identity. The laws discussed in this section are *facially neutral*, meaning that they do not identify the class of person to be protected or targeted. In reality, however, while protecting a privileged subset of gay people, they are deployed foremost against low-income, homeless, and marginally housed people, including disproportionate populations of LGBTQ people and people of color who rely on public space.[99] The effect is to set up a security divide that operates principally in gentrifying urban areas between upper- and lower-income LGBTQ people.

Gentrification patterns repeatedly set up conflicts of interest organized around race and class distinctions, resulting in clashes over local uses of law. Gay men have long been associated with gentrification in urban areas as earners without children seek tolerant enclaves that support vibrant arts, restaurant, and retail scenes. The phenomenon is so well known (and well documented)[100] that developers and planners have caught on. One of the proposals to rescue the bankrupt city of Detroit is to cultivate a "gayborhood" along the lines of San Francisco's Castro or Boston's South End. The founder of Kick, a black LGBT center in Detroit, met with bankers and community developers to gain support for a district that would include retail, housing, and gay bars.[101]

According to the gay community's leading demographer, Gary Gates, gay gentrification trends are not a consequence of gay men earning higher incomes than straight men; gay men are, however, less likely to have children, while lesbians, who are more likely than gay men to have children, tend to do so a bit later than their straight, female counterparts. Consequently, when gay men and lesbians buy real estate, they may be less concerned with the neighborhood schools and more inclined to invest their income in raising the value of their property.[102]

Gentrification has well-rehearsed revitalization benefits but also displacement costs, and in several cities it has positioned propertied and high-rent gays in direct conflict with LGBTQ people who live more of their lives in public space. In the West Village of New York, during Rudolph Giuliani's mayoral administration, affluent residents of condominiums located in Hudson River Park and near the Christopher Street Pier battled with LGBTQ youth—many of color, not infrequently homeless, and in many cases involved in the sex trade—who historically have congregated on the pier. The West Village has a long history of hipster and gay culture and is home to such landmarks as the Village Vanguard and the Stonewall Inn. The mid-1990s saw an increase in policing of the youth in the area, including arrests for petty offenses such as blocking a sidewalk—part of Giuliani's "quality of life" initiative that cracked down on "public drinking, noise, and loitering."[103] Youth seeking community and refuge in the area joined together in 2000 to form the grassroots organization FIERCE (Fabulous Independent Educated Radicals for Community Empowerment) and engaged in community organizing, training, and activism.[104] The group coalesced specifically in response to the closing of the pier for development, depriving youth of a crucial gathering place. Even after the pier reopened in 2003, a host of property value-enhancing measures threatened their access to their terrain. The measures were pushed by a vocal group of West Village residents calling itself RID (Residents in Distress). At neighborhood meetings, FIERCE and RID clashed; RID called for a curfew, enhanced police presence, and aggressive permit enforcement for service vehicles. Against this opposition, FIERCE was remarkably effective. Among its victories are the defeat of a curfew on the pier, the defeat of a measure that would have closed public restrooms on the pier overnight, and the rescinding of a $25,000 parking fee that was imposed on the service vehicles that were serving young people's medical needs.[105]

Similar clashes have taken place in Chicago's Boystown, a Lakeview neighborhood so named when gay men began moving into the area in the 1970s and '80s. The black population there shrank as real estate prices rose and gay bars and bookstores flourished. LGBTQ youth—many of color, often homeless—still seek refuge in Boystown, but this younger generation increasingly has been picked up for loitering, apparently to quell the anxiety of more established residents in the wake of a series of violent incidents, one of which was recorded and widely viewed on the Internet.[106] Responding to what were undoubtedly legitimate fears, a group of residents ominously calling itself Take Back Boystown, formed and launched a Facebook page with a brilliant, swaying rainbow flag.[107] (The group was apparently unselfconscious about antecedent white gay gentrification when it decided on its name.) Members have called for curfews, bicycle patrols, and increased police presence, while youth have complained of being harassed and profiled.[108]

Gates has argued that the presence of gays and lesbians in a community signals a general atmosphere of tolerance for diversity and that gays and lesbians themselves improve a community's level of tolerance.[109] According to Gates, it is no coincidence that San Francisco is among the leading cities in the United States for both gay presence and innovation (measured in patents per capita). Tolerance for diversity may explain the correlation. Innovators want to live in open-minded places.[110]

Tolerance, however, is not always the experience of the most marginalized and low-income members of even very gay-friendly communities. In the words of one black, transgender young person surviving on the streets of Boystown, "I don't identify with the upscale faggotry of the neighborhood. I don't identify with the yuppie ignorance here. I hate this neighborhood. . . . I have no tolerance for misogyny, racism, or classism, and that's all there is in this neighborhood."[111]

In San Francisco, a controversy erupted over the obviously nominal fee charged to Silicon Valley tech companies for the use of public bus stops to shuttle their employees to work ($1 per stop per day). The fee was charged only after a period of total nonenforcement of the rules regarding private use of the stops. The shuttles made it convenient for tech company employees to live in San Francisco while displacing low-income, disproportionately LGBTQ and of color, residents of the Polk Gulch, or Outer Tenderloin, and other gentrifying neighborhoods. This gave rise to protests, including an instance of local activists' surrounding a Google shuttle.[112]

While Gates may be right about the presence of gay people signaling an attitude of tolerance, it may also be the case that this attitude has its limits, sometimes observable as intra-LGBT conflict along axes of race and class. Zoning and fees imposed on service organizations, curfews, escalated police presence, and enforcement of laws against petty offenses such as loitering often emerge as contested legal territory in gentrification conflicts. Such disputes implicate the LGBT community not because they are equality- or identity-oriented but because (on one side) they involve mostly white, middle- and upper-income urban dwellers, often including gay people who have participated in (or even led) the process of gentrification, for both its good and its ill. Meanwhile, on the other side are LGBTQ people and others fighting not for equal rights but to avoid displacement and for access to public space, services, freedom from excess police attention, and so on.

Moreover, as Christina Hanhardt noted (with regard to the conflict in Greenwich Village), "Many observers saw the actions of the local community board as representing the viewpoint of a gay neighborhood. Thus, regardless of the actual identities of the key actors, the dominant identity of the neighborhood supported both a broad assumption that a residents-based campaign against LGBT youth and transgender adult women of color was not anti-LGBT as well as a counteractivist argument that residents' efforts fundamentally represented white, middle-class, lesbian and gay interests that collude with those of the police."[113] Because the reputation of the neighborhood is that it is gay—and, in fact, many of its residents are so identified—harassment and ousting of LGBTQ youth does not read as homophobic. That illegibility is an artifact of LGBTQ equal rights discourse. Gay residents were able to access the police in defense of their domestic tranquility and property values. That access was gained through a shift that placed some sectors of the LGBTQ community on the lucky side of the security divide, protected against discrimination and hate crimes, sanctified by marriage, ennobled by non-reliance on public funds and spaces, enjoying privacy, and already having triumphed in the battle against legal oppression.

But the immediate needs of the more marginalized members of the LGBTQ community do not sound in the key of antidiscrimination. Same-sex marriage in particular not only offers them little; it has probably done them more harm than good. This is true partly because the pursuit of same-sex marriage took place in discursive terms such as privatization and securitization, collaborating with identical themes in neoliberal policy argument. The logo for Wolfson's Freedom to Marry organization was an equal sign undergirding a heart and a house—a perfect symbolic coalescence of gay equality, virtuous love, and private domesticity. That ideal fusion, so enticing to so many, excludes a broad swath of LGBTQ people from the emancipatory destination; it treats low-income LGBTQ people as threats to domesticity and attempts to use law to curtail their bodily freedom and access to public resources. This cost to those on the margins is constantly being compounded by the endless reproduction of the archetypal gay subject on whose behalf efforts to promote equal rights are succeeding, reinvigorating the pursuit of reforms that benefit that subject.

The reforms that would be of greatest service to the marginalized LGBTQ populations in gentrification conflicts are not the same reforms as those generated by and for the archetypal gays. For those who lack a home, not even privacy-oriented reforms such as constitutional protection for sodomy that takes place within the home will be of much help and may be a hindrance. Police maintain a quiver full of arrows—including lewdness, indecency, and loitering statutes—that give them plenty of discretion to exercise against LGBTQ people in the wrong place at the wrong time.[114] To address these issues, advocates would have to shift attention away from recognition of partnerships and protections of privacy to small-time, local legal reforms that affect the power dynamic between police and youth or between high-income residents and low-income people who may be homeless or marginally or transitionally housed. LGBT equal rights discourse is in the way.

A Tale of Two City Ordinances

In 2005–2006, the District of Columbia passed two laws that lawmakers apparently viewed as unrelated.[115] The first added gender identity protections to the city's antidiscrimination law. This was a step forward in the march of equal rights, as the campaign to incorporate coverage for transgender people was logging in some wins at state and local levels.

The other law under consideration at the time was one amid a cluster of legal tools designed to interrupt sex work, especially in gentrifying areas of DC. This law empowered police to identify problem areas based on prior arrests or reports of prostitution activity and temporarily designate those areas "prostitution-free zones." The zones could be up to one thousand square feet, marked with signs, and could remain so designated for up to ten days. Police could then arrest—without probable cause—people suspected of prostitution who were congregating within those zones and refusing to disperse or who returned after a dispersal order. Penalties for violating a dispersal order could include jail time, as well as fines.

According to the report "Move Along: Policing Sex Work in Washington D.C.," produced by the Alliance for a Safe and Diverse DC, the law was new, but the strategies it embodied were not.[116] Prior to the law's enactment, police habitually detained suspected sex workers for jaywalking and other petty offenses; the city posted street signs prohibiting right turns at certain intersections during nighttime hours to prevent patrons of sex workers from circling; and judicial "stay away" orders barred repeat offenders from congregating in known sex-work areas.

The prostitution-free zones were initially designed to be confined to limited areas and to temporarily enhance police authority, but enthusiasts subsequently attempted to expand the zones and make them permanent. Constitutional concerns halted their progress, and the law was finally repealed in 2015.[117] For nine years, however, among those most susceptible to dispersal orders based on suspicion of prostitution were transgender women, especially of color. At the same moment that one hand of the law purported to shield transgender people with antidiscrimination legislation, the other hand of the law virtually invited attention from law enforcement and forced transwomen's dislocation while also driving some sex work into more remote (read, less safe) areas of the city. Anticipating this result, local activists worked to thwart the crusade against sex work and pleaded with lawmakers to understand that the antiprostitution law would endanger transwomen (among others) and undermine all of the good intentions of the antidiscrimination legislation, but to no avail. What, after all, does a prostitution-free zone have to do with equality?

The major LGBT advocacy organizations have been remarkably quiet in relation to the raging controversy over the regulation of sex work. Like ciswomen, LGBTQ populations are deeply implicated in this issue. Homeless LGBTQ youth are overrepresented in the trade, and transgender women of color perform sex work at especially high rates, due at least in part to rampant discrimination in the aboveground economy. Trans women of color also report an excess of attention and abuse from law enforcement, whether they actually engage in the practice or are merely assumed to do so.[118] The widely publicized case of Monica Jones, a black transwoman in Phoenix who was arrested on suspicion of "manifesting an intent" to engage in prostitution for talking to passersby, has been a weathervane for the issue. Her offense was an example of what has been sarcastically referred to as "walking while trans."[119] Jones was convicted, but an appeals court vacated her conviction, and after two years the charges were finally dropped.

Criminalization subjects sex workers to a host of dangers. The more sex workers have to worry about arrest, the less empowered they are to negotiate terms with customers, including price, location, and condom use, rendering them vulnerable to violence and HIV. Criminalization also enables police abuse of sex workers, including forced sex. For the most marginalized members of the LGBTQ community, this is a pressing matter of survival.

Some of the major LGBT advocacy organizations have "come out of the closet" on the issue of sex work. Lambda belatedly joined an alliance of sex work organizations in New York City to oppose the use of condoms found on one's person as evidence of prostitution because of the obvious effect it could have on safe-sex practices and the spread of HIV.[120] A raid by the Department of Homeland Security on the on-line male escort service Rentboy.com in August 2015 elicited a statement from Lambda, as well.[121] Acknowledging that many LGBT people rely on participation in street economies to survive, Lambda defended the site, arguing that "escorts and sex workers say [the site provided] access to work and an additional measure of safety, allowing them to screen potential customers."[122] Finally, Amnesty International recently ratified a policy favoring decriminalization of consensual sex work, including all of its incidents.[123] Amnesty argues that criminalization of any aspect of sex work creates opportunities for abuse by police. Pro-sex worker feminist organizations have come out in force in favor of the policy with petitions and electronic media blasts. A subset of the big LGBT organizations (Lambda, GLAD, NCLR, the Transgender Law Center, and the National Center for Transgender Equality) issued a supportive statement, as well, pointing to the particular importance of underground economies for LGBTQ youth and trans women of color.[124]

Feminist organizations have embroiled themselves for decades in a global struggle over the regulation of this field, including the definitional question of the relationship between sex work and trafficking, the funding of HIV-related services for sex workers, and the desirability of criminalizing associated activities (such as solicitation, purchasing sexual services, or earning an income from the sale of sex by another—that is, pimping or operating a brothel).[125] International human rights organizations such as Human Rights Watch have positioned themselves on the front lines of decriminalization, yet the major LGBT advocacy organizations have just begun to peep.

Before same-sex marriage crowded the agenda, LGBT legal organizations frequently positioned their advocacy on the lawbreakers' side of the "law and order" divide, combatting prohibitions on sodomy, defending casualties of police raids, and representing "tearoom" cruisers. Given the reality of LGBTQ participation in the sex trade, it is nonsensical for the major LGBT advocacy organizations to be AWOL on the legal issues associated with sex work. *Discursively*, however, it makes complete sense. LGBT equal rights as a discourse comprises a number of familiar strands. The discourse is teleological, setting forth the steps to eradicating discrimination. Where is sex work in the march toward the *telos* of equality? The discourse emphasizes love, commitment, and privatized responsibility. How does sex work illustrate those themes? The discourse coalesces with carceral policies that secure the private family against criminal threats, favoring punitive rather than welfarist social policies. What is sex work but a threat to fidelity, health, and property values?

The discourse of LGBT equal rights has made it hard to see issues such as sex work as central to the larger equality project. For many in the LGBT community, this may be just fine. *If it does not sing in the key of LGBT equality, it is not an LGBT issue. After all, LGBT equality cannot be all things to all people. It is not the same as a movement to salvage the social safety net or to mitigate the racism of the criminal justice system. We have enough on our plate.* Some leaders within the LGBT advocacy community, such as Urvashi Vaid, have urged their comrades to give matters of race and class greater prominence.[126] Following the shooting and killing of an unarmed black eighteen-year-old named Michael Brown by a police officer in Ferguson, Missouri, a statement of protest signed by more than a dozen major LGBT rights organizations provided cause for optimism that the message was getting through.[127] As more and more incidents involving the deaths of unarmed black people gained national attention, the LGBT advocacy community continued to issue antiracist statements and support campaigns such as Black Lives Matter. These are important gestures. Still, LGBT equal rights discourse narrows our conceptual frame considerably, making a real expansion in the understanding of the LGBT law reform agenda cognitively difficult. As a result, while many of the major LGBT advocacy organizations make genuine efforts to address disparities linked to race and class, especially in the area of trans law reform, those efforts continue to be marginal to the march toward the equality telos. From a leftist perspective, the tone-deafness of the major organizations to cross-cutting political issues that take place outside the strict confines of LGBT equal rights sets up an uneasy, even debilitating, conundrum over how to favor equality without simultaneously lending support to conservative trends with which LGBT equal rights has joined its fate, including sexual moralism, privatization, carceral politics . . . and retrogressive foreign policy.

Over There

One context in which the conundrum over how to favor LGBT equality without lending support to conservative causes arises is in the debate over "pinkwashing," a term that has more than one meaning but has come into frequent use to describe Israel's making a big show of its increasingly liberal attitudes toward gay people in an effort to distract from its occupation of the West Bank and Gaza.[128] The connection has flummoxed some proponents of gay rights, such as Arthur Slepian, longtime leader of the LGBT Jewish community in San Francisco. In 2012, in an issue of the progressive Jewish magazine *Tikkun* that was dedicated entirely to the pinkwashing debate, Slepian protested, "The fundamental problem with anti-pinkwashing rhetoric is that it proceeds from imagined motives to imagined outcomes, projecting invented intentions onto Israeli and American Jewish and LGBT leaders. Then it takes two unrelated topics—Israel's LGBT communities and their progress in the struggle for equality and inclusion, and the Israel-Palestinian conflict—and asserts that they are inextricably intertwined."[129] Slepian charges critics of pinkwashing with "errors of fact and logic."[130] Indeed, it must be maddening to him how analytically inept are those who cannot seem to disentangle these obviously unconnected issues. Viewed inside the logic of LGBT equal rights discourse, to give a Palestinian answer to an LGBT question is simply inapposite, as if one person had asked, "Isn't it great that the majority of students in law school are now women?" and a second had responded, "But the white rhino is still endangered."

As Katherine Franke explained in the same issue of *Tikkun*, however, the pinkwashing charge is not merely a depressive admonition against enjoyment of one group's advances while another group founders. It is a critique of "Israeli *state policy* that uses members of our community and/or our interests to burnish its own international reputation. In this respect, the concern is how LGBT rights get taken up by the state as a marketing tool and are served up to an international audience as part of a national rebranding project."[131] Franke published a more elaborate law review article discussing Israeli pinkwashing (along with related strategies used by the United States and the European Union).[132] Her work should provoke a pang in the conscience of anyone who takes pride in Israel's progress on LGBT issues. The evidence Franke has amassed leaves little doubt that the Israeli government has developed specific projects through its Tourism Ministry and consulates to tout its record on gay rights and to promote Tel Aviv as a gay travel destination to distinguish itself from its Arab neighbors, establish itself as hip and modern, and gain liberal political sympathies. Writing in the English version of the Israeli daily *Haaretz*, the Israeli law professor Aeyal Gross observed, "After the flotilla incident in 2010, when the Israeli navy killed nine activists aboard the Gaza-bound *Mavi Marmara*, [Israeli Prime Minister Benjamin] Netanyahu urged peace activists: 'Go to the places where they oppress women. Go to the places where they hang homosexuals in town squares and deny the rights of minorities. . . . Go to Tehran. Go to Gaza.'"[133]

So what will we do? Will we just take our gay rights and have a parade, or will we pause to consider that the improving legal conditions enjoyed by LGBT Israelis are not merely contemporaneous with an evil on the same planet but *being exploited for reputational gain* by a country that is denying human rights and the rudiments of democracy to millions of people? The pinkwashing critique offers a rich opportunity to wrestle with the responsibilities of success, although it has not been received that way in all quarters.

Discourse on LGBT equal rights leads us to the pinkwashing problem in at least two ways. First, the teleological dimension of LGBT equal rights renders that discourse particularly opportune for exploitation by countries seeking to prove their modernity. Jasbir Puar makes a similar point when she argues that the "progress narrative" of gay rights pointedly distinguishes enlightened Western cultures from lagging Eastern ones (see chapter 2).[134]

Second, as Slepian aptly demonstrated, the discourse produces a limited range of questions, and in the international arena the question "Are people like me equal over there, in that other country?" bubbles right to the surface. Slepian is not more lucidly deductive than Franke; he is more beholden to discursive constraints. By insisting on them, and on the exclusion from the realm of LGBT politics issues that do not sit squarely within the confines of LGBT equal rights logic, he puts many principled leftists in the position of having to decide whether to sit out pro-LGBT efforts and events they might otherwise support (which, in addition to Franke, Rabbi Rebecca Alpert, Judith Butler,

Sarah Shulman, and other respected LGBT Jewish intellectuals have done) because they chafe at the prospect of being complicit in "unrelated" reactionary political projects.

The international arena provides many more examples of the astigmatic thinking that can sometimes characterize zeal for LGBT equal rights. In 2013, Vladimir Putin's government passed a so-called ban on gay propaganda, a vague and sweeping prohibition against outness or advocacy of any kind that effectively has served as a license to brutalize and arrest gay Russians.[135] The law, along with reports of public beatings of gay (or apparently gay) citizens by civilian thugs in which the police have failed to intervene and the hostile comments of Putin and other Russian officials, generated an international response in the months leading up to the Winter Olympics in Sochi in 2014. President Obama, in a shrewd maneuver that sent a clear message of protest while avoiding forced sacrifice on the part of American Olympians, sent a presidential delegation that included stellar out gay and lesbian athletes.[136]

In addition, some gay activists around the world, spurred by the American sex columnist and social commentator Dan Savage, launched a (literally) splashy boycott of Russian vodka, replete with YouTube scenes of gay bartenders pouring Stoli and other brands into the sewers.[137] Stoli in particular claims to be not a Russian company but a Latvian one, although this seems not to have made an impression on Savage or the other vodka activists. According to the *New York Times*,

> The exact nationality of Stolichnaya, like many global brands, is hard to pin down. It was made for a time in Russia and simply bottled in Riga [Latvia] but has in recent years been filtered and blended in Latvia. Yet while its water comes from Latvian springs, its main ingredient, raw alcohol distilled from grain, still comes from Russia. Its bottles are from Poland and Estonia, its caps from Italy.
>
> All of the roughly 100,000 bottles of Stolichnaya produced each day for sale in the United States and elsewhere . . . come from a factory here in Riga.[138]

Moreover, Stoli pointed to a certain injustice in its being the target of these protests, arguing that it has sponsored gay events, donated to gay rights causes, and in general been a supporter of the gay community.[139] Again, its claims fell on deaf ears.

Supporters of the boycott argued that if people were conducting web searches about the boycott (which apparently they were) or talking about it (even if they were saying it made no earthly sense), then they were learning about the plight of gay Russians and the boycott was per se effective, regardless of whether it created incentives toward better behavior on the part of Russia. Supporters *did not* contend with the possibility that Western criticism of Russian homophobia provoked anti-Western sentiment, fueling antigay violence with nationalist fervor, although a number of Russia experts advised that a sensational display of Western excoriation could indeed prove counterproductive in exactly that fashion. This is a problem into which LGBT equal rights activists have catapulted themselves, some with greater awareness and sensitivity than others.

Reports of violence against and persecution of LGBT people in Egypt, Jamaica, Uganda, Zimbabwe, and elsewhere have prompted demands in the United States and Western Europe for identity-based protections and equality guarantees. Further, Western governments as well as private foundations, corporations, and advocacy organizations based in the West have put their money where their mouths are. HRC, Arcus Foundation, Deloitte LLP, Hilton Worldwide, Royal Bank of Canada, and others promote LGBT equality around the world by supporting the Global Equality Fund, which was launched by the U.S. State Department in 2011 and has given millions of dollars to LGBT advocacy groups in more than fifty countries. It says it provides emergency assistance to advocates, organizations, and individuals; documents human rights abuses; develops institutional capacity; prevents and responds to violence; works with faith leaders to cultivate tolerance; and promotes nondiscrimination and access to health.[140] In 2013, the U.S. Agency for International Development launched the "Global Development Partnership," a $16 million public-private partnership (again, including charitable foundations as well as corporations) to fund LGBT advocacy in the developing world. According to its webpage, the program, which operates in fifteen countries, "strengthens LGBT civil society organizations, enhances LGBT participation in democratic processes, undertakes research to inform national and global policy and programs, and supports LGBT entrepreneurship and LGBT-owned small and medium sized enterprises."[141]

In late 2015, Norimitsu Onishi, chief of the *New York Times*'s southern Africa bureau, published a lengthy piece entitled "U.S. Support of Gay Rights in Africa May Have Done More Harm than Good." Reporting from Nigeria, Onishi interviewed gay Nigerians who blamed the United States for worsening conditions. The United States has put hundreds of millions of dollars into promoting gay rights in sub-Saharan Africa, raising the profile of the issue but also putting gay Africans at greater risk: "African activists [told Onishi] they must rely on the West's support despite often disagreeing with its strategies." Some of the antigay laws in Africa were "colonial laws that had been largely forgotten until the West's push to repeal them in recent years." The result has been a spate of new and harsher laws—a reaction to a sense that gay rights are a feature of "cultural imperialism." If the United States had not been interfering, one man who resented the pressure and supported the Nigerian anti-homosexuality law told Onishi, "the law would not have come in the form in which it did." Before the Western push for gay rights, according to Stella Iwuagwu, executive director of the Center for the Right to Health, described as "an H.I.V. patient rights group based in Lagos, . . . these people were leading their lives quietly, and nobody was paying any attention to them. . . . [A] lot of people didn't even have a clue there was something called gay people. But now they know and now they are outraged. Now they hear that America is bringing all these foreign lifestyles."[142]

Western funders have to tread carefully to avoid backfiring. In part, this is because gay identity has not evolved identically in every culture, and pushing for gay equality as an identity-based right is not the most effective approach everywhere. As the legal scholar Sonia Katyal and the political scientist Joseph Massad explained in simultaneous critiques in 2002, American gay identity is historically and culturally specific.

Katyal pointed to the catastrophe of *Bowers v. Hardwick* as a major determinant of the contemporary conceptualization of gay identity in the United States.[143] When the U.S. Supreme Court made clear in 1986 that it was entirely permissible to criminalize homosexual sodomy, it stripped away a number of advocacy options. Criminal offenders, defined by their prohibited acts, were not good candidates for advancing an agenda of fair treatment in the workplace or in child custody proceedings. Legal advocates therefore made a hard turn toward sexual orientation, which, like race, would be defined by a trait rather than by an act. In this case, the trait would be one's preference for a sexual object.

George Chauncy's history of gay men in New York City in the first half of the twentieth century offers additional explanatory factors.[144] Faced with police-enforced virtue campaigns, white middle-class men muted any flamboyancy as a tool of self-preservation and began to insist on a reserved, bourgeois identity determined by the choice of sexual object alone. This turn distinguished middle-class men from effeminate, lower-class, black and immigrant "fairies," who were defined not by object preference but by gender deviance, setting up an eventual split between sexual orientation and gender identity.[145]

The historian John D'Emilio points to industrialization, urbanization, and the separation of domestic production from market production as the key economic conditions that enabled gay communities and identities to take form in American cities.[146] Margot Canaday puts the crucial period a bit later, around

World War II, when the regulation of immigration, welfare, and the military imbued categories of sexual orientation with new significance in terms of administration and distribution.

Whatever the determinants, sexual orientation in the United States has come to be defined principally by sexual object preference. The American Psychological Association adopted guidelines in 2011 for treatment of gay, lesbian, and bisexual clients stating that *"sexual orientation* refers to the sex of those to whom one is sexually and romantically attracted."[147] In the course of determining the level of review for classifications based on sexual orientation in *Kerrigan*, Connecticut's decision on same-sex marriage, the court almost offhandedly observed that the defining trait of the relevant class was "attraction to persons of the same sex."[148] Consistent with this discourse, associations of homosexuality with gender deviance, while a sometimes earnest and sometimes campy facet of gay and lesbian subcultures, are often condemned as *stereotyping*.[149] The recent minor slew of college and professional male athletes coming out as gay has been embraced as especially valuable to social progress because it contradicts long-standing stereotypes of gay men as weak and effete. When Michael Sam, the Missouri Tigers' All-American defensive lineman and Defensive Player of the Year, came out in advance of the NFL draft in 2014, he said to ESPN on the topic of antigay stereotypes, "If you led the [Southeastern Conference] with 11.5 sacks and 19 tackles for losses? . . . If a gay person did that, I wouldn't call that person weak."[150] This established his toughness and drew a crisp distinction between homosexuality and effeminacy.

The conceptual order that has evolved in the United States that distinguishes the choice of sexual object from femininity or masculinity has not, however, been the prevailing typology everywhere or at all times. Femininity and performance of an anally receptive, rather than insertive, role has taken on greater meaning for men's sexual identity in some African contexts. Participation in homosexual sex may carry no significance in some Arab contexts if a person is living an otherwise heterosexual lifestyle. Western LGBT equal rights advocacy can go awry by assuming a universal map of sexual orientations.

Further, some of the same-sex sexual acts committed in non-Western contexts may be absorbed without notice or opprobrium precisely because they do not occur under the banner of gay identity, a category increasingly associated with Western imperialism—and, not unjustifiably, in light of insights by Katyal, Chauncy, D'Emilio, Canaday, and others that the category has evolved in culturally and historically specific ways. Massad bitterly attacked Western gay rights advocates for their response to the prosecution of the Queen's 52, a group of men arrested in 2001 for "debauchery" during a visit to a discotheque boat on the Nile. The arrest was part of a "crackdown" prompted by "increasing visibility of Westernized, Cairo-based, upper- and middle-class Egyptian men who identified as gay and consort with European and American tourists."[151] Many of the urbane and relatively privileged Egyptians arrested on the Nile had arranged liaisons on an English-language website to which most Egyptian men who practice same-sex sex would have had no access. This distinction (in class, Internet access, English fluency, and international hobnobbery), Massad argues, is crucial. When the police raided the boat, they were targeting *gay-identified* men who socialize with Westerners, not ordinary Egyptians who practice same-sex sex. Western gay rights advocates, Massad alleged, overlooked that specificity, launching a highly public international campaign to condemn Egypt's actions. This provoked an antigay, nationalist response in Egypt that included further targeting by police of those who were viewed as a threat to the nation's virility. It also prompted Egyptian reactionaries to call for new laws to criminalize same-sex sex—laws that would legislatively link sexual *acts* to gay *identity* in a way that could introduce new forms of repression and have an impact on Egyptians who were neither previously gay-identified nor part of an urbane, international gay scene. Entering the Queen's 52 situation with gay identity guns ablaze backfired, Massad charged, putting ordinary Egyptian practitioners of sodomy at increased risk.

The discourse of LGBT equal rights sets up these errant cross-cultural assumptions, first by the pretense to a universal teleological process that implies that some countries must simply be a number of steps behind in a natural sequence. That conception is the perfect corollary to the resentful, nationalist idea that the arrival of the West portends moral decay. Second, LGBT equal rights discourse propels every thought down the same avenue: "Am I equal?" In the international context, the question materializes as "Are people like me being treated equally over in that other country?" It is the question that LGBT equal rights discourse thrusts again and again to the forefront, because inside the discursive logic of LGBT equal rights the stage is set: Identities align, and progressive and conservative forces stand ready at their marks. Whatever is extraneous is excluded, like an irrelevance from a formal proof.

Conclusion: Am I Equal with a Fox? Am I Equal in a Box?

In the debate on gay issues among Democratic presidential contenders televised in 2007, after responding to Melissa Etheridge's question about spousal health insurance, John Edwards, in an apparent non sequitur, described a visit he had made to the Los Angeles Gay and Lesbian Center:

An extraordinary place, which I'm sure some people here are familiar with . . . they are doing amazing, amazing work.

But there's a message from my visit there that I think is really important for America to hear, which is I met a whole group of young people who were there because they were homeless, and they were homeless because they came out of the closet and told their parents the truth, and their parents kicked them out of the home.

And there they were—the only place—they were living on the street, had nowhere to go. Thank God for the LA Gay and Lesbian Center being there for them, and an extraordinary woman who runs the center. But without that place, where would these young people go?

And it just can't be that in America people think that's OK. They can't believe that's OK. And they need to hear and see exactly what I saw when I was there, because it was moving. It was touching, and I actually believe that that kind of experience would have a huge impact on the American people if they could just see.[152]

Etheridge and her co-panelists did not seem moved by Edwards's story. None asked a follow-up question, such as, "What legal changes would you work to achieve as president to help these young people?" Instead, Etheridge asked Edwards whether he was uncomfortable around gay people, and the panelist from HRC brought the brief discussion back around to the topic of marriage. We will never know how many opportunities have been lost to the myopia of LGBT equal rights discourse or how much of dire importance seemed immaterial or extraneous because it lay outside the bounded world of reason that we have produced.

LGBT equal rights discourse has produced a finite range of objectives, forcing nonconforming needs and proposals into a marginal and sometimes entirely neglected position. It tells us not only what we are, but what we want—and even what is possible.

PART I HAS parsed constituent strands that together compose LGBT equal rights discourse. Chapters 1 and 2 examined the components of judicial neutrality, bourgeois sexlessness, and the double-binds of likeness and unlikeness and injury and health. Chapter 3 emphasized the teleological dimension of the discourse and its constricting effect on LGBT political range, as well as its concurrence and compatibility with crescent aspects of neoliberalism. These elements have not merely stunted the LGBT reformist imagination but, while advancing equal rights objectives with astonishing success, have also stymied progress in those areas in which LGBT identity intersects with, or may not be as important as, forms of legal subordination that track closely to race and class.

The argument in part I is *not* that same-sex marriage and other equal rights objectives have damaged LGBT interests by absorbing all of the resources needed to fight for less spectacular reforms. That criticism of the same-sex marriage campaign may be right, but it may not be. It is equally plausible that the rapid progress and excitement of the past two decades have brought in contributions and invited corporate and political mainstreaming and have therefore resulted in an overall advantage in terms of resources. Either way, diversion of resources is *not* the argument here. The argument of part I, I am afraid, is probably more contentious. It is that despite the actual and possible benefits that have accrued to the LGBT community as a result of equal rights work, the discourse of LGBT equal rights in which the mainstream objectives have been pursued is inflicting underappreciated costs. To make the point painfully but necessarily clear, the discourse of LGBT equal rights—including its moralism, its legitimation of unjust distributions, its contradictory and unstable archetypes, its collusion with and bolstering of neoliberal themes of privatized dependence and policing—has imposed real harms on vulnerable people.

My claim is not that this has been intentional or racist or classist. It is crucial to appreciate that even our most savvy and sophisticated leaders—the ones who sit in the conference room with the focus group data and the strategy memoranda at their fingertips—are "subjects," too; they are "subjected," or shaped by the same knowledge that shapes the rest of us. Their identities, their desires, and the limits of their imaginations are no more natural than anyone else's. Neither are they merely strategic actors who can exploit the terms of LGBT equal rights discourse for purely instrumental purposes when addressing courts or other pertinent audiences and then put their tools down at the end of the day, as carpenters do their hammers and nails. The discourse of LGBT equal rights affects even the most calculating lawyers. This is what it means to produce knowledge in the Foucauldian sense. While information is something we can stand outside of and study, we *inhabit* knowledge. The best we can do is to make a purposeful move into a critical position and hold that knowledge up for examination, even if we can never be entirely free of its grip. Implicitly, the examination is of ourselves and of our organizing assumptions.

It is for a reason that Chad Griffin of HRC does not think of housing law while standing in a youth homeless shelter (see the introduction). Advocates are not delivering an effect on a system that is external to themselves. The discourse produces the questions that occur to its subjects, as well as the reforms that we are capable of wanting.

What questions do *not* arise while uncritically inhabiting the discourse of LGBT equal rights? What desires do *not* stir? To know them requires a deliberate step off a well-lit path.

PART II. A Step Off the Well-Lit Path

4

BRINGING LEGAL REALISM
TO POLITICAL ECONOMY

What's Next?

A bit more than a year after the U.S. Supreme Court's decision in *United States
v. Windsor*,[1] the court declined to review five appeals from states in which federal courts had struck down bans on same-sex marriage, leaving the lower court
rulings in place.[2] As a result, by October 2014 same-sex couples could marry in
thirty states, and it looked to most observers as if the boulder could continue
rolling only in one direction. The next month, the Sixth Circuit *upheld* bans in
Michigan, Ohio, Tennessee, and Kentucky,[3] but the majority opinion was so
poorly conceived that some commentators actually suggested that the decision
could have been an underhanded ploy to create a split among the Courts of Appeals, thereby prompting the Supreme Court to get it over with already. Early
in 2015, the Supreme Court agreed to hear the cases. It appeared inevitable that
by June of that year, same-sex marriage would be a constitutional right guaranteed to everyone in the country. The campaign for same-sex marriage in the
United States went from gathering steam to barreling downhill.

On the eve of the anticipated decision, the *Washington Blade* (a leading
LGBT news outlet) published a "what comes next?" story. Would major financial contributors consider the game over and put away their checkbooks? A
"prominent gay donor in New York" indicated some uncertainty as to whether
his peers would continue to support the major organizations after the right to
marry was secured: "There is no question that some people and institutions

became engaged as donors because they were inspired by the promise of the freedom to marry.... We may well lose some number of those folks."[4]

One major LGBT advocacy organization, Evan Wolfson's Freedom to Marry, announced that it would shut its doors and distribute its assets in the wake of a favorable decision. Other major organizations, however, began sending out new and different messages to prepare their constituencies for imminent pivots. After all, having committed themselves to the telos of marriage equality for the better part of the previous two decades, the organizations faced a new challenge: How would they continue to engage their supporters? Three major themes could be discerned.

First, the organizations signaled an invigoration of advocacy work in regions of the country that had yet to protect LGBT people from discrimination. Those mostly northern and coastal states that had led the way to same-sex marriage ordinarily did so atop a foundation of antidiscrimination legislation and case law governing legal sectors that included housing, employment, and family. The states that had to be dragged along by federal court order, however, still typically lacked those basic protections. Antidiscrimination protection for transgender people was even further behind, with a handful of states providing antidiscrimination coverage on the basis of sexual orientation but still excluding gender identity. A detailed story in the *Washington Post* described renewed outreach by Human Rights Campaign (HRC) in the South.[5] The *New York Times* reported that HRC, the American Civil Liberties Union, and Lambda were launching a push for federal legislation on the scale of the Civil Rights Act of 1964, noting that gay people could still be discriminated against in employment and housing in a number of southern and mountain states.[6] The Williams Institute hosted an event and released the study "The LGBT Divide: A Data Portrait of LGBT People in Midwestern, Mountain and Southern States."[7] The e-mail missive promoting the study declared, "The Williams Institute has released a new, interactive resource, sponsored by Credit Suisse, estimating that the nationwide economic boost from marriage of same-sex couples could be up to $2.6 billion in just the first three years. It also shows that $750 million nationwide remains unlocked by states that have not yet extended marriage to same-sex couples—largely by states in the South."[8] Notwithstanding the breakneck speed of their advance in the Northeast and on the West Coast, LGBT advocacy organizations indicated their intent to do some back-filling where progress had foundered.

Second, more eyes turned to the international sphere. One report was entitled "LGBTI rights—still not there yet."[9] The "still" and the "yet," one surmises, were intended to chasten potentially complacent American readers, who—when they saw recent advances for same-sex marriage in the United States—might have imagined that the war had been won. According to the report, seventeen national jurisdictions permitted same-sex marriage, and a few South Asian countries were in some respects ahead of Western states on transgender issues, recognizing a "third sex" category for legal purposes. Still, the report warned, violence against sexual and gender minorities remained widespread; many countries retained prohibitions on sodomy; and a couple of African countries had emerged as fresh culture war territory for American advocates for LGBT equal rights and their evangelical opponents. In Uganda, for example, criminalization of homosexuality was escalating to a lunatic level with proposals to make it a capital crime. While American evangelicals poured support into the campaign against homosexuality there, pro-LGBT Westerners were nonetheless the ones depicted as imperialist in the Ugandan national debate. As unfair as this may have been, many local activists in developing countries had been critical of their Western counterparts, admonishing them to overcome their national biases and attend to those issues that were most pressing in the relevant locales: often violence and poverty much more than marriage. While the horrendous treatment of LGBT populations in countries such as Uganda and Russia were more visible and outrageous to the Western LGBT community than poverty, some LGBT advocacy organizations heeded the call to address the latter. The Williams Institute, for example, produced a study and hosted a forum together with U.S. Agency for International Development on "LGBT Inclusion and Economic Development in Emerging Economies."[10]

Third, organizations whose resource allocations and rhetoric evinced a laser focus on antidiscrimination started suggesting that questions of economic justice might just be scaling the priority list. GLBTQ Legal Advocates and Defenders (GLAD), the premier LGBT civil rights organization in New England, has a long history of wide-ranging legal work, from representing sex offenders to advocating for LGBTQ children in the foster care system, but for the preceding two decades or so it had made same-sex marriage its foremost campaign. In the summer and fall of 2014, GLAD co-sponsored with Harvard the seminar "After Marriage: The Future of LGBT Activism." While some of the work of the seminar was an extension of the campaign for marriage and formal equality (e.g., discussing the danger of religious exemptions), one session was on class, race, and poverty in the LGBT movement and another was on criminalization of LGBTQ people.

Around the same time, GLAD also posted a column on its website entitled "Equality Is Not the Finish Line," by Janson Wu, who was then deputy director but at the time of this writing is executive director of the organization.[11] The column affirmed the inadequacy of formal equality and announced that the real goal all along has been justice. *Justice,* according to Wu, means legal treatment that would "address the obstacles that we face as a community, instead of treating us exactly the same as everyone else." The column went on to sketch out some of the elements of this general vision: It "means no one is left behind, especially the most vulnerable in our community—our youth, our elders, transgender and HIV-positive folks, as well as LGBT people of color, prisoners, and immigrants." It mentions access to medical care associated with gender transition and asylum for a gay activist from Uganda. "Economic justice" came next and is exemplified by protection against employment discrimination and the effort to ensure that religious exemptions do not come to swallow up those protections. Every family form must be recognized by the law, the column declared, and LGBT people must be "not just protected—[but] celebrated," perhaps, Wu suggested, by introducing LGBT history to school curricula.

One can see in this list a continuation of conventional equality/antidiscrimination strategies as well as a shift—albeit a bit equivocal—to economic priorities. The expanse of reformist possibility is far broader, however, than what the mainstream LGBT advocacy organizations appear to be contemplating. The next chapter provides a glimpse of that expanse.

But first, this chapter steps back from the details of specific legal reforms to ask broader questions facing LGBT advocates and other movements for social justice about *how to use law.* Social movements have long wrestled with the extent of law's capacity to contribute to a civil rights struggle that is working toward progressive change on behalf of a constituency that is both defined and hindered by an elusive alloy of civil inequality and economic privation. How much is to be gained and lost by the acquisition of formally equal rights? Can economic reform alone advance the objectives of an identity-based constituency? How are race, gender, sexual orientation, and other identity categories embedded in the logic of political economy? The LGBT movement does not grapple with these vexing questions on a blank slate. Debates over these issues are long-standing and have produced a wealth of insight, if not resolution. Previous movements have in some respects pre-constructed some of the questions, as well as the analytical categories we rely on to address them.

Nor is the LGBT movement the first American movement for civil rights to make the kind of adjustment evident in the GLAD program or to struggle with the problem of how to pursue social justice for a constituency whose oppression occurs in multiple registers, including discrimination and economic marginalization. The next section glances back at the early- to mid-twentieth-century movement for black civil rights and identifies a recurring dilemma common to it and the LGBT movement. The claim is not that the two movements or the challenges facing them are exactly the same but that a powerful thematic tension between formal equality and economic reform emerges and persists as reformers, serving complex and diverse constituencies, evaluate competing legal possibilities and establish priorities.[12]

After glancing back, the chapter proceeds to inquire whether there is something distinctive about the LGBTQ constituency that makes it uniquely suited to a civil equality focus. This question has been debated perhaps most elaborately by Nancy Fraser and Judith Butler. Their disagreement—over whether LGBTQ people are principally creatures of cultural value or political economy—is reviewed here in an effort to identify the conceptual limits around such a debate while working with a reified vision of political economy. Leftist legal thinkers from the American legal realist and critical legal theory traditions saw political economy in less static terms. Their image is of a massive constellation of rapidly changing law at every level of governance, including the degree of official discretion enabled under any regulatory regime and the extent to which any law is enforced. This discussion tees up the next chapter, which, using dozens of small, moving pieces, will identify concrete opportunities to improve the political-economic position of especially vulnerable LGBTQ people.

A Glance Back

Advocates for black civil rights have been embroiled for many years in a conversation about how to advance the interests of African Americans in the context of a tangled array of legal conditions, some of which sound precisely in the key of race and some of which may appear "race-neutral" but nonetheless result in extreme disproportionality in rates of poverty, joblessness, educational deprivation, and incarceration. Whether to emphasize civil rights and equality or economics and redistribution is just one of several dilemmas that has characterized the struggle for racial justice (radicalism or conciliation? legal and legislative advocacy or direct action? separatism or integration? nonviolence or self-defense?[13]). The question of civil rights or distributive justice is, however, a persistent theme in the history of this struggle and has emerged as one of the most tenacious quandaries facing social justice movements more generally.

Some observers of electoral politics seemed flummoxed by the targeting of the presidential candidate Bernie Sanders in 2015 by Black Lives Matter, the activist group that arose to protest police and vigilante violence against African Americans. Sanders's supporters and others wondered why the group would disrupt the campaign of the lefty candidate, an avowed socialist, when the entire presidential field, Democrat and Republican, sat to Sanders's right. With a glance back at American history, however, it is really not all that surprising. Sanders's rhetoric and program of economic reform were—before the activists interrupted his events—race-blind. The divide between those who see social injustice primarily through an economic lens and those who see it primarily through a racial lens is at least a century old.

In 1913, Woodrow Wilson took office as the first Southerner elected to the U.S. Presidency in more than a half-century. His administration segregated federal buildings and practiced racist hiring; he presided over racist military practices during World War I; and he never spoke out against the scourge of lynching or took seriously any major proposals to improve the conditions facing African Americans. Black activists and thinkers advocated a range of strategies during this bleak period, including "retaliatory violence," "united action by white and black workers against the capitalist class," trade unionism, interracialism, the building of separate black economies in American cities, and Marcus Garvey's Back to Africa separatism.[14] At times, adherents of competing philosophies exhibited rancor toward one another, with the nationalist Garvey labeling the interracial NAACP "worse enemies . . . than the KKK," and W. E. B. Du Bois (a founder of the NAACP) calling Garvey "the most dangerous enemy of the Negro race in America and the world."[15]

The National Association for the Advancement of Colored People (NAACP) was founded in 1909, spurred by lynching and other incidents of riotous violence against black people. It dedicated itself to securing the promises of the Reconstruction amendments, including equality before the law and universal (male) suffrage. Its principal strategies were legislative advocacy, litigation, and public education campaigns in an effort to combat race discrimination, lynching, and interference with the franchise. In its first couple of decades, the NAACP maintained a civil rights focus, eschewing the kind of economic campaigns promoted by coexisting leftist organizations.

In 1911, Du Bois—one of the civil rights organization's most prominent black leaders—joined the Socialist Party, thinking a socialist economic program was the most promising avenue to relief for African Americans. He quickly became disenchanted, however, by the party's failure to grasp the significance of race. He left the Socialist Party in 1912, and in an address in Harlem, confronted what he understood to be the commonly held view among socialists that "we must not turn aside from the great objects of socialism to take up this issue of the American Negro; let the question wait; when the objects of socialism are achieved, this problem will be settled along with other problems."[16] Identifying what he called a "logical flaw" in this thinking, Du Bois asked, "Can the problem of . . . ten million be properly considered as 'aside' from any program of socialism?"[17] Du Bois answered his rhetorical question: "The essence of social democracy is that there shall be no excluded or exploited classes in the socialistic state. . . . I have come to believe that the test of any great movement toward social reform is the excluded class."[18]

But Du Bois appreciated that he was contending not only with the ideological belief that a purely economic program would settle the problem of racial hierarchy, but also with a question of political strategy. Socialism would gain fewer adherents in the South if black advancement were an explicit goal. Du Bois attempted to reverse the calculus: "What is anti-Negro socialism doing but handing its enemies the powerful weapon of four and one-half million men who will find it not simply in their interest, but a sacred duty to underbid the labor market, vote against labor legislation, and fight to keep their fellow laborers down."[19] The Socialist Party, Du Bois concluded, "finds itself in this predicament: If it acquiesces in race hatred, it has a chance to turn the tremendous power of southern white radicalism toward its own party; if it does not do this, it becomes a 'party of the Negro.' . . . [I] ask . . . after you have gotten the radical South and paid the price which they demand, will the result be socialism?"[20]

Du Bois realized early "that the symbolic struggles for black rights and recognition within the nation-state could not be separated from material struggles over distribution."[21] He continued to wrestle with the complex relationship between race and class for decades, into the New Deal and beyond, certain on the one hand that economic reform alone was insufficient to address the distinctive conditions facing African Americans, but arguing on the other hand that access to suffrage had no effect on private corporations and left unaddressed the problems of workers; he therefore advocated unionization and socialist reforms.[22]

The issue was a pointed one for Du Bois and many of his contemporaries. At a convention of black intellectuals and activists in 1933, participants—including Du Bois—made "an effort to combine the older liberal emphasis on civil rights with a recognition of the importance of political economy to [what Du Bois called] 'the welfare of the great mass of Negro laboring people.'"[23] But Du Bois recalled that they "could not really reach agreement as a group because of the fact that so many of us as individuals had not made up our own minds on the essentials of coming social change."[24] At ninety-three, Du Bois joined the Communist Party, which—as early as the 1920s and '30s—had maintained a much more pronounced focus on race than the Socialist Party did, making appeals to black nationalists as well as to interracialists and taking up the causes of the Scottsboro Boys (black teens falsely prosecuted for gang rape in Alabama) and Angelo Herndon (an African American communist organizer prosecuted for "insurrection").[25]

In the 1930s, when leftist economic ideas were incorporated into and over-taken by liberal welfarism, the New Deal "not only evaded issues of racial re-form, in some respects it expanded and legitimized racist practice on a wider scale."[26] As the historian Nikhil Pal Singh explains, Social Security "exempted domestic and agricultural laborers, who were disproportionately black. Hous-ing loans and subsidies under the Fair Housing Administration . . . were allocated along racial lines, expanding rather than diminishing segregation. . . . Crop reduction payouts under the Agricultural Adjustment Administration . . . were notoriously discriminatory and barely trickled down from plantation owners to poor tenant farmers and share croppers."[27]

Much of the New Deal legislation, including the Fair Labor Standards Act, which established maximum hour, minimum wage, and overtime protections, and the National Industrial Recovery Act, which authorized industry codes reg-ulating wages and hours, was negotiated by President Franklin Delano Roosevelt with powerful southern congressmen who consistently required that a whole range of protections exclude black workers to preserve the plantation system. Plantation owners were seeking to protect their supply of cheap, mostly black labor. Legislation did not specify by race who was to be excluded from labor protections, but it did typically exclude sectors of the economy, especially agri-cultural and domestic labor, in which black workers were known to predomi-nate.[28] Plantations' interests influenced the distribution of relief, as well. The short-lived Federal Emergency Relief Administration, which provided cash grants for the poorest Americans in the early to mid-1930s, allocated much of the administrative authority over distribution to states and localities, which—in the South—sought to preserve an oversupply of farm labor by restricting grants to poor black people, notably during planting and harvest seasons.[29] Characterizing the New Deal as a "Faustian bargain," the historian and politi-cal scientist Ira Katznelson explained, "The compromise [securing passage of labor and social welfare reforms at the expense of black workers] reached to the core of the New Deal. By not including the occupations in which African Americans worked, and by organizing racist patterns of administration, New Deal policies for Social Security, social welfare, and labor market programs re-stricted black prospects while providing positive economic reinforcement for the great majority of white citizens."[30]

Black activists and intellectuals were profoundly frustrated by the New Deal, many linking its failure to assist black people to capitalism itself. During this period, the NAACP expanded its purposes, pushed at least in part by dire economic need among the black masses as well as by competition from the Communist Party and other organizations that had an agenda for black advancement that included an anti-poverty or labor component.

The second term of President Roosevelt saw a good deal of improvement, with the First Lady and others close to the president pushing for attention specifically to the plight of black Americans, as well as continued agitation by activists.[31] The administration hired dozens of black officials into the ranks of its agencies. A group of officials spread throughout New Deal agencies came to be called the "Black Cabinet" and began meeting regularly to ensure the administration's attention to black civil rights and fair treatment by New Deal programs.[32] Thanks to Eleanor Roosevelt, the Black Cabinet, and white allies within the administration, the Works Progress Administration (WPA) emerged as a crucial support for black workers and artists and for providing adult education.[33] Discrimination abated in federal relief projects, as well.

Labor reforms by the administration were initially enacted with southern support. That support held out until unionization began to spread to southern cotton, tobacco, steel, and other industrial settings and might have begun to include black workers.[34] Labor reform then stalled, especially in the South, as a result of abandonment by southern Democrats and effectively left "the South's political, social, and economic structure . . . largely unchallenged."[35] Katznelson identifies this crucial result: "The emerging judicial strategy and mass movement to secure black enfranchisement and challenge Jim Crow developed independently of the labor movement . . . [and] the incipient civil rights impulse rarely tackled the economic conundrums of southern black society directly, focusing instead mainly on civic and political, rather than economic, inclusion."[36]

It cannot be said that the dual tracks of civil rights and labor reform remained entirely separate. A. Philip Randolph founded the Brotherhood of Sleeping Car Porters as early as 1925 and gained admittance for the black organization into the historically all-white American Federation of Labor (AFL) in 1937. Racial exclusion from unions, over the years, had exactly the effect predicted by Du Bois: it created incentives for black workers to cross picket lines. The unions accordingly denounced them as "scabs," sustaining a long-standing antipathy between black activists and union activists.[37]

But by the 1940s, the NAACP had joined forces with unions of the Congress of Industrial Organizations (CIO) to pressure Roosevelt on matters of both civil rights and jobs. The irrepressible Ella Baker, who worked for the NAACP in the early 1940s first as a field secretary and then as director of branches, viewed the trade unions as "a natural ally" of her own organization.[38] She urged the NAACP in a memo to view its struggle as part of a larger democratic vision, arguing that "the fight for up-grading of Negro workers might well gain support if a given local branch would also take the leadership in support of the labor movement's fight against anti-labor legislation."[39] Throughout her career as an organizer Baker believed that the labor and civil rights struggles were inextricable, and in 1942 she participated in CIO efforts to organize shipyard workers in Virginia.[40] Randolph, too, was crucial to the NAACP-CIO alliance. A longtime opponent of Garveyist separatism; an organizer of black shipyard workers, elevator operators, and sleeping car porters; and an advocate for higher wages, Randolph maintained the inextricability of black civil rights and workers' unity.[41] He got the AFL to address its own racist practices and prompted labor leaders to speak out on behalf of the Scottsboro Boys and Angelo Herndon.[42]

Still, while the NAACP joined forces with Randolph and the unions during the New Deal to accomplish a series of economic goals, many of the achievements of civil rights and economic reform of the next couple of decades occurred along distinct tracks. In the 1960s, while the NAACP did support Lyndon B. Johnson's War on Poverty, it largely resumed its focus on civil rights strategies, including equal treatment under the new antipoverty legislation.

In addition to courtroom victories such as *Brown v. Board of Education* (1954), the focus on civil inequality—not only by the NAACP, but also by Martin Luther King Jr.'s Southern Christian Leadership Conference (SCLC) and other groups acting inside and outside the legal system—led to the successes of the Civil Rights Act of 1964 and the Voting Rights Act of 1965. As American cities erupted into violence in the mid- to late 1960s, however, these reforms began to disclose their own inadequacy. The poverty of inner-city African Americans meant the continuation of *lived* inequality by millions, quite apart from whatever formal legal equality was by then "on the books."

Reflecting on the limits of *Brown*, "the Holy Grail of racial justice,"[43] the late law professor and civil rights attorney Derrick Bell wrote:

> While civil rights lawyers worked to remove the most obvious legal symbols of segregation, we left it to A. Philip Randolph and the National Urban League to address the major changes in the economic outlook of a great many black people. Living in inner-city areas across the country, they were finding it increasingly difficult to find jobs. Employers were moving to the suburbs where public transportation was almost nonexistent but discrimination in hiring was rampant. Without work, family

instability followed. Those able to leave the old neighborhoods did so, taking with them the stability of middle-class educations and aspirations. Public services, including schools ... all but collapsed under the burden. For those left behind, joblessness and hopelessness were eased with alcohol and drugs, sedatives that quickly worsened conditions for individuals and their communities. Neither the *Brown* decision nor our efforts to give it meaning had any relevance to the plight of those whom we had not forgotten, but had no real idea how to help.[44]

The NAACP, long reputed to be elitist and mainstream compared with many of its fellow legal and activist organizations, was uncomfortable with rising radicalism in the late 1960s, including Black Power and activism against the war in Vietnam; it doubled down on its traditional civil rights focus and tried to maintain its mainstream appeal.[45] This, as Bell observed, left others to focus on economics and, specifically, on the conditions in American cities.

Martin Luther King Jr. attributed the outbreak of urban violence to economic conditions that the civil rights victories had done little to alleviate. The resources that were supposed to go into President Johnson's so-called War on Poverty went instead to the war in Vietnam as unemployment and hunger ran rampant in black communities. Gerald McKnight explains, "Despite the civil rights victories since 1954, King was painfully aware that most black Americans had barely moved forward at all. The legislative triumphs embodied in the 1964 Civil Rights Act and the Voting Rights Act of 1965 did precious little to improve the lot of millions of blacks living in the ghettos of the North, a bitter irony recognized by King."[46] As a consequence, King turned his attention to economic justice. He started to advocate a radical reorganization of society and such objectives as a "guaranteed annual wage," advanced years before by economic leftists such as Bayard Rustin and Randolph.[47]

In 1967, a young NAACP lawyer, now known to the world as Marian Wright Edelman, founder and president of the Children's Defense Fund, came up with the idea to bring the nation's poor to Washington, DC, to protest. King and the SCLC dubbed this the Poor People's Campaign.[48] Its purpose was to spur President Johnson and Congress to enact additional federal legislation, this time to alleviate poverty for Americans of all races by addressing housing, joblessness, education, and health care.

At Victory Baptist Church in Los Angeles in June 1967, King said, "You see our struggle in the first phase was a struggle for decency. Now we are in the phase where there is a struggle for genuine equality. Now this is much more difficult. We aren't merely struggling to integrate a lunch counter now. We're struggling to get some money to buy a hamburger or a steak when we get to the counter." He went on to call for a "radical redistribution of economic and political power."[49]

King was assassinated before the major demonstration of poor people he planned for Washington, DC, in the spring of 1968. He was in Memphis to lend his support to a sanitation workers' strike. Although Johnson signed the Fair Housing Act shortly thereafter and attributed it to King's legacy, the Poor People's Campaign foundered and has been looked on by history as a failure.

The challenges facing African Americans, a hundred years ago and now, exist in multiple and overlapping registers. The struggle for racial justice accordingly has had to negotiate dilemmas of philosophy and strategy. At each historical moment, competing emphases have vied for prominence. While some activists worked for civil rights and voting rights legislation and litigated to erode and eventually eradicate the "separate but equal" doctrine, others formed or joined labor unions, participated in communist or socialist organizing, or fought for an expanded WPA. These efforts sometimes coincided and at other times followed separate or even competing tracks, but to leaders such as Du Bois, Baker, and Randolph, the deficiencies of a pure civil rights liberalism, as well as of economic reformism lacking in racial consciousness, were painfully evident from early on.

The difficult but crucial question of where to concentrate emancipatory efforts along a continuum that stretches from the most purely symbolic equality for an identity-based constituency to a completely economic program and the jettisoning of identities as if they were "snake skins which have been cast off by *history*,"[50] has occupied leftist political thinkers for more than a century. The question has not lost its urgency for African Americans, but its relevance has multiplied as other social movements have unfolded on behalf of complex constituencies.

Recognition and Redistribution: The Place of Sexuality

In a broadly influential essay first published in 1995, "From Redistribution to Recognition? Dilemmas of Justice in a 'Postsocialist Age,'" the social theorist Nancy Fraser framed an apparent contradiction facing progressive reformers between pursuing identity-based equality strategies and pursuing a redistributive economic agenda.[51] Fraser took up race, class, gender, and sexual orientation in her essay and provoked a storm of reaction.[52] In particular, Fraser inaugurated her now famous dialogue with Judith Butler over the extent to which homophobia is amenable to interpretation through the lens of political economy or whether—in contrast to racism and sexism—homophobia is "merely cultural."[53]

The debate erupted over a highly provisional typology offered by Fraser as part of an effort to overcome what she viewed as a division within the left between those who would address injustice principally as a problem of "recognition" and those who would address injustice principally as a problem of distribution. While conceding that the objectives of recognition and redistribution often "overlap," Fraser observed that in the 1990s, at the moment of her writing, "identity-based claims tend to predominate, as prospects for redistribution appear to recede."[54] Fraser was writing during an apogee of identity politics.

According to the American studies scholar Lisa Duggan, *identity politics* refers to a "rights-claiming focus of balkanized groups organized to pressure the legal and electoral [and I think we have to add university] systems for inclusion and redress."[55] Economic conservatives in the 1980s made a strategic move to align themselves with "civil rights/equality politics" in a way that "minimized any downwardly redistributing impulses and effects."[56] Consequently, many writers on the left have been critical of the amenability of identity politics to corporate aims and upward distribution of wealth. Some have attributed the rise of identity politics "to the conservative tendencies of American jurisprudence."[57] According to this view, "Law secures substantive rights, but always in favor of preserving . . . existing power relations."[58] Moreover, some leftist critics of identity politics have expressed impatience with people they see as recognition-obsessed liberals whom they accuse of introducing toxicity and divisiveness into leftist politics and allowing themselves to be distracted from material concerns.[59] Finally, the rise of identity politics was accompanied by increasing "NGO-ization," including large, financially endowed, and centralized representative organizations that purport to speak for economically diverse—if ethnically or in some other respect discrete—constituencies, essentializing complex and contingent identities, setting the terms of the culture war, and establishing the credentials for political righteousness.

Writing into this moment and the contest over identity politics, Fraser articulated a "recognition-redistribution" conundrum and distinguished between two leftist conceptions of injustice, each demanding its own kind of remedy. *Socioeconomic injustice* is "rooted in the political-economic structure" and can be characterized by "exploitation . . . economic marginalization . . . and deprivation." *Cultural or symbolic* injustice, by contrast, is "rooted in social patterns of representation" and is characterized by "stereotyp[ing]," "disrespect" and "nonrecognition."[60] Fraser's taxonomy crystallized the terms of those who had come to loggerheads over identity politics in the 1980s and '90s, echoing competing approaches to black advancement in prior decades.

Butler may have been allergic to any overtones coming from the socialist Fraser that identity politics were a mere distraction from the "real" issue of distributive justice. She chastised Fraser for underestimating the gravity of cultural injustice in the title of her response essay, "Merely Cultural."[61] Fraser does, however, convey her appreciation for the seriousness of symbolic injury by excerpting a leading liberal voice on the issue: the Canadian political theorist Charles Taylor, who argued that nonrecognition "can be a form of oppression, imprisoning someone in a false, distorted, reduced mode of being."[62] He went on to explain, "Beyond simple lack of respect, it can inflict a grievous wound, saddling people with crippling self-hatred. Due recognition is not just a courtesy but a vital human need."[63]

Taylor's widely cited *Multiculturalism and "The Politics of Recognition"* was written amid two crises: Heated on-campus battles between traditionalists and multiculturalists over the content of liberal arts education and the potentially imminent secession of Quebec. Taylor seemed to be searching for a way to quell the strife around him, each instance of which he understood as a struggle over recognition between a culturally demeaned and a culturally dominant group. He turned to Hegel and, in particular, to the master-slave dialectic to conceptualize these controversies.

Hegel's master-slave dialectic attributes the formation of identity to an exchange of recognition between emerging, striving, and demanding consciousnesses. Our identities evolve not internally (not "monologically") but through a "dialogical" process of social intercourse in which we seek recognition in another. Taylor observed that the process of recognition described by Hegel occurs in "intimate" contexts (e.g., between lovers or parent and child) as well as at a social level, between groups. He warned, "Inwardly derived, personal, original identity doesn't enjoy . . . recognition *a priori*. It has to win it through exchange, and the attempt can fail."[64] Mis- or nonrecognition by another can inflict significant damage, as poor reflections of the self come to constitute the self.[65]

According to Taylor, the tragedy of Hegel's master-slave dialectic is that the terrible thirst for recognition devolves into a battle. A superordinate and subordinate emerge, and as the "master" extracts recognition from the "slave," the master defeats himself, because the slave is so demeaned that his recognition is no longer of value.[66] Adapting this devolution from the Hegelian story, Taylor argued that compelling the dominant culture to recognize the equal value of a subordinate culture's contributions cannot in the end be a worthwhile form of recognition at all. Indeed, Taylor observed, recognition under such conditions cannot possibly be "a genuine act of respect" and is in fact "condescending."[67] Paradoxically, Taylor cast the culturally and politically dominant groups (old, white, male professors and Anglo-Canadians) as the slaves, whose recognition—if forcibly extracted—would mean little to the more marginalized groups (proponents of Third World, minority, and women's contributions to arts and literature and the Quebecois) who are figured as the masters.

In an effort to break out of the dialectic and to ease the acrimony of contemporary debates over respect and inclusion, Taylor proposed a middle ground. Rather than arrogantly refusing recognition to another culture (as some of his more dismissive contemporaries did) while also avoiding condescension by attributing equal value as a matter of right, Taylor would employ a "presumption of equal worth . . . a stance we take in embarking on the study of the other."[68] Taylor's solution is a kind of liberal open-mindedness with a retention of the right, even obligation, to evaluate quality based on merit.[69]

The moment of defeat features prominently in Taylor's account of Hegel precisely because he is proposing a way out: a lightly held presumption of value and the chance for earnest, authentic recognition. Antagonists in the controversies that compelled him to write appear in the essay as chronically dissatisfied, stubborn, and closed-minded, so Taylor offers a reasonable intervention that would occur to the kind of guy who can see both sides. He might say, "It need not spiral into a Hegelian death match, if we could all just keep our heads." This deflates the dialectic a bit but strictly because of Taylor's faith in liberal tolerance, open-mindedness, and merit—not because he fails to appreciate what is at stake in recognition. In fact, the entire mission of Taylor's essay is to infuse gestures of recognition with believability so that recognition will hold up against doubt and do its job of constituting positive identities effectively.

By relying on Taylor, Fraser conveys that nonrecognition is serious business for her, too, although she differs from Taylor in key respects. Fraser is not Hegelian in her conception in the sense that she does not engage the dialectic or even appear to consider the possibility that a culturally dominant group also needs recognition. Neither is she psychoanalytically inclined—social, or group, recognition is Fraser's concern rather than individual identity formation. As she states explicitly, Fraser regards "misrecognition [as] an institutionalized social relation, not a psychological state,"[70] by which I take her to mean that it is a form of domination built into social and political structures and effectively a unidirectional matter. Fraser is also not a liberal, on the hunt like Taylor for an open-minded multiculturalism that accommodates everyone in a reasonable way. Indeed, Fraser concludes her essay with rejection of identity-based claims for multicultural inclusion in favor of a deconstructive approach to identity. She sees "destab[ilization of] group differentiation" as a more promising avenue to "restructuring... relations of recognition" in the long run than strategies that rely on and thereby entrench categories of identity.[71]

One might expect "destabilizing identity" to appeal to Butler, herself among the world's most influential social theorists of that enterprise, yet she does not find an ally in Fraser because she views Fraser's approach as "disparagement of the cultural."[72] The crucial bone of contention between Butler and Fraser arises out of Fraser's theorizing "lesbian and gay struggles" as cultural and homophobia as lacking roots in political economy.[73] Central to Fraser's analysis is "a conceptual spectrum of different kinds of social collectivities," defined on one end by socioeconomic injustice and the need for redistribution, and on the other end by cultural injustice and the need for recognition. Along this spectrum, Fraser locates ideal types.[74] Marx's "exploited class" resides squarely on the socioeconomic/redistributive end because it is entirely a creature of the political economy, constituted by "its relation to other classes."[75] Gays and lesbians, by contrast, sit on the cultural/recognition end of the spectrum because they "are distributed throughout the entire class structure... [and] occupy no distinctive position in the division of labor." The problem facing gays and lesbians is, according to Fraser, one of "cultural devaluation." Fraser concedes that anti-gay discrimination may result in economic harm (in employment, social welfare benefits, and so on), but at root, she contends, is nonetheless a problem most appropriately addressed by "positive recognition."[76]

Fraser posits race and gender as "bivalent," in that cultural valuation and political economy operate together to create the injustice faced by racial minorities and women.[77] She appreciates the quandary confronted by Du Bois and others who struggled with inequalities in dual registers. Racial minorities and women occupy exploited and marginalized positions in the economic structure, but both are also subject to devaluing representations, and their devaluation is tied up with their economic position. Domestic labor, for example, is both low-paying and "coded" in racial and gendered ways. Fraser insisted that "political economy and culture are mutually intertwined, as are injustices of distribution and recognition" and that she presented "sexuality in a highly stylized theoretical way in order to sharpen the contrast" with the other ideal types.[78]

These provisos were of no solace to Butler. She faulted Fraser for overlooking a basic socialist feminist insight that "sought not only to identify the family as part of the mode of production, but to show how the very production of gender had to be understood as part of the 'production of human beings themselves,' according to norms that reproduced the heterosexually normative family."[79] As a consequence, "Both 'gender' and 'sexuality' become part of 'material life' not only because of the way in which it serves the sexual division of labor, but also because normative gender serves the reproduction of the normative family."[80] For Butler, the pertinent lesson to be gleaned from the socialist feminists is the vital importance of normative gender and sexuality to the capitalist economy, perpetuating the division of labor but also—crucially—reproducing the family structure that supports that economy.

It follows for Butler that "struggles to transform the social field of sexuality do not become central to political economy to the extent that they can be directly tied to questions of unpaid and exploited labor, but also because they cannot be understood without an expansion of the 'economic' sphere itself to include both the reproduction of goods as well as the social reproduction of persons."[81] Despite Fraser's appreciation for the centrality of *gender* to the political economy, she fails, according to Butler, to "pursue radically enough the implications. . . . She does not ask how the sphere of reproduction that guarantees the place of 'gender' within political economy is circumscribed by sexual regulation. . . . Is there any way to analyze how normative heterosexuality and its 'genders' are produced within the sphere of reproduction without noting the compulsory ways in which homosexuality and bisexuality, as well as transgender, are *produced* as the sexually 'abject'?" The normative family and marginalization of "non-normative sexualities" are taken by Butler not as "merely cultural," but as suffused with political economic implication. Disruptions of heterosexist normativity, should, therefore, be regarded as political-economic interventions.[82]

Butler's quarrel with Fraser's initial essay, in sum, is with Fraser's characterizing the injustice facing sexual minorities as cultural rather than economic. Butler's objection is not only that Fraser appeared to devalue the injustice facing sexual minorities, but also that she failed to appreciate the crucial function that sexual normativity performs under capitalism.

Fraser made her rejoinder in a second essay, "Heterosexism, Misrecognition, and Capitalism: A Response to Judith Butler." She charged Butler with de-historicizing twentieth-century capitalism, in which "intimate relations, including sexuality, friendship and love . . . can no longer be identified with the family and . . . are lived as disconnected from the imperatives of production and reproduction."[83]

Indeed, in his classic of gay history "Capitalism and Gay Identity," historian John D'Emilio reads the historical evidence to suggest "gay men and

lesbians . . . are a product of history. . . . Their emergence is associated with relations of capitalism; it has been the historical development of capitalism—more
specifically, its free-labor system—that has allowed large numbers of men and
women in the late twentieth century to call themselves gay, to see themselves
as part of a community of similar men and women, and to organize politically
on the basis of that identity."[84] According to D'Emilio's account, the predominance of self-sufficient agrarian households during the colonial period allowed
"no 'social space'" for the development of gay identity or community. Children
typically contributed their labor to the household, and (while same-sex erotic
acts no doubt occurred) moral and legal codes aligned with economic imperatives by confining sexuality to marriage and procreation and condemning non-
procreative sex of all kinds. The gradual transformation of the economy into
one of capitalist free labor and the end of household self-sufficiency, however,
meant that adults would leave home to work, and urbanization would give
rise to the possibility of meeting places such as bars. Meanwhile, birthrates
dropped as children became mouths to feed from an adult worker's income
earned in the wage labor market. The purpose of sexuality shifted toward being
companionate rather than procreative.[85]

Capitalist developments, therefore, can be credited with providing conditions precedent for gay identity and community. To the extent that Butler
suggests that—in empirical terms—"capitalism . . . 'needs' or benefits from
compulsory heterosexuality [and] that gay and lesbian struggles against heterosexism threaten the 'workability' of the capitalist system," the contention
simply is not borne out by current reality. Capitalism, "in its actually existing
historical form," does not seem the least bit threatened by gay identity, community, or rights.[86]

It may once have seemed that it was, but for reasons of right-wing politics and paranoia rather than because of any rational entailment. During the
Red Scare of the 1950s, homosexuality and communism were closely associated forms of menace. As D'Emilio reports, McCarthyites stoked the fear that
homosexuals, "slaves of their sexual passions, would stop at nothing to gratify
their desires until the satisfaction of animal needs finally destroyed their moral
sense. Communists taught their children to betray their parents; 'mannish'
women mocked the ideals of marriage and motherhood. Lacking toughness,
the effete men of the eastern establishment lost China and Eastern Europe to
the enemy, while weak-willed, pleasure-obsessed homosexuals—'half-men'—
feminized everything they touched and sapped the masculine vigor that had
tamed a continent."[87] McCarthy and his allies uttered "Communists and
queers" in a single breath, branding one disloyal and the other a "security risk"

due to moral weakness and vulnerability to blackmail. Republicans pursued a public mission to ferret both out of federal government jobs.[88] "The congruence between the stereotypes," D'Emilio writes, "made the scapegoating of gay men and women a simple matter."[89] One right-wing pundit of the era, Arthur Guy Mathews, "accused Communists of encouraging homosexuality in the West to make us 'physically weak.' 'Homosexuality,' he proclaimed, 'was "Stalin's Atom Bomb." ' "[90]

But this association between communism and homosexuality long ago waned, along with the Cold War itself. As Fraser points out, the "principal opponents of gay and lesbian rights today are not multinational corporations, but religious and cultural conservatives."[91] Economic and cultural politics have diverged so that it is entirely legible to be conservative in the former category and liberal in the latter. Moreover, it is easy to find instances of capitalist support for gay rights, such as tech companies that began offering benefits for same-sex partners early on and banks that sponsor gay pride parades.

Indeed, it turns out that nothing about being gay, in the sense of having same-sex desire, reliably predicts a broader political allegiance to people on the margins. As the queer theorist Leo Bersani observed with some resentment, "To want sex with another man is not exactly a credential for political radicalism."[92] And Bersani did not even discuss the Log Cabin Republicans; or the insistence by Human Rights Campaign (HRC), the nation's largest LGBT advocacy organization, that it is nonpartisan; or the intra-community dissension between prominent LGBT figures of the right, such as Andrew Sullivan, and of the left, such as Urvashi Vaid—all of which are testament to the notion that being gay, even being a gay activist, does not entail any particular larger ideological commitment.

The ideological pliability of gay rights may account in part for the movement's recent success. Fraser is surely correct that over the past two decades, guardians of global capitalism have shown themselves to be utterly unafraid of gay rights and in many instances have aligned themselves with its progress. Dozens of large corporations (including AIG, Citigroup, eBay, Goldman Sachs, Google, Nike, Starbucks, and Xerox) signed on to an *amicus* brief urging the Supreme Court to strike down Section 3 of the Defense of Marriage Act (DOMA) in the *Windsor* case,[93] arguing that DOMA imposed administrative costs on them and forced them to discriminate in contravention of their corporate missions. Then again in *Obergefell*, nearly four hundred corporations (including Aetna, Amazon, American Airlines, Coca-Cola, DuPont, JetBlue, Marriott, Starbucks, Target, and Xerox) argued in an *amicus* brief that state laws banning same-sex marriage injure their corporate cultures and impede their efforts to obtain the best talent by driving qualified people from jurisdictions in which they do business.[94] HRC scratched many of these backs when in 2015 it published its Corporate Equality Index, a list of top places for LGBT employees to work based on LGBT antidiscrimination coverage, insurance coverage for same-sex partners, the existence of an employer-supported "diversity" group for employees, and support for the "External LGBT Community." No other corporate conduct was considered when HRC lent its imprimatur to the 366 corporations that received "100 Percent" ratings, including AIG, Bank of America, Bristol-Myers Squibb, Chevron, Citigroup, Goldman Sachs, Lockheed Martin, Merck, Pfizer, and Raytheon.[95]

Furthermore, many companies seem to find in the increasing acceptance of gays fresh marketing opportunities. The sociologist Suzanna Danuta Walters has catalogued extensive advertising to the gay consumer by beer, wine, and liquor companies; clothing retailers; car manufacturers; insurance companies; financial advisers; and airlines. Some of these companies place targeted advertisements in gay magazines; some proffer "secret handshakes" in more general ad venues that most heterosexual viewers will not detect but may give gay readers that "knowing" feeling; and some borrow androgynous and gender-bending imagery to generate for their products or services a sense of hip cosmopolitanism.[96]

All of this would seem to confirm Fraser's view that capitalism is sufficiently elastic to embrace homosexuality and gay rights. The socialist feminists did not get it exactly right that capitalism requires compulsory heterosexuality. (In their defense and Butler's, they wrote decades before an ad for Alaska Airlines in *The Advocate* would feature two handsome, buff white men in an embrace with the caption, "Who you love is not a choice. How you fly with them is.")[97] This is not to say that capitalism, in its neoliberal form, does not need family; it does. As discussed in chapter 3, familial interdependence as a moral code provides crucial support to the neoliberal economic objective of increasingly privatized responsibility and concomitant relief to the public sector. Still, that family, it turns out, need not be heterosexual.

But whether capitalism can accommodate gay rights may not have been the right question. Perhaps instead the question of non-normative sexualities and genders and their relationship to political economy is best raised by an inquiry into the *specific manifestation of LGBT advancement*. Law professor Angela Harris has argued that "the political economy of the Right is well able to absorb queers as long as they stand ready to get married, move to the suburbs, and vote for lower taxes."[98] But would *any* instantiation of LGBT progress be so easily absorbed into the capitalist enterprise, or has the particular way in which

LGBT progress has been pursued in the past two or three decades, especially the foregrounding of same-sex marriage, been uniquely amenable?

In yet a third essay revisiting the same recognition-redistribution dichotomy, Fraser cited exclusion from marriage as her prime example of misrecognition of gay people, or—as she explains it—an "institutionalized pattern" of "cultural value," that stigmatizes "same-sex partnerships as illegitimate and perverse."[99] Many people in the gay and lesbian community undoubtedly experienced denial of the right to marry in exactly the way she describes: stigmatizing and delegitimizing of their most significant relationships. Still, Fraser betrays her lack of familiarity with queer critiques of same-sex marriage as *itself* distinctly misrecognizing. For example, Michael Warner regards same-sex marriage as a betrayal of a more radical queer normativity that is avowedly pro-sex.[100] David Eng condemns the quest for same-sex marriage as a racially and class privileged project.[101] The late José Esteban Muñoz depicted the pursuit of marriage equality as assimilationist and directed his readers' attention to the "not yet here"—a deliberately less pragmatic and aesthetic realm of queer potentiality and longing.[102] Nancy Polikoff argues that the gay rights movement ought not to have made marriage the centerpiece of its fight for equality because doing so bolstered the privilege of marriage as a beneficiary of state recognition to the exclusion of a wide variety of family constellations that historically have not been valued by the law.[103] Collections such as *Against Equality*, edited by Ryan Conrad, burst with full-throated rejections of same-sex marriage as assimilationist, religious, romantic (in a bad way), anti-sex, patriarchal, imperialist, capitalist, bourgeois, and so on.[104]

I could go on because there are more. I refer you to the sources themselves for the details of each critique. Some of these writings resonate for me more than others; I do not cite any of them to endorse them in their particularity, but only to make the point that the prioritization of marriage by mainstream advocacy organizations has engendered a good deal of alienation, disaffection, resentment, and even outrage in leftist and queer segments of the community and among LGBTQ writers of color. At least some of this negative response arises out of a problem that could *itself* be characterized as one of misrecognition. This misrecognition is perhaps in the first instance on the part of the architects of the LGBT reform agenda, but the discourse of LGBT equal rights and marriage as the exemplar of gay progress now predominate in the mind of the general public. As a result of this predominance, the great victories of the past few years have left many LGBTQ people with the feeling that the train has left without them.

Denial of the right to marry may appear to be a paradigmatic example of nonrecognition to Fraser precisely because she conceptualizes recognition as flowing (or not) in one direction, from the dominant to the subordinate in a hierarchical social structure—not unlike the conception urged by the mainstream LGBT advocacy community in counter-majoritarian forums. Marriage is a central institution of American life, a key indicator of one's status as a rights-endowed person, and (until recently) the majority had been withholding it from a disrespected minority, thereby conveying a clear message of devaluation and second-class status. In this respect, the socialist Nancy Fraser echoes the conservative Andrew Sullivan: Admission to the institution of marriage figures as a central remedy to gay exclusion. Fraser's simplistic structure of dominance and subordination obscures the queer critiques, as well as the multiplicity of LGBTQ experiences.

Recognition through Redistribution

In 2012, a group of queer-identified activists, writers, and academics joined forces to produce "A New Queer Agenda," published in the Barnard web journal *Scholar and Feminist Online*.[105] A preface by political scientist Lisa Duggan and editor of *The Nation* Richard Kim, decried the mainstream LGBT advocacy organizations' agenda that has prioritized access to the military and marriage and "gay representation in the corporate media," and focused on "exclusively 'gay' issues . . . [making] formal, legal equality the end goal."[106] As Duggan and Kim acknowledged, progress toward these objectives has been manifest, but "meanwhile, queer immigrants, homeless youth, unemployed and impoverished transgender workers, and queers of color are getting hit even harder since the 2008 crash. This great divergence makes it more than clear—the time has come to change the agenda of lesbian, gay, bisexual, transgender, and queer politics in the United States."[107] In the remainder of the edition, contributors propose features of a "New Queer Agenda" that address a span of economic justice issues, including rural poverty, urban gentrification, health care access, homelessness, immigration, sex work, elder care, incarceration, police violence, and reproductive justice. Duggan and Kim emphasize that much of the agenda comes from people who are "activist, on-the-ground."

The Center for Gender and Sexuality Law at Columbia Law School, directed by Professor Katherine Franke, issued a report in 2014 entitled *Our Fair City: A Comprehensive Blueprint for Gender and Sexual Justice in New York City* that goes into real policy detail.[108] Like "The New Queer Agenda," this report was assembled in consultation with street-level providers. It urges New York

City's Mayor Bill de Blasio to institute an array of reforms that—in the words of the center—"address the day-to-day manifestations of sexual and gender injustice in New York."[109] The report offers recommendations such as ending enforcement of a vague criminal statute that empowers police to arrest people for "Loitering for the Purposes of Engaging in Prostitution" without any evidence of prostitution itself; making self-identification the sole determinant of gender on city documents; expanding housing availability for people living with HIV-AIDS; conducting mental health assessments of arrested LGBTQ youth and developing alternatives to incarceration; settling a pending lawsuit that challenges the pay discrepancy between mostly female school safety agents and other officers; and delivering "cultural competency training" to providers who work with LGBTQ elders.

The kind of redistributive programs envisioned in "The New Queer Agenda" and *Our Fair City* may well offer greater recognition than even the most sensational successes of the mainstream LGBT advocacy organizations, at least for some sectors of the LGBTQ population. Indeed, one possible response to Fraser is that a redistributive approach to justice already contains within it the possibility of recognition. The philosopher Axel Honneth effectively takes this position in his own response to Fraser: "Rules of distribution cannot simply be derived from the relations of production, but are rather to be seen as the institutional expression of a sociocultural dispositive that determines in what esteem particular activities are held at a specific point in time. Conflicts over distribution . . . are always symbolic struggles over the legitimacy of the sociocultural dispositive that determines the value of activities, attributes and contributions. In this way, struggles over distribution, contrary to Nancy Fraser's assumption, are themselves locked into a struggle for recognition."[110] For Honneth, economic marginalization conveys a society's low valuation of a person or group's qualities and contributions; it follows that redistribution represents a recalibration of both resources and value.

Fraser seems to appreciate this when it comes to her "bivalent collectivities," but she adheres to the sharp distinction when it comes to her exemplars of the two opposed poles (the working class and gays, respectively). According to Fraser's view, "The economic disabilities of homosexuals are better understood as effects of heterosexism in the relations of recognition than as hard-wired in the structure of capitalism."[111] An "institutionalized pattern" of cultural devaluation can *result in* economic injury, but the primary injustice is one of nonrecognition. This reflects a deep concession to the logic of LGBT equal rights discourse, which accords primacy to the symbolic. Fraser does not appear to consider the possibility that an agenda that directly engages the political economy (as "The New Queer Agenda" and *Our Fair City* endeavor to do) may itself offer recognition.

Fraser does fleetingly note in her original essay that some LGBT people experience *intersecting* forms of injustice.[112] A gay person could be working class, for example. She does not begin to theorize this kind of "intersection," however, framing sexual identity as its own, independent, if sometimes cross-cutting, condition, itself amenable to a recognition solution. Fraser's thin and offhand version of intersectionality does not accomplish much.[113]

Is there a way to conceptualize the needs of economically marginalized LGBTQ people to accomplish more? What would take Honneth's insight on board and simultaneously address distribution and recognition? In "A New Queer Agenda" and *Our Fair City*, queer/leftist thinkers are trying to do both, shifting to a distributive focus but without jettisoning LGBTQ identity. Can we change how we think about law reform and advance this effort?

To situate the matter historically, progressive social movements have wrestled with the dual objectives of civil equality and economic justice for some time. Our progenitors, from Marx to Du Bois, from King to the socialist feminists, have bestowed on us a rich canon of thought about civil rights, discrimination, and economic disparity. As we on the left grapple with the breathtakingly successful, but in some respects disconcerting, legal agenda of the mainstream movement for LGBT equal rights, how might we more subtly apprehend the place of sexuality and gender identity in the political economy and use law to advance the interests of constituencies that are disadvantaged along axes of both resources and knowledge?

Selves, Repeating

In an essay on Robert L. Hale and Michel Foucault, law professor Duncan Kennedy brings together key assets from two seemingly unrelated thinkers. Theories of distribution (Hale) and of knowledge (Foucault), in concert, can reveal much about the dynamic process by which law endows differently situated people with both material resources and knowledge of themselves and others: "Law is one of the things that constitute the bargaining power of people across the whole domain of private and public life. One of the things this power produces is a distribution of income, understood as a distribution of whatever people value that is scarce. But another product of the deployment of power in unequal relations is knowledge, meaning particular understandings of the world and how it works."[114] Like Honneth, Kennedy sees both the distribution of material resources and the production of knowledge as entwined consequences of law.

Kennedy adds this insight: The lawmaking process repeats itself, but a bit differently each time. "Knowledge conditions the valuation process, indeed creates valuing subjects, as well as the particular values of valuing subjects. The knowledges produced by those empowered in earlier processes of . . . lawmaking alter . . . future lawmaking, and future knowledge production. Thus individuals and groups . . . are themselves reconstituted through exercises of power that seem merely instrumental to preexisting goals."[115] Each instance of lawmaking can affect the next in ways that are constrained by the resource allocations and knowledge production effectuated in the prior instance. The result is something like a spiral—cyclical, but moving to a new level, with each iteration burying the prior one. "Those empowered in earlier processes" accentuate maldistribution as they "alter . . . future lawmaking."

The excerpt reads as ominous in the sense that, while Kennedy surely is urging on the left an analytical toolkit to interrupt the spiral, the spiral he depicts is decidedly downward from a leftist perspective. It begins with inequality, which compounds itself. The most and least endowed with value act from their revalued positions again and again, while the process by which that value gets produced and reproduced is obscured.

The debate between Butler and Fraser, on whether the political economy can absorb gay equality, misses this constant dynamic production. Part of the problem with Fraser's formulation is surely that she has not taken seriously enough the range of experiences of sexuality on axes of race and class so that she fails to offer a satisfying answer to Butler's questions: "How are we to understand the production of the HIV population as a class of permanent debtors? Do poverty rates among lesbians not call to be thought of in relation to the normative heterosexuality of the economy?"[116] Yes, they do. Butler is right that Fraser erred in her typology—perhaps so grievously as to sabotage her entire recognition-redistribution framework.[117] A weak nod to the fact that some gays and lesbians are also working class extracts little value from intersectionality as a theoretic tool. To move beyond Fraser's perfunctory acknowledgment of the multiple features of identity and derive real analytic value from the intersections *would require that we be informed about the legal conditions facing highly localized constituencies.* It would require an awareness of background rules and their distributional effects on specific populations. It would require an intervention into the processes by which inequalities of resources and meaning reproduce and compound themselves. In the daily imminence of law and its enforcement,

LGBTQ people who are low-income or of color encounter conditions that can be interrupted or reformed, creating possibilities for redistribution and—in Honneth's sense rather than Fraser's or Taylor's—recognition, as well.

Sexual orientation and gender identity *are* profoundly bound up with the fiber of political economy, but not because capitalism depends on compulsory heterosexuality. Instead, this is so because law emerges out of existing distributions of resources and knowledge. Those distributions are to specific subconstituencies that are defined in part by their sexualities but also by intersecting identity traits and aspects of their economic positions. *Law then effectuates new distributions out of which more law emerges.* Background legal conditions that determine aspects of the daily lives of LGBTQ people go underexamined, as does the knowledge that produces them. The resulting distributions compound and elide the relations of power and valuation that led to them in the first instance.

This cycle presents a predicament but also an opportunity. The opportunity is not for an all-at-once revolution, but for *repetition that is a bit different each time*. The feminist philosopher Jana Sawicki, advocating an analogous idea she called "radical pluralism," described a similar shift she envisioned for feminist thought. "It is based on a form of incrementalism in which the distinction between reform and revolution is collapsed. Yet, this is not an incrementalism . . . that denies the need for major structural transformation. . . . It is an incrementalism that recognizes domination, but also represents the social field as a dynamic, multidimensional set of relationships containing possibilities for liberation as well as domination."[118] Sawicki was bringing a Foucauldian conception of power's perpetual motility to feminist analysis. Hale saw similar motion in law, which is why Kennedy brought them together in his essay. This dynamism is complex to perceive, but it provides constant opportunity.

We could conceptualize the law reformer's job to be to appreciate the process of navigating the immediate legal conditions in a local population's experience. Where are the obstacles to work, safety, nutrition, housing, health care, and so on? What legal reforms—however low-profile and regardless of their apparent symbolic significance—might ease the experience of maneuvering among adverse material conditions? Where are those levers that result in shifting resources to a specific constituency in need?

Reforms conceived in this way would not fundamentally upset capitalism or reset relations of value. They would occur on the grid of economic disparity, homophobia, transphobia, racism, and sexism. They would be repetitions, but just a bit different.

Outside the context of law reform, Butler is in fact a pioneer of this way of thinking. In *The Psychic Life of Power*, she outlined a structurally similar idea about the individual psyche: "I propose to take account of... a paradox.... How can it be that the subject, taken to be the condition for and instrument of agency, is at the same time the effect of subordination, understood as the deprivation of agency?"[119] Butler is wrestling here with a fundamental problematic of critical theory: The individual human "subject" is conceptualized in contradictory yet coexistent ways. On the one hand, Marx, Foucault, and others contested the classical liberal ideal of the atomistic, preference-holding, bargain-seeking, rights-bearing subject. In Marxist, structuralist, and post-structuralist theory originating mostly in continental Europe, the subject is taken to be an *effect* of existing power structures, including language and discourse. To be an *effect* of power means that one is legible only within existing terms. Discursively produced "social categories [rendering the subject legible] signify subordination and existence at once."[120] To be a subject, therefore, is to be "subjected"—to be formed by existing structures of power and to "exist" as legible only within the terms of those structures.

Simultaneously, however, having subjectivity is the basic precondition for agency—that is, for having the capacity to desire and to act in a way that is not already entirely subordinated to those same power structures. Once acquired, subjectivity is credited with "any effort to oppose... subordination."[121] Yet how is opposing subordination, or *resistance*, possible if the agent of that resistance exists only by being subjected? Will not "any effort to oppose... subordination... necessarily presuppose and reinvoke it"?[122]

The way out of the enigma is repetition. "For Foucault," Butler explains, "the subject who is produced through subjection is not produced at an instant in its totality. Instead, it is in the process of being produced, it is repeatedly produced."[123] Butler argues, "If conditions of power are to persist, they must be reiterated; the subject is precisely the site of such reiteration."[124] In acting, the subject always reenacts power, but not by producing an exact copy of its enabling conditions. "It is precisely the possibility of a repetition which does not consolidate... the subject, but which proliferates effects which undermine the force of normalization."[125] In each repetition—required to sustain the existence of the subject—lies the possibility of resistance, error, or change. "A subject only remains a subject through a reiteration or rearticulation of itself as a subject, and this dependency of the subject on repetition for coherence may constitute that subject's incoherence, its incomplete character. This repetition or better, iterability thus becomes the non-place of subversion, the possibility of a re-embodying of the subjectivating norm that can redirect its normativity."[126] Resistance, or "redirect[ion of] normativity," is made possible by the need for the subject to *keep acting*. Although power continues to act on the subject, to be sure, it is also the case that to perpetuate its own existence as a subject, the subject must act—again and again.

The *again and again* is key. While power is reproduced through the acting subject, "power is not a straightforward task of taking power from one place, transferring it intact, and then and there making it one's own; the act of appropriation may involve an alteration of power such that the power assumed or appropriated works against the power that made the assumption possible."[127] Even digital copies vary slightly from one reproduction to the next. Similarly, each repetition opens up a possibility for "alteration."

"The subject is compelled to repeat the norms by which it is produced, but that repetition establishes a domain of risk. . . . And yet, without a repetition that risks life—in its current organization—how might we begin to imagine the contingency of that organization, and performatively reconfigure the contours of the conditions of life?"[128] Subjection, Butler is telling us, is neither stable nor permanent in its form. Instead, it is a process in which subjects themselves participate. With each act, a subject reproduces relations of power that gave rise to its existence, perpetuating both those relations and its own existence, but not in the form of an identical copy. It is in the imperfection of the next iteration that the possibility of resistance resides.

This does not mean that the subject is fully an agent, entirely free of its subordination. "That agency is implicated in subordination is not the sign of a fatal self-contradiction at the core of the subject. . . . But neither does it restore a pristine notion of the subject, derived from some classical liberal-humanist formulation, whose agency is always and only opposed to power."[129] Borrowing an example from Foucault, Butler observes that the social category of homosexuality "will be deployed first in the service of normalizing heterosexuality and second in the service of its own depathologization. This term will carry the risk of the former meaning in the latter, but it would be a mistake to think that simply by speaking the term one either transcends heterosexual normalization or becomes its instrument."[130] The homosexual subject becomes legible by its discursive production, by its categorization, and by its contrast to the heterosexual. It is a reproduction of power relations to articulate the subject in the way that it is already legible, but that is not end of the story. The act of repeating the legibility of the homosexual contains the possibility of partial resignification— not utter liberation, but neither precise duplication.

Butler's unwinding of this paradox avoids both an overly determined subject entirely lacking in agency and the resort to the liberal, atomistic, preference-bearing individual that springs forth unconstrained by the conditions of power in which it exists. And this is not merely pertinent to the individual psyche; it also responds to "a larger cultural and political predicament, namely, how to take an oppositional relation to power that is, admittedly, implicated in the very power one opposes."[131] How? By repetition—but just a bit differently.

Imperfect repetition by a perennially forming subject has an analogue in legal thought. That analogue is in an understanding of law as perpetually allocating and reallocating resources and value. Working in what in legal theory are called "background rules" is a method of intervening in the conditions that produce existing distributions (of power, resources, knowledge, and so on). A tweak in the rules works within the existing legal regime and is therefore constrained by existing power relations. It also, however, contains the capacity to disturb the process of reproducing those relations, effectuating a small redistribution.

Here is another way to visualize the idea: The French anthropologist Claude Lévi-Strauss used the metaphor of *bricolage* to explain the structure of mythical thought.[132] A *bricoleur* in France is something like a handyman (if perhaps a bit less reputable). His tools and materials are his *bricolage*. The bricoleur is distinguished by being

> adept at performing a large number of diverse tasks; but, unlike the engineer, he does not subordinate each of them to the availability of raw materials and tools conceived and procured for the purpose of the project. His universe of instruments is closed and the rules of his game are always to make do with "whatever is at hand," that is to say with a set of tools and materials which is always finite and is also heterogeneous because what it contains bears no relation to the current project, or indeed to any particular project, but is the contingent result of all the occasions there have been to renew or enrich the stock or to maintain it with the remains of previous constructions or destructions.[133]

Like Butler's subject, the bricoleur is not in a position to envision something completely new, to shed all priors and innovate from scratch. The materials he brings to his work are not driven by his next goal; rather, they are entirely conditioned by his past—they are remnants of his previous undertakings. He therefore addresses a new problem with what already exists: "His first practical step is retrospective. He has to turn back to an already existent set made up of tools and materials, to consider or reconsider what it contains and, finally and above all, to engage in a sort of dialogue with it and, before choosing between them, to index the possible answers which the whole set can offer to his problem."[134] The purpose of Lévi-Strauss's metaphor is to illustrate how myths are "pre-constrained," made up of "constitutive units" in one among their "possible combinations."[135]

The lesson that law reformers can take away, however, is in both the limits and the potential of working with what already exists, in recombination and to new effect: "In the continual reconstruction from the same materials, it is always earlier ends which are called upon to play the part of means. . . . so that a result can be defined which will always be a compromise between the structure of the instrumental set and that of the project."[136]

Using existing tools (with apologies to Audre Lorde[137]) may not bring about revolution—at least, not in one fell swoop. It will carry forward the components of the past, but it can still effectuate a meaningful shift. Like the law reformer, "The 'bricoleur' may not ever complete his purpose but he always puts something of himself into it." That "self" is evident in "the choices he makes between the limited possibilities."[138] It is the same "self" that (in Butler) must reiterate the prior discursive terms that gave rise to it as a subject, but inexactly and perhaps with slightly altered normativity. This is not an all-at-once revolution, but it is resistance. It is also a vision for the role of law—a medium that is at once moored to its priors and rich with possibilities for reform.

5

MAKING THE DISTRIBUTIVE TURN

Spotting Reform Opportunities

A few years ago, I joined forces with the Poverty Law Clinic at Northeastern University School of Law, taught by my colleague Professor Jim Rowan, to put on a training at an LGBTQ youth center in Boston. The center serves predominantly homeless and marginally housed youth, largely of color and typically hailing from the low-income Boston neighborhoods of Dorchester, Roxbury, and Mattapan. The two of us, along with five law students, trained the staff and youth at the center on the process for obtaining aid from the Supplemental Nutrition Assistance Program (SNAP), also known as food stamps. The training covered how to complete an application, how awards are calculated, what to do if your application is denied, and other basic matters. We sat together in a roomy lounge with about a dozen youth, some of whom were transgender or gender nonconforming and all of whom were familiar with survival on the street. We began with the first line of the application: *name.* The youth immediately ran into an obstacle. *What if my name is not my legal name? What if my name is not the same as it was on the SSI application I filed six months ago?* The application offers the option of "alias." (Grumbling.) Next line: gender, M or F? (Not grumbling—more like extreme irritation.) Farther down the application, applicants must identify people with whom they live (again, including name and gender). SNAP wants to know with whom applicants prepare their meals. Some urban LGBTQ youth are in and out of a parental home, some couch-surf, some live in ball houses or similar constellations.[1] Housing can be unstable; "family" can be a fluctuating concept; and meals can be hard to come by. One of the ways the youth center attracts kids is by having food around—there were cheese and crackers, fruit. The application asks about minors (not your children) living with you and about boarders. Many LGBTQ street youth sell sex to survive. Sometimes they sell it for cash; sometimes for a place to sleep. How does one characterize a situation in which an adult houses a young person in an informal, possibly affectionate, exchange of sex for food? What are the young person's earnings? How much is her rent?

By sitting together in the youth center and listening to the youth react to the questions on the application we came to appreciate the complexities of low- or no-income LGBTQ youth navigating what was supposed to be a simple benefits form. Food stamp application forms do not spring forth fully drafted from the head of Zeus; government agency regulators draft them, and they do so within discursive confines of gender identity, sexuality, family, and race. Those applications and the resulting awards condition the availability of nutrition—to the detriment of people whose identities and social ties chafe against the norm. That experience led us to insight about counseling individual clients and suggested some reformist possibilities in as low-profile and rudimentary a site as an application form.

Changing Priorities

A growing number of studies document LGBT poverty. The Williams Institute at the University of California, Los Angeles, in particular, has been a source of fresh and high-quality empirical data on hunger, homelessness, and other incidents of economic marginalization in the LGBT population.

One function that these studies perform is to support traditional facets of the LGBT equal rights project. They bolster the case for counter-majoritarianism by combatting the stereotype of the white, wealthy homosexual exerting outsized influence on the political system in service of a minority recognition project (see chapter 1). They also provide evidence of the concrete economic injuries inflicted by employment discrimination and lack of access to marriage. The need for antidiscrimination protections as well as for relationship recognition is prominent in the conclusions of many of these studies.

The studies may also be taken as an indicator of rising consciousness of a broader range of needs in the socially, economically, regionally, and racially diverse LGBT population than the mainstream LGBT equal rights movement has addressed. Many of the studies highlight wage disparities as well as deficiencies in the social welfare net, suggesting the possibility of an expanding agenda.

Prior to the ascent of the Williams Institute, the National LGBT Task Force was the movement's closest approximation to a think-tank.[2] The Task Force conducted a study of LGBT youth homelessness in 2006, before there were a lot of studies documenting LGBT poverty. Together with the National Coalition for the Homeless, the Task Force, led by the author Nicholas Ray, produced the comprehensive report "Lesbian, Gay, Bisexual and Transgender Youth: An Epidemic of Homelessness" (known as the Ray report).[3] It detailed the best available empirical data on LGBT homeless youth, the causes of their homelessness, the risks they face (including substance abuse, mental health risks, sexual health risks, and risks of victimization), the resources available to them, and some of the legal landscape against which they struggle to survive. While the nearly two hundred-page document does mention the bar to same-sex marriage—notably, as an obstacle to legal immigration—marriage is a bit player in the larger scene depicted in the Ray report.

Discrimination more generally does play a role in the hardship that the report depicts. Some shelters, especially those administered by faith-based organizations, have been sites of hostility and even violence rather than solace or safety for LGBTQ youth. Some legal and human service professionals remain oblivious about how to approach the topics of sexuality and gender identity with their clients or how those features of identity may affect their clients' interests. And obviously, family rejection, a particularly intimate form of discrimination, plays a causal role in the homelessness of many of the youth.

But the Ray report also stresses factors unrelated to discrimination and cultural competence that contribute to homelessness among LGBT youth and to the risks associated with that condition. Some of the factors that show up in the report are the dearth of funding for programs for homeless youth (including shelters, drop-in centers, street outreach, and transitional living); lack of affordable housing and rising rents brought on by gentrification; scarcity of opportunities for adequately paying work; the "criminalization of homelessness" through prohibitions against sleeping in public places, combined with the impact of criminal records on prospects for obtaining jobs and housing; difficulties obtaining documentation and photo identification that accurately and uniformly reflect one's name and gender identity, which in turn make it hard to get a job; and barriers to accessing gender-appropriate medical screenings and gender-affirming health care such as hormone therapy.

The report concludes with policy recommendations, several of which have nothing whatsoever to do with equal rights or antidiscrimination. For example, it proposes a reauthorization and increase in federal funding for homeless youth programs; it endorses legislation that would empower unaccompanied minors to consent to a wide range of medical services as well as a mandatory expansion of Medicaid coverage for youth (up to age twenty-four) who do not live with their families or who have aged out of the foster care system; it urges a broadened definition of *homelessness* for U.S. Department of Housing and Urban Development (HUD) programs so that people who live in motels or sleep on friends' couches would qualify for services; and it calls for an end to the criminal prohibitions against sleeping, sitting, or lying down in public spaces that effectively render homeless people de facto criminals. Finally, the Ray report advocates an increase in the minimum wage that would enable more working people to afford housing.

Attacking the problem of LGBT youth homelessness from a wider angle than an antidiscrimination lens affords yields insights and policy recommendations well beyond those that have dominated the LGBT law reform agenda in recent decades. Low-income LGBTQ people are contending with a vast array of disadvantageous legal conditions, well beyond those that sound in an equal rights or antidiscrimination key. The slow opening of reformist eyes to a more expansive range of legal issues that have a considerable and daily impact on marginalized members of the LGBTQ community is a salutary development, but there is much more to see.

This chapter pries the angle wider still—busts it open, I hope. It prioritizes the distribution of income, housing, food, health, safety, and jobs as it endeavors to step off of the path of LGBT equal rights discourse. To attend to those priorities, it will examine closely some of the low-profile but very concrete legal conditions that affect the daily lives of marginalized LGBTQ subpopulations.

The effort requires a reconceptualization of the relevant constituency. This chapter will not present LGBT people as an undifferentiated, rights-bearing identity group seeking equality. Instead, the chapter examines vulnerable LGBTQ subpopulations seeking the best possible bargains for themselves in a world in which their prospects and decisions are heavily conditioned by law. Myriad statutes, regulations, common law doctrines, and everyday routine practices and exercises of legal discretion together compose a legal landscape against which a situated constituency must make choices. A small adjustment in the legal network, even one that is utterly illegible in LGBT equal rights discourse, has the potential to improve the bargaining position of marginalized LGBTQ subpopulations, understood as differentially endowed players operating in an imminent legal and economic environment. This perspectival shift will fix the spotlight anew on under-examined legal conditions that may be amenable to change.

The chapter illustrates its method by weaving together two narratives. One follows LGBTQ youth along a path that begins in their families of origin but too often continues with homelessness and a struggle to survive. It examines the legal conditions the youth face as they bargain with their parents, the foster care system, landlords, employers, police, and "johns." These legal conditions are disparate—they are not all incidents of discrimination. That is precisely the point. Highlighting obstacles faced by LGBTQ youth navigating their legal environment makes evident that many of the reforms that could provide a real benefit to a marginalized constituency are obscure, low profile, and not obviously connected to one another.

At the same time, the chapter introduces a set of analytical tools drawn from American legal realism, a critical intervention into mainstream legal thought that began in the late nineteenth century and early twentieth century and steered attention to law's distributive capacities. Methodological insights will slowly pour into the mix: the construction of bargaining endowments, the distinction between rules of permission and rules of prohibition, the significance and dimensions of enforcement, the availability of official discretion, and the problem of unintended consequences of well-intended laws. As the need arises, we will turn to the legal theory to make visible the legal obstacles that the youth face, as well as alternatives that could improve their circumstances.

By examining, alternatively, a constituency's regular encounters with the law and a set of theoretic tools for understanding and intervening in those encounters, the chapter will distill a process for generating fresh possibilities for law reform that would not be self-evident from within the confines of LGBT equal rights discourse. Attention to the legal background and to its distributive effects can enable those who are concerned with economically marginalized LGBTQ constituencies to identify new avenues to reform. Even a seemingly minor adjustment to the kinds of legal conditions that are elucidated in this chapter could meaningfully alter the position of a vulnerable population.

The chapter concludes by moving beyond LGBTQ youth. It profiles other marginalized LGBTQ subpopulations and imagines some possible starting points for bringing the same method to bear.

Background Rules and Legally Constructed Alternatives

We begin with Robert L. Hale. A lawyer and economist, Hale wrote in the first half of the twentieth century, a period of struggle and reform in the industrial labor market. His most widely read article, "Coercion and Distribution in a

Supposedly Non-Coercive State," confronts a dogma advanced by those who advocated minimal state intrusion into the wage labor market: that laissez-faire is a form of freedom. Hale illustrated that the employment market is riddled with coercion, revealing those who advocated that the market remain "free" to be either disingenuous or naïve.[4]

All eyes, at this time, were on the dazzling spectacle of contract. It was the era of *Lochner* and Franklin Delano Roosevelt's court-packing plan (see chapter 1), when the U.S. Supreme Court was striking down laws that interfered with "freedom of contract." The Court imagined contract to be a space of genuine individual autonomy within which men could negotiate their bargains on the basis of free will. The law that governed this ennobled endeavor occupied the foreground.

Hale's chief contribution was to draw attention away from the pageant of contract to *background rules*. In the absence of regulations such as a minimum wage or maximum hour rule, it may seem that an employer and employee are "free" to negotiate whatever contractual terms they choose. Hale showed, however, that property rules operating unnoticed in the background limit the range of choices available to negotiating parties. His crucial insight into law's role in the construction of alternatives provides a new way to understand the conditions LGBTQ young people face.

Hale inquired, "What is the government doing when it 'protects a property right'? . . . [I]t is forcing the non-owner to desist from handling [the thing owned] unless the owner consents."[5] The non-owner, in other words, has a legally enforceable *duty* to abstain from infringing on the owner's "sole right to enjoy the thing owned." Of course, "The owner can remove the [non-owner's] legal duty" if he chooses, but he is likely to do so only on some condition that is to his advantage:

> The non-owner may be willing to obey the will of the owner, provided that the obedience is not in itself more unpleasant than the consequences to be avoided. Such obedience may take the trivial form of paying five cents for legal permission to eat a particular bag of peanuts, or it may take the more significant form of working for the owner at disagreeable toil for a slight wage. In either case the conduct is motivated, not by any desire to do the act in question, but by a desire to escape a more disagreeable alternative.[6]

The *construction of alternatives* is crucial to Hale's argument: Property law vests a "right" in an owner of property and a "duty" in the non-owner to avoid interference with that right. The owner may relieve the non-owner of his duty but can refuse to do so unless the non-owner succumbs to some wish of the owner's, giving the non-owner two choices. If, for example, the property in question is money, the non-owner must abstain from taking any of it *or* could be relieved of that duty in exchange for performing labor:

> In the case of labor, what would be the consequence of refusal to comply with the owner's terms? It would be either absence of wages, or obedience to the terms of some other employer. If the worker has no money of his own, the threat of any particular employer to withhold any particular amount of money would be effective in securing the worker's obedience in proportion to the difficulty with which other employers can be induced to furnish a "job." . . . If the non-owner works for anyone, it is for the purpose of warding off the threat of at least one owner of money to withhold that money from him (with the help of the law). Suppose, now, the worker were to refuse to yield to the coercion of any employer, but were to choose instead to remain under the legal duty to abstain from any use of any of the money which anyone owns. He must eat. While there is no law against eating in the abstract, there is a law which forbids him to eat any of the food which actually exists in the community—and that is the law of property. . . . There is no law to compel [the owners of food] to part with their food for nothing. Unless, then, the non-owner can produce his own food, the law compels him to starve if he has no wages, and compels him to go without wages unless he obeys the behests of some employer. It is the law that coerces him into wage-work under penalty of starvation—unless he can produce food. Can he? Here again, there is no law to prevent the production of food in the abstract; but in every settled country there is a law which forbids him to cultivate any particular piece of ground unless he happens to be an owner. This again is the law of property.[7]

Hale's analytical triumph was in refuting the convention that bargaining for a contract without governmentally imposed terms (e.g., a minimum wage) meant that the parties were "free"—that is, not subject to coercion. *Coercion* here means something less than brute force and is more like having one's choices powerfully influenced by legal conditions. One chooses from among alternatives that have been constructed in part by background legal rules. A worker is coerced into working for an owner/employer on undesirable terms by facing alternatives that are worse. Similarly, the owner is "counter-coerced" into paying for labor if he requires it to conduct his business. The range and desirability of alternatives available to each party determine the relative bargaining power each brings to negotiating the employment contract. Each "coerces" the other by pressing him with demands that are only incrementally preferable to his other options.[8]

It is crucial that these background rules are neither "neutral" nor "natural." Realist property law professors instruct their students that property is "a bundle of rights." The phrase fragments property ownership into constituent strands rather than conceptualizing it as a natural whole. For example, if you own a plot of land, do you own the sky above it? May airplanes pass through the airspace above your parcel unhindered by your wish that they would not? Can you build on your land as high as you like, even if you block your neighbor's view of the ocean? Can you dump your trash into the creek that runs through your land and continues into the neighboring parcel? If you lease your parcel to a tenant, can you enter the premises at will? Can you use your parcel to open an all-night tavern? A noxious chemical plant? A porn shop? Can you build a high-rise condominium complex on your eroding beachfront? Do your neighbors have an easement that entitles them to cross your land to get to the road? In each of these cases, there may be a limit—whether contained in a zoning ordinance, in the common law, or in a deed—on the right to enjoy or the right to exclude, both of which are critical features of property ownership.

Courts, legislatures, agencies, and zoning boards answer questions regularly about the exact ambit of particular instances of property ownership or about which rights one holds in the "bundle." These choices do much of the work of shaping a parcel's market value. The rules or restrictions may look like givens, but someone decided them, allocating an advantage somewhere and a disadvantage somewhere else. In this way, background conditions are *distributive*.[9]

Employment contracts, Hale showed, result in part from distributions that appear to be *ex ante* but are actually products of property law and the range of alternatives into which it coerces employer and employee. The analytical method Hale used to illustrate the importance of background rules to comprehending what may seem to be the outcomes of freely made choices, has applicability beyond the employment contract. In what follows, LGBTQ youth will be understood as bargain-seekers, navigating legal conditions as they negotiate the terms of their lives with other—competing—bargain-seekers, including family members, employers, landlords, police, and others. This will influence where and how they live, whether they are safe, what they have to eat, as well as what kind of sex they have and with whom. At each turn, it will pay to be mindful of the legally constructed alternatives the youth have at their disposal.

Permission and Prohibition

The lives of LGBTQ youth begin under a legal regime that concedes tremendous deference to their parents to raise them in accordance with parental values. This deferential posture has constitutional roots. Parental autonomy, an incident of family privacy, was elevated to the level of constitutional principle in the early twentieth century, in the middle of the *Lochner* era and around the same time that Hale and his contemporaries were critiquing the allegedly free market to which that Supreme Court was devoted. The court decided a pair of cases on the heels of World War I that established what came to be known as the "fundamental right to parent."[10] In each case, a state law forbade a choice that parents might make with respect to their children's education—to send them to parochial rather than public school and to seek instruction in a foreign language, respectively. In each case, the Supreme Court struck down the challenged law as an unconstitutional restraint on parental liberty under the due process clause "to direct the upbringing and education of children."[11] The twin cases are often cited as antecedents to the modern right to privacy.[12]

The parenting right is not, however, without limits. California made news in 2012 when it enacted a statute outlawing the use of "conversion therapy" on minors—a psychotherapeutic practice discredited in all but cultural conservative circles—that is alleged to relieve patients of "unwanted" homosexual desire or gender deviance. (Presumably when minors are involved, "unwanted" refers to the wishes of the parents.) The law was challenged in federal court on constitutional grounds—specifically, that it infringed on parental rights as well as on the speech rights of the therapists. The U.S. Court of Appeals for the Ninth Circuit upheld the law, finding that parental rights were not unlimited and that the therapy was professional conduct rather than speech.[13] Since then, New Jersey, Oregon, Illinois, and the District of Columbia have enacted similar bans (New Jersey's has been upheld by the Court of Appeals for the Third Circuit); more than a dozen states have introduced legislation; and President Barack Obama, responding to an online petition, expressed his disapproval of the practice and called for its end. A jury in New Jersey found that a conversion therapy center's promises of heterosexuality were fraudulent in violation of consumer protection law and awarded damages to plaintiffs who had undergone the treatment.[14] Federal legislation was introduced in 2015 (but never passed) that would have approached the issue similarly, treating it as consumer fraud and granting enforcement authority to the Federal Trade Commission.[15] Oklahoma briefly considered a bill that would protect the practice of conversion therapy, but it did not get far. LGBT advocacy organizations are, of course, deeply engaged in the controversy and working toward the eradication of the faux-therapeutic practice.

Outlawing conversion therapy is a big win for kids who might otherwise be exposed to it, but what about gay and trans kids who are regularly subjected to lower-profile practices that discourage or even punish them for their emerging identities? It is difficult to imagine a federal court decision coming along and curtailing homo- or transphobic parenting per se.

The real effects of the conflict between the parenting right and the protection of gay and trans kids are felt in routine decisions by lower courts and administrative agencies and even in parenting practices in which law appears not to tread. If a parenting approach rises to a level that would be considered child abuse or neglect, then the child welfare system could take an interest. Actively discouraging homosexuality or gender nonconformity through ordinary discipline or religious instruction, however, has not been classified as abuse or neglect and is generally permitted. This legal condition has tremendous implications for LGBTQ youth whose parents employ permissible practices to prohibit or condemn the youths' emerging identities.

The significance of this condition may, however, go under-recognized because—unlike bans on conversion therapy—the *absence* of a rule against homo- or transphobic parental discipline or religious instruction is *permissive*. As Duncan Kennedy has written, "We don't think of ground rules of permission as ground rules at all, by contrast with ground rules of prohibition.... [T]he legal order permits as well as prohibits, in the simple-minded sense that it *could* prohibit."[16] When the law permits, it may seem absent, but just like prohibitions, permissions help to establish the range of alternatives available to bargainers.

The presence of law in permitting as well as prohibiting was a key insight of the American legal realists. For Hale, the absence of regulatory prohibitions was mythologized as "free." Political opponents still debate the extent to which the state should intervene in the market for fairness, with laissez-faire enthusiasts arguing for minimal governmental intrusion and reformers advocating greater regulation. But Hale showed that regardless of how many (or how few) regulatory prohibitions were enacted, the market could never be "free."

Law professor Frances E. Olsen, a feminist and devotee of critical legal studies (a "fem-crit"), adapted Hale's analysis of laissez-faire to the family. In her widely cited article "The Family and the Market" and her follow-up piece, "The Myth of State Intervention in the Family," Olsen drew an analogy between laissez-faire and the allegedly private family.[17] Like the market, the family is mythically private in its natural state, or "free" of the state's presence. The state may "intervene" to protect a weaker party—for example, by prohibiting abuse. Olsen illustrated, however, that the family is never really free of the state's presence. To begin with, to know precisely what sphere it is supposed to stay out of, the state must define the contours of the family and insulate the family from outsiders: "Imagine . . . if the state stood idly by while . . . neighbors prepared to take [a] child on their vacation against the wishes of the parents, or if the child decided to go live with his fourth grade teacher. Once the state undertakes to prevent such third-party action, the state must make numerous policy choices, such as what human grouping constitutes a family and what happens if parents disagree."[18]

Furthermore, the concept of "nonintervention" in the family lacks the capacity to determine a logical outcome: "Suppose a good-natured, intelligent sovereign were to ascend to the throne with a commitment to end state intervention in the family. . . . Is she intervening if she makes divorces difficult, or intervening if she makes them easy? Does it constitute intervention or nonintervention to grant divorce at all? If a child runs away from her parents to go live with her aunt, would nonintervention require the sovereign to grant or to deny the parents' request for legal assistance to reclaim their child?"[19] Olsen concludes, "Because the state is deeply implicated in the formation and functioning of families, it is nonsense to talk about whether the state does or does not intervene in the family. Neither 'intervention' nor 'nonintervention' is an accurate description of any particular set of policies, and the terms obscure rather than clarify the policy choices that society makes."[20]

Permissions appear at first blush to be noninterventionist, or pre-regulatory, but one way to reveal their regulatory nature is to examine them in conjunction with accompanying prohibitions. In the 1980s, when Olsen wrote her seminal articles, for example, opponents of domestic violence reforms "argue[d] that the state should not interfere to prevent wife abuse."[21] The family, they argued, should remain private, and the state should maintain a noninterventionist stance. But what about wives who kill their battering husbands? Should they be subject to criminal prosecution?[22] Would an unswervingly noninterventionist approach permit both the husband's beating of his wife *and* the wife's killing of her husband? If the state permits the former but criminalizes the latter, is the first instance fairly understood as nonintervention? When these possibilities are considered together, it becomes clear that a policy of "nonintervention" in spousal abuse presses wives into a tight range of alternatives while putting the power of the state behind husbands. Similarly, if the law tolerates homo- and transphobic parenting but treats running away and chronic disobedience as an offense,[23] the law can hardly be said not to be intervening. It is putting the power of the state behind the parents.

One of the reforms to domestic violence law instituted in many U.S. jurisdictions since the time of Olsen's writing is *mandatory arrest*—that is, police must make an arrest on every domestic violence call.[24] One consequence of this policy has been increased arrests of trans youth who are in violent conflict with their parents. In the typical scenario, a neighbor hears fighting and calls the police. When the police arrive on the scene, uncertain who the aggressor is, they arrest the person who looks fishy: the awkward young person in the midst of a gender transition.[25] This effectively puts the power of the police behind the parents, with potentially severe consequences for transgender youth, including a criminal record and all of its ramifications (discussed later).

Another way to express Olsen's critique of "nonintervention" is that the state cannot be "neutral" toward the family: "For example, if a court were to allow a child to recover in tort damages from her parents for confining her to her room as punishment, most people would consider this a serious state intrusion in the family, even though the parents' act would have been false imprisonment had it been committed by a third party. The notion of noninterference in the family depends upon some shared conception of proper family roles, and 'neutrality' can be understood only with reference to such roles."[26] In this scenario, the parent is *permitted* to confine the child to her room—that is, no legal cause of action arises. Put in the language of Hale, the child has no "right" against being sent to her room, and the parents have no corresponding "duty" to abstain from sending her there.

Parents are not, of course, free to do anything at all in the name of discipline; they may not, for example, confine a child to her room for days without food or water. That would be deemed abusive or neglectful and would be prohibited. Once these situations are viewed in juxtaposition, the state's presence comes into relief: It is the entity responsible for drawing the line between ordinary discipline and abuse, permitting conduct it deems to belong in the former category.

It is obvious that the state "intervenes" in the parent-child relationship when it statutorily prohibits parents from subjecting their children to conversion therapy, but it also "intervenes" when it merely permits parents to threaten their children with eternal damnation or to punish them for exhibiting homosexual desire or for dressing in attire thought to be inconsistent with their assigned birth sex. Once prohibition and permission are understood as a set, the state's role in determining which homo- or transphobic parenting behaviors are acceptable comes into view. The law's acquiescence to some parenting practices and not others forms the background of the parent-child relationship and the range of options available to each—in other words, their respective bargaining positions.

Bargaining

Bargaining does not refer strictly to financial matters. Family members constantly bargain with one another over a vast array of issues. Can Johnny experiment with mascara? Can Sally be seen in public holding hands with her girlfriend? Law is one factor in the bargaining environment in which parents and kids understand their power to determine the answers to these questions. The more parenting behaviors the law permits, the greater the bargaining endowment parents enjoy.

In 1979, a decade after California first adopted a no-fault divorce regime and as the no-fault model swept through the rest of the nation, two law professors, Robert H. Mnookin and Lewis Kornhauser, published "Bargaining in the Shadow of the Law," an article that became essential reading in family law and beyond. They observed what few would guess from watching television legal dramas but lawyers know very well: Most lawsuits are not resolved in courtrooms. Most divorces, for example, are settled over a conference table and finalized with a judicial stamp of approval that is often all but pro forma. Mnookin and Kornhauser offered a theory about what influences the bargains struck at those tables: settling property distribution, child custody and visitation, alimony, and child support.[27]

To understand Mnookin and Kornhauser's argument, it helps to take a visual cue from the title. Imagine a conference room in a private law office, far from any courthouse. Even there, as the parties negotiate the terms of their divorce, the law casts its shadow. As the parties negotiate, the thought of what *could* happen if they do not come to a resolution outside the courtroom looms: "The outcome that the law will impose if no agreement is reached gives each parent certain bargaining chips—an endowment of sorts."[28]

To illustrate these endowments, Mnookin and Kornhauser discuss custody rules. An old rule known as the "tender years doctrine" provided that in the case of young children, courts were to favor mothers over fathers as sole physical custodians. In cases in which both mother and father wished for a share of the custodial privilege, the mother began with a bargaining advantage: If the couple could not reach an agreement and resorted to judicial resolution, the mother could usually be confident that she would prevail regarding custody.

In negotiations, therefore, the mother did not have to agree to share custody. She might, however, decide to give up all or some custody if she got something in return. If the husband agreed to grant her more property than a court would be likely to order, for example, she would have an incentive to grant him more time with the children. The tender years doctrine, therefore, endowed the mother with a chip that she could use at the bargaining table. What a court *would have done* was important even in those cases that barely involved a court. The parties "bargained in the shadow" of their expectations of how the law would be applied if they wound up before a judge.

Mnookin and Kornhauser wrote their article in the 1970s, by which time the tender years doctrine was already largely outdated. The ostensibly gender-neutral "primary caretaker" presumption, however, continued to favor mothers over fathers in the majority of custody determinations for the next couple of decades. The current trend is toward *shared* custody. From a human services perspective, there are psychological advantages in most cases to children maintaining strong ties with both parents after a divorce. From the perspective of a legal realist, however, another consequence ought to be considered. The trend in favor of shared custody withdraws a key bargaining chip from mothers, who are vulnerable to losing out not only on the custody side, but also on the property or support side of a negotiated settlement because they have less with which to bargain.

What would improve the bargaining position of LGBTQ youth in relation to their parents? Many face a choice among self-abnegation, enduring whatever discipline their parents decide to mete out, running away, or suicide. To help, we would need to expand the array of alternatives available to them. One possibility is a more aggressive child welfare system.

Enforcement

If the child welfare system were to protect LGBTQ kids with greater zeal, responding to a wider array of homo- and transphobic parenting practices, some parents would curb their injurious behavior. Some would not, resulting in more removal of children. Would this improve the lot of LGBTQ kids? Could the child welfare system actually provide a viable alternative for children of homo- or transphobic parents?

The major advocacy organizations see LGBT fostering and adoption as a matter of equal rights not only for the LGBT adults who wish to adopt but also for LGBTQ kids who would benefit from having LGBT parents as particularly empathetic role models. Domestically, no jurisdiction maintains a total ban on gay adoption any longer. The parenting rights of transgender people are less settled. LGBT advocacy organizations have litigated a number of cases seeking to eradicate the use of sexual orientation and gender identity as formal obstacles to adoption. Cultural conservative adversaries of LGBT adoption, meanwhile, have attempted to exempt religious social service organizations from having to place children with same-sex couples, even where state law protects those couples from discrimination. The exemptions have been dubbed *conscience clauses* by their proponents. This clash between LGBT equality and religious freedom is a classic conflict of rights (see chapter 1).

A route from a punitive homo- or transphobic home into the arms of LGBT caretakers would represent an alternative for youth, as would an assuredly LGBT-positive environment provided by straight foster or adoptive parents. Youth in the foster care system do not, however, exert control over their placement. They risk winding up in the homes of foster or adoptive parents whose attitudes are more homo- or transphobic than those of their original parents. To alleviate that risk would require grappling with another policy problem: whether homophobia and transphobia ought to constitute a bar to foster and adoptive parenting.

Foster parents and petitioners for adoption do not benefit from the constitutional pedigree of biological parenting and therefore do not enjoy parental rights.[29] Fostering and adoption are public acts; petitioners entering those processes voluntarily submit themselves to state investigation and oversight.[30] States typically require foster parents or people who seek to adopt through the child welfare system to express a willingness to cultivate a positive racial identity in the child, just as international adoption agencies often seek affirmation of an applicant parent's willingness to create positive encounters for a foreign-born adopted child with the culture of his or her national heritage. It is less common, however, to find a rule like the one in Massachusetts that provides that to qualify for licensure as a foster/pre-adoptive parent, a person "must demonstrate ... the ability ... to promote the physical, mental, and emotional well-being of a child placed in his or her care, including supporting and respecting a child's sexual orientation or gender identity."[31]

This rule is obviously designed to protect LGBTQ foster youth from homo- or transphobic prospective foster or adoptive parents. The degree of *enforcement* that one can expect of such regulatory protections, however, will prove as significant as the regulation itself. The legal realist and Supreme Court Justice Oliver Wendell Holmes Jr. famously wrote that the study of law is about learning to make predictions: "The prophecies of what the courts will do in fact, and nothing more pretentious, are what I mean by the law."[32] Courts and other legal authorities do not always do what they say they will do. If social service officials and juvenile courts do not regularly mandate that would-be parents "demonstrate" their "ability" to support a gay or trans identity, the regulation will offer youth little protection. A report released in 2015 by the Urban Institute suggests that, while the child welfare agency in New York City maintains policies designed to protect LGBTQ youth ("to respect preferred pronouns, provide gender-appropriate placement and clothing, and maintain confidentiality of youths' gender identity and sexual orientation"), youth reported a lack of conformity with such policies, including placement in hostile foster homes.[33]

Law professor Marc Galanter refers to the phenomenon of rule changes made at a high level actually effectuating change at the "field level" as *penetration*.[34] Despite the formal hierarchy, rule changes made in the higher echelons do not always make an impact on ground-level practice. Galanter raises the issue of penetration as part of an effort to distinguish the capacities of two different kinds of litigants: "repeat players" and "one-shotters." Repeat players are regular users of forums for resolving legal disputes; examples include prosecutors and insurance companies. One-shotters are more likely to be ordinary individuals facing a one-time legal problem. Numerous advantages accrue to the repeat players, from easy access to legal counsel to the ability to play a "long game" that is attentive to the evolution of rules. One-shotters are unlikely to be invested in what happens after the outcome of their individual cases. To a repeat player, however, any single case may be of less importance than a rule change that, over the course of many cases, could provide an advantage. Repeat players may settle or not depending on their long-term interests. Moreover, repeat players are better positioned to predict which rule changes are valuable to them (or, alternatively, pose a risk to their interests) due to the likelihood that a rule change will *penetrate*—that is, actually make a difference in practice.

Social service professionals may easily undermine a regulation that governs them in theory by inconsistently ascertaining at the case level that prospective foster or adoptive parents are indeed prepared to support non-normative sexual and gender identities. If juvenile courts that oversee foster care cases and finalize adoptions do not hold social service agencies accountable, they are in effect reversing a rule over which they have no formal authority.

Even if social workers reliably enforce the regulation in cases of adolescents, an infant or young child placed in a foster or adoptive home before sexual orientation or gender identity becomes perceptible may run into trouble down the road if the parents were not vetted. Preventing those less foreseeable clashes would require a high level of enforcement: The child welfare agency would have to vet *all* prospective foster and adoptive parents for their attitudes on sexual orientation and gender variance, as they already do for financial and emotional security and—in Massachusetts—for attitudes regarding corporal punishment. The Massachusetts regulation requiring foster and adoptive parents to be willing and able to affirm a child's sexual orientation or gender identity rises and falls on the willingness of every social worker in the commonwealth to actually vet *all* prospective parents and of every juvenile court to insist on it when it reviews the agency's work.

Consistent enforcement, however, may run counter to the interests of the agency, which is hardly looking for obstacles to placement. In fact, federal law creates incentives for adoption with rewards to states. Adoptions of children older than nine result in higher rewards.[35] The social service agency, a "repeat player" in Galanter's schema, is in a good position to know the extent of juvenile courts' insistence on compliance with the regulation. The youth, of course, are not likely to have the wherewithal even to be aware of the regulation, much less to ensure its enforcement, and there is no reason to think that their lawyers will reliably attend to the issue, particularly when it comes to preadolescent clients.

Moreover, even if there were universal vetting for the "demonstrate[d] . . . ability" to support a non-normative sexual or gender identity, that could easily give rise to a legal challenge after a few conservative religious couples were deemed ineligible to become foster or adoptive parents. A coexisting regulation in Massachusetts prohibits the denial of eligibility to foster or adopt based on religion,[36] setting up a conflict within the regulatory scheme. Even without this regulation one could imagine a maximally enforced exclusion against homo- and transphobic applicants facing a challenge under the Free Exercise Clause of the First Amendment. The devotion to fostering and adoption prevalent among evangelical Christians makes such a clash especially plausible.

Nonenforcement of a rule protecting LGBTQ youth and the expectations that nonenforcement engenders are effectively an intervention on behalf of would-be parents. The right to foster or adopt a child while maintaining one's homo- or transphobic attitudes requires neither a copy of the rule nor a moral compass; rather, it requires the capacity to anticipate official response to one's actions. As Holmes urged, to acquire "a businesslike understanding of" the law, one should approach it "as a bad man, who cares only for the material consequences which . . . [studying the law] enables him to predict, not as a good one, who finds his reasons for conduct . . . in the vaguer sanctions of conscience."[37] If prospective parents who hold an antigay/anti-trans bias are routinely permitted to foster and adopt notwithstanding the apparent conflict between their attitudes and regulatory policy as written, such would-be parents would have all of the information they need to proceed as they wish. Navigating the law is an exercise in "avoid[ing] an encounter with the public force"[38]—not an exercise in compliance with the law's purpose or letter. The expectation of enforcement is crucial to a law's efficacy.

The leeway that the law invisibly grants to prospective foster and adoptive parents to express and enforce their disapproval of homosexuality or gender nonconformity is part of the background against which *original* parents and their children are situated in the struggle over youths' sexual and gender identity. In the absence of any cause for reassurance that the child welfare system offers a better alternative for kids suffering at the hands of homo- or transphobic original parents, kids have one less alternative to which they might turn.

Predictably, the homo- and transphobia left undisturbed by constitutional and child welfare norms result in elevated rates of running away by LGBTQ youth. Some youth are forced out, as well. Religious parents, unsurprisingly, are more likely than nonreligious parents to kick their gay or trans kids out of the house.[39] Even as the country witnesses increasing visibility and tolerance for homosexuality, the average age of "coming out" has dropped, and the number of youth being kicked out by their parents has increased.[40] The result is continuing extreme overrepresentation of LGBTQ youth in the population of homeless minors—as high as 40 percent.[41] According to a report from 2013 co-written by more than a dozen advocacy organizations, 44 percent of LGBT-identified homeless youth identify as black and 26 percent as Latino.[42] These young people predict that being at home with their original families or taking their chances with the child welfare system are worse than life on the streets.

Bargaining in the Street

Once LGBTQ youth are living on the street as runaways or "throwaways," they face a fresh array of conditions. Like Hale's non-owner, they must eat; they also must sleep.

WHERE TO SLEEP?

Many homeless youth sleep outside, literally under bridges, in parks, on subway trains, on benches, on heat grates, and in doorways. In a growing number of locales, however, sleeping in public places, including on public transportation, is illegal and could subject a person to arrest. The sit-lie ordinance in San Francisco is part of that trend (see the introduction). Parks often simply close—at dusk or at an appointed hour—rendering nighttime presence an offense, whether sleeping or waking.[43] These kinds of laws have collectively earned the moniker "criminalization of homelessness," because the barest act of survival in public space, resting, subjects a person to criminal sanction.

For some youth, arrest may come as a relief in that it brings with it free meals and a cot, but it is not all perks. In many states, for example, juveniles are routinely shackled.[44] Moreover, depending on the reason that a police officer takes a minor into custody, the first preference is typically to release the child to his or her parents or foster parents.[45] Youth fleeing abusive homes are not likely to find that placement viable. A young person may also be placed in a jail or juvenile lockup facility. There, a number of specific rules may determine the degree of tolerability, and kids who have been in lockup before or have heard about it from peers will be familiar with the details. For example, Massachusetts recently began assigning juveniles to facilities based on gender identity (rather than assigned birth sex),[46] but that is unusual: Many youth are placed in settings inconsistent with their gender identities. In addition, many jurisdictions mandate strip searches upon admission to a youth detention facility. Obviously, for any young person who has already endured her share of trauma, this can be painful, but for youth grappling with gender transition, it can be especially humiliating. If a young person is moved from one facility to another, she could undergo the search at each entry. For many youth, the streets are preferable.

Youth shelters are available to homeless youth in some places. A decent shelter may provide a young person living on the street with a place to sleep, shower, eat, and obtain counseling or referrals to a range of services, including medical care. Some shelters have earned appalling reputations for discriminatory behavior, religious moralizing, and even abuse of youth. The Ray report discusses youth shelters extensively, singling out for criticism Covenant House in New York City, which is operated by a faith-based organization. Stories of antigay and anti-trans discrimination and harassment at Covenant House were once legion, although its leadership has since met with LGBT advocates in an effort to become more hospitable. The Ray report highlights the good work of Urban Peak in Denver and Ozone House in Ann Arbor, both of which have dedicated themselves to providing positive shelter environments to LGBTQ youth.

Short-term shelters typically rely on federal grant funding, the terms of which are governed by statute and regulation. The Senate defeated S. 262, the Runaway and Homeless Youth and Trafficking Prevention Act.[47] This bipartisan legislation would have reauthorized the Runaway and Homeless Youth Act (RHYA), which expired in 2013.[48] The RHYA funded so-called *basic center programs*, which provide temporary shelter for minors for up to twenty-one days (the period would have been increased to thirty days by the proposed legislation) and emergency assistance such as food, clothing, and access to health care. The same law also dedicated funding to street outreach programs and transitional living programs.[49]

The U.S. Department of Health and Human Services (HHS) administered the RHYA. According to HHS regulations, funding decisions under the statute were based on a number of factors, including "plans for meeting the best interests of the youth involving, when possible, both the youth and the family. These must include contacts with the families. This contact should be made within 24 hours, but must be made no more than 72 hours following the time of the youth's admission into the runaway and homeless youth project. The plans must also include assuring the youth's safe return home or to local government officials or law enforcement officials and indicate efforts to provide appropriate alternative living arrangements."[50] Some youth do not consider returning home a viable alternative and would be unwilling to remain in the shelter long enough to trigger the parental notification requirement. The shelters are designed to be temporary, in any event, and cannot serve as a long-term housing option.

In some places, temporary shelter is available for women fleeing intimate partner violence. Shelters designed for adult women, however, typically do not accept minors who are not with their mothers. Many are also notoriously exclusive when it comes to transwomen, regardless of age.

In New York City, youth who test positive for HIV are eligible for a range of services that are unavailable to HIV-negative people, including substantial housing assistance and free medical care. As a result, there have been reports for years of homeless people "bug chasing"—that is, intentionally seeking out infection—to become eligible for a subsidized apartment.[51]

What about entering into an ordinary apartment lease? Setting aside for the moment the question of how to procure money for rent, young people face a legal hurdle in trying to enter a lease or any other contract. Minors are not entirely lacking in contractual capacity, but they are effectively limited by a common law doctrine called *the power of disaffirmance*. This doctrine permits minors to void their contracts unilaterally for any reason or no reason. The power resides exclusively with the minor; an adult with whom a minor has entered a contract may not void the contract on the grounds that the other party is a minor. In some U.S. jurisdictions, the power stays with the person into adulthood with regard to any contracts entered into while still a minor, and in some jurisdictions even the fact that the minor falsely represented herself as an adult is no bar to her exercise of the power. Why would any landlord in his right mind enter into a lease with a minor—a lease to which the landlord is bound but that the tenant may void?

Some landlords may be willing to rent to a minor without a lease; most low-income tenants do not have the protections of a lease anyway. Tenants with leases are difficult and costly to evict. Landlords must have "cause" (generally a violation of the terms of the lease such as nonpayment of rent). Many therefore prefer to offer what is called a "tenancy at will," meaning that either the landlord or the tenant can terminate the tenancy at any time without a reason. In most jurisdictions, landlords not bound by a lease must still send a proper notice and obtain a court judgment to evict a tenant-at-will, which does take some time. The more knowledgeable about that process a tenant-at-will is, the more empowered he is to delay his eviction, although in most cases he probably cannot prevent it.

Given the constricted range of places to sleep for youth who have run away or been kicked out of their homes, whatever a landlord offers will probably have to do. Other terms of the rental agreement (price, repairs, pets, and so on) will be negotiated under the same bargaining conditions.

Let us return now to the bracketed question of how to pay the rent. How can a minor obtain an income?

IN SEARCH OF A LEGAL INCOME STREAM:
THE FORMAL ECONOMY

Can a minor borrow money to pay for her housing and other necessities? The disaffirmance doctrine affects not only leases but also just about any effort by a minor to obtain an extension of credit. No commercial lender, such as a credit card company or bank, would knowingly permit a minor to take out a line of credit without an adult co-signer because the minor can disaffirm the debt.[52] As a result, a minor would not be able to secure a car loan, or gain use of a credit card to respond to emergencies or to manage a large purchase, such as a refrigerator.

In the adult context, the significance of full contractual autonomy and the capacity to bind oneself to a promise of performance can hardly be overstated in Anglo-American law. It is generally regarded as a right-leaning value, which competes with a left-leaning value of protecting weaker parties from the dangers of bargaining autonomy. For example, should borrowers of subprime mortgages have been more cautious and face foreclosure if they are unable to pay, *or* did more informed and powerful lenders prey on them, entitling them to protection against loss of their homes? Is exorbitant credit card debt the responsibility of careless spenders who have not exercised their contractual autonomy judiciously, *or* is that debt the product of exploitative banks eager to lure people of modest means into such a hole that they never have the chance to diminish their principal balances? The prior framings in each pair are arguments from the right, while the latter echo left-leaning Senator Elizabeth Warren (D-MA).

In the case of minors, however, even rightist legal thinkers agree that denying paternalistic protection against misspent bargaining autonomy is unjustified. The competence of the parties to a contract is an essential ingredient to its legitimacy. The law does not treat a person who has not yet attained the age of maturity as it does a mentally competent adult. *Incompetence* and *infancy*, in the law's charming terminology, undermine the general principle that binds a person to perform his end of bargains to which he agreed.

Is this protective consensus a good one, however, for homeless youth? Limits on youths' capacity to enter contracts are designed to safeguard those who are not mentally equipped to exercise it, but it also erects hurdles to self-support, and some of those hurdles do not disappear even after the young person has reached eighteen. The inability to gradually develop a positive credit history may mean that even a newly minted adult faces obstacles to obtaining a lease or a loan.

Where the power of disaffirmance presents youth with a legal disability, however, emancipation provides an alternative. Emancipation is a status declared by a court after a minor, his parents, or his representative petition for it. The law governing this status varies considerably from state to state, but in general, an emancipated minor gains many of the rights and responsibilities of adulthood. Not every privilege of adulthood comes with emancipation—not, for example, the right to drink alcohol or the right to vote. Still, the usual litany of acquired rights includes full contractual capacity and the right to manage one's assets, along with the right to sue (and be sued) and the right to make one's own medical decisions. While standards governing emancipation are not uniform (e.g., the age at which a minor is eligible varies from state to state), judges are generally less than freewheeling in doling out emancipation declarations—and with good reason. Emancipation means permanently giving up the right to be taken back in or supported by one's parents. Moreover, once one is vested with contractual autonomy, the power of disaffirmance evaporates forever. The minor must be prepared to face fully the consequences of his bargains.

The responsibilities of contractual autonomy are great and have serious and long-lasting consequences that sometimes even fully competent adults find themselves unable to manage. The risk is compounded for LGBTQ kids, who are overrepresented not only among the homeless but also in the foster care system.[53] A stunningly high number of youth who come through that system are victims of identity theft, probably because their names and Social Security numbers have been in the hands of so many people.[54] Thieves open credit card and utility accounts in the names of foster kids and then leave the accounts delinquent so that by the time the youth reach the age of majority, their credit histories are already in ruins. While technically they should be able to disaffirm debts incurred before age eighteen, repairing a credit history is costly and time-consuming and may be a more onerous bureaucratic task than most young people emerging from foster care are prepared to navigate. If they were fully responsible for their debts even as minors, the challenge of repairing that history would be made even more daunting.

Enabling young people to accrue debt, of course, is not our main objective; we are looking for access to any legal means of self-support. By what methods could a minor obtain an income stream?

Child support law requires parents to support their children even when those children are not in their physical custody. This includes circumstances such as divorce, where physical custody may be divided between parents or rest entirely with one parent. A residential parent or guardian may receive support on the child's behalf. If the family receives public assistance, the state reimburses itself for those expenditures from child support collected. Child support law also requires parents of children in the foster care system to pay support into state coffers to reimburse the state for the support of the child. (Foster parents receive a small allowance from the state for providing care.) Dependent minors, however, are not themselves eligible payees—that is, they may not receive child support on their own behalf even if they live apart from their parents or guardians.[55] That rule cuts off one avenue to youths' self-support.

What other routes are there to accessing a stream of income? Could a homeless gay or trans young person do what Hale's non-owner does: work at "disagreeable toil" to pay for her necessities? The law erects a number of obstacles.

For starters, youth who are not living with their parents may not have documentation that establishes who or how old they are. Employers need to see ID to comply with Social Security and other requirements, so the lack of ID impedes access to wage work. Moreover, as law professor Dean Spade has described, for transgender people of any age, identification that consistently reflects one's name and gender may be difficult to obtain. Different ID-issuing agencies (e.g., motor vehicle registries, the State Department, the Social Security Administration) vary widely in their policies regarding gender reclassification so that the same person may carry a driver's license identifying a male and a passport identifying a female or may present a driver's license identifying him as male at the time of hire, only to have the Social Security Administration send a letter to the employer indicating that the gender in the hiring paperwork does not match the gender associated with the person's Social Security number.[56] This creates real problems (ranging from outing and discrimination to violence) not only in obtaining employment but also in applying for benefits. Minors, meanwhile, may have no identification at all, making job prospects even dimmer. Some employers run credit checks to assess the character of job applicants, which puts former foster youth who have been subjected to identity theft at a disadvantage even into adulthood. (In Massachusetts, a bill was proposed in 2016 that would have made that practice illegal, but the legislature did not act on it.)[57]

Beyond the ID problem, the law restricts minors' ability to support themselves through wage work in a number of ways. An exception to federal minimum wage requirements applies to workers younger than twenty during their first ninety days of employment; employers need only pay them an hourly wage of $4.25.[58] Proponents urge that this "opportunity wage" creates incentives to hire young people, but it also seems to be premised on the assumption that the pay is not for self-support.

Federal law also generally prohibits employing a person younger than fourteen (with a few exceptions, such as babysitting and delivering newspapers).[59] It further imposes limits on the number of hours a person younger than sixteen may work—for example, a fifteen-year-old may work no more than eighteen hours per week while school is in session (even if she is not attending school because she lives on the street).[60] Exemptions to some of these rules apply where minors work for their parents, but that will not help our constituency. Federal law also imposes prohibitions on employing minors in jobs that involve driving and jobs performed in hazardous conditions.[61] State laws vary in the extent to which they prohibit people younger than twenty-one to serve alcohol, with some permitting it in restaurants but not bars and others prohibiting it altogether.

The legal obstacles to wage work in the formal economy for minors and young adults are substantial. A number of these barriers to work were erected with child welfare in mind. Child labor and compulsory schooling reforms were advanced during the Industrial Revolution in part by children's advocates. Few among us would wish to return to the days before these reforms. Still, one of the *effects* of these reforms has been to eliminate options that some of the most vulnerable people in the country have for self-support. A legal realist analysis of child labor law would steer our attention toward those effects.

This was a key point in Karl Llewellyn's classic article "A Realistic Jurisprudence—The Next Step" (1930).[62] Llewellyn picked up on Holmes's admonition regarding prediction and tried to draw attention away from the "words on the statute books" or even their underlying purposes, and toward what actual *practices* result—"on the level of isness and not of oughtness."[63] A contract, for example, is thought to give each party a right to the other's performance. One really "ought" to perform one's voluntarily undertaken contractual duties: "It is a heresy when [the British jurist Sir Edward] Coke or Holmes speaks of a man having liberty under the law to perform his contract, or pay damages, at his option."[64] In reality, if a party to a contract would rather pay damages than perform his obligation, nothing stops him from electing to breach the contract and pay the damages instead.

> It would likewise be a heresy to argue that . . . the right could rather more accurately be phrased somewhat as follows: if the other party does not perform as agreed, you can sue, and *if* you have a fair lawyer, and nothing goes wrong with the witnesses or the jury, *and* you give up four or five days of time and some ten to thirty percent of the proceeds, and wait two to twenty months, you will *probably* get a judgment for a sum considerably less than what the performance would have been worth—which, if the other party is solvent and has not secreted his assets, you can in further due course collect with six percent interest for delay.[65]

By shifting from *ought* to *is*, we can see that while the existence of a contract *should* enjoin the parties to perform their promises, the law in effect gives them the option to perform or be liable for damages. No matter how ironclad a contract may be, the option *not* to perform one's obligation is always available. What the contract really does is *create alternatives* for an obligated party.

"The question," Llewellyn urged, "is how, and how much, and in what direction, do the accepted rule [the *ought*] and practice [the *is*] diverge? . . . You cannot generalize on this, *without investigation*."[66] Llewellyn was proposing a shift in focus from what the contract says a party *should* do to an investigation of the actual *effects* of a contract, including the choices it establishes, the law governing its enforcement, judicial willingness to enforce, and the resultant conduct of the parties.

Llewellyn's expansion of the Holmesian kernel forms the basis of what is now referred to in legal theory as *consequentialism*, a stance from which one views the desirability of some law (contractual or otherwise): What will be its consequences once we account for the behavior of the relevant decision makers and actors?[67] This is to be distinguished from assessing a law for the good or ill intentions of its proponents or for the law's symbolic value or logical consistency with an overarching set of principles.[68]

The policy makers who gave us child labor restrictions, along with those who promulgated a child support rule establishing a limited range of eligible payees, had largely beneficent purposes in mind. These laws serve the interests of the vast majority of children—those who reside at home with a parent or guardian, free of abuse and adequately supported until they develop the skills necessary to live independently.

Still, the consequences of these well-intended laws radically restrict the ability of homeless youth to support themselves. Framed as an *ought*, this should inure to the objective of parents maintaining their children at home until they develop into self-sufficient adults, but with our population, that is not the *is*. Instead, the laws conditioning parenting practices combined with the laws conditioning youth self-support structure survival alternatives for youth. The real consequence of these restrictions on youth is to push them into the informal, or underground, economy.

IN SEARCH OF AN INCOME STREAM CONTINUED:
THE INFORMAL ECONOMY

What does one do if one cannot find wage work? As Duncan Kennedy explained, "In our system, there are well-established alternatives to wage labor, and each has a legal structure that affects how available and desirable it is."[69] For example, working in the "gig economy"—that is, engaging in a string of short-term contracts or freelance jobs, often via an Internet platform such as TaskRabbit or Uber—is one alternative to wage work. Other "examples include welfare; criminal activity; independent petty commerce, from the corner store to the street vendor; the status of franchisee; independent professional activity, from the therapist to the real estate broker working on commission, to the 'consultant'; and providing household services in a marriage, or equivalent form, in exchange for support."[70] Most of these options are unrealistic for homeless young people for legal reasons (e.g., limits on contractual capacity to secure loans and insurance) and for reasons of education and training. Many homeless LGBTQ young people therefore turn to the informal economy.

Some, for example, engage in under-the-table but otherwise noncriminal enterprises, such as braiding hair, babysitting, or sewing.[71] Others panhandle. Panhandling, like other incidents of homelessness, is a criminal or ticketing offense in many locales. While absolute bans run into First Amendment obstacles, aggressive panhandling or panhandling in certain places (such as within a perimeter around ATMs or on traffic medians) is increasingly prohibited. To circumvent the free speech issue, some localities have attacked panhandling by forbidding passersby from giving anything to panhandlers rather than prohibiting the panhandling request itself.

Finally, some homeless youth engage in criminal activity, including drug dealing, robbing people, or shoplifting, thereby subjecting themselves to the possibility of arrest. And a high percentage of LGBTQ homeless minors and young adults, as has now been compendiously documented, trade sex for what they need to survive.[72] African American and Latino/a youths are vastly overrepresented within this population.[73]

According to one study, between a quarter and half of homeless youth engage in sex work during their period of homelessness.[74] LGBT—especially T—youth are statistically more likely than straight kids to sell sex, but straight kids (including boys) do it, too. Some hustle or trick in swift and transient encounters, while others exchange sex for food and a warm place to sleep in the context of a longer-term, sometimes affectionate, relationship. Legal rules associated with sexual exchange form a complex background against which youth bargain with their customers to meet their basic needs. The array of rules, the degree to which they are enforced, and the extent of predictability they afford all contribute to structuring the bargaining environment.

As discussed in chapter 3, prostitution-free zones can force sex workers (of any age) to more remote (and therefore more dangerous) areas of a city, and the use of condoms as evidence of prostitution can create disincentives for sex workers to carry a supply. In Canada it was illegal before 2014 to solicit, which put street sex workers at risk of arrest as they hung in car windows, negotiating terms and assessing their safety with prospective customers. By criminalizing solicitation, Canada effectively rushed street sex workers into cars, disabling a key self-protection mechanism.[75] It is no longer criminal to negotiate the *sale* of sex, but its *purchase* remains illegal. This strategy takes its cue from the "Swedish Model," according to which customers are treated as criminals, but sex workers are understood to be victims of exploitation. This approach offers lessons about the construction of a bargaining relationship in which sex workers seek both to maximize their income and protect themselves from violence. Sex workers living under a regime that criminalizes their customer base report that it pushes the phenomenon underground and impedes their safety.[76] In the United States, the FBI's decision to raid online escort services such as Rentboy.com impaired the bargaining position of some sex workers. When it was active, the website enabled a subset of male sex workers to raise their rates and afforded them the opportunity to make deliberate assessments about their safety.[77] The channeling of law enforcement resources against such web platforms probably increases the risk of violence against sex workers by pushing them in the direction of street hustling.

As Brendan Connor has explained, youth in the U.S. sex trade risk becoming caught in the criminal justice system, but about half of the states have enacted so-called Safe Harbor provisions that divert minors who have been arrested for prostitution from delinquency proceedings to state supervision as child welfare cases.[78] The concept underlying these new laws is that youth should be treated as victims of exploitation rather than as criminals. That sounds well intended, but many of the youth subjected to this diversionary approach may not be entirely sanguine about its consequences. In New York, for example, the penalty for prostitution is up to ninety days in jail, while a minor under the supervision of the child welfare system may be detained in an appropriate facility until he reaches eighteen, which could be much longer than the criminal penalty would have been.[79]

When youth sex workers bargain with customers, law is one of the factors that structures the alternatives available to them, but an array of additional conditions—ranging from the weather to the availability of comprehensive medical care—also factor in. Homeless youth need money, food, and a place to sleep. Some may be addicted to drugs, which imposes an additional physical and financial burden. Those youth who are making a gender transition may require funds to pay for associated expenses, including hormones or silicone (either of which can be dangerous if purchased on the street). Some may be saving for a surgical intervention. Just how desperate any one young person is will affect the price she is willing to accept for sex, the particular sexual services she is willing to perform, the use of condoms, and where she is willing to go (cars? homes?) with a customer.

Many youth engaged in the sex trade, however, report the benefits of peer networks and the development of a "street sense" that enable them to minimize dangers. These resources are endowments of sorts in that they empower youth as they negotiate price, location, and so on. Moreover, buyers of sex face a limited range of choices that may include forgoing sex, investing in unwanted interpersonal relations to obtain sex for free, paying more for sex using a high-end escort service, or traveling farther away from home or work to obtain sex. Customers also face the risk of legal sanction, public humiliation, and being left by a spouse or lover if they are found out. Legal and other conditions "coerce" the buyer as well as the seller of sex, although this is not to assert that their bargaining power is equal.

Youth on the street, whether or not they engage in the sex trade, must routinely interact with the police, and that relationship, too, is one of bargaining that is structured in part by law. How deferentially must the youth behave toward the police? How great is the pressure to grant the police sexual favors or to act as informants?

As Joey L. Mogul, Andrea J. Ritchie, and Kay Whitlock have written, a high degree of "discretionary policing" characterizes the enforcement of "quality of life offenses including 'lewd conduct,' 'public indecency,' and 'loitering with the intent to solicit.'"[80] Police campaigns against homeless young people who spend time in public spaces are often designed to accommodate the needs of gentrification and respond to complaints from more established members of an urban community.[81] The discretion vested in police to enforce laws against loitering, public urination, and "obscenity," as well as against incidents of homelessness such as sleeping on sidewalks, endows the police with immense power. If a rigorous judicial check were in place, the youth would be in a stronger position not only to resist police abuse but also to rein in the latitude of police discretion. But to the extent that police operate with little sense that their discretion to enforce minor offenses will be subject to any accountability (e.g., for profiling or harassment), youth are radically disempowered in their relations with police.

Enhancing that disparity in bargaining power even more are the ramifications of having a criminal record. For starters, a criminal record can interfere with future employment prospects, introducing another steep obstacle to success in the formal economy for many LGBTQ people of any age. While states often limit information about criminal records that is available to employers (e.g., blocking information about juvenile offenses or arrests that did not result in convictions), agencies that maintain criminal records sometimes send unauthorized recipients too much information or incorrect information. Moreover, criminal record sheets may be difficult for a person who does not work in the field of criminal justice to read and understand, and a prospective employer can mistakenly read an arrest as a conviction. "Banning the box" would eliminate inquiries about an applicant's criminal record on job applications, and the effort to bring about that reform has had some limited success. In November 2015, President Obama directed federal agencies to eliminate the box from job applications, and a handful of states have done the same for public and private employers.

Criminal records can also interfere with access to public housing and certain public assistance benefits, and the problem of misreading exists in this context, too.[82] Moreover, judges are sometimes reluctant to a grant a name change to someone pursuing a gender transition if that person is saddled with a criminal record. Possible consequences for immigration include denial of a green card and even deportation.

This snowball effect of arrest slants powerfully against those who are vulnerable to even minor criminal charges. Police discretion along with the subsistence needs of homeless youth, compounded by the severe consequences of a criminal record, radically weight the bargaining relationship in favor of the police. This may affect everything from how polite the youth must be in the face of harassing treatment to having to perform sexual favors to avoid arrest. The heightened vulnerability of people of color to arrest is widely recognized. The elevated police attention to lesbians is less well known but has been documented.[83] High rates of incarceration among transgender people, as well as the personal testimony of individual transwomen, especially of color, attest to extreme over-policing of that population.

Changing the Landscape

Homeless LGBTQ youth are ensnared in a web of conditions that create a very constricted range of legal and extralegal options for survival. Some of these rules affect adults and straight youth, as well, while some allocate effects more often or more severely to youth living on the margins of sexuality or gender and to youth of color. To see these legal conditions requires a cognitive shift: Rather than understanding LGBTQ youth as an identity group in need of equal rights, we have to envision them as vulnerable subpopulations navigating a multitude of legal and nonlegal conditions. They may contend with parents, foster parents, landlords, sex purchasers, police, and others, all of whom are endowed with bargaining strengths and weaknesses. Law does a lot of the work of constructing those bargaining relationships and therefore is at least partially responsible for the distribution of income, safety, housing, and nutrition. Statutes, regulations, common law doctrines, and exercises of discretion together constitute a complex landscape against which LGBTQ youth fight to survive.

Broad latitude for parents, coupled with the lack of any guarantee that the child welfare system offers a better alternative, results in high rates of homelessness among LGBTQ youth. The life on the street that awaits these young people after running away or being kicked out is an experience of hunger and violence. What should law reformers who are concerned about these kids do?

We should engage not only prohibitions on homo- and transphobic parenting (such as the spreading prohibition against subjecting youth to conversion therapy) but also those untold permissions that empower parents in the struggle over their children's sexual and gender identity. We should reconsider rules and practices that deny LGBTQ youth any recourse in the face of ordinary discipline.

More parents might think twice about forcing their children to live outside the home if we were to modify the child support payee rule so that minors could receive their own support directly. This would put a powerful enforcement apparatus—including wage garnishment—at the disposal of a young person.[84] For those youth who found themselves on the street despite the disincentive provided to parents by the expanded rule, the change would provide a source of income.

On the street, neither full contractual autonomy nor the protections of legal infancy are ideal for young people trying to gain access to apartments or credit. Getting rid of the power of disaffirmance would have benefits but also come with real risks. It would enable accrual of a positive rental or credit history, which in turn would further enhance access to housing and credit. However, it would also leave youth vulnerable to all of the consequences of ill-advised bargains. While the responsibilities of adulthood and the disabilities of infancy present difficulties, intermediate or partial adjustments to the status of minors could make a real impact. An exception to the power of disaffirmance for apartment leases, not unlike those that apply in the context of educational loans, for example, would help some young people. Minors could be held fully liable for lines of credit capped at a low sum to prevent debt spirals. It seems entirely possible to require free and accelerated credit history repair for young adults. We should push for exceptions to existing law governing minors' access to credit and to wage labor so that youth can pay for necessities without being forced into the underground economy.

The status of emancipation could be reformed to grant some contractual rights while protecting against some of the losses. In the arena of medical decision-making, the "mature minor doctrine" enables minors who can establish their maturity to acquire some control over medical treatment without input from their parents or guardians. A similar doctrine could be instituted for limited financial purposes. Emancipation could also be reformed so that an emancipated minor does not instantly lose the right to child support.

Youth shelters should not only be fully funded but should be relieved of the uniform obligation to notify parents of a child's whereabouts when the child is opposed. Time periods for shelter stays could be extended and a modest amount of rent could be charged after a certain length of time to allow minors to develop a rental history.

If sex work were decriminalized, including on web platforms, sex workers (minors and adults) could engage in that enterprise more safely. Decriminalization of homelessness (including panhandling, sitting down on sidewalks, sleeping on park benches, and so on) and "ban the box" should be considered LGBTQ issues. Highly discretionary petty offenses such as loitering and lewdness should be amended to reduce police discretion.

These "rule ticks," as Janet Halley dubs them, may seem like small potatoes compared with the big news of constitutional protection for same-sex marriage,[85] but they would intervene in the very immediate conditions facing LGBTQ young people as they negotiate with parents, landlords, the police, and so on. Once we turn our attention to these legal conditions and their distributive effects, we can develop more and more reformist ideas that would shift the bargaining weight in LGBTQ young people's favor and secure for some of them an income, a safe place to sleep, and something to eat.

Whatever reforms are implemented will not be without costs; existing law is in place to serve sound policy purposes. The question is the extent to which some cost might be bearable in exchange for an expected benefit—and our best predictions may not pan out or may have effects we did not anticipate. We should be prepared, therefore, to assess and reassess the consequences of any reforms we undertake.

Taking the Method on the Road

Many of the legal conditions discussed in the foregoing sections, such as the laws governing sex work and the extent of police discretion when it comes to enforcing "lewdness" laws, affect LGBT adults as well as youth. LGBTQ youth do, however, face some unique circumstances due to their status as minors (e.g., labor laws, foster care rules). Age is among the most significant intersecting dimensions of identity and experience in terms of understanding the legal conditions that circumscribe the choices of an LGBT subpopulation. Other intersecting dimensions include region of the country and nature of the surrounding community in which a person lives (e.g., urban, rural), race, being HIV-positive or HIV-negative, being coupled or single, having children or no children, immigration status, and disability. Following is a glimpse into some of the conditions that could yield law reform targets.

For urban dwellers, zoning law is a crucial rule regime that affects job oppor-tunities and safety. While working in background rules, Katherine Silbaugh, a law professor and expert on women's uncompensated care work and devaluation in the paid labor market, observed the significance of zoning law to her con-stituency's interests:

> Researchers have argued that women are more likely to choose workplaces closer to home in order to manage dual responsibilities [of family and work]. If this is so, we have workforce participation patterns determined in a gendered fashion according to attributes of land use patterns. The landscape separating work from home places constraints on employment decisions of workers who take greater responsibility for family work. This constraint on job mobility should be expected to negatively influence women's wage equality. When a worker makes a residential decision for her family based on the location of her employer, or an employment deci-sion based on family, a greater portion of family stability is tied to stability in a single job. This should give an employer a bargaining advantage once employment has begun, because her exit options are impaired.... [I]f an entire area is more densely developed [than single-use zoning generally permits], it is possible that a larger array of employment options would be available.... This improves a worker's exit strategy, which in turn im-proves her bargaining position with her current employer.[86]

Zoning is not typically on the front burner for feminist law reform, but Sil-baugh observes how it operates quietly in the background to construct women's bargaining power.

Zoning affects LGBTQ constituencies, as well. Some large cities and resort areas have "gayborhoods"—areas where a concentration of LGBT residents, shops, and culture can be found. Those neighborhoods depend in part for their existence on zoning. In a typical gayborhood, one can find cafés and bou-tiques as well as shops that sell porn or sex toys. In the 1990s, during Rudolph Giuliani's mayoral administration, New York City used its zoning powers to disrupt the clustering of sexually oriented business, imposing limits on their number, size, and placement.[87] The queer theorists Lauren Berlant and Michael Warner observed that Giuliani's amended zoning regime

> aims to restrict any counterpublic sexual culture by regulating its eco-nomic conditions; its effects will reach far beyond the adult businesses

it explicitly controls. The gay bars on Christopher Street draw customers from people who come there because of its sex trade. The street is cruisier because of the sex shops. The boutiques that sell freedom rings and "Don't Panic" T-shirts do more business for the same reasons. Not all of the thousands who migrate or make pilgrimages to Christopher Street use the porn shops, but all benefit from the fact that some do.... The street becomes queer. It develops a dense, publicly accessible sexual culture. It therefore becomes a base for nonporn businesses, like the Oscar Wilde Bookshop. And it becomes a political base from which to pressure politicians with a gay voting bloc.[88]

Geographic dispersion imposed by zoning rules has the capacity to obstruct gay culture and politics. Dispersion also endangers people marked as sexual minorities who, denied a protected enclave, seek out LGBT businesses in less concentrated neighborhoods.[89] Dismantling the gayborhood is also likely to result in job loss for the staff at the shops, bars, and cafés that go out of business as the area's allure diminishes.[90] Zoning, not typically regarded as a major LGBT law reform issue, is a significant factor in jobs and safety.

OUTSIDE THE COASTAL CITIES

Of course, not all LGBTQ people live in gayborhoods. A report issued in 2013 by the Movement Advancement Project (MAP), a pro-LGBT think tank, states that "people of color in same-sex relationships are less likely to live in predominantly 'gay' areas than in places that are home to people of the same ethnicity." [91]

According to a study by the Williams Institute, LGBT African Americans are more highly represented in the South than in other regions of the country.[92] This "regional study" assembles a goldmine of data. It was framed to distinguish the twenty-one mostly northeastern and Pacific states that have employment antidiscrimination laws based on sexual orientation and gender identity from the twenty-nine southern, midwestern, and mountain states that do not and in which more than half of LGBT-identified Americans reside. In 2013, the Williams Institute published another excellent study, this one on poverty in the LGB (not T) community.[93] Read together, the regional study and the poverty study offer tremendous insight (although because they precede *Obergefell* by a couple of years, most states did not yet have married same-sex couples to compare with married heterosexual couples).[94]

The poverty study points to slightly elevated rates of poverty for individual lesbian, gay, and bisexual adults, compared with heterosexuals, and for lesbian couples, compared with gay male and married heterosexual couples. Once race and children are introduced into the picture, the disparities become more pronounced. The poverty rate of African Americans in same-sex couples is higher than that of both married heterosexual couples generally and white people in same-sex couples (by a multiple of six for men and three for women). Children being raised in households with same-sex parents are nearly twice as likely to be poor as those being raised in households with married heterosexual parents, but it seems that disparity is almost entirely located in lesbian households and—to an even more dramatic extent—in African American households headed by same-sex parents. The poverty rate is 37.7 percent for children in black lesbian households (compared with 15.2 percent in black married heterosexual households). Children in households headed by black gay men fare the worst, with a poverty rate of 52.3 percent.

According to the regional study, while higher rates of *parenting* among same-sex couples can be found in the twenty-nine (southern, midwestern, and mountain) states without antidiscrimination protections, the *adoption* rate for those couples is lower. The study speculates that this could be due to stigma pushing gay and lesbian people into heterosexual relations early, resulting in biological children. Perhaps. It could also be related to poorer sex education, less frequent use of reproductive control methods, more flexible sexual orientation identities and practices, or earlier childbearing due to less postsecondary education. African American gay and lesbian individuals, as well as couples, are more likely to live in those states, especially in the South, that lack antidiscrimination protections.

The regional study observes some educational and average income *advantages* to same-sex couples compared with heterosexual couples in every region (only very slightly in the Midwest), but this has to be viewed in concert with the elevated rates of *poverty* and associated challenges such as food insecurity and lack of health insurance. These coexisting facts—of gay advantage and gay disadvantage—suggest a sizeable gap between the gay haves and have-nots. Some of us are living in a world of relative economic privilege even compared with heterosexuals, while others are in dire straits. We have heard quite a bit about the wealth gap in recent years; that gap seems to be exacerbated by the gay factor.

The Williams Institute's studies speculate on the importance of antidiscrimination protection in employment, but, of course, antidiscrimination law applies only in the formal economy. People working under the table, dealing drugs, selling sex, and so on do not glean any benefit from such protections. For those working in the informal economy, the relevant legal conditions are more likely to concern the conduct of law enforcement and police, as well as the enforcement of licensure schemes (e.g., for plumbers or carpenters). The presence of migrants and the nature and enforcement of immigration rules are also bound to affect not only the migrants themselves but also other low-income populations in the area, especially their prospects for formal and informal work, as well as the pay scale in sectors such as childcare and sex work.[95]

The regional and poverty studies emphasize that lack of access to marriage in a given jurisdiction created economic disadvantages for some LGBT people. Recall, however, that some of the advantages—such as asset pooling, sharing employer-based health insurance and pensions, and distribution of property and alimony upon divorce—accrue only to those with some means because they are effectively the privatization of obligation mechanisms; they do not inject new resources into a low-income family. Social welfare will be more important to this constituency, and in that marriage is not all advantages. Depending on the specific circumstances, the combined assets or income of a newly married low-income couple could reduce or eliminate benefits one of them previously received from Temporary Assistance for Needy Families, Supplemental Security Income, Medicaid, SNAP, or the Earned Income Tax Credit. Penalties built into these already stingy regimes create disincentives for low-income people to marry.[96]

We know that people living in "red" regions of the country tend to view sex more moralistically and have less access to high-quality sex education and contraception than those living in "blue" regions. They are also less likely to attend college. These factors, as law professors Naomi Cahn and June Carbone have shown, are linked to higher divorce rates, higher rates of teen pregnancy, and higher rates of poverty.[97] Counterintuitively, lesbian, gay, and bisexual teens appear to experience higher rates than their heterosexual peers of becoming pregnant or causing a pregnancy.[98] According to one study, this may be explained by the fact that LGB adolescents are disproportionately subjected to a number of risk factors that are linked to teen pregnancy, including early "sexual debut," a history of sexual abuse, a high number of sexual partners, homelessness, engagement in survival sex, and failure to use any or effective contraception.[99] The study also proposed that LGB youth may use heterosexual sex and pregnancy as a method of "stigma management" (i.e., to conceal their sexual orientation); they may neglect to pay attention in sex education class because it seems irrelevant to their lives; and they may receive less social support from schools and families, putting them at risk for an array of adolescent difficulties. Whatever the reasons (and they have not been ascertained), various studies of North American youth have suggested a pregnancy rate from two to ten times higher for LGB adolescents than for their heterosexual counterparts.

As teen parents emerge into adulthood, issues of poverty—the Williams Institute studies suggest—are likely to dominate their lives. This is especially the case for black gay and lesbian couples, who are more likely than whites to reside in red states and whose children are the most likely to be impoverished. Antidiscrimination laws might provide some fresh leverage to this subpopulation, but it is difficult to imagine that the accumulated disadvantage that results in all of child poverty's terrible dimensions can be meaningfully blunted by that kind of measure; the red states are already bound by antidiscrimination rules regarding race. Low-income people who have children at a young age and no longer live in the relationships that produced those children will be concerned with traditional poverty issues, such as wages, childcare, public assistance, housing, access to health care, and schools. Neither marriage nor employment nondiscrimination laws have much to offer this subpopulation, especially while marriage imposes penalties on people who access social insurance and public assistance benefits and poor people are pushed into the informal economy.

What specific levers might reformers adjust in an effort to effectuate real change for LGBT people living in red states, who are disproportionately African American, have low incomes, and are raising children? The answers will be less obvious than antidiscrimination; they will be hidden in the background legal rules that construct the range of alternatives available to each localized constituency.

This is a more robust version of intersectionality than the one envisioned by Nancy Fraser in chapter 4, because it is entwined with concrete, local conditions, including the legal background against which a constituency makes choices. It is to that background that we should divert our gaze.

Law's Bad Rep

Some scholars of social movements object to the inflated role lawyers play in social change and note a perception prevalent among grassroots organizers of lawyerly arrogance. Scott Barclay, Mary Bernstein, and Anna-Marie Marshall have published a volume entirely addressed to the relationship of LGBT activism to LGBT legal advocacy.[1] In their introductory chapter, they reflect on both the potential and the limitations of legal strategies for social change, noting that for decades scholars "have ... been critical of the effects of legal strategies on social movements" on the grounds that legal strategies can be "too conservative" and "often ... compromise on goals, ideals and values." Moreover, lawyers' "elite control over legal strategies is often blamed for demobilizing grassroots organizations whose participation in strategic decision-making can be limited by their lack of expertise."[2] Cause lawyers "mold ... movement demands into legally recognizable claims .... [making them] appear to be double agents, subverting the LGBT movement ideologies and values for the sake of winning narrowly defined victories."[3]

Law professor Gwendolyn M. Leachman conducted a study of LGBT activism and advocacy in California from 1985 to 2008 and found that "litigation received the most news coverage of any movement tactic and that the movement organizations that used litigation had a greater likelihood of survival than organizations using other tactics."[4] Interestingly, Leachman found that this not only influenced the direction of reform; it may actually have altered the agendas of the nonlegal organizations:

> Protest groups seized on the mainstream media coverage of the movement to set their own agendas; protest groups organized actions in response to recent headlines (rather than members' primary issues of concern) to attract publicity and participants to the protest's timely and newsworthy

focus. Because the media primarily reported on litigated issues, protest organizations' reactivity to media coverage appears to have redirected those organizations away from their original priorities and toward legal goals. The protest groups' agendas came to be centered not on their members' priorities, but rather the more limited set of issues that could be translated into formal legal claims.[5]

In another volume covering a broader array of social movements,[6] sociologist and lawyer Sandra R. Levitsky outlined additional possible reasons for the perception that lawyers wield outsized influence.[7] She investigated the role of litigation strategies in social movements using LGBT organizations in Chicago as a case study. Levitsky found that while litigation can be just one among many social movement strategies and legal advocacy organizations can be one type among a "heterogen[eous]" array of groups organizing for social change within a single movement, that characterization "occlude[s] important differences in resource capacities" that affect the dynamics among the organizational players.[8] Large organizations such as the American Civil Liberties Union and Lambda tend to be well funded, bureaucratized, and professionalized. They have access to elites and maintain expertise not only in law but also in using the press to advance the interests they deem most important.[9] The influence of smaller, less well-resourced grassroots organizations with a higher rate of turnover suffers by comparison.

Moreover, while Levitsky identified several ways in which grassroots participants in social movements have called on lawyers and benefited from their expertise (e.g., conducting legal workshops or handling cases that directly benefited their constituents), she nonetheless noted that the legal organizations "had a reputation . . . as being 'white' or 'elitist.'"[10] Moreover, rather than an exchange of expertise or a genuinely mutual enterprise of strategizing for social change, Levitsky describes the sharing of expertise as "*unidirectional*. There was little evidence that law organizations in turn relied on the expertise of, or input from nonlegal . . . organizations."[11] As a result, the priorities of the legal organizations predominated.

Grassroots organizers interviewed by Levitsky repeatedly cited same-sex marriage as a case in point. Levitsky reports, "Nearly all of the activists of color and self-identified radical leftists in [the] study independently brought up the subject of the gay marriage campaign . . . as an example of a *top-down strategy*, conceived of and implemented by attorneys with little attention to the needs and desires of the greater GLBT community."[12] One activist described the marriage campaign as a "highjack[ing]." As a "cofounder of Chicago Black Lesbian and Gays" put it to Levitsky, "You go into the black lesbigay community and ask them what are the most important things to you and you will not hear marriage.... What you will hear are employment and housing." Similarly, a "cofounder of Khuli Zaban, an organization for South Asian and Middle Eastern lesbians and bisexuals," told Levitsky, "I feel like marriage is important, and yes it would give validation in huge ways, but if there's people that don't have enough food to eat, you know, where is our sense of priority?"[13]

Where, indeed? But this need not be the way movement lawyers do business. The social movement literature lamenting the relationship between LGBT activists and lawyers routinely conflates law generally with litigation, rights, and formal equality.[14] And no wonder: The major LGBT legal advocacy organizations have in fact emphasized these themes. Law, however, has far broader potential, and lawyers carry around a truckload of possibilities. But the choice among them cannot be made until a lawyer sees the problem up close. In other words, a legal agenda should be driven by what is gleaned on the ground, in a local assessment of constituencies' needs. The problem posed by the role of lawyers in social movements is not, in my view, with being elite; it is with being wrapped up in LGBT equal rights discourse. Nothing will alter the reality that the lawyer class has training and access that the grassroots lacks, but that does not relieve lawyers of responsibility for thinking critically about the effects of the discourse on the legal agenda or for appreciating their clients' daily encounters with conditions that are formed, at least in part, by law.

The sense among Levitsky's interviewees that the relationship between grassroots activists and lawyers was "unidirectional" is entirely understandable but not at all a necessary description of the activist-lawyer relationship. Method matters. A method that carefully attends to the experiences of people who are navigating legal conditions and examines the background rules that construct those conditions would suffer less from this "unidirectionality." Such an approach multiplies the terrains of reform and makes room for the kind of genuine cooperation that social movement scholars envision.

LGBTQ grassroots activists have been clear for decades that same-sex marriage and hate crimes legislation were never going to address the pressing needs of the most disadvantaged. The Williams Institute has provided a trove of research on the economic realities facing large swaths of the LGBTQ community. And since *Obergefell*, even those major LGBT organizations that were most consumed with civil rights and marriage have warmed up to economic priorities. Yet the tentative shift from equal rights to distributive justice is groping and maladroit. Reformist logic has not caught up with the newly formulating objectives; the shift looks like a practice in search of a theory. The moral clarity with which the mainstream movement pursued same-sex marriage felt impermeable, yet the new economic priorities are articulated without nearly the same vision or confidence. Why? Because the LGBT movement is still very much in the grip of its dominant discourse: that of LGBT equal rights. It has not made sense out of economic priorities yet.

The job of lawyers, though, is to construct arguments. By "argument" I do not mean a stand-alone rationale for why something is a good idea, but a whole logic within which distributive priorities cohere. We should start by assuming a deliberately critical posture in relation to the discursive setting in which we have, for the past few decades, been operating. We may never escape it fully, but we can drive toward an altered iteration. It was easy to sing in the tune of LGBT equal rights discourse, but it has left too many behind. *Resistance* now means critiquing our own discourse and pushing toward discursive adjustments within which desperately needed revisions of value and resource distribution will make sense.

Priorities

Lawyers in the trenches could be forgiven for chafing at the ivory tower ring of *critique*, but critique is not an intellectual holiday; it is a necessary doing. We can commit to critical practices that make new forms of resistance possible. We have tools that can be used to broadly assess and perpetually reassess the needs of a complex constituency and the extent to which law is effectuating distributions that address those needs. The continuous practice of critique is vital to law reform.

Movement lawyers who represent the LGBT community's interests should embrace a two-fold moral imperative. Their agenda should prioritize the interests of the poorest and most marginalized sectors of the community *and* they should redirect their considerable talent and dedication to a method of lawyering that attends to those populations' regular and life-shaping encounters with law.

Law can do more than make mega-rights claims like the ones that make the front page. The problems are varied, but the toolbox is deep. It is past time to reach inside and make use of all that we have.

Introduction

1 *Christian Legal Society Chapter of the University of California, Hastings College of the Law v. Martinez.*
2 San Francisco Police Code, Art. 2, §168 (added by Prop L, app. November 2, 2010), available at http://www.amlegal.com/nxt/gateway.dll/California/police/policecode ?f=templates$fn=default.htm$3.0$vid=amlegal:sanfrancisco_ca$sync=1.
3 Ray, "Lesbian, Gay, Bisexual and Transgender Youth," 1.
4 "Homeless Point-in-Time Count and Survey Comprehensive Report 2015," Applied Survey Research, available at https://sfgov.org/lhcb/sites/default/files /2015%20San%20Francisco%20Homeless%20Count%20%20Report_0.pdf, accessed August 30, 2016.
5 Chad Griffin, "Connecting with Our Nation's Homeless Youth," HRC blog, June 9, 2012, http://www.hrc.org/blog/entry/connecting-with-our-nations-homeless -youth.
6 Chris Johnson, "HRC President on the Road Ahead for LGBT Movement," *Washington Blade*, July 12 2013, available at http://www.washingtonblade.com/2013/07 /12/griffins-envisions-enda-marriage-progress-in-the-movement.
7 Foucault, "Two Lectures," 78–108.
8 This stance on identity is meant to avoid "foundationalism," or the belief in the existence of an "Archimedean point" from which to view reality neutrally, without relying on the knowledge or identity categories with which we are familiar. I thank Karl Klare for help sorting through this crucial question.
9 *Straight* in this book means *not LGBT*. Some transgender people identify as heterosexual, so for that reason and others the term as I use it may not feel like a good fit for everyone. I nonetheless chose a single word for reading and writing fluidity over the awkward, endless, and doomed effort to designate every identity category that exists in our complicated and fast-changing world. LGBT as used throughout the book refers to the full range of identities that deviate from the heterosexual, cisgender, and gender-conforming ideal. Straight and LGBT identities are *diacritically related* according to my usage, meaning that they are mutually defining, each by being *not* the other. This is characteristic of sexuality and gender identities and

is part of why they are so vulnerable to critique. The identities have enormous contingencies built into them; it should be understood that these terms (along with *gay, lesbian, transgender*, etc.) as I use them refer more to archetypes that are produced discursively and identities that are held, sometimes quite dearly, than to any naturally occurring fixities. *Queer* is a term I use to indicate a theory and politics that are characterized by a critique of identity, but I also make some select usage of *queer* or *LGBTQ* to refer to identities that have been adopted in resistance to both straight identity and the increasingly normalized identities associated with mainstream gay rights advocacy.

10 Foucault, "Two Lectures," 78–108.

11 Cf. Foucault, *The Archaeology of Knowledge*, 23.

12 "Children Reared by Female Couples Score Higher on Good Citizenship than Children Reared by Heterosexual Parents," Williams Institute, Los Angeles, September 17, 2013, http://williamsinstitute.law.ucla.edu/press/press-releases/17-sept-2013.

13 Menand, *The Metaphysical Club*, 339–58.

14 Hale, "Coercion and Distribution in a Supposedly Non-coercive State," 470–94.

15 Cf. Kennedy, *A Critique of Adjudication*, 8–20, 262–63.

16 Dan Eggen, "The Influence Industry: Same-Sex Marriage Issue Shows Importance of Gay Fundraisers," *Washington Post*, May 9, 2012, available at https://www.washingtonpost.com/politics/same-sex-marriage-debate-many-of-obamas-top-fundraisers-are-gay/2012/05/09/gIQASJYSDU_story.html.

Chapter 1. THE INDETERMINACY TRAP

1 *Huff v. Chapel Hill Chancy Hall School.*

2 Mass. Gen. Laws Annotated 151b § 1 (2000).

3 Mass. Gen. Annotated 151b § 1 (2000).

4 Mass. Gen. Laws Annotated 151b § 1 (2000).

5 *Huff v. Chapel Hill Chancy Hall School* at 1619–20.

6 Klare, "Critical Perspectives on Social and Economic Rights, Democracy and Separation of Powers," 3, 11. "Judges [and administrative adjudicators] should be self-conscious and transparent about the values they bring to their adjudicative practice." As Klare explains, the indeterminacy critique is not " 'against reason' [but] against . . . unwillingness to acknowledge the limitations of reason."

7 *Obergefell v. Hodges.*

8 The "Third Branch" refers to the federal judiciary, the powers of which are delineated in Article III of the U.S. Constitution. The legal scholar Alexander M. Bickel famously called the judiciary "the least dangerous branch" in his book by that name: Bickel, *The Least Dangerous Branch*. He borrowed the phrase from Alexander Hamilton, who described the judicial department envisioned by the Federalists as the "least dangerous" of the three proposed branches. Hamilton, in *The Federalist No. 78*, was attempting to mitigate concern about the fact that the judicial branch—unelected and unaccountable—would review the work of the elected branches. The Court, Hamilton argued, would only have the power to impose

the law of the Constitution, which would be ratified using a super-majoritarian process, and therefore would pose no real threat to majority rule. Bickel, on the other hand, used the phrase "least dangerous branch" with some irony, introducing as well the term of art *counter-majoritarian difficulty*—that is, the conceptual problem in American constitutionalism that an unelected department can reverse the work of an elected one and how such decisions can be justified. This led Bickel to a cautious constitutional theory, one that criticized the most celebrated decisions of the Warren Court as unrestrained and viewed judicial passivity as virtuous.

In an interesting twist on this usual narrative of the problematic of counter-majoritarianism, the contemporary legal scholar Steven L. Winter argues, "The countermajoritarian difficulty begins to pale once we recognize the courts' dependence on the cultural understandings that enable meaning. The conventional concern is that judges will impose their values in contravention of the policy choices of democratically elected legislatures. But . . . judges cannot even think without implicating the dominant normative assumptions that shape their society and reproduce their political and cultural context. . . . [Moreover,] it remains perfectly possible to have the worst of both worlds: judicial review (or interpretation) that overturns (or undermines) democratic decision-making, but that nevertheless fails to transcend the dominant normative assumptions implicit in our background conceptions": Winter, "An Upside/Down View of the Countermajoritarian Difficulty."

9 *Bowers v. Hardwick.*

10 *Bowers v. Hardwick* at 190.

11 *Bowers v. Hardwick* at 190.

12 *Bowers v. Hardwick* at 194.

13 There have been a couple of exceptions. Judge Douglas Ginsburg of the U.S. Court of Appeals for the DC Circuit, briefly a nominee to the U.S. Supreme Court, came up with the term *Constitution in Exile* to rehabilitate the way that the due process and commerce clauses were construed during the *Lochner* era. He regarded those readings as truer to their original meaning: Jeffrey Rosen, "States of Nature," *New Republic*, April 23, 2008, available at https://newrepublic.com/article/61952/states-nature. This view is not that different from that of Supreme Court Justice Clarence Thomas, but even Thomas has had little influence on the thinking of the Court or the legal profession on this topic, except in a few extremist corners. The contemporary right-wing Fox News commentator Andrew Napolitano, for example, wrote a book entitled *The Constitution in Exile.*

14 *Lochner v. New York.*

15 *Brown v. Board of Education of Topeka.* See also Horwitz, *The Warren Court and the Pursuit of Justice.*

16 Horwitz, "The Jurisprudence of Brown and the Dilemmas of Liberalism," 600.

17 Horwitz, "The Jurisprudence of Brown and the Dilemmas of Liberalism," 602.

18 Other dimensions of the due process clause remain highly controversial (e.g., abortion cases are litigated under that clause) and the extent to which congressional power under the commerce clause ought to keep pace with economic realities

also continues to divide the Court. On the constitutionality of key provisions of the Affordable Care Act, see e.g., *National Federation of Independent Business v. Sebelius*.

19 The Bowers opinion included an inquiry into whether "history and tradition" supported finding "a fundamental right [of] homosexuals to engage in sodomy." Dozens of commentaries observe the selectivity of the historical account. Without reviewing all of that material here, suffice it to say that Justice White framed that constitutional question in a deliberately narrow fashion and also made careful choices, as judges do, in assembling the history that answered it. See Eskridge, "Hardwick and Historiography," 631. Justice Scalia, who was not yet on the Court for Bowers but was a fan, believed that history is the best guide we have for determining the nature and extent of fundamental rights. He laid out his argument about this elaborately in *McDonald v. City of Chicago*, one of two modern cases construing the Second Amendment to provide an individual right to bear arms. (The other is *District of Columbia v. Heller.*) These two decisions split the Court and their historical bases have come under especially intense criticism by historians.

20 "Anti-formalist criticism is not 'against reason.' It is against misuse or unwillingness to acknowledge the limitations of reason": Klare, "Critical Perspectives on Social and Economic Rights, Democracy and Separation of Powers," 11.

21 Blackstone, *Blackstone's Commentaries*.

22 *Bowers v. Hardwick* at 197.

23 *Bowers v. Hardwick* at 197.

24 Alexander Hamilton, *The Federalist No. 78*, http://thomas.loc.gov/home/histdox /fed_78.html, accessed July 27, 2014.

25 *Marbury v. Madison.*

26 And I do mean relative. During the period of Reconstruction, the country saw three constitutional amendments that harbored the potential to transform the relationship between federal and state governments through the mechanism of national citizenship and its attendant rights and privileges. Judicial decisions of the late nineteenth century, however, undermined much of this potential (see, e.g., *Slaughter-House Cases*), construing the privileges and immunities clause of the Fourteenth Amendment so narrowly as to effectively repeal it. The constitutional scholar Bruce Ackerman has made the influential argument that the New Deal should also be understood as a transformational era in American constitutional history, due not to formally ratified amendments but, rather, to an effective ratification of a transformation in the federal-state relationship expressed by the New Deal and the profusion of federal bureaucratic authority, as well as the subsequent efforts by the federal judiciary to assimilate these new realities to longstanding constitutional requirements: Ackerman, *We the People*, 105–30.

27 *Lawrence v. Texas*. The Texas sodomy statute under consideration in *Lawrence* differed from the Georgia law upheld in *Bowers* in two respects. First, the Texas law prohibited only same-sex sodomy while the Georgia law—at least on its face— prohibited sodomy between any two persons, though Georgia claimed to enforce the law only against homosexuals. Second, the specific acts that were prohibited

under the two laws were not identical. Texas prohibited penetration with an object, but Georgia's statute did not contemplate that act: see Tex. Penal Code Ann. § 21.01(1) (Vernon 2003); Ga. Code Ann. § 16–6–2 (1984).

28 Carpenter, *Flagrant Conduct*, 87.
29 *Lawrence v. Texas* at 586.
30 *Lawrence v. Texas* at 605.
31 *Goodridge v. Department of Public Health*.
32 *Goodridge v. Department of Public Health* at 357.
33 *Goodridge v. Department of Public Health* at 358.
34 *Goodridge v. Department of Public Health* at 350.
35 *Goodridge v. Department of Public Health* at 353.
36 *Goodridge v. Department of Public Health* at 319–20.
37 *Obergefell v. Hodges* at 2584.
38 *Obergefell v. Hodges* at 2590.
39 *Obergefell v. Hodges* at 2600.
40 *Obergefell v. Hodges* at 2628.
41 *Obergefell v. Hodges* at 2602.
42 *Obergefell v. Hodges*, Brief for Respondent at 23 (internal quotations omitted).
43 *Obergefell v. Hodges*, Reply Brief for Petitioners at 5.
44 *Obergefell v. Hodges* at 2613.
45 *Obergefell v. Hodges* at 2611.
46 *Obergefell v. Hodges* at 2612.
47 *Obergefell v. Hodges* at 2624.
48 *Obergefell v. Hodges* at 2616.
49 *Obergefell v. Hodges* at 2616–17.
50 *Dred Scott v. Sandford*, 60 U.S. 393 (1857).
51 *Obergefell v. Hodges* at 2626.
52 *Obergefell v. Hodges* at 2627.
53 *Obergefell v. Hodges* at 2628.
54 *Obergefell v. Hodges* at 2629.
55 *Obergefell v. Hodges* at 2632.
56 *Romer v. Evans*.
57 *Romer v. Evans* at 636.
58 *Romer v. Evans* at 636.
59 *Lochner v. New York* at 65.
60 *Plessy v. Ferguson*.
61 *Lochner v. New York* at 75.
62 *Lochner v. New York* at 76.
63 *Lochner v. New York* at 75.
64 *Lochner v. New York* at 76.
65 *Lochner v. New York* at 76.
66 Bickel, *The Least Dangerous Branch*, 16–23.
67 Klare, "Critical Perspectives on Social and Economic Rights, Democracy and Separation of Powers," 10.

68 Klare, "Critical Perspectives on Social and Economic Rights, Democracy and Separation of Powers," 11.

69 Kennedy, "The Critique of Rights in Critical Legal Studies," 185.

70 Kennedy, "The Critique of Rights in Critical Legal Studies," 185.

71 Kennedy, "The Critique of Rights in Critical Legal Studies," 185.

72 Some antagonists (and even some fans) interpret the CLS critique of rights to mean that rights are bogus and useless, but that is a crude misreading of a much subtler point about the limits of their deductive capacities. Rights have a very powerful legacy in American law that the CLS writers whom I have cited do not underestimate. Rights are the conceptual vehicle responsible for advances that few would give back. Moreover, as many writers in the "race crit" and "fem crit" traditions have emphasized, "For minorities . . . rights serve as a rallying point and bring us closer together": Delgado, "The Ethereal Scholar," *Harvard Civil Rights-Civil Liberties Law Review* 22:305.

73 The terms *formal equality* and *substantive equality* are used here to indicate whether differences ought to be ignored or accommodated. If, however, one reads broadly in antidiscrimination law and scholarship, it becomes clear that not everyone uses these terms the same way. In some contexts, substantive equality is regarded as "equality of outcome" and implies a redistributive agenda. Moreover, some writers juxtapose formal equality against "anti-subordination," which seems to imply a more aggressive remedial agenda. Some distinguish equal opportunity from equal consideration and then from equal outcome, where the middle possibility refers to consideration of difference.

74 Civil Rights Act of 1964, 42 U.S.C.A. § 2000e-2 (1991).

75 *Ulane v. Eastern Airlines, Inc.*

76 See, e.g., *Sommers v. Budget Marketing, Inc.*

77 *Price Waterhouse v. Hopkins.*

78 *Rosa v. Park West Bank and Trust Company*; Equal Opportunity Credit Act, 15 U.S.C.A. §§1691 et seq. (1974).

79 *Smith v. City of Salem, Ohio.*

80 *Schroer v. Billington.*

81 *Macy v. Holder.*

82 *Macy v. Holder* at 4.

83 *Goins v. West Group.*

84 *Goins v. West Group* at 723.

85 *Goins v. West Group* at 726.

86 "GLAD—Our Work—Cases—*Freeman v. Denny's*," Gay and Lesbian Advocates and Defenders, http://www.glad.org/work/cases/freeman-v-dennys, accessed July 26, 2014.

87 "Sex-Segregated Facilities," Transgender Legal Defense and Education Fund, http://www.transgenderlegal.org/work_show.php?id=6, accessed July 26, 2014.

88 "Victory! Coy Mathis Wins Equal Access to Girls' Bathrooms at School," Transgender Legal Defense and Education Fund, http://www.transgenderlegal.org/headline_show.php?id=415, accessed July 26, 2014.

89 *Mathis v. Fountain-Fort Carson School District 8.*

90 *Doe v. Regional School Unit 26.*

91 Me. Rev. Stat. tit. 5, ch. 337 (2005).

92 20 U.S. Code § 1681 et seq.

93 Public Facilities Privacy and Security Act, H.R. 2, Gen. Assembly of N.C. (2016), http://www.ncleg.net/Sessions/2015E2/Bills/House/PDF/H2v1.pdf.

94 *Texas et al. v. United States.*

95 The terms *ciswoman* and *cisman* refer to people whose gender identity aligns with their assigned sex at birth.

96 Eskridge, "Comparative Law and the Same-Sex Marriage Debate," 641.

97 Eskridge, *The Case for Same-Sex Marriage.*

98 *Loving v. Virginia.*

99 Koppelman, "Why Discrimination against Lesbians and Gay Men Is Sex Discrimination"; Law, "Homosexuality and the Social Meaning of Gender."

100 *Washington v. Davis.*

101 Osagie Obasogie, "The Supreme Court Is Afraid of Racial Justice," *New York Times,* June 7, 2016, http://www.nytimes.com/2016/06/07/opinion/the-supreme-court-is-afraid-of-racial-justice.html.

102 For in-the-know con law readers, this obviously assumes a level of review comparable to the one applied in *Loving,* an argument Eskridge also made but that I do not recount here.

103 *Pace v. Alabama.*

104 *Brown v. Board of Education of Topeka; McLaughlin v. State of Florida.*

105 Eskridge, *The Case for Same-Sex Marriage.*

106 *Washington v. Davis* had not yet been decided, but Warren could have relied on an earlier case also cited by Eskridge: *Yick Wo v. Hopkins.*

107 Holmes, *The Common Law,* 1.

108 Chief Justice Roberts's view invokes Justice Harlan's dissent in *Plessy*: "Our Constitution is color blind . . ." *Parents Involved in Community Schools v. Seattle School District No. 1,* quoting *Plessy v. Ferguson*; Steele, *The Content of Our Character.*

109 Feminists who come down on the latter side of this debate also sometimes argue that efforts to advance women's equality that assume that women will bear and raise children are constructive of women's identity, marginalizing women who do not fit the mold and, in the long run, entrenching women's responsibility for a disproportionate share of child-rearing. Law reforms and arguments on behalf of LGBT people are also rife with identity-shaping potential. Chapter 2 explores that potential in detail.

110 Case, "How High the Apple Pie."

111 Cf. Walters, *The Tolerance Trap,* 265–66. Walters goes a bit further, arguing that "gay navigations of kinship and sexuality are not only pioneering models but have much to teach all of us, gay and straight alike." Her argument is that gay people should be seeking more than tolerance; there are specific aspects of gay life that should be ratified by and incorporated into the larger culture.

112 Crenshaw, "Race, Reform, and Retrenchment," 1336–41.

113 *Brown* also can be (and has been) read as representing an anti-subordination version of equality: see, e.g., Fiss, "Groups and the Equal Protection Clause," 147–70.
114 Bell, *Silent Covenants*, 6–7.
115 Stone, *Policy Paradox*, 376.

Chapter 2. THE LGBT RIGHTS-BEARING SUBJECT

1 *Hollingsworth v. Perry*; *Perry v. Brown*; *Perry v. Schwarzenegger*.
2 *Bush v. Gore*.
3 *In re Marriage Cases*.
4 *Strauss v. Horton*.
5 *Obergefell v. Hodges*.
6 For a complete timeline on same-sex marriage in the United States, see
http://www.freedomtomarry.org/pages/history-and-timeline-of-marriage.
7 1 U.S. Code § 7; 28 U.S. Code § 1738C (permitting states not to recognize
same-sex marriages performed in other states and denying federal recognition
to same-sex marriages performed validly in states where same-sex marriage was
available).
8 *Hollingsworth v. Perry*.
9 Transcript of Trial Proceedings at 240, *Perry v. Schwarzenegger* (No. C 09–
2292-VRW), 2010.
10 Transcript of Trial Proceedings at 241, *Perry v. Schwarzenegger* (No. C 09–2292-
VRW), 2010.
11 Transcript of Trial Proceedings at 241, *Perry v. Schwarzenegger* (No. C 09–2292-
VRW), 2010.
12 Transcript of Trial Proceedings at 243–44, *Perry v. Schwarzenegger* (No. C 09–2292-
VRW), 2010.
13 Transcript of Trial Proceedings at 244, *Perry v. Schwarzenegger* (No. C 09–2292-
VRW), 2010.
14 *Perry v. Schwarzenegger* at 993.
15 Transcript of Trial Proceedings at 1333, *Perry v. Schwarzenegger* (No. C 09–2292-
VRW), 2010.
16 Becker, *A Treatise on Family*.
17 Badgett, *Money, Myths and Change*, 149.
18 Badgett, *Money, Myths and Change*, 150.
19 Badgett, *Money, Myths and Change*, 160.
20 Transcript of Trial Proceedings at 1333, *Perry v. Schwarzenegger* (No. C 09–2292-
VRW), 2010.
21 In her book, Badgett responds to authors who seriously propose that butch-femme
roles might influence the allocation of labor within a same-sex household, mar-
shaling evidence to demonstrate that the two aspects of life appear to be unrelated:
Badgett, *Money, Myths and Change*, 157–58. I assert no such empirical connection.
22 *Perry v. Schwarzenegger* at 978.
23 *Perry v. Schwarzenegger* at 967.

24 Transcript of Trial Proceedings at 584, *Perry v. Schwarzenegger* (No. C 09–2292-VRW), 2010.

25 Transcript of Trial Proceedings at 617, *Perry v. Schwarzenegger* (No. C 09–2292-VRW), 2010.

26 Transcript of Trial Proceedings at 2020, *Perry v. Schwarzenegger* (No. C 09–2292-VRW), 2010.

27 Transcript of Trial Proceedings at 2025, *Perry v. Schwarzenegger* (No. C 09–2292-VRW), 2010.

28 Transcript of Trial Proceedings at 2073, *Perry v. Schwarzenegger* (No. C 09–2292-VRW), 2010.

29 Transcript of Trial Proceedings at 2026, *Perry v. Schwarzenegger* (No. C 09–2292-VRW), 2010.

30 Transcript of Trial Proceedings at 2055, *Perry v. Schwarzenegger* (No. C 09–2292-VRW), 2010.

31 Transcript of Trial Proceedings at 2203, *Perry v. Schwarzenegger* (No. C 09–2292-VRW), 2010.

32 Transcript of Proceedings at 622:14–24, *Log Cabin Republicans v. United States* (No. CV 04–08425-VAP [Ex]).

33 Transcript of Proceedings at 624:13–16, *Log Cabin Republicans v. United States* (No. CV 04–08425-VAP [Ex]).

34 Humphreys, *Tearoom Trade.*

35 Benoit Denizet-Lewis, "Double Lives on the Down Low," *New York Times*, August 3, 2003, http://www.nytimes.com/2003/08/03/magazine/double-lives-on-the-down-low.html. See also Collins, *Black Sexual Politics*, 173–74, 274.

36 Snorton, *Nobody Is Supposed to Know*, 3.

37 Stone, "The Down Low and the Sexuality of Race," 41.

38 Stone, "The Down Low and the Sexuality of Race," 44.

39 Stone, "The Down Low and the Sexuality of Race," 45.

40 Stone, "The Down Low and the Sexuality of Race," 47.

41 Announcement on file with author.

42 Transcript of Trial Proceedings at 2071, *Perry v. Schwarzenegger* (No. C 09–2292-VRW), 2010.

43 Transcript of Trial Proceedings at 2128, *Perry v. Schwarzenegger* (No. C 09–2292-VRW), 2010.

44 Transcript of Trial Proceedings at 2128, *Perry v. Schwarzenegger* (No. C 09–2292-VRW), 2010.

45 Transcript of Trial Proceedings at 2129, *Perry v. Schwarzenegger* (No. C 09–2292-VRW), 2010.

46 Transcript of Trial Proceedings at 2225, *Perry v. Schwarzenegger* (No. C 09–2292-VRW), 2010.

47 Transcript of Trial Proceedings at 2227, *Perry v. Schwarzenegger* (No. C 09–2292-VRW), 2010.

48 *Perry v. Schwarzenegger* at 964.

49 Goldberg, "Social Justice Movements and LatCrit Community," 630–31.

50 Chauncy, *Gay New York*.
51 Announcement on file with author.
52 Sedgwick, *Epistemology of the Closet*, 40.
53 Sedgwick, *Epistemology of the Closet*, 10.
54 Blankenhorn, *Fatherless America*.
55 *Perry v. Schwarzenegger* at 946.
56 *Perry v. Schwarzenegger* at 943, 980.
57 *Florida Department of Children and Families v. Adoption of X.X.G.*
58 *Florida Department of Children and Families v. Adoption of X.X.G.* at 87.
59 One of the state's experts, the conservative psychologist and Southern Baptist minister George Rekers, embarrassed Florida's attorney-general while the appeal was pending by getting caught returning from a European trip with a male escort hired from the (now defunct) website Rentboy.com. Rekers claimed implausibly that the young man was hired to help with the luggage. Rentboy.com was raided, and the site was shut down by federal authorities in August 2015 for promoting prostitution.
60 *Goodridge v. Department of Public Health* at 358 (Sosman, J., dissenting).
61 Regnerus, "How Different Are the Adult Children of Parents Who Have Same-Sex Relationships?"
62 Transcript of Trial Proceedings at 828, *Perry v. Schwarzenegger* (No. C 09–2292-VRW), 2010.
63 Transcript of Trial Proceedings at 872, *Perry v. Schwarzenegger* (No. C 09–2292-VRW), 2010.
64 *Florida Department of Children and Families v. Adoption of X.X.G.* at 88.
65 *Florida Department of Children and Families v. Adoption of X.X.G.* at 89.
66 Transcript of Trial Proceedings at 883, *Perry v. Schwarzenegger* (No. C 09–2292-VRW), 2010.
67 Transcript of Trial Proceedings at 884, *Perry v. Schwarzenegger* (No. C 09–2292-VRW), 2010.
68 Transcript of Trial Proceedings at 900, *Perry v. Schwarzenegger* (No. C 09–2292-VRW), 2010.
69 Transcript of Trial Proceedings at 1142–1143, *Perry v. Schwarzenegger* (No. C 09–2292-VRW), 2010.
70 Ely, *Democracy and Distrust*, 87–104.
71 *Kerrigan v. Commissioner of Public Health*.
72 *Kerrigan v. Commissioner of Public Health* at 208.
73 Brown, *States of Injury*, 21.
74 The doctrinal application of elevated tiers of scrutiny moves in and out of contact with representation-reinforcement theory. Explicit racial classifications, for example, now receive strict scrutiny even where a classification is alleged to discriminate against white people, who can vindicate their interests using majoritarian power. This development can also be understood as a victory for *formal* over *substantive* equality because it treats everyone the same rather than taking differences into account.

75 *Obergefell v. Hodges*, Brief of Petitioner, Obergefell v. Hodges, 2015 WL 860738 (U.S.) (No. 14–556).

76 *Obergefell v. Hodges*, Brief of Constitutional Law Scholars Supporting Petitioners.

77 *Obergefell v. Hodges*, Brief of Petitioner.

78 *Obergefell v. Hodges*, Brief for the American Psychological Association as Amici Curiae Supporting Petitioners.

79 Halley, "Rhetorics of Justification in the Same-Sex Marriage Debate," 100n7.

80 *Schroer v. Billington.*

81 Spade, "Documenting Gender."

82 *Batch checking* refers to a cross-checking process among different governmental databases designed to prevent fraud, as well as to alert authorities to possible terrorists or criminals. If the process generates a "no match" letter, it could "out" a person who has transitioned, subjecting the person to discrimination or even violence. Dean Spade's work alerted scholars and activists to the significance of this practice for trans people.

83 Puar, *Terrorist Assemblages*, xxiii.

84 Puar, "Rethinking Homonationalism," 337.

85 "Florida Shooting: Live Updates," *New York Times*, June 12, 2016, http://www .nytimes.com/live/orlando-nightclub-shooting-live-updates.

86 Warner, *The Trouble with Normal*, 82.

87 Warner, *The Trouble with Normal*, 98.

88 *Goodridge v. Department of Public Health* at 326.

89 Warner, *The Trouble with Normal*, 115.

90 Ahmed, "When Men Are Harmed," 17–18.

91 It may not always go this way. The East has alternatively been depicted as exotically liberated on matters of sexuality: cf. Otto, "Transnational Homo-Assemblages," 87–88.

92 "Lexington, Mass., father of 6-year-old arrested, spends night in jail over objections to homosexual curriculum in son's kindergarten class": MassResistance, http://www.massresistance.org/docs/parker/main.html.

93 Mass. Gen. Laws ch. 71 § 32A (2002).

94 *Parker v. Hurley*, Brief for Amicus ACLU of Massachusetts at 19.

95 James Vaznis and Tracy Jan, "In Storm over Gay Books, a Principal Holds Ground," *Boston Globe*, April 27, 2006.

96 Evan Thomas, "The War over Gay Marriage," *Newsweek*, March 3, 2010, http:// www.newsweek.com/war-over-gay-marriage-139539.

97 *United States v. Windsor.*

98 Ariel Levy, "The Perfect Wife: How Edith Windsor Fell in Love, Got Married, and Won a Landmark Case for Gay Marriage," *New Yorker*, September 30, 2013, http://www.newyorker.com/magazine/2013/09/30/the-perfect-wife.

99 *Goodridge v. Department of Public Health* at 313.

100 *Goins v. West Group.*

101 *Cruzan v. Special School District No. 1.*

102 Zack Ford, "Anti-LGBT Group Admits It Invented Story about Transgender Student Harassing Classmates [Updated]," Think Progress (blog), October 17,

2013, http://thinkprogress.org/lgbt/2013/10/17/2797141/pacific-justice-institute -invented-transgender.

103 *Women's Liberation Front v. U.S. Department of Justice.*

104 See, e.g., Janell Ross, "In Houston, Gay Rights Debate Degenerates into Feud Over 'Bathroom Bill,' " *Washington Post*, October 28, 2015, https://www.wash ingtonpost.com/news/the-fix/wp/2015/10/28/in-houston-gay-rights-debate -degenerates-into-feud-over-bathroom-bill.

105 "New Law Allows Transgender Students to Choose Bathrooms and Sports Teams," National Public Radio, January 8, 2014, http://www.npr.org/2014/01 /07/260455851/new-law-allows-transgender-students-to-choose-bathrooms-and -sports-teams.

106 Pacific Justice Institute, October 23, 2013, https://www.facebook.com /PacificJusticeInstitute/posts/10151727646358660, accessed August 21, 2014.

107 An Act Relative to Gender Identity, H. 3810, 187th Leg. (Mass. 2011).

108 Mass. Gen. Laws. ch. 272 § 98 (2016).

109 The U.S. Supreme Court's protection of the right to desecrate the flag as a form of expression under the First Amendment is the reason we have seen repeated attempts—all failed—to protect the flag with a constitutional amendment. An amendment protecting the flag presumably would override that expressive right.

110 Tushnet, "The Critique of Rights," 31.

111 Compare *Roe v. Wade* with *Planned Parenthood v. Casey.*

112 *McDonald v. City of Chicago.*

113 Olsen, "Statutory Rape," 387.

114 Transcript of Proceedings at 615:13–626:11, *Log Cabin Republicans v. United States* (No. CV 04–08425-VAP [Ex]).

115 Transcript of Proceedings at 622:14–24, *Log Cabin Republicans v. United States* (No. CV 04–08425-VAP [Ex]).

116 *Boy Scouts of America v. Dale.*

117 The organizers of the Boston St. Patrick's Day Parade began admitting the partici- pation of a gay group in 2015.

118 This policy was modified on January 1, 2014 to permit gay-identified youth to par- ticipate but to continue excluding gay-identified adult leaders. It was modified yet again in July, 2015, lifting the ban on gay-identified adult volunteers and leaders, but still permitting individual units to exclude gay adults.

119 *Boy Scouts of America v. Dale* at 649.

120 *Fabrizio v. City of Providence.*

121 *Romer v. Evans.*

122 Mike Pence signed a similar bill into law when he was the governor of Indiana, but after public outcry (especially by business groups) he signed a follow-up measure that watered it down considerably. Since then, bills that would seem to grant businesses license to discriminate have died in several state legislatures, and Governor Asa Hutchinson of Arkansas vetoed one.

123 *Burwell v. Hobby Lobby.*

124 Tushnet, "The Critique of Rights," 34.

125 Goldberg-Hiller, *The Limits to Union*, 63.

126 Tushnet, "The Critique of Rights," 31.

127 Ely, *Democracy and Distrust*, 87–104.

128 Badgett et al., "New Patterns of Poverty in the Lesbian, Gay, and Bisexual Community."

129 Gates, "LGBT People Are Disproportionately Food Insecure."

130 Bersani, "Is the Rectum a Grave?" 203.

131 De Tocqueville, *Democracy in America*, 239.

Chapter 3. REFORMIST DESIRE

1 *United States v. Windsor*; 1 U.S. Code § 7; 28 U.S. Code § 1738C.

2 Roberta Kaplan, quoted in *Harvard Law Today*, Lana Birbrair, symposium on Marriage Equality, Harvard Law School, November 1, 2013. Link no longer available; on file with the author.

3 "Inaugural Address by President Barack Obama," White House, http://www.whitehouse.gov/the-press-office/2013/01/21/inaugural-address-president-barack-obama, accessed September 27, 2014.

4 "Inaugural Address by President Barack Obama," White House, http://www.whitehouse.gov/the-press-office/2013/01/21/inaugural-address-president-barack-obama, accessed September 27, 2014.

5 "Once again, even in this historic moment of presidential recognition, the vast panoply of sexual and civil rights is reduced to access to this one institution: marriage." Walters, *The Tolerance Trap*, 257.

6 Waaldijk, "Small Change," 439.

7 Waaldijk, "Small Change," 440.

8 Waaldijk, "Small Change," 439.

9 Eskridge, "Comparative Law and the Same-Sex Marriage Debate," 648.

10 *Bowers v. Hardwick*.

11 *Lawrence v. Texas*.

12 *Goodridge v. Department of Public Health*.

13 Hirshman, *Victory*.

14 Sullivan, *Virtually Normal*.

15 *Baehr v. Lewin*.

16 Sedgwick, *Touching Feeling*, 5.

17 A rich literature—psychoanalytic, queer, and literary—wrestles with the nature and origin of desire: see, e.g., Dean, "Queer Desire, Psychoanalytic Hermeneutics, and Love Lyric." The questions are fascinating, but it is not my purpose to engage them here. This chapter argues that LGBT equal rights discourse plays a powerful role in producing the objectives of the LGBT movement. Discursive constraints funnel our capacity to ask questions and identify reformist goals down a narrow path, blinding us to possibilities for change that lie outside the confines of the discourse.

18 Freedom to Marry shut its doors after *Obergefell v. Hodges*. It now appears to be a website and archive.

19 Wolfson, *Why Marriage Matters.*

20 Wolfson, *Why Marriage Matters*, 8.

21 Wolfson, *Why Marriage Matters*, 8.

22 *Turner v. Safley.*

23 Wolfson, *Why Marriage Matters*, 9.

24 Wolfson, *Why Marriage Matters*, 9.

25 *Lawrence v. Texas.*

26 Wolfson, *Why Marriage Matters*, 9.

27 Wolfson, *Why Marriage Matters*, 12.

28 Polikoff, *Beyond (Straight and Gay) Marriage.*

29 *Goodridge v. Department of Public Health* at 314.

30 *Goodridge v. Department of Public Health* at 322.

31 *Goodridge v. Department of Public Health* at 312.

32 "The Unnecessary Doctrine of Necessaries."

33 Ershow-Levenberg, "Court Approval of Medicaid Spend-Down Planning by Guardians," 200.

34 Rand, "The Real Marriage Penalty," 94–97.

35 Waggoner, "The Uniform Probate Code's Elective Share," 1.

36 Duggan, *The Twilight of Equality?* 10.

37 Brown, *Undoing the Demos*, 28.

38 Brown, *Undoing the Demos*, 30–31.

39 Cossman, "Family Feuds."

40 *M. v. H.*

41 *M. v. H.*

42 *M. v. H.*

43 Cossman, "Family Feuds," 188.

44 "Yes on 1: Mainers United for Marriage: Pat and Dan Lawson of Monroe," YouTube, https://www.youtube.com/watch?v=FdUCLgjxanQ last modified October 19, 2012.

45 "The Gardner Family: Why Marriage Matters Maine," YouTube, https://www .youtube.com/watch?v=gvJrmMK8Hlo, last modified July 25, 2012.

46 Judy Harrison, "Mainers Approve Gay Marriage Referendum," *Bangor Daily News*, November 6, 2012, http://bangordailynews.com/2012/11/06/politics/both-sides -of-gay-marriage-question-optimistic-as-polls-close.

47 "Grandparents for Marriage Equality," YouTube, https://www.youtube.com/watch ?v=FgDH-kbfv9E, last updated February 25, 2012.

48 Duggan, *The Twilight of Equality?* 10.

49 "The Visible Vote '08: A Presidential Forum," co-sponsored by the Human Rights Campaign and LOGO, August 9, 2007, transcript.

50 "Victory! Transgender Man's Surviving Spouse Wins Pension Benefits," Trans- gender Legal Defense and Education Fund, http://www.transgenderlegal.org /headline_show.php?id=458, accessed September 27, 2014.

51 The bill was actually drafted broadly enough to permit a businessperson to use free exercise of religion as a defense to a range of legal claims so that, for example,

a religious store owner's free exercise would trump any antidiscrimination claim that a would-be customer might make. The bill would have been overkill in Arizona, where antidiscrimination law does not protect gay people anyway. Business owners in that state can probably refuse to serve gay people without any special authorization.

52 See, e.g., Jennifer Oldham, "Apple, American Oppose Arizona Bill Targeting Gay People," *Bloomberg News*, February 25, 2014, http://www.bloomberg.com/news /2014–02–25/american-airlines-to-apple-oppose-arizona-bill-that-targets-gays .html; Mike Florio, "NFL Won't Rule Out a Move of Super Bowl XLIX," *NBC Sports*, February 25, 2014, http://profootballtalk.nbcsports.com/2014/02/25/nfl -wont-rule-out-a-move-of-super-bowl-xlix.

53 Chad Griffin, "Corporate America Becomes a Beacon of Progress for Gay Rights," MSNBC, February 26, 2014, http://www.msnbc.com/msnbc/corporations—gay -rights-arizona.

54 D'Arcy Kemnitz to LGBT Bar Members and Supporters mailing list, "Thanking Corporate America: You Can Help," March 13, 2014, on file with the author.

55 *Hollingsworth v. Perry*, Brief of Amici Curiae Kenneth B. Mehlman et al. Supporting Respondents.

56 *Obergefell v. Hodges*, Brief of Kenneth B. Mehlman et al. as Amici Curiae Supporting Petitioners.

57 *Obergefell v. Hodges*, Brief of Kenneth B. Mehlman et al. as Amici Curiae Supporting Petitioners, 1.

58 *Obergefell v. Hodges*, Brief of Kenneth B. Mehlman et al. as Amici Curiae Supporting Petitioners, 3.

59 *Obergefell v. Hodges*, Brief of Kenneth B. Mehlman et al. as Amici Curiae Supporting Petitioners, 6.

60 *Obergefell v. Hodges*, Brief of Kenneth B. Mehlman et al. as Amici Curiae Supporting Petitioners, 11.

61 Andrew Coyne and David Frum, "How Far Do We Take Gay Rights," *Saturday Night*, vol. 110, no. 10, December 1995, 72.

62 David Frum, "I Was Wrong about Same-Sex Marriage," FrumForum, June 27, 2011, http://edition.cnn.com/2011/OPINION/06/27/frum.gay.marriage.index.html ?andhpt=hp_c2.

63 David Blankenhorn, "How My View on Gay Marriage Changed," *New York Times*, June 22, 2012, http://www.nytimes.com/2012/06/23/opinion/how-my-view-on -gay-marriage-changed.html.

64 Blankenhorn, "How My View on Gay Marriage Changed."

65 Blankenhorn, *Fatherless America*.

66 Blankenhorn, *The Future of Marriage*.

67 Blankenhorn, *The Future of Marriage*, 243.

68 Blankenhorn, "How My View on Gay Marriage Changed."

69 Richard Kim, "What's Still the Matter with David Blankenhorn," *The Nation*, June 24, 2012, http://www.thenation.com/blog/168545/whats-still-matter-david -blankenhorn.

70 U.S. Department of Labor, Office of Policy, Planning and Research, *The Negro Family*.

71 Cohen, "Punks, Bulldaggers, and Welfare Queens," 455.

72 Cohen, "Punks, Bulldaggers, and Welfare Queens," 458.

73 Murray, *Losing Ground*.

74 Williams, "The Ideology of Division," 718.

75 42 U.S. Code § 601 et seq. The act is premised on the congressional finding that "marriage is the foundation of a successful society" and states as part of its purpose to "end the dependence of needy parents on government benefits by promoting job preparation, work, and marriage": Act August 22, 1996, P.L. 104–93, Title I, § 101, 110 Stat. 2110 (2); 42 U.S. Code § 601(a)(2).

76 Alexander, *The New Jim Crow*, 60.

77 Alexander, *The New Jim Crow*, 57.

78 Adam Liptak, "One in One Hundred Adults behind Bars, New Study Says," *New York Times*, February 28, 2008, http://www.nytimes.com/2008/02/28/us/28cnd -prison.html; "State of Recidivism: The Revolving Door of America's Prisons," Pew Center on the States, April, 2011, 1, http://www.pewtrusts.org/~/media/legacy /uploadedfiles/pcs_assets/2011/pewstateofrecidivismpdf.pdf.

79 Alexander, *The New Jim Crow*, 60.

80 Harcourt, *The Illusion of Free Markets*, 203.

81 Harcourt, *The Illusion of Free Markets*, 52.

82 Harcourt, *The Illusion of Free Markets*, 136–39.

83 Bernstein, "Carceral Politics as Gender Justice?"

84 Ben Pershing, "Senate Passes Hate Crimes Bill That Would Extend Protection to Gays, Lesbians," *Washington Post*, October 23, 2009, http://www.washingtonpost .com/wp-dyn/content/article/2009/10/22/AR2009102204689.html.

85 Matthew Shepard and James Byrd Jr. Hate Crimes Prevention Act, 18 U.S. Code § 249(a)(2) (2009).

86 Matthew Shepard and James Byrd Jr. Hate Crimes Prevention Act.

87 "ACLU Cheers Free-Speech Friendly Hate Crimes Legislation," ACLU, September 27, 2007, https://www.aclu.org/lgbt-rights_hiv-aids/aclu-cheers-free-speech -friendly-hate-crimes-legislation.

88 See, e.g., "SRLP on Hate Crimes Laws," Sylvia Rivera Law Project, accessed September 28, 2014, http://srlp.org/action/hate-crimes.

89 For a discussion of the unintended consequences of hate crime statutes for communities of color, see Crooms, "Everywhere There's War," 41.

90 See, e.g., Zaibert, "Punishment and Revenge."

91 In his classic article "The Expressive Function of Punishment," Joel Feinberg argues that punishment serves a crucial "expressive function," symbolizing public condemnation of certain bad acts. That criminal punishment serves this purpose enjoys broad acceptance, but the additional element I point to in the main text is a "recognition function"—that is, of certain identity groups as legitimate minorities vulnerable to prejudice.

92 *Romer v. Evans*.

93 Mass. Gen. Laws ch. 71 § 370 (2010) (updated in 2014).

94 Mass. Gen. Laws ch. 71 § 370(d)(2).

95 Mass. Gen. Laws ch. 71 § 370(d)(2).

96 Mass. Gen. Laws ch. 71 § 370(d)(4). That training must cover the specific categories of "students who have been shown to be particularly at risk for bullying."

97 "Who Is at Risk," stopbullying.gov, accessed September 28, 2014, http://www.stopbullying.gov/at-risk/index.html.

98 Mass. Gen. Laws ch. 71 § 370(d)(3) (2010) (updated in 2014).

99 At this point in the book LGBTQ comes into more frequent use. The addition of the Q is meant to indicate that a more marginal sector of the community is under discussion, including younger, lower-income, and more gender-variant people. These populations are more likely to refer to themselves using the term *queer*. I include the Q in deference to that preference.

100 See, e.g., Gates and Ost, *The Gay and Lesbian Atlas*, 39–41.

101 Ross Benes, "The Latest Plan to Save Detroit: Build a Gay Neighborhood," Outward (blog), *Slate*, November 25, 2013, http://www.slate.com/blogs/outward/2013/11/15/detroit_is_bankrupt_could_a_gay_neighborhood_save_the_city.html.

102 Christina B. Hanhardt, discussing conflicts over gentrification that involve LGBTQ populations, explains that "gay men (and, to a lesser degree, lesbians) are seen as the arbiters of risk, their vulnerability to violence—or their protected presence—a measure of an urban region's vitality": Hanhardt, *Safe Space*, 8.

103 Hanhardt, *Safe Space*, 186.

104 Gio Ross, "Youth Fight Displacement—and Win!" FIERCE, March 1, 2008, http://www.fiercenyc.org/media/mentions/youth-fight-displacement-and-win.

105 For an excellent and comprehensive account of this story, see Hanhardt, *Safe Space*, 185–220.

106 "Third Boystown Stabbing in as Many Weeks Caught on Video," *Huffington Post*, July 5, 2011, http://www.huffingtonpost.com/2011/07/05/third-boystown-stabbing-i_n_890411.html.

107 Take Back Boystown's Facebook page, https://www.facebook.com/TakeBackBoystown, accessed September 28, 2014.

108 Kate Sosin, "Hundreds Pack into Boystown Violence Forum," *Windy City Times*, July 13, 2011, http://www.windycitymediagroup.com/gay/lesbian/news/ARTICLE.php?AID=32676.

109 "The Demographics of Diversity: Why Cities Are Courting the Gay and Lesbian Community," June 3, 2003, http://www.urban.org/publications/900634.html.

110 "The Demographics of Diversity." Richard Florida writes, "Regional economic growth is powered by creative people, who prefer places that are diverse, tolerant and open to new ideas": Florida, *The Rise of the Creative Class*, 249.

111 Elly Fishman, "Pariahs amid the Rainbow: Young, Queer, and Homeless in Boystown," *Chicago Reader*, July 18, 2012, http://www.chicagoreader.com/chicago/boystown-as-home-to-the-young-gay-homeless/Content?oid=6990871.

112 Karen Gullo, "San Francisco Google Buses Attacked in Lawsuit," *Bloomberg News*, May 2, 2014, http://www.bloomberg.com/news/2014-05-01/san-francisco-sued-over-google-bus-project-by-community-group.html; Dan Brekke, "Yet Another

Protest against Tech Buses as San Francisco Adopts Shuttle Plan," KQED News, January 21, 2014, http://blogs.kqed.org/newsfix/2014/01/21/yet-another-protest-against-tech-buses.

113 Hanhardt, *Safe Space*, 7.

114 Mogul et al., *Queer (In)Justice*, 56–57.

115 I thank Darby Hickey for putting these two events together for me.

116 Alliance for a Safe and Diverse DC, "Move Along: Policing Sex Work in Washington D.C.," report, 2008.

117 Repeal of Prostitution Free Zones Amendment Act of 2014, S. 20–760 (2014).

118 Erin Fitzgerald, Sarah Elspeth, and Darby Hickey, "Meaningful Work: Transgender Experiences in the Sex Trade," December 2015, http://www.transequality.org/sites/default/files/Meaningful%20Work-Full%20Report_FINAL_3.pdf.

119 Chase Strangio, "Arrested for Walking while Trans: An Interview with Monica Jones," Speak Freely (blog), April 2, 2014, https://www.aclu.org/blog/arrested-walking-while-trans-interview-monica-jones.

120 Memorandum of Support from Lambda Legal Defense and Education Fund for Bill S. 323/A.1008, prepared by Lambda Legal Defense and Education Fund (New York, April 2012), http://www.lambdalegal.org/sites/default/files/ltr_ny_20120405_condoms-as-evidence_0.pdf.

121 Stephanie Clifford, "Raid of Rentboy, an Escort Website, Angers Gay Activists," *New York Times*, August 26, 2015; Hayley Gorenberg, "Raiding Rentboy.com Threatens Our Safety," blog entry dated August 27, 2015, http://www.lambdalegal.org/blog/20150827_raiding-rentboy-threatens-our-safety.

122 Hayley Gorenberg, "Raiding Rentboy.com Threatens Our Safety," Lambda Legal (blog), August 27, 2015, http://www.lambdalegal.org/blog/20150827_raiding-rentboy-threatens-our-safety.

123 "Q&A Policy to Protect the Human Rights of Sex Workers," Amnesty International, https://www.amnesty.org/en/qa-policy-to-protect-the-human-rights-of-sex-workers. Last accessed July 1, 2017.

124 "LGBT Rights Organizations Join Amnesty International in Call to Decriminalize Sex Work," National Center for Lesbian Rights, August, 20, 2015, http://www.nclrights.org/press-room/press-release/lgbt-rights-organizations-join-amnesty-international-in-call-to-decriminalize-sex-work.

125 See, e.g., Ahmed, "Think Again."

126 Vaid, *Irresistible Revolution*.

127 Daniel Reynolds, "LGBT Groups Sign Letters of Support for Michael Brown's Family," *The Advocate*, August 13, 2014, http://www.advocate.com/crime/2014/08/13/lgbt-groups-sign-letter-support-michael-browns-family.

128 *Pinkwashing* also refers to corporate displays of pink ribbons to promote breast cancer awareness while simultaneously profiting from the sale of products linked to the disease.

129 Slepian, "An Inconvenient Truth."

130 Slepian, "An Inconvenient Truth."

131 Franke, "The Greater Context of the Pinkwashing Debate."

132 Franke, "Dating the State."

133 Aeyal Gross, "Pinkwashing Debate: Gay Rights in Israel Are Being Appropriated for Propaganda Value," *Haaretz*, June 10, 2015, http://www.haaretz.com/opinion/.premium-1.660349.

134 Puar, "Rethinking Homonationalism," 337.

135 Harvey Fierstein, "Russia's Anti-Gay Crackdown," *New York Times*, July 21, 2013, http://www.nytimes.com/2013/07/22/opinion/russias-anti-gay-crackdown.html.

136 Travis Waldron, "Why Obama Is Sending Openly Gay Athletes to Russia's Olympics," *Think Progress*, December 18, 2013, http://thinkprogress.org/sports/2013/12/17/3079061/openly-gay-athletes-billie-jean-king-caitlin-cahow-obama-delegation-sochi-olympics/.

137 "Anti-Gay Russian Laws Lead to Stoli Vodka Boycott: The Rubin Report," YouTube, https://www.youtube.com/watch?v=zuplkaBfiJc, last modified December 5, 2013.

138 Andrew Higgins, "Facing Fury over Antigay Law, Stoli Says 'Russian? Not Really,'" *New York Times*, September 7, 2013, http://www.nytimes.com/2013/09/08/world/europe/facing-fury-over-antigay-law-stoli-says-russian-not-really.html?pagewanted=all and_r=0.

139 Daniel Reynolds, "Stoli Responds to LGBT Boycott of Russian Products," *The Advocate*, July 25, 2013, http://www.advocate.com/politics/2013/07/25/stoli-responds-lgbt-boycott-russian-products.

140 "About the Fund," U.S. Department of State, http://www.state.gov/globalequality/about/index.htm, accessed February 19, 2016.

141 "LGBT Global Development Partnership," U.S. Agency for International Development, https://www.usaid.gov/sites/default/files/documents/2496/CTP_Program_LGBTGlobalPartnership_Targeted%20Outreach_FINAL2.pdf.

142 Norimitsu Onishi, "U.S. Support of Gay Rights in Africa May Have Done More Harm than Good," *New York Times*, December 20, 2015, http://www.nytimes.com/2015/12/21/world/africa/us-support-of-gay-rights-in-africa-may-have-done-more-harm-than-good.html?_r=1.

143 Katyal, "Exporting Identity," 103–14.

144 Chauncy, *Gay New York*.

145 Minter, "Do Transsexuals Dream of Gay Rights?" 147–48.

146 D'Emilio, "Capitalism and Gay Identity."

147 "Definition of Terms: Sex, Gender, Gender Identity, Sexual Orientation," American Psychological Association, http://www.apa.org/pi/lgbt/resources/sexuality-definitions.pdf, accessed September 28, 2014.

148 *Kerrigan v. Commissioner of Public Health*.

149 See, e.g., Battles and Hilton-Morrow, "Gay Characters in Conventional Spaces."

150 Chris Connelly, "Mizzou's Michael Sam Says He's Gay," *ESPN Outside the Lines*, February 10, 2014, http://espn.go.com/espn/otl/story/_/id/10429030/michael-sam-missouri-tigers-says-gay.

151 Massad, "Re-Orienting Desire," 182.

152 "The Visible Vote '08."

Chapter 4. LEGAL REALISM TO POLITICAL ECONOMY

1 *United States v. Windsor.*

2 Robert Barnes, "Supreme Court Declines to Review Same-Sex Marriage Cases, Allowing Unions in Five States," *Washington Post*, October 6, 2014, https://www .washingtonpost.com/politics/courts_law/supreme-court-declines-to-review -same-sex-marriage-cases/2014/10/06/ee822848–4d5e-11e4-babe-e91da079cb8a _story.html.

3 *DeBoer v. Snyder.*

4 Chris Johnson, "After Marriage, What's Next for the LGBT Movement?" *Washington Blade*, June 11, 2015, http://www.washingtonblade.com/2015/06/11/after -marriage-whats-next-for-lgbt-movement.

5 Sandhya Somashekhar, "Gay Rights Group, after Recent Victories, Turns to a New Frontier: The South," *Washington Post*, September 10, 2014, https://www.washing tonpost.com/politics/gay-rights-group-after-recent-victories-turns-to-a-new-frontier -the-south/2014/09/10/22c72a68–3761–11e4-bdfb-de4104544a37_story.html.

6 Sheryl Gay Stolberg, "Rights Bill Sought for Lesbian, Gay, Bisexual, and Transgender Americans," *New York Times*, December 4, 2014, http://www.nytimes .com/2014/12/05/us/advocates-seek-civil-rights-bill-for-lesbian-gay-bisexual-and -transgender-americans.html.

7 Hasenbush et al., "The LGBT Divide."

8 E-mail on file with author.

9 Kyle Knight, "LGBTI Rights: Not There Yet," *Irin*, August 14, 2014, http://www .irinnews.org/report/100487/lgbti-rights-still-not-there-yet.

10 Badgett et al., "LGBT Inclusion and Economic Development in Emerging Economies."

11 Janson Wu, "Equality is Not the Finish Line," GLAD (blog), July 29, 2014, http://www.glad.org/current/post/equality-is-not-the-finish-line.

12 Contemporary historians have transcended the "big men" theory of black civil rights, pointing out that many of the acts of organizing and resistance that have constituted the movement over time have been performed by regular people, neither all "big" nor all men. My brief account, however, will pay particular attention to a few leaders who, like the current LGBT organizational leadership, struggled with the civil rights-distributive justice dichotomy as they ushered their movement forward.

13 Peller, "Race Consciousness," 760.

14 Sitkoff, *A New Deal for Blacks*, 20–24.

15 Sitkoff, *A New Deal for Blacks*, 23–25.

16 Foner, "Socialism and the Negro Problem," 240.

17 Foner, "Socialism and the Negro Problem," 240.

18 Foner, "Socialism and the Negro Problem," 241–42.

19 Foner, "Socialism and the Negro Problem," 242.

20 Foner, "Socialism and the Negro Problem," 243.

21 Singh, *Black Is a Country*, 213.

22 Singh, *Black Is a Country*, 73

23 Singh, *Black Is a Country*, 72–73.

24 Singh, *Black Is a Country*, 73.

25 Sitkoff, *A New Deal for Blacks*, 139–68.

26 Singh, *Black Is a Country*, 88.

27 Singh, *Black Is a Country*, 87.

28 Linder, "Farm Workers and the Fair Labor Standards Act," 1335.

29 Katznelson, *When Affirmative Action Was White*, 37–40.

30 Katznelson, *When Affirmative Action Was White*, 29.

31 Sitkoff, *A New Deal for Blacks*, 58–83.

32 Sitkoff, *A New Deal for Blacks*, 79.

33 Sitkoff, *A New Deal for Blacks*, 71.

34 Katznelson, *When Affirmative Action Was White*, 67–79.

35 Katznelson, *When Affirmative Action Was White*, 77–78.

36 Katznelson, *When Affirmative Action Was White*, 78.

37 Sitkoff, *A New Deal for Blacks*, 170.

38 Ransby, *Ella Baker and the Black Freedom Movement*, 132.

39 Ransby, *Ella Baker and the Black Freedom Movement*, 132.

40 Ransby, *Ella Baker and the Black Freedom Movement*, 133.

41 Sitkoff, *A New Deal for Blacks*, 173.

42 Sitkoff, *A New Deal for Blacks*, 173–89.

43 Bell, *Silent Covenants*, 3.

44 Bell, *Silent Covenants*, 8. Although Bell points to Randolph and the National Urban League in a single sentence, they ought to be sharply distinguished. The National Urban League was reputed to be much more conservative in its economic policy preferences than Randolph, who was decidedly a leftist. Indeed, while this chapter does not run through all of the distinctions, the range of policy preferences among those organizations and individuals who focused on economics was wide. Trade unionists, socialists, communists, advocates for welfare and social insurance, and capitalists with a modest regulatory or antidiscrimination agenda would be separately considered in a comprehensive discussion.

45 Hall, "The NAACP and the Challenges of 1969's Radicalism," 7585.

46 McKnight, *The Last Crusade*, 3.

47 McKnight, *The Last Crusade*, 13. Rustin was a close adviser to King and a major influence in King's adoption of Gandhian nonviolence. He was in and out of King's inner circle, apparently due to the public relations implications of his having been convicted of lewdness for having sex with two other men in a parked vehicle.

48 McKnight, *The Last Crusade*, 20.

49 Kate Ellis and Stephen Smith, *King's Last March: New Front in the Fight for Freedom*, online recording. http://americanradioworks.publicradio.org/features/king /b1.html.

50 Marx and Engels, "On the Jewish Question," 28.

51 Fraser, "From Redistribution to Recognition?"

52 Fraser, "From Redistribution to Recognition?"

53 Butler, "Merely Cultural," 48.
54 Fraser, "From Redistribution to Recognition?" 13.
55 Duggan, *The Twilight of Equality?* xviii.
56 Duggan, *The Twilight of Equality?* xix.
57 Harris, "From Stonewall to the Suburbs?" 1565.
58 Harris, "From Stonewall to the Suburbs?" 1565.
59 See, e.g., Klein, *No Logo*, 122.
60 Fraser, "From Redistribution to Recognition?" 14.
61 Butler, "Merely Cultural," 42.
62 Taylor, *Multiculturalism and "The Politics of Recognition,"* 25.
63 Taylor, *Multiculturalism and "The Politics of Recognition,"* 26.
64 Taylor, *Multiculturalism and "The Politics of Recognition,"* 34–35.
65 This is among the more psychoanalytic readings of Hegel.
66 Taylor, *Multiculturalism and "The Politics of Recognition,"* 50.
67 Taylor, *Multiculturalism and "The Politics of Recognition,"* 70–71.
68 Taylor, *Multiculturalism and "The Politics of Recognition,"* 72.
69 Taylor briefly addressed in his essay the problem of settling on a metric for judgment, though not very satisfactorily.
70 Fraser, "Heterosexism, Misrecognition, and Capitalism," 59.
71 Fraser, "From Redistribution to Recognition?" 29–30.
72 Butler, "Merely Cultural," 48.
73 Fraser, "From Redistribution to Recognition?" 20–22.
74 Fraser, "From Redistribution to Recognition?" 18–27.
75 Fraser, "From Redistribution to Recognition?" 20.
76 Fraser, "From Redistribution to Recognition?" 22.
77 Fraser, "From Redistribution to Recognition?" 23.
78 Fraser, "From Redistribution to Recognition?" 19, 21n18.
79 Butler, "Merely Cultural," 50, quoting Engels, *The Origin of the Family, Private Property and the State*, 71–72.
80 Butler, "Merely Cultural," 51.
81 Butler, "Merely Cultural," 51.
82 Butler, "Merely Cultural," 51–52.
83 Fraser, "Heterosexism, Misrecognition, and Capitalism," 64.
84 D'Emilio, "Capitalism and Gay Identity," 5.
85 D'Emilio, "Capitalism and Gay Identity," 7.
86 Fraser, "Heterosexism, Misrecognition, and Capitalism," 65.
87 D'Emilio, "The Homosexual Menace," 64.
88 Johnson, *The Lavender Scare*, 37.
89 D'Emilio, "Homosexual Menace," 64.
90 Mathews, quoted in Johnson, *The Lavender Scare*, 37. The pioneering gay rights organization the Mattachine Society rose and fell in the grip of this anxious association. Harry Hay and a small group of gay men, all communists or communist sympathizers, founded the initially secret organization in Los Angeles in 1950. The conditions at the time for both homosexuals and communists were frightening, as

the House Un-American Activities Committee (HUAC) wielded its investigatory power and police regularly raided gay bars and entrapped homosexuals in cruising areas, destroying reputations and careers. John D'Emilio writes, "An atmosphere of insecurity and vulnerability infected the entire gay subculture": D'Emilio, "Dreams Deferred," 29. As the Mattachine Society grew beyond its initial membership, internal conflicts erupted, perhaps the most destructive of which was whether to resist the abuses of HUAC or to purge the organization of communists by instituting loyalty oaths: D'Emilio, "Dreams Deferred," 42–49. The organization fractured. A Washington, DC, chapter arose, however, specifically in defiance of anti-gay firings and denials of federal government jobs: Johnson, *The Lavender Scare*, 179–208.

91 Fraser, "Heterosexism, Misrecognition, and Capitalism," 65.

92 Bersani, "Is the Rectum a Grave?" 205. In an essay designed in part to excavate the obscure politics of sex acts, Bersani disposed of one theory, writing, "There has been a lot of confusion about the real or potential political implications of homosexuality. Gay activists have tended to deduce those implications from the status of homosexuals as an oppressed minority. . . . While it is indisputably true that sexuality is always being politicized, the ways in which having sex politicizes are highly problematical. Right-wing politics can, for example, emerge quite easily from a sentimentalizing of the armed forces or of blue collar workers, a sentimentalizing which can itself prolong and sublimate a marked sexual preference for sailors and telephone linemen": Bersani, "Is the Rectum a Grave?" 206.

93 *United States v. Windsor*, Brief of 278 Employers and Organizations Representing Employers as Amici Curiae in Support of Edith Schlain Windsor.

94 *Obergefell v. Hodges*, Brief of 379 Employers and Organizations Representing Employers as Amici Curiae in Support of Petitioners.

95 "Best Places to Work 2015," *Human Rights Campaign*, accessed February 2, 2016, http://www.hrc.org/resources/best-places-to-work-2015.

96 Walters, *All the Rage*, 235–72.

97 "LGBT: The Coming Out of Alaska Airlines Pays Off 2096 Percent," *ETN: Global Travel Industry News*, December 16, 2015, http://www.eturbonews.com/66858 /lgbt-coming-out-alaska-airlines-pays-2096-percent.

98 Harris, "From Stonewall to the Suburbs?" 1570.

99 Fraser, "Rethinking Recognition," 113–14.

100 Warner, *The Trouble with Normal*.

101 Eng, *The Feeling of Kinship*.

102 Muñoz, *Cruising Utopia*.

103 Polikoff, *Beyond (Straight and Gay) Marriage*.

104 Conrad, *Against Equality*.

105 "A New Queer Agenda," special issue, *Scholar and Feminist Online* 10, nos. 1–2 (Fall 2011–Spring 2012), http://sfonline.barnard.edu/a-new-queer-agenda, accessed February 2, 2016.

106 Duggan and Kim, "Preface."

107 Duggan and Kim, "Preface."

108 *Our Fair City.*
109 *Our Fair City.*
110 Honneth, "Recognition or Redistribution?" 54.
111 Fraser, "Heterosexism, Misrecognition, and Capitalism," 65.
112 Fraser, "From Redistribution to Recognition?" 40.
113 The term *intersectionality* originates with Kimberlé Williams Crenshaw: see, e.g., Crenshaw, *Mapping the Margins.* For the life of, and variations in, that theoretic tool, see Sumi Cho, Kimberlé Williams Crenshaw, and Leslie McCall, eds., "Toward a Field of Intersectional Studies: Theory, Applications, and Praxis," special issue, *Signs* 38, no. 4 (Summer 2013): 785–810. Fraser invokes the term in its weakest possible usage here. My goal is to make richer use of intersectionality by integrating it with insights from American legal realism so that the low-profile legal conditions facing highly localized constituencies come into the foreground.
114 Kennedy, "The Stakes of Law, or Hale and Foucault!" 124.
115 Kennedy, "The Stakes of Law, or Hale and Foucault!" 124.
116 Butler, "Merely Cultural," 52.
117 For continuing discussion of the framework, especially as it regards the challenges facing feminism, see also Fraser, "Feminism, Capitalism and the Cunning of History."
118 Sawicki, *Disciplining Foucault,* 9.
119 Butler, *The Psychic Life of Power,* 10.
120 Butler, *The Psychic Life of Power,* 20.
121 Butler, *The Psychic Life of Power,* 12.
122 Butler, *The Psychic Life of Power,* 12.
123 Butler, *The Psychic Life of Power,* 93.
124 Butler, *The Psychic Life of Power,* 16.
125 Butler, *The Psychic Life of Power,* 93.
126 Butler, *The Psychic Life of Power,* 99.
127 Butler, *The Psychic Life of Power,* 13.
128 Butler, *The Psychic Life of Power,* 28–29.
129 Butler, *The Psychic Life of Power,* 17.
130 Butler, *The Psychic Life of Power,* 93.
131 Butler, *The Psychic Life of Power,* 17.
132 Lévi-Strauss, *The Savage Mind,* 16–21.
133 Lévi-Strauss, *The Savage Mind,* 17.
134 Lévi-Strauss, *The Savage Mind,* 18.
135 Lévi-Strauss, *The Savage Mind,* 19.
136 Lévi-Strauss, *The Savage Mind,* 21.
137 Lorde, "The Master's Tools Will Never Dismantle the Master's House," 110.
138 Lévi-Strauss, *The Savage Mind,* 21.

Chapter 5. MAKING THE DISTRIBUTIVE TURN

1 Ball houses are chosen familial constellations comprising LGTBQ people of color in urban settings. Some of the houses compete with one another in runway-style

competitions: see Arnold and Bailey, "Constructing Home and Family." Boston is not a major hub for the ball house scene, but the houses are a significant phenomenon in big cities such as New York and Chicago.

2 The task force was formerly known as the National Gay and Lesbian Task Force (NGLTF).

3 Ray, "Lesbian, Gay, Bisexual and Transgender Youth."

4 Hale, "Coercion and Distribution in a Supposedly Non-coercive State."

5 Hale, "Coercion and Distribution in a Supposedly Non-coercive State," 471.

6 Hale, "Coercion and Distribution in a Supposedly Non-coercive State," 472.

7 Hale, "Coercion and Distribution in a Supposedly Non-coercive State," 472–73.

8 On the significance of Hale's analysis and its historical context, see Horwitz, *The Transformation of American Law*, 195–98.

9 Kennedy, "The Stakes of Law," 93.

10 *Pierce v. Society of Sisters*; *Meyer v. Nebraska*.

11 *Pierce v. Society of Sisters* at 534.

12 See, e.g., *Griswold v. Connecticut*.

13 *Pickup v. Brown*, 728 F.3d 1042 (9th Cir. 2013). Cert denied, 134 S. Ct. 2871 (2014).

14 *Ferguson v. JONAH*.

15 Therapeutic Fraud Prevention Act, H.R. 2450, 114th Cong. (2015).

16 Kennedy, "The Stakes of Law," 90.

17 Olsen, "The Family and the Market"; Olsen, "The Myth of State Intervention in the Family."

18 Olsen, "The Myth of State Intervention in the Family," 837.

19 Olsen, "The Myth of State Intervention in the Family," 842.

20 Olsen, "The Myth of State Intervention in the Family," 837.

21 Olsen, "The Family and the Market," 1509.

22 Olsen, "The Family and the Market," 1509.

23 In Massachusetts, parents may petition the juvenile court to take action against a child who repeatedly runs away or refuses to obey: see under Mass. Gen. Laws ch. 119 § 39E.

24 Suk, "Criminal Law Comes Home," 12.

25 I thank Chase Strangio for this account.

26 Olsen, "The Family and the Market," 1505–6.

27 Mnookin and Kornhauser, "Bargaining in the Shadow of the Law."

28 Mnookin and Kornhauser, "Bargaining in the Shadow of the Law," 968.

29 Once an adoption is finalized, the fundamental right to parent fully attaches. The adoptive family is treated differently during the process from how it is treated after finalization.

30 See *Smith v. Organization of Foster Families for Equality and Reform*, 431 U.S. 816 (1977); *Lofton v. Secretary of the Department of Children and Family Services*, 358 F.3d 804 (11th Cir. 2004).

31 110 Mass. Code. Regs. 7.104(1)(d).

32 Holmes, "The Path of the Law," 457.

33 Dank et al., "Locked In."

34 Galanter, "Why the 'Haves' Come Out Ahead," 97.

35 42 U.S. Code § 673b.

36 110 Mass. Code Regs. 1.09(3).

37 Holmes, "The Path of the Law," 459.

38 Holmes, "The Path of the Law," 461.

39 Alex Morris, "The Forsaken: A Rising Number of Homeless Gay Teens Are Being Cast Out by Religious Families," *Rolling Stone*, September 3, 2014, http://www .rollingstone.com/culture/features/the-forsaken-a-rising-number-of-homeless-gay -teens-are-being-cast-out-by-religious-families-20140903.

40 Morris, "The Forsaken."

41 Durso and Gates, "Serving Our Youth." This number is based on the population accessing services.

42 Movement Advancement Project et al., "A Broken Bargain for LGBT Workers of Color."

43 In Massachusetts, "no person is allowed [in public parks] except during the hours from dawn to dusk unless specified otherwise at the site, or by permit": 700 Mass. Code Regs. 5.201(2)(b).

44 "States That Limit or Prohibit Juvenile Shackling and Solitary Confinement," National Conference of State Legislatures website, July 26, 2016, http://www .ncsl.org/research/civil-and-criminal-justice/states-that-limit-or-prohibit-juvenile -shackling-and-solitary-confinement635572628.aspx.

45 See e.g., Mass. Gen. Laws ch. 119 § 39H.

46 Commonwealth of Massachusetts, Department of Youth Services (DYS), "Prohibition of Harassment and Discrimination against Youth," policy no. 03.04.09, effective July 1, 2014, in *DYS Guidelines for Lesbian, Gay, Transgender, Questioning, Queer, Intersex, and Gender Non-Conforming Youth*, § III(B).

47 The vote was 56–43 in favor, but supporters were unable to garner the sixty votes necessary to overcome the now routinely invoked filibuster.

48 42 U.S. Code § 5701 et seq.

49 These are longer-term programs, up to eighteen months, but only for older youth, age sixteen to twenty-one.

50 45 C.F.R. § 1351.18(e).

51 Maral Noshad Sharifi, "The Men Who Want AIDS—and How It Improved Their Lives," *OUT Magazine*, August 8, 2013, http://www.out.com/news-opinion/2013 /08/02/men-who-want-aids-bronx-new-york. For more in-depth discussion of "bug chasing" and "bare backing," including their subtler psychic dimensions, see Bersani and Phillips, *Intimacies*.

52 Federal and state laws carve out exceptions for educational loans, many types of which are fully enforceable against a person who signed as a minor: Higher Education Act of 1965, 20 U.S. Code § 1070 et seq. (1992). Also, some proposals contemplate making certain contracts entered into online enforceable against minors: see Preston and Crowther, "Infancy Doctrine Inquiries," 47, 66–77.

53 Knauer, "LGBT Youth," 255. See also Wilson et al., *New Report*. In addition, kids (LGBTQ and otherwise) who have been in foster care are at increased risk of

homelessness: Fowler et al., "Pathways to and from Homelessness and Associated Psychosocial Outcomes among Adolescents Leaving the Foster Care System," 1453. In other words, the three populations (LGBTQ kids, kids who have been in foster care, and homeless kids) overlap.

54 See Jesse Ellison, "Fostering Children Targets for Identity Theft," *Newsweek*, February 6, 2009, http://www.newsweek.com/foster-children-targets-identity-theft -82561#.

55 See 45 C.F.R. § 302, establishing the federal rules for collection and distribution of support payments.

56 Spade, "Documenting Gender," 737.

57 An Act Regulating the Use of Credit Reports by Employers, Bill MA H. 1736, 189th Gen. Ct. (2015).

58 29 U.S. Code § 206(g)(1).

59 29 C.F.R. § 570.119.

60 29 C.F.R. § 570.35(a)(3).

61 29 C.F.R. § 570.120.

62 Llewellyn, "A Realistic Jurisprudence," 431.

63 Llewellyn, "A Realistic Jurisprudence," 431, 448.

64 Llewellyn, "A Realistic Jurisprudence," 437.

65 Llewellyn, "A Realistic Jurisprudence," 437–38.

66 Llewellyn, "A Realistic Jurisprudence," 444.

67 Consequentialism is also a philosophy of ethics related to utilitarianism. The use of the term in legal theory is pretty close. It eschews judging a law ethical or not by reference to its text or purpose, instead considering the law's effects in the real world.

68 Holmes and Llewellyn wrote before the administrative state really took hold in the course of the New Deal; their thinking therefore reflects a focus on the decisions of courts. Llewellyn addressed administrative agencies briefly in his article, which was published in 1930. (Holmes was dead by 1935.) Later realists addressed themselves to the decision-making of administrative agencies once the New Deal led to their profusion: see, e.g., Landis, *The Administrative Process*. Landis served in several administrative capacities under FDR, including chairman of the Securities and Exchange Commission, and later wrote a report on the functioning of federal agencies to President John F. Kennedy. Contemporary consequentialists are interested in the conduct of such agencies and, really, any arm of the state charged with enforcing the law, as well as in the effects of that conduct on private actors.

69 Kennedy, "The Stakes of Law," 98.

70 Kennedy, "The Stakes of Law," 98.

71 Dank et al., "Girls Do What They Have to Do to Survive."

72 See, e.g., Dank et al., *Surviving the Streets of New York*.

73 Dank et al., *Surviving the Streets of New York*.

74 Lankenau et al., "Street Careers," 11.

75 Eliyanna Kaiser, remarks at "Beyond Coercion: Radical Voices on Sex Work, Feminism and the Law," final panel in Unbound: Harvard Journal of the Legal Left

Speaker Series, April 16, 2008. See Foohey, "Panel Discusses Prostitution and the Sex Industry."

76　Ahmed, "Think Again."

77　See "Rentboy Wasn't My 'Brothel': It Was a Tool to Stay Alive in This Economy of Violence," *The Guardian*, September 1, 2015, http://www.theguardian.com /commentisfree/2015/sep/01/rentboy-online-brothel-tool-economy-sex-work.

78　Connor, "In Loco Aequitatis," 48.

79　Connor, "In Loco Aequitatis," 49.

80　Mogul et al., *Queer (In)justice*, 53.

81　Mogul et al., *Queer (In)justice*, 53–60.

82　One of my earliest experiences in law practice was trying to convince a hearing officer for a public housing program that the front-line worker had misread my client's sheet. The sheet listed three court dates, but they were all for the same offense. The housing official insisted that my client had three offenses, which (passing the limit of two) would have rendered her ineligible for housing for the elderly and disabled.

83　Morgan et al., "The School Discipline Consensus Report"; Wilber, *Lesbian, Gay, Bisexual and Transgender Youth in the Juvenile Justice System*.

84　For a critique of the child support enforcement system, see Adler and Halley, "You Play, You Pay." Making minors eligible payees would put some muscle on their side, but there is plenty to object to about this system. See also Brito, "Fathers behind Bars."

85　Halley, "Doing a Distributional Analysis."

86　Silbaugh, "Women's Place," 1808.

87　New York City Zoning Resolution Amendment N 950384 ZRY (October 25, 1995). See also *Stringfellows of New York Ltd. v. City of New York* upholding amendments against constitutional challenge.

88　Berlant and Warner, "Sex in Public," 551–52.

89　Berlant and Warner, "Sex in Public," 551n9. See also Blank and Rosen-Zvi, "The Geography of Sexuality," 987–89.

90　Pendleton and Goldschmidt, "Sex Panic!" 30. The Oscar Wilde Bookshop, which opened in 1967 as the first gay and lesbian bookshop in the country, did in fact shut its doors in 2009 for economic reasons. Given the recession of 2008 and the advent of Amazon.com, it is difficult to know for certain whether efforts by the city to "clean up" Greenwich Village were determinative.

91　Movement Advancement Project et al., "A Broken Bargain for LGBT Workers of Color."

92　Hasenbush et al., "The LGBT Divide."

93　Badgett et al., "New Patterns of Poverty in the Lesbian, Gay, and Bisexual Community."

94　*Obergefell v. Hodges*, 135 S. Ct. 2071 (2015).

95　In a premier example of background rules analysis, the Israeli law professor Hila Shamir studied the effects of a range of administrative regimes on the allocation of domestic responsibilities between men and women in heterosexual households. She argued that "high tolerance for employment [and immigration] law violation" in the heavily migrant U.S. pool of child-care workers, enables middle- and upper-income women to join the paid work force and privatize significant portions of domestic labor at low costs": Shamir, "The State of Care," 969.

96 For details on how a "marriage penalty" is built into an array of social insurance, public assistance, and other programs aimed at low-income people, see Rand, "The Real Marriage Penalty," 93.

97 Cahn and Carbone, *Red Families v. Blue Families*, 1–4.

98 Saewyc et al., "Stigma Management?"

99 Saewyc et al., "Stigma Management?"

Conclusion

1 Barclay et al., *Queer Mobilizations*.

2 Barclay et al., *Queer Mobilizations*, 5.

3 Barclay et al., *Queer Mobilizations*, 10.

4 Leachman, "From Protest to Perry," 1673.

5 Leachman, "From Protest to Perry," 1673.

6 Sarat and Scheingold, *Cause Lawyering and Social Movements*.

7 Levitsky, "To Lead with Law."

8 Levitsky, "To Lead with Law," 157–59.

9 Levitsky, "To Lead with Law," 148, 157.

10 Levitsky, "To Lead with Law," 151, 153.

11 Levitsky, "To Lead with Law," 150.

12 Levitsky, "To Lead with Law," 155–56.

13 Levitsky, "To Lead with Law," 156.

14 See, e.g., Barclay et al., *Queer Mobilizations*, 7.

Case Law and Legal Briefs

Baehr v. Lewin. 852 P.2d 44 (1993), as clarified on reconsideration (May 27, 1993).

Bowers v. Hardwick. 478 U.S. 186 (1986).

Boy Scouts of America v. Dale. 530 U.S. 640 (2000).

Brown v. Board of Education of Topeka. 387 U.S. 483 (1954).

Burwell v. Hobby Lobby. 134 S. Ct. 2751 (2014).

Bush v. Gore, 531 U.S. 98 (2000).

Christian Legal Society Chapter of the University of California, Hastings College of the Law v. Martinez. 561 U.S. 661 (2010).

Craig v. Boren. 429 U.S. 190 (1976).

Cruzan v. Special School District No. 1. 294 F.3d 981 (8th Cir. 2002).

DeBoer v. Snyder. 772 F.3d 388 (6th Cir. 2014).

District of Columbia v. Heller. 554 U.S. 570 (2008).

Doe v. Regional School Unit 26. 86 A.3d 600 (Me. 2014).

Fabrizio v. City of Providence. 104 A.3d 1289 (R.I. 2014).

Ferguson v. JONAH. No. HUD-L-5473–12 (N.J. Super. Ct. Law Div. June 6, 2014). https://www.splcenter.org/sites/default/files/d6_legacy_files/downloads/case /ferguson_v_jonah_-_psj_-_6-6-14_-_final.pdf.

Florida Department of Children and Families v. Adoption of X.X.G. 45 So. 3d 79 (Fla. Dist. Ct. App. 2010).

Goins v. West Group. 635 N.W.2d 717 (Minn. 2001).

Goodridge v. Department of Public Health. 440 Mass. 309 (Mass. 2003).

Griswold v. Connecticut. 381 U.S. 479, 483 (1965).

Hollingsworth v. Perry. 133 S. Ct. 2652, 186 L. Ed. 2d 768 (U.S. 2013).

———. Brief of Amici Curiae Kenneth B. Mehlman et al. Supporting Respondents, Hollingsworth v. Perry, 133 S.Ct. 2652 (2013). No. 12–144.

Huff v. Chapel Hill–Chancy Hall School. 16 MDLR 1605 (Massachusetts Commission against Discrimination, 1994).

Hurley v. Irish-American Gay, Lesbian and Bisexual Group of Boston. 515 U.S. 557 (1995).

In re Marriage Cases. 183 P.3d 384 (Cal. 2008).

Kerrigan v. Commissioner of Public Health. 289 Conn. 135, 957 A.2d 407 (2008).

Lawrence v. Texas. 539 U.S. 558 (2003).

Lochner v. New York. 198 U.S. 45 (1905).

Lofton v. Secretary of the Department of Children and Family Services. 358 F.3d 804 (11th Cir. 2004).

Log Cabin Republicans v. United States. 716 F.Supp.2d 884 (C.D.Cal. 2010).

Loving v. Virginia. 388 U.S. 1 (1967).

Macy v. Holder. EEOC doc. 0120120821, 2012 WL 1435995.

Marbury v. Madison. 1 Cranch, 137 (1803).

Mathis v. Fountain-Fort Carson School District 8. Charge no. P20130034X (2013). http://www.transgenderlegal.org/media/uploads/doc_529.pdf.

McDonald v. City of Chicago. 130 S. Ct. 3020, 3108 (2010).

McLaughlin v. State of Florida. 379 U.S. 184 (1964).

Meyer v. Nebraska. 262 U.S. 390 (1923).

M v. H. (1999) 2 S.C.R. 3 (Can.).

National Federation of Independent Business v. Sebelius. 132 S. Ct. 2566 (2012).

Obergefell v. Hodges, 135 S. Ct. 2584 (2015).

———. Brief for the American Psychological Association as Amici Curiae Supporting Petitioners, Obergefell v. Hodges, 135 S. Ct. 2584 (2015). WL 1004713 (U.S.). Nos. 14–556, 14–562, 14–571, 14–574.

———. Brief of Constitutional Law Scholars Supporting Petitioners, Obergefell v. Hodges, 135 S. Ct. 2584 (2015). WL 1022689 (U.S.). Nos. 14–556, 14–562, 14–571, 14–574.

———. Brief for Respondent, Obergefell v. Hodges, 135 S. Ct. 2584 (2015). WL 1384100 (U.S.). No. 14–556.

———. Brief of 379 Employers and Organizations Representing Employers as Amici Curiae in Support of Petitioners, Obergefell v. Hodges, 135 S. Ct. 2584 (2015).

———. Brief of Kenneth B. Mehlman et al. as Amici Curiae Supporting Petitioners, Obergefell v. Hodges, 135 S. Ct. 2584 (2015). WL 981540 (U.S.). Nos. 14–556, 14–562, 14–571, 14–574.

———. Reply Brief for Petitioners, Obergefell v. Hodges, 135 S. Ct. 2584 (2015). WL 1776076 (U.S.) (No. 14–556).

Pace v. State. 106 U.S. 583 (1883).

Parents Involved in Community Schools v. Seattle School District No. 1. 551 U.S. 701, 772 (2007).

Parker v. Hurley. 474 F. Supp. 2d 261 (D. Mass. 2007) aff'd, 514 F.3d 87 (1st Cir. 2008).

———. Brief for Amicus ACLU of Massachusetts at 19, Parker v. Hurley, 474 F. Supp. 2d 261 (D. Mass. 2007) aff'd, 514 F.3d 87 (1st Cir. 2008). No. 06-CV-10751-MLW, 2006.

Perry v. Brown. 671 F.3d 1052 (9th Cir. 2012), vacated and remanded sub nom.

Perry v. Schwarzenegger. 704 F. Supp. 2d 921 (N.D. Cal. 2010), aff'd sub nom.

Pickup v. Brown. 728 F.3d 1042 (9th Cir. 2013). Cert denied, 134 S. Ct. 2871 (2014).

Pierce v. Society of Sisters. 268 U.S. 510 (1925).

Planned Parenthood v. Casey. 505 U.S. 833 (1992).

Plessy v. Ferguson. 163 U.S. 537 (1896).

Price Waterhouse v. Hopkins. 490 U.S. 228 (1988).

Roe v. Wade. 410 U.S. 113 (1973).

Romer v. Evans. 517 U.S. 620 (1996).

Rosa v. Park West Bank and Trust Company. 214 F.3d 213 (1st Cir. 2000).

Schroer v. Billington. 577 F. Supp. 2d, 293 (D.C. Cir. 2008).

Slaughter-House Cases. 83 U.S. 36 (1873).

Smith v. City of Salem, Ohio. 378 F.3d 566 (6th Cir. 2004).

Smith v. Organization of Foster Families for Equality and Reform. 431 U.S. 816 (1977).

Sommers v. Budget Marketing, Inc. 667 F.2d 748 (8th Cir. 1982).

Strauss v. Horton. 207 P.3d 48 (Cal. 2009).

Stringfellows of New York Ltd. v. City of New York. 91 N.Y.2d 382 (1998).

Texas et al. v. United States. Case 7:16-cv-00054-O (N.D. Tex. 2016).

Turner v. Safley. 482 U.S. 78, 95–96 (1987).

Ulane v. Eastern Airlines, Inc. 742 F.2d 1081 (7th Cir. 1984).

United States v. Windsor. 133 S. Ct. 2675 (2013).

———. Brief of 278 Employers and Organizations Representing Employers as Amici Curiae in Support of Edith Schlain Windsor, Windsor v. U.S., 133 S. Ct. 2675 (2013).

Washington v. Davis. 426 U.S. 229 (1976).

Women's Liberation Front v. U.S. Department of Justice. 1:16-cv-00915 (D.N.M. 2016).

Yick Wo v. Hopkins. 118 U.S. 356 (1886).

Secondary Sources

Ackerman, Bruce. *We the People: Foundations.* Cambridge. MA: Harvard University Press, 1991.

Adler, Libby, and Janet Halley. "You Play, You Pay." In *Governance Feminism: Notes from the Field,* ed. Janet Halley, Prabha Kotiswaran, Hila Shamir, and Rachel Rebouché. Minneapolis: University of Minnesota Press, forthcoming.

Ahmed, Aziza. "Think Again: Prostitution: Why Zero-Tolerance Makes for Bad Policy on the World's Oldest Profession." *Foreign Policy,* January 19, 2014. http://foreignpolicy.com/2014/01/19/think-again-prostitution.

———. "When Men Are Harmed: Feminism, Queer Theory, and Torture at Abu Ghraib." UCLA *Journal of Islamic and Near Eastern Law* 11 (2012): 1–19.

Alexander, Michelle. *The New Jim Crow: Mass Incarceration in the Age of Colorblindness.* New York: New Press, 2012.

Arnold, Emily A., and Marion M. Bailey. "Constructing Home and Family: How the Ballroom Community Supports African American GLBTQ Youth in the Face of HIV/AIDS." *Journal of Gay and Lesbian Social Services* 21 (2–3) (January 1, 2009): 171–88. https://www.ncbi.nlm.nih.gov/pmc/articles/PMC3489283.

Badgett, M. V. Lee. *Money, Myths and Change.* Chicago: University of Chicago Press, 2001.

Badgett, M. V. Lee, Laura E. Durso, and Alyssa Schneebaum. "New Patterns of Poverty in the Lesbian, Gay, and Bisexual Community." Report. Williams Institute, University of California, Los Angeles, School of Law, 2013. http://williamsinstitute.law.ucla.edu/wp-content/uploads/LGB-Poverty-Update-Jun-2013.pdf.

Badgett, M. V. Lee, Sheila Nezhad, Kees Walldijk, and Yana van der Meulen Rodgers. "LGBT Inclusion and Economic Development in Emerging Economies." Report. Williams Institute, University of California, Los Angeles, School of Law, November 2014. http://williamsinstitute.law.ucla.edu/wp-content/uploads/lgbt-inclusion-and-development-november-2014.pdf.

Barclay, Scott, Mary Bernstein, and Anna-Marie Marshall, eds. *Queer Mobilizations: LGBT Activists Confront the Law*. New York: New York University Press, 2009.

Battles, Kathleen, and Wendy Hilton-Morrow. "Gay Characters in Conventional Spaces: *Will and Grace* in the Situation Comedy Genre." *Critical Studies in Media Communication* 19, no. 1 (March 2002): 87–105. http://www.csun.edu/~vcspcoog/301/will%26grace-csmc.pdf.

Becker, Gary S. *A Treatise on Family*. Cambridge, MA: Harvard University Press, 1981.

Bell, Derrick. *Silent Covenants*. New York: Oxford University Press, 2004.

Berlant, Lauren, and Michael Warner. "Sex in Public." *Critical Inquiry* 24, no. 2 (1998): 551–52.

Bernstein, Elizabeth. "Carceral Politics as Gender Justice? The 'Traffic in Women' and Neoliberal Circuits of Crime, Sex, and Rights." *Theory and Society* 41, no. 3 (2012): 233–59.

Bersani, Leo. "Is the Rectum a Grave?" *AIDS: Cultural Analysis/Cultural Activism* 43 (October 1987): 197–222.

Bersani, Leo, and Adam Phillips. *Intimacies*. Chicago: University of Chicago Press: 2008.

Bickel, Alexander M. *The Least Dangerous Branch: The Supreme Court at the Bar of Politics*. New Haven, CT: Yale University Press, 1962.

Blackstone, William. *Blackstone's Commentaries*. London: Forgotten, 2012.

Blank, Yishai, and Issi Rosen-Zvi. "The Geography of Sexuality." *North Carolina Law Review* 90, no. 4 (2012): 955–1025.

Blankenhorn, David. *Fatherless America: Confronting Our Most Urgent Social Problem*. New York: Harper Perennial, 1996.

———. *The Future of Marriage*. New York: Encounter, 2007.

Brito, Tonya L. "Fathers behind Bars: Rethinking Child Support Policy toward Low-Income Noncustodial Fathers and Their Families." *Iowa Journal of Gender, Race and Justice* 15 (2012): 617–73.

Brown, Wendy. *States of Injury: Power and Freedom in Late Modernity*. Princeton, NJ: Princeton University Press, 1995.

———. *Undoing the Demos: Neoliberalism's Stealth Revolution*. New York: Zone, 2015.

Butler, Judith. "Merely Cultural." In *Adding Insult to Injury: Nancy Fraser Debates Her Critics*, ed. Kevin Olsen, 42–56. New York: Verso, 2008.

———. *The Psychic Life of Power: Theories in Subjection*. Stanford, CA: Stanford University Press, 1997.

Cahn, Naomi, and June Carbone. *Red Families v. Blue Families: Legal Polarization and the Creation of Culture*. New York: Oxford University Press, 2010.

Carpenter, Dale. *Flagrant Conduct: The Story of Lawrence v. Texas*. New York: W. W. Norton, 2012.

Case, Mary Anne. "How High the Apple Pie—A Few Troubling Questions about Where, Why, and How the Burden of Care for Children Should Be Shifted." *Chicago-Kent Law Review* 76 (2001): 1753–88.

Chauncy, George. *Gay New York: Gender, Urban Culture, and the Making of the Gay Male World, 1890–1940.* New York: Basic, 1995.

Cohen, Cathy J. "Punks, Bulldaggers, and Welfare Queens: The Radical Potential of Queer Politics?" *GLQ* 3, no. 4 (1997): 437–65.

Collins, Patricia Hill. *Black Sexual Politics: African Americans, Gender, and the New Racism.* New York: Routledge: 2005.

Connor, Brendan M. "In Loco Aequitatis: The Dangers of 'Safe Harbor' Laws for Youth in the Sex Trades." *Stanford Journal of Civil Rights and Civil Liberties* 12, no. 1 (2016): 43–120.

Conrad, Ryan, ed. *Against Equality: Queer Revolution, not Mere Inclusion.* Oakland, CA: AK, 2014.

Cossman, Brenda. "Family Feuds: Neo-Liberal and Neo-Conservative Visions of the Reprivatization Project." In *Privatization, Law, and the Challenge to Feminism,* ed. Brenda Cossman and Judy Fudge, 169–217. Toronto: University of Toronto Press, 2002.

Crenshaw, Kimberlé Williams. "Mapping the Margins: Intersectionality, Identity Politics, and Violence against Women of Color." *Stanford Law Review* 43, no. 6 (1991): 1241–99.

———. "Race, Reform, and Retrenchment: Transformation and Legitimation in Anti-discrimination Law." *Harvard Law Review* 101, no. 7 (1988): 1331–87.

Crooms, Lisa A. "Everywhere There's War: A Racial Realist's Reconsideration of Hate Crimes Statutes." *Georgetown Journal of Gender and Law* 1 (1999): 41–66.

Dank, Meredith. "Locked In: Interactions with the Criminal Justice and Child Welfare Systems for LGBTQ Youth, YMSM, and YWSW Who Engage in Survival Sex." Urban Institute, Washington, DC, 2015. http://www.urban.org/sites/default/files/publication/71446/2000424-Locked-In-Interactions-with-the-Criminal-Justice-and-Child-Welfare-Systems-for-LGBTQ-Youth-YMSM-and-YWSW-Who-Engage-in-Survival-Sex.pdf.

———. *Surviving the Streets of New York: Experiences of LGBTQ Youth, YMSM, and YWSW Engaged in Survival Sex.* Washington, DC: Urban Institute, February 2015. http://www.urban.org/sites/default/files/publication/42186/2000119-Surviving-the-Streets-of-New-York.pdf.

Dean, Tim. "Queer Desire, Psychoanalytic Hermeneutics, and Love Lyric." In *A Concise Companion to Psychoanalysis, Literature, and Culture,* ed. Laura Marcus and Ankhi Mukherjee, 151–66. Chichester, UK: John Wiley and Sons, 2014.

Delgado, Richard. "The Ethereal Scholar: Does Critical Legal Studies Have What Minorities Want?" *Harvard Civil Rights-Civil Liberties Law Review* 22, no. 2 (1987): 301–22.

D'Emilio, John. "Capitalism and Gay Identity." In *Making Trouble: Essays on Gay History, Politics, and the University,* 3–16. London: Routledge, 1992.

———. "Dreams Deferred." In *Making Trouble: Essays on Gay History, Politics, and the University,* 17–56. London: Routledge, 1992.

———. "The Homosexual Menace." In *Making Trouble: Essays on Gay History, Politics, and the University*, 57–73. London: Routledge, 1992.

De Tocqueville, Alexis. *Democracy in America* (1835), ed. Harvey C. Mansfield and Delba Winthrop. Chicago: University of Chicago Press, 2000.

Duggan, Lisa. *The Twilight of Equality? Neoliberalism, Cultural Politics, and the Attack on Democracy*. Boston: Beacon, 2003.

Duggan, Lisa, and Richard Kim. "Preface." In "A New Queer Agenda," special issue, *Scholar and Feminist Online* 10, nos. 1–2 (Fall 2011–Spring 2012). http://sfonline .barnard.edu/a-new-queer-agenda/preface.

Durso, Laura E., and Gary J. Gates. "Serving Our Youth: Findings from a National Survey of Services Providers Working with Lesbian, Gay, Bisexual and Transgender Youth Who Are Homeless or at Risk of Becoming Homeless." Report. Williams Institute, University of California, Los Angeles, School of Law, 2012. http:// williamsinstitute.law.ucla.edu/wp-content/uploads/Durso-Gates-LGBT-Homeless -Youth-Survey-July-2012.pdf.

Ely, John Hart. *Democracy and Distrust: A Theory of Judicial Review*. Cambridge, MA: Harvard University Press, 1980.

Eng, David. *The Feeling of Kinship: Queer Liberalism and the Racialization of Intimacy*. Durham, NC: Duke University Press, 2010.

Engels, Friedrich. *The Origin of the Family, Private Property and the State* (1884), ed. Eleanor Burke Leacock. New York: International Publishers, 1972.

Ershow-Levenberg, Linda S. "Court Approval of Medicaid Spend-Down Planning by Guardians." *Marquette Elder's Advisor* 6, no. 2 (2005): 197–215.

Eskridge, William N., Jr. *The Case for Same-Sex Marriage: From Sexual Liberty to Civilized Commitment*. New York: Free Press, 1996.

———. "Comparative Law and the Same-Sex Marriage Debate: A Step-by-Step Approach toward State Recognition." *McGeorge Law Review* 31, no. 3 (2000): 641–72.

———. "Hardwick and Historiography." *University of Illinois Law Review* 1999 (1999): 631–702.

Feinberg, Joel. "The Expressive Function of Punishment." *The Monist* 49, no. 3 (1965): 397–423.

Fiss, Owen M. "Groups and the Equal Protection Clause." *Philosophy and Public Affairs* 5, no. 2 (1976): 107–77.

Florida, Richard. *The Rise of the Creative Class: And How It's Transforming Work, Leisure, Community, and Everyday Life*. New York: Basic, 2002.

Foner, Philip S., ed. "Socialism and the Negro Problem." In *W. E. B. Du Bois Speaks: Speeches and Addresses 1890–1919*, ed. Philip S. Foner, 240. New York: Pathfinder, 1970.

Foohey, Pamela. "Panel Discusses Prostitution and the Sex Industry." *Harvard Law Record* (September 10, 2008). http://hlrecord.org/2008/09/panel-discusses -prostitution-and-the-sex-industry.

Foucault, Michel. *The Archaeology of Knowledge*, trans. A. M. Sheridan Smith. New York: Harper Torch, 1972.

———. "Two Lectures." In *Power/Knowledge: Selected Interviews and Other Writings, 1972–1977*, ed. Colin Gordon, trans. Colin Gordon, Leo Marshall, John Mepham, and Kate Soper, 78–108. New York: Pantheon, 1980.

Fowler, Patrick J., Paul A. Toro, and Bart W. Miles. "Pathways to and from Homelessness and Associated Psychosocial Outcomes among Adolescents Leaving the Foster Care System." *American Journal of Public Health* 99, no. 8 (2009): 1453–58.

Franke, Katherine. "Dating the State: The Moral Hazards of Winning Gay Rights." *Columbia Human Rights Law Review* 49, no. 1 (2012): 1–46.

———. "The Greater Context of the Pinkwashing Debate." *Tikkun*, July 3, 2012. http://www.tikkun.org/nextgen/the-greater-context-of-the-pinkwashing-debate.

Fraser, Nancy. "Feminism, Capitalism and the Cunning of History." *New Left Review* 56 (2009).

———. "From Redistribution to Recognition? Dilemmas of Justice in a 'Postsocialist Age.'" In *Adding Insult to Injury: Nancy Fraser Debates Her Critics*, ed. Kevin Olsen, 9–41. New York: Verso, 2008.

———. "Heterosexism, Misrecognition, and Capitalism: A Response to Judith Butler." In *Adding Insult to Injury: Nancy Fraser Debates Her Critics*, ed. Kevin Olsen, 57–68. New York: Verso, 2008.

———. "Rethinking Recognition." *New Left Review* 3 (May–June 2000): 107–20. https://newleftreview.org/II/3/nancy-fraser-rethinking-recognition.

Galanter, Marc. "Why the 'Haves' Come Out Ahead: Speculations on the Limits of Legal Change," *Law and Society Review* 9, no. 1 (1974): 95–160.

Gates, Gary. "LGBT People Are Disproportionately Food Insecure." Report. Williams Institute, University of California, Los Angeles, School of Law, 2014.

Gates, Gary J., and Jason Ost. *The Gay and Lesbian Atlas*. Washington, DC: Urban Institute Press, 2004.

"Girls Do What They Have to Do to Survive: Illuminating Methods Used by Girls in the Sex Trade and Street Economy to Fight Back and Heal, a Participatory Action Research Study of Resilience and Resistance." Young Women's Empowerment Project, Chicago, 2009, 7. https://ywepchicago.files.wordpress.com/2011/06/girls-do-what-they-have-to-do-to-survive-a-study-of-resilience-and-resistance.pdf.

Goldberg, Suzanne. "Social Justice Movements and LatCrit Community: On Making Anti-Essentialist and Social Constructionist Arguments in Court." *Oregon Law Review* 81, no. 3 (2002): 629–62.

Goldberg-Hiller, Jonathan. *The Limits to Union: Same-Sex Marriage and the Politics of Civil Rights*. Ann Arbor: University of Michigan Press, 2004.

Hale, Robert L. "Coercion and Distribution in a Supposedly Non-coercive State." *Political Science Quarterly* 38, no. 3 (1923): 470–94.

Hall, Simon. "The NAACP and the Challenges of 1969's Radicalism." In *Long Is the Way and Hard: One Hundred Years of the NAACP*, ed. Kevern Verney and Lee Sartain. Fayetteville: University of Arkansas Press, 2009.

Halley, Janet. "Doing a Distributional Analysis." In *Governance Feminism: An Introduction*, ed. Janet Halley, Prabha Kotiswaran, Hila Shamir, and Rachel Rebouché. Minneapolis: University of Minnesota Press, forthcoming.

———. "Rhetorics of Justification in the Same-Sex Marriage Debate." In *Legal Recognition of Same-Sex Partnerships: A Study of National, European and International Law*, ed. Mads Andenaes and Robert Wintemute. Oxford: Hart, 2001.

Hanhardt, Christina B. *Safe Space: Gay Neighborhood History and the Politics of Violence*. Durham, NC: Duke University Press, 2013.

Harcourt, Bernard E. *The Illusion of Free Markets: Punishment and the Myth of Natural Order*. Cambridge, MA: Harvard University Press, 2011.

Harris, Angela P. "From Stonewall to the Suburbs? Toward a Political Economy of Sexuality." *William and Mary Bill of Rights Journal* 14, no. 4 (2006): 1539–82.

Hasenbush, Amira, Andrew R. Flores, Angeliki Kastanis, Brad Sears, and Gary J. Gates. "The LGBT Divide: A Data Portrait of LGBT People in the Midwestern, Mountain and Southern States." Report. Williams Institute, University of California, Los Angeles, School of Law, 2014. http://williamsinstitute.law.ucla.edu /wp-content/uploads/LGBT-divide-Dec-2014.pdf.

Hirshman, Linda. *Victory: The Triumphant Gay Revolution*. New York: Harper Perennial, 2012.

Holmes, Oliver Wendell. *The Common Law*. Boston: Little, Brown, 1881.

———. "The Path of the Law." *Harvard Law Review* 10 (1897): 457–88.

Honneth, Axel. "Recognition or Redistribution? Changing Perspectives on the Moral Order of Society." *Theory, Culture and Society* 18, nos. 2–3 (2001): 43–55.

Hooker, Evelyn. "The Adjustment of the Male Overt Homosexual." *Journal of Projective Techniques* 21 (1957): 18–31.

Horwitz, Morton J. "The Jurisprudence of Brown and the Dilemmas of Liberalism." *Harvard Civil Rights-Civil Liberties Law Review* 14, no. 3 (1979): 599–613.

———. *The Transformation of American Law, 1870–1960: The Crisis of Legal Orthodoxy*. New York: Oxford University Press, 1992.

———. *The Warren Court and the Pursuit of Justice*. New York: Hill and Wang, 1998.

Humphreys, Laud. *Tearoom Trade: Impersonal Sex in Public Places (Observations)*. Chicago: Aldine Transaction, 1975.

Johnson, David K. *The Lavender Scare: The Cold War Persecution of Gays and Lesbians in the Federal Government*. Chicago: University of Chicago Press, 2004.

Katyal, Sonia. "Exporting Identity." *Yale Journal of Law and Feminism* 14, no. 1 (2002): 97–176.

Katznelson, Ira. *When Affirmative Action Was White: An Untold History of Racial Inequality in Twentieth-Century America*. New York: W. W. Norton, 2005.

Kennedy, Duncan. *A Critique of Adjudication (Fin de Siècle)*. Cambridge, MA: Harvard University Press, 1997.

———. "The Critique of Rights in Critical Legal Studies." In *Left Legalism/Left Critique*, ed. Wendy Brown and Janet Halley. Durham, NC: Duke University Press, 2002.

———. "The Stakes of Law, or Hale and Foucault!" In *Sexy Dressing Etc.*, ed. Duncan Kennedy, 83–125. Cambridge, MA: Harvard University Press, 1993.

Klare, Karl. "Critical Perspectives on Social and Economic Rights, Democracy and Separation of Powers." In *Social Economic Rights in Theory and Practice: Critical*

Inquiries, ed. Helena Alviar García, Karl Klare, and Lucy Williams, 3–22. London: Routledge, 2015.

Klein, Naomi. *No Logo: No Space, No Choice, No Jobs*. New York: Picador, 2000.

Knauer, Nancy J. "LGBT Youth: Reconciling Family, Pride, and Community." *Temple Political and Civil Rights Law Review* 23, no. 2 (2014): 253–62.

Koppelman, Andrew. "Why Discrimination against Lesbians and Gay Men Is Sex Discrimination." *New York Law Review* 69, no. 2 (1994): 197–287.

Landis, James M. *The Administrative Process*. New Haven, CT: Yale University Press, 1938.

Lankenau, Stephen E., Michael C. Clatts, Dorinda Welle, Lloyd A. Goldsamt, and Marya Viost Gwadz. "Street Careers: Homelessness, Drug Use, and Sex Work among Young Men Who Have Sex with Men (YMSM)." *International Journal of Drug Policy* 16, no. 1 (2005): 10–18.

Law, Sylvia. "Homosexuality and the Social Meaning of Gender." *Wisconsin Law Review* 1988 (1988): 187–235.

Leachman, Gwendolyn M. "From Protest to Perry: How Litigation Shaped the LGBT Movement's Agenda." *University of California Davis Law Review* 47 (2014): 1668–751.

Lévi-Strauss, Claude. *The Savage Mind*, trans. George Weidenfeld. Chicago: University of Chicago Press, 1966.

Levitsky, Sandra R. "To Lead with Law: Reassessing the Influence of Legal Advocacy Organizations in Social Movements." In *Cause Lawyering and Social Movements*, ed. Austin Sarat and Stuart Scheingold, 145–63. Stanford, CA: Stanford University Press, 2006.

Linder, Marc. "Farm Workers and the Fair Labor Standards Act: Racial Discrimination in the New Deal." *Texas Law Review* 65 (1987): 1335–93.

Llewellyn, Karl L. "A Realistic Jurisprudence—The Next Step." *Columbia Law Review* 30, no. 4 (1930): 431–65.

Lorde, Audre, "The Master's Tools Will Never Dismantle the Master's House." In *Sister Outsider: Essays and Speeches*, 110–13. Freedom, CA: Crossing, 1984.

Marx, Karl, and Friedrich Engels. "On the Jewish Question." In *The Marx-Engels Reader*, ed. Robert C. Tucker, 26–52. New York: W. W. Norton, 1978.

Massad, Joseph. "Re-orienting Desire: The Gay International and the Arab World." *Public Culture* 14, no. 2 (2002): 361–85.

McKnight, Gerald. *The Last Crusade: Martin Luther King, Jr., the FBI, and the Poor People's Campaign*. Boulder, CO: Westview, 1998.

Menand, Louis. *The Metaphysical Club: A Story of Ideas in America*. New York: Farrar, Straus and Giroux, 2001.

Minter, Shannon. "Do Transsexuals Dream of Gay Rights? Getting Real about Transgender Inclusion." In *Transgender Rights*, ed. Paisley Currah, Richard Juang, and Shannon Price Minter. Minneapolis: University of Minnesota Press, 2006.

Mnookin, Robert H., and Lewis Kornhauser. "Bargaining in the Shadow of the Law: The Case of Divorce." *Yale Law Journal* 88, no. 5 (1979): 950–97.

Mogul, Joey L., Kay Whitlock, and Andrea K. Ritchie. *Queer (In)Justice: The Criminalization of LGBT People in the United States*. Boston: Beacon, 2011.

Morgan, Emily, Nina Salomon, Martha Plotkin, and Rebecca Cohen. "The School Discipline Consensus Report: Strategies from the Field to Keep Students Engaged in School and Out of the Juvenile Justice System." Council of State Governments Justice Center, New York, 2014. https://csgjusticecenter.org/wp-content/uploads/2014/06/The_School_Discipline_Consensus_Report.pdf.

Movement Advancement Project, Freedom to Work, National Black Justice Coalition, Human Rights Campaign, Center for American Progress, FIRE, "A Broken Bargain for LGBT Workers of Color," 2013. http://www.lgbtmap.org/file/a-broken-bargain-for-lgbt-workers-of-color.pdf.

Muñoz, José Esteban. *Cruising Utopia: The Then and There of Queer Futurity*. New York: New York University Press, 2009.

Murray, Charles. *Losing Ground: American Social Policy, 1950–1980*. New York: Basic, 1984.

Napolitano, Andrew. *The Constitution in Exile*. Nashville, TN: Thomas Nelson, 2006.

Olsen, Frances E. "The Family and the Market: A Study of Ideology and Legal Reform." *Harvard Law Review* 96, no. 7 (1983): 1497–578.

———. "The Myth of State Intervention in the Family." *Michigan Journal of Law Reform* 18, no. 4 (1985): 835–64.

———. "Statutory Rape: A Feminist Critique of Rights Analysis." *Texas Law Review* 63, no. 3 (1984): 387–432.

Otto, Diane. "Transnational Homo-Assemblages: Reading 'Gender' in Counter-terrorism Discourses." *Jindal Global Law Review* 4, no. 2. (2013): 79–98.

Our Fair City: A Comprehensive Blueprint for Gender and Sexual Justice in New York City. New York: Columbia Law School, 2014. http://web.law.columbia.edu/sites/default/files/microsites/gender-sexuality/our_fair_city.pdf.

Peller, Gary. "Race Consciousness." *Duke Law Journal* 39, no. 4 (1990), 758–847.

Pendleton, Eva, and Jane Goldschmidt. "Sex Panic!—Make the Connections." *Harvard Gay and Lesbian Review* 5, no. 3 (1998): 30–33.

Polikoff, Nancy. *Beyond (Straight and Gay) Marriage: Valuing all Families under the Law*. Boston: Beacon, 2008.

Preston, Cheryl B., and Brandon T. Crowther. "Infancy Doctrine Inquiries." *Santa Clara Law Review* 52 (2012): 47–80.

Puar, Jasbir. "Rethinking Homonationalism." *International Journal of Middle East Studies* 45, no. 2 (2013): 336–39.

———. *Terrorist Assemblages: Homonationalism in Queer Times*. Durham, NC: Duke University Press, 2007.

Rand, Spencer. "The Real Marriage Penalty: How Welfare Law Discourages Marriage despite Public Policy Statements to the Contrary—and What Can Be Done about It." *University of the District of Columbia Law Review* 18, no. 1 (2015): 93–143.

Ransby, Barbara. *Ella Baker and the Black Freedom Movement: A Radical Democratic Vision*. Chapel Hill: University of North Carolina Press, 2003.

Ray, Nicholas. "Lesbian, Gay, Bisexual and Transgender Youth: An Epidemic of Homelessness." National Gay and Lesbian Task Force Policy Institute and the

National Coalition for the Homeless, 2006. http://www.thetaskforce.org/static
_html/downloads/reports/reports/HomelessYouth.pdf.

Regnerus, Mark. "How Different Are the Adult Children of Parents Who Have Same-
Sex Relationships? Findings from the New Family Structures Study." *Social Science
Research* 41, no. 4 (July 2012): 752–70.

Saewyc, Elizabeth M., Colleen S. Poon, Yuko Homma, and Carol L. Skay. "Stigma
Management? The Links between Enacted Stigma and Teen Pregnancy Trends
among Gay, Lesbian, and Bisexual Students in British Columbia." *Canadian Journal
of Human Sexuality* 17, no. 3 (2008): 123–39. https://www.ncbi.nlm.nih.gov/pmc
/articles/PMC2655734.

Sarat, Austin, and Stuart Scheingold, eds. *Cause Lawyering and Social Movements*.
Stanford, CA: Stanford University Press, 2006.

Sawicki, Jana. *Disciplining Foucault: Feminism, Power, and the Body*. New York: Routledge, 1991.

Sedgwick, Eve Kosofsky. *Epistemology of the Closet*. Oakland: University of California
Press, 2008.

———. *Touching Feeling: Affect, Pedagogy, Performativity*. Durham, NC: Duke University Press, 2003.

Shamir, Hila. "The State of Care: Rethinking the Distributive Effects of Familial Care
Policies in Liberal Welfare States." *American Journal of Comparative Law* 58, no. 4
(2010): 953–86.

Silbaugh, Katherine B. "Women's Place: Urban Planning, Housing Design, and Work-
Family Balance." *Fordham Law Review* 76, no. 3 (2007): 1797–852.

Singh, Nikhil Pal. *Black Is a Country: Race and the Unfinished Struggle for Democracy*.
Cambridge, MA: Harvard University Press, 2004.

Sitkoff, Harvard. *A New Deal for Blacks: The Emergence of Civil Rights as National
Issue, Volume 1: The Depression Decade*. New York: Oxford University Press, 1978.

Slepian, Arthur. "An Inconvenient Truth: The Myths of Pinkwashing." *Tikkun*,
July 3, 2012. http://www.tikkun.org/nextgen/an-inconvenient-truth-the-myths-of
-pinkwashing.

Snorton, C. Riley. *Nobody Is Supposed to Know: Black Sexuality on the Down Low*.
Minneapolis: University of Minnesota Press, 2014.

Spade, Dean. "Documenting Gender." *Hastings Law Journal* 59, no. 1 (2008):
731–841.

Steele, Shelby. *The Content of Our Character: A New Vision of Race in America*. New
York: Harper Perennial, 1990.

Stone, Brad Elliott. "The Down Low and the Sexuality of Race." *Foucault Studies* 12
(2011): 36–50.

Stone, Deborah. *Policy Paradox: The Art of Political Decision Making*. New York:
W. W. Norton, 2002.

Suk, Jeannie. "Criminal Law Comes Home." *Yale Law Journal* 116, no. 1 (2006): 2–70.

Sullivan, Andrew. *Virtually Normal*. New York: Vintage, 1996.

Taylor, Charles. *Multiculturalism and "The Politics of Recognition."* Princeton, NJ:
Princeton University Press, 1992.

Tushnet, Mark. "The Critique of Rights." *Southern Methodist University Law Review* 47, no. 1 (1993–94): 23–36.

"The Unnecessary Doctrine of Necessaries." *Michigan Law Review* 82, no. 7 (June 1984): 1767–99.

U.S. Department of Labor, Office of Policy, Planning and Research. *The Negro Family: The Case for National Action*. Washington, DC: U.S. Government Printing Office, 1965.

Vaid, Urvashi. *Irresistible Revolution: Confronting Race, Class and the Assumptions of Lesbian, Gay, Bisexual, and Transgender Politics*. New York: Magnus, 2012.

Waaldijk, Kees. "Small Change: How the Road to Same-Sex Marriage Got Paved in the Netherlands." In *Legal Recognition of Same-Sex Partnerships: A Study of National, European and International Law*, ed. Mads Andenaes and Robert Wintemute, 437–64. Oxford: Hart, 2001.

Waggoner, Lawrence W. "The Uniform Probate Code's Elective Share: Time for a Reassessment." *University of Michigan Journal of Law Reform* 37, no. 1 (2003–4): 1–37.

Walters, Suzanna Danuta. *All the Rage: The Story of Gay Visibility in America*. Chicago: University of Chicago Press, 2001.

———. *The Tolerance Trap: How God, Genes, and Good Intentions Are Sabotaging Gay Equality*. New York: New York University Press, 2014.

Warner, Michael. *The Trouble with Normal: Sex, Politics, and the Ethics of Queer Life*. Cambridge, MA: Harvard University Press, 1999.

Wilber, Shannan. *Lesbian, Gay, Bisexual and Transgender Youth in the Juvenile Justice System: A Guide to Juvenile Detention Reform*. Annie E. Casey Foundation, 2015. http://www.issuelab.org/resource/lesbian_gay_bisexual_and_transgender_youth _in_the_juvenile_justice_system#sthash.z761aGMR.dpuf.

Williams, Lucy A. "The Ideology of Division: Behavior Modification Welfare Reform Proposals." *Yale Law Journal* 102, no. 3 (1992): 719–46.

Wilson, Bianca D. M., Khush Cooper, Angel Kastanis, and Sheila Nezhad. *New Report: Sexual and Gender Minority Youth in Foster Care*. Los Angeles: Williams Institute, University of California, Los Angeles, School of Law, 2014.

Winter, Steven L. "An Upside/Down View of the Countermajoritarian Difficulty." *Texas Law Review* 69 (1991): 1881–1927.

Wolfson, Evan. *Why Marriage Matters: America, Equality, and Gay People's Right to Marry*. New York: Simon and Schuster, 2004.

Zaibert, Leo. "Punishment and Revenge." *Law and Philosophy* 25, no. 1 (2006): 81–118.

conscience clause, 189
consent as legal concept, 32, 180
consequentialism, 199–200, 243n67
Constitution. *See* U.S. Constitution
constitutional interpretation, 24, 27–31
Constitution in Exile (term), 219n13
Constitution in Exile, The (Napolitano), 219n13
consumer debt and minors, 195–98, 205
contract rights, 41, 180–82, 194–96, 199–200, 242n52. *See also* due process clause
contractual autonomy, 196–97
conversion therapy, 183–86, 205
Corporate Equality Index (HRC), 164
corporate support of LGBT equality, 116–17, 135, 163–64, 234n128
Cossman, Brenda, 112–13
Cott, Nancy, 63–64
counter-majoritarian body, 24, 79, 218n8
counter-rights claims, 89–98
Court Packing Plan (Roosevelt), 25–26, 180
Covenant House (shelter), 193
coverture, 63–64, 106
credit and LGBT youth, 195–97, 198, 205
Crenshaw, Kimberlé Williams, 240n113
criminal justice system, 120–22, 202–4
criminal records and discrimination, 203–4, 206, 244n82
critical legal studies (CLS), overview of, 8–10, 14, 44, 222n72
Cruzan v. Special School District No. 1, 90
custody in divorce cases, 187–88. *See also* child support law; family law

"Dear Colleague" letter on transgender discrimination, 50
De Blasio, Bill, 167
DeBoer v. Snyder, 236n3
deductive reasoning, 10, 22–23, 40–43, 55–56. *See also* indeterminacy of law
Defense of Marriage Act (1996), 62, 87–88, 100, 163
Deloitte LLP, 135
D'Emilio, John, 136, 161–63, 239n90
Denny's (restaurant), 49
desire, 229n17

discipline vs. abuse, 186
disparate impact claims, 20
disparate treatment claims, 20–21
District of Columbia, 36, 47, 53, 128–29, 183
District of Columbia v. Heller, 220n19
divorce, 65, 110, 185, 187–88, 210. *See also* child support law
DOMA. *See* Defense of Marriage Act (1996)
domestic labor, 56, 64–65, 108, 152, 160, 207, 244n95
domestic violence laws, 185–86
Don't Ask, Don't Tell policy, 2, 8, 9, 67–68, 93–94, 103–4
double-bind argument, 71–72, 97–98
"down low" sexual encounters, 68–69
Dred Scott v. Sandford, 37
Du Bois, W. E. B., 150–51
due process clause: in *Bowers v. Hardwick*, 25, 33, 38, 220n19; controversial aspects of, 92–93, 219n18; Douglas Ginsburg on, 219n13; in *Huff v. Chapel Hill–Chauncy Hall School*, 32; Kennedy on, 32; in *Lawrence v. Texas* (2003), 32, 38; in *Lochner* era, 26, 28, 40–41; in parental liberty cases, 183. *See also* contract rights; equal protection clause
Duffy, Michael T., 20–24
Duggan, Lisa, 111, 114, 157, 166
Dworkin, Andrea, 121

economic argument of marriage, 64–66, 98, 118–19
economic landscape for LGBT youth, 195–204
economic reform: vs. racial justice reform, 149–56, 236n12, 237n44; and redistribution, 156–168. *See also* labor laws; LGBT reform objectives
Edelman, Marian Wright, 155
educational loans, 205, 242n52
Edwards, John, 115, 138–39
effeminacy, 136–37
Egypt, 137–38
emancipation status, 196, 205
employment discrimination: affirmative action against, 45–46, 57; batch checking, 82, 227n82; with benefits, 115–16;

employment discrimination (*continued*)
cases on, 19–24, 46–49, 89–90; and
contracts, 180–82; criminal record
applicants, 203–4, 206, 244n82; labor
laws, 26, 37, 40–42, 100–101, 152, 198–99;
by race, 154–55; union activism, 153–54;
Wu on, 148; of youth, 197–98
Employment Non-Discrimination Act
(ENDA), 100–101
enforcement, 188–92
Eng, David, 165
Equal Employment Opportunity Commission (EEOC), 47–48
"Equality Is Not the Finish Line" (Wu),
147–48
equality of outcome, 222n73. *See also* substantive vs. formal equality
equal protection clause, 38–39. *See also* due
process clause
equal rights: formal equality vs. other
versions of equality, 56–58; formal vs.
substantive equality, 45–51; and indeterminacy, 51–56; terminology in, 222n73.
See also formal equality; LGBT equal
rights; women's equality
Eskridge, William N., Jr., 51–54, 102
Etheridge, Melissa, 115, 138

Fabrizio v. City of Providence, 228n120
facial neutrality, 53, 125
Fair Housing Act (1968), 152, 156
Fair Labor Standards Act (1938), 152
"Family and the Market, The" (Olsen),
184–85
family law: bargaining, 187–88; child support law, 197–98, 205, 244n84; divorce
in, 65, 110, 185, 187–88, 210; for foster and
adoptive families, 73, 188–92, 241n29;
privacy rights, 183–85; on runaways,
241n23. *See also* gay parenting; parenting
family rejection, 4–5, 12, 177. *See also*
parenting
family values as advocacy strategy, 112–19
Fatherless America (Blankenhorn),
72, 118
Federal Emergency Relief
Administration, 152
Federalist No. 78 (Hamilton), 30, 218n8

federal judiciary, 24, 30–31, 218n8. *See also*
U.S. Supreme Court; *and specific cases*
Feinberg, Joel, 232n91
Feldblum, Chai, 47
feminism: carceral, 121; organizations on
sex industry, 130–31; on women's identity
and child-rearing, 56, 223n109. *See also*
women's equality
FIERCE (Fabulous Independent Educated
Radicals for Community Empowerment), 126
First Amendment (U.S. Constitution), 92,
94, 191, 228n109
fiscal conservatism and family values,
118–19
flag-burning, 92, 228n109
Florida, 73
Florida, Richard, 233n110
*Florida Department of Children and Fami-
lies v. Adoption of X.X.G. and N.R.G.*,
73–75
food insecurity, 2, 16, 98, 155, 176, 204,
209, 214
food stamps. *See* Supplemental Nutrition
Assistance Program (SNAP)
formal economy and LGBT youth, 195–200,
209
formal equality: and indeterminacy,
51–56; vs. other versions of equality,
56–58; vs. substantive equality, 45–51,
226n74; as term, 222n73. *See also* equal
rights
foster care, 73, 188–92, 197, 242n53. *See also*
parenting
Foucault, Michel, 10, 12, 81
Fourteenth Amendment (U.S. Constitution), 27
Franke, Katherine, 132–33, 166
Fraser, Nancy, 14, 149, 156–61, 163, 165, 168,
240n113
freedom of contract, 180. *See also* contract
rights
Freedom to Marry (organization), 106, 146,
229n18
free exercise clause, 191
"From Redistribution to Recognition"
(Fraser), 156–57
Frum, David, 117

functional vs. formal equality, 45–51, 222n73, 226n74

Future of Marriage, The (Blankenhorn), 118

Galanter, Marc, 190
Garner, Tyron, 32
Garvey, Marcus, 150
Gates, Gary, 69–71, 98, 125–26. *See also* Williams Institute
gayborhoods, 125–27, 207–8
gay men: Mattachine Society, 103, 238n90; and military service, 67–68; periods of defining, 136–37; sexuality of, 67–70; "tearoom trade" of, 68. *See also* transgender equality; *and under* LGBT *entries*
Gay New York (Chauncy), 70, 136
gay parenting: and child welfare system, 73, 188–89; judicial opinion of, 34–35; mental health argument against, 75–77; in *Perry v. Schwarzenegger*, 72–80; *Who's in the Family?* case on, 85–86; *X.X.G.* case on, 73–75. *See also* marriage equality; parenting
gender discrimination. *See* LGBT equal rights; sex discrimination; transgender equality; women's equality
gendered roles in marriage, 63–65
gender identities, terminology on, 217n9, 223n95, 233n99
gentrification, 124–28, 177, 203, 233n102
Georgia, 24, 28–29, 220n27
gig economy, 200
Gill, Martin, 74
Ginsburg, Douglas, 219n13
Ginsburg, Ruth Bader, 1, 100
Giuliani, Rudolph, 125–26, 207–8
GLAD (GLBTQ Legal Advocates & Defenders), 130, 147
Global Equality Fund, 135
Goins, Julienne, 48
Goins v. West Group, 48–49, 89–90
Goldberg, Suzanne, 70–71
Goldberg-Hiller, Jonathan, 96
Goodridge v. Department of Public Health, 33–35, 74, 84, 88, 98, 102–3, 110
Griffin, Chad, 4–5, 116, 140
Grimm, Gavin (G.G.), 50

Griswold v. Connecticut, 241n12
Gross, Aeyal, 133
gun control, 92–93

Haaretz, 133
Hale, Robert, 14, 168–70, 179–84
Halley, Janet, 81
Hamilton, Alexander, 30, 218n8
Hanhardt, Christina, 127, 233n102
harassment in schools, 76. *See also* bullying
Harcourt, Bernard, 120–21
Harlan, John Marshall, 40, 223n108
Harris, Angela, 164
Hastings College of Law, 1, 2, 4, 105
hate crimes, 121–24, 233n96
Hawaii, 103–4
Hay, Harry, 103, 238n90
HB2 (North Carolina), 50
health insurance, 64–65, 108, 115–16, 138, 210
Hegel, Georg, 158
Herek, Gregory, 67, 69, 71
Herndon, Angelo, 152, 154
"Heterosexism, Misrecognition, and Capitalism" (Fraser), 161
Hilton Worldwide, 135
Hirshman, Linda, 103–4
HIV/AIDS, 68, 130–31, 167, 194
Holder, Eric, 110
Holmes, Oliver Wendell, Jr., 40–42, 55, 189, 191, 243n68
homeless population: criminalization of, 1–2, 192–93, 206, 242n43; LGBT youth among, 2, 129–30, 175–78, 192–95; rates of black and Latina/o youth, 2, 192, 201; reforms for, 177–78; and sit-lie ordinances, 1–2, 105, 192, 242n43; youth shelters for, 4–5, 140, 193, 205–6. *See also* housing discrimination and housing laws
homonationalism, 83
Honneth, Axel, 167
Hooker, Evelyn, 76
Horwitz, Morton, 27
hostile work environment, 89–90. *See also* employment discrimination
House Un-American Activities Committee (HUAC), 162–63, 238n90

Lodewyks, Chris, 108
Lofton v. Secretary of the Department of Children and Family Services, 241n30
Log Cabin Republicans, 19–20, 163
Logo forum (2007), 115, 138–39
Los Angeles Gay and Lesbian Center, 138–39
Losing Ground (Murray), 119
Loving, Mildred and Richard, 52–56
Loving v. Virginia, 52–56
low-income households. *See* poverty

MacKinnon, Catherine, 121
Macy, Mia, 47
Macy v. Holder, 47
Maine, 49, 61, 113–14
Maine Human Rights Act, 49
Maines, Nicole, 49
Marbury v. Madison, 30, 43
marriage as institution: benefits and obligations of, 109–11; and choice, 84; divorce, 65, 110, 185, 187, 210; economic argument of, 64–66, 98, 118–19; historical argument of, 63–64, 72–73; Marshall on, 109–10; and poverty considerations, 210; under U.S. Constitution, 23, 35; Wolfson on, 106–107. *See also* family law; parenting
marriage equality: as capstone in equal rights movement, 101–6, 220n5; for immigrants, 177; interracial marriage, 52–56, 106; Kennedy on, 35, 39; LGBT movement's priorities of, 2–3, 12–13; for prisoners, 107; relationship comparison, 66–67; Roberts on, 37–38; San Francisco legislation on, 1–2, 5; Scalia on, 37–39; as top-down strategy of LGBT advocacy, 213–14. *See also* gay parenting; *and specific cases and states*
Marriage Project (Lambda Legal), 106
Marshall, Anna-Marie, 212
Marshall, Margaret, 84, 88, 102–3, 109–10
Maryland, 61
Massachusetts: bullying laws in, 123–24, 233n96; constitutional amendment acts in, 96; foster/pre-adoptive rule in, 189, 191; *Hurley v. Irish-American Gay, Lesbian and Bisexual Group of Boston*, 94;

judicial system of, 33; juvenile detention rules in, 193; marriage equality cases in, 19–24, 33–35, 65; runaway law in, 241n23; sit-lie ordinance in, 242n43; trans rights in, 91
Massachusetts Commission against Discrimination (MCAD), 19–20
Massad, Joseph, 136–37
MassResistance, 85
master-slave dialectic, 158
Mathews, Arthur Guy, 163
Mathis, Coy, 49, 90
Mathis v. Fountain-Fort Carson School District 8, 223n89
Mattachine Society, 103, 238n90
Matthew Shepard and James Byrd, Jr., Hate Crimes Prevention Act (2009), 121
McCarthyism, 162–63, 238n90
McDonald v. City of Chicago, 220n19
McKnight, Gerald, 155
McLaughlin v. State of Florida, 54
Medicaid, 110, 116, 178, 210
medical care, 205. *See also* health insurance
Meneghin, Cindy, 87, 89, 98, 108
mental health argument, 75–77
"Merely Cultural" (Butler), 158
Meyer, Ilan, 75–77
Meyer v. Nebraska, 241n10
Michigan, 74, 145
military service inclusion, 2, 8–9, 67–68, 93–94, 103–4
Miller, Kenneth, 79
Minnesota, 48–49, 89–90
Minnesota Human Rights Act, 48
minoritizing conception, 71
"minority stress," 75–76
Missouri, 107
Mnookin, Robert H., 187–88
Mogul, Joey L., 203
Money, Myths and Change (Badgett), 64, 224n21
moral equivalency, 109, 111
Movement Advancement Project (MAP), 208
Moynihan, Daniel Patrick, 119
Multiculturalism and "The Politics of Recognition" (Taylor), 158–59
Muñoz, José Esteban, 165

performativity, 104, 137, 172, 195, 199

permission vs. prohibitions, legal, 184–87

Perry v. Schwarzenegger: about, 61–62; economic marriage argument in, 64–66, 98, 117–18; gay advocacy groups on, 62; gay parenting arguments in, 72–80; gay political power argument in, 79; historical marriage argument in, 63–64; knowledge production in, 60, 66, 71–72; political *amicus* brief in, 116–17; sexual orientation arguments in, 67–70, 109

Pew Center on the States, 120

Pickup v. Brown, 241n13

Pierce v. Society of Sisters, 241n10, 241n11

pinkwashing, 132–33, 234n128

Planned Parenthood v. Casey, 228n11

Plessy v. Ferguson, 40–41, 223n108

police abuse, 2, 130, 202–4

Polikoff, Nancy, 109, 165

political vs. legal reasoning, 43

Poor People's Campaign, 155–56

poverty, 119, 154–56, 208–11. *See also* economic reform; homeless population; social welfare system

Poverty Law Clinic, 175

power and redistributive justice, 168–74

power of disaffirmance, 194, 205

pregnancy, 2, 210–11

Price-Waterhouse v. Hopkins, 46

prisoner's rights, 107, 110–11. *See also* incarceration

privacy rights: as concept, 32, 45; and Don't Ask, Don't Tell policy, 2, 8, 9, 67–68, 93–94, 103–4; for families and parents, 183–85; in *Lochner* era, 26–29; and sodomy laws, 24–25, 28–29, 32–33, 102, 138; for women seeking abortions, 92

property rights, 180–81

Proposition 8 (California), 61–63. See also *Perry v. Schwarzenegger*

prostitution, 129, 167, 226n59. *See also* sex industry

Psychic Life of Power, The (Butler), 171

Puar, Jasbir, 83, 84, 133

Pulse nightclub massacre (2016), 83

punishment, 232n91. *See also* penal system

Putin, Vladimir, 134

Queen's 52, 137–38

queer (term), 218n9, 233n99. *See also* LGBT community; *and under* LGBT *entries*

Queers for Economic Justice, 122

queer theory, overview of, 6–9, 83, 104, 218n9

racial discrimination: affirmative action against, 45–46; Black Lives Matter on, 131, 149–50; *Brown v. Board of Education of Topeka*, 27, 54, 57, 154–55, 224n113; civil rights movement on, 13, 149–56, 236n12, 237n44; and colorblindness, 56, 223n108; *Dred Scott v. Sandford*, 37; vs. economic justice goals, 149–56, 236n12, 237n44; and gentrification, 124–28; LGBT advocacy community on, 131–32; *Loving v. Virginia*, 52–56; in military, 150; *Plessy v. Ferguson*, 40–41, 223n108; *Washington v. Davis*, 53, 223n106. *See also* African Americans; Civil Rights Act (1964); intersectionality

Randolph, A. Philip, 153, 154, 155, 237n44

rape, 130

rational basis, 77–78

Rauch, Jonathan, 118

Ray Report, 177–78, 193

reaction-formation, 43

Reagan, Ronald, 111, 120

"Realistic Jurisprudence, A" (Llewellyn), 199

recognition-redistribution claims, 156–68

Regnerus, Mark, 74

Regnerus Study, 74–75

Rehnquist, William, 32

Rekers, George, 226n59

religion and LGBT discrimination, 191–92

religious freedom claims, 94–95, 189, 230n51

Rentboy.com, 130, 201, 226n59

repeat litigants vs. one-shotters, 190

representation-reinforcement, 77–79, 96–98, 226n74

Rhode Island, 61, 94

RID (Residents in Distress), 126

rights claims, summary of, 44–45, 89–98, 222n72

rights of survivorship, 116

rights of victims, 92

right to bear arms, 92–93

right to contract. *See* contract rights

right to desecrate the American flag, 92, 228n109

right to privacy. *See* privacy rights

Ritchie, Andrea J., 203

Roberts, John, 37

Roberts, Owen, 27

Romer v. Evans, 38–40, 94, 123

Romney, Mitt, 85, 96

Roosevelt, Eleanor, 153

Roosevelt, Franklin D., 25–26, 152–53, 180

Rosa v. Park West Bank and Trust Company, 46

Rowan, Jim, 175

Royal Bank of Canada, 135

Rubio, Marco, 83

Runaway and Homeless Youth Act (2008), 193–94

Runaway and Homeless Youth and Trafficking Prevention Act, 193

runaways, 4–5, 12, 177. *See also* homeless population

Russia, 134–35, 147

Rustin, Bayard, 155, 237n47

same-sex marriage. *See* marriage equality

Sams, Michael, 137

Sanders, Bernie, 149–50

San Francisco, 1–2, 105, 126, 127, 192

Savage, Dan, 134

Sawicki, Jana, 170

SB 1062 (Arizona), 116, 230n51

Scalia, Antonin: constitutional interpretation of, 31; on history and fundamental rights, 220n19; on *Lawrence v. Texas* (2003), 32; on *Romer v. Evans*, 38–39, 40, 42, 123

Schroer, Diane, 46–47, 81–83

Schroer v. Billington, 46–47, 81–83

Scottsboro Boys, 152, 154

Second Amendment (U.S. Constitution), 92–93

Sedgwick, Eve Kosofsky, 12, 71–72, 80, 104

Segura, Gary, 79

Selma, civil rights movement in, 101

Seneca Falls Convention (1848), 101

sex discrimination, 46–47, 50, 103. *See also* employment discrimination; transgender equality; women's equality

sex education, 85–86, 209–10

sex industry: carceral feminism on, 121; LGBT youth in, 129–32, 201–4; in New York City, 130, 166–67; Rentboy.com, 130, 201, 226n59; trans rights in, 130, 132, 201

sexual abuse, 122, 130, 210

sexuality and sexual orientation: D'Emilio on, 161–63; Don't Ask, Don't Tell on, 2, 8, 9, 67–68, 93–94, 103–4; and norm production, 85–88; *Perry v. Schwarzenegger* on, 67–70, 109; sexual object and defining, 136–37

sex workers. *See* sex industry

Shamir, Hila, 244n95

shared custody, 188

Shulman, Sarah, 134

Silbaugh, Katherine, 207

Singh, Nikhil Pal, 152

sit-lie ordinances, 1–2, 105, 192, 242n43. *See also* homeless population

slavery, 37, 106

Slepian, Arthur, 132, 133

small steps theory (Waaldijk), 102

SNAP. *See* Supplemental Nutrition Assistance Program (SNAP)

Snorton, C. Riley, 68

Sochi Olympics. *See* Olympic Games (2014)

social construction argument, 69–70

socialism, 150–54

Social Security system, 152

social welfare system: adoption, 73, 188–92, 209, 241n29; foster care, 73, 188–92, 197, 242n53; Medicaid, 110, 116, 178, 210; SNAP, 98, 110, 116, 120, 175–76. *See also* poverty

sodomy laws, 24–25, 28–29, 32–33, 102, 138. *See also* privacy rights

Solmonese, Joe, 121

Sommers v. Budget Marketing, Inc., 222n76

Sosman, Martha, 34, 74

Southern Christian Leadership Conference (SCLC), 154

Spade, Dean, 82, 197, 227n82

specialization, 64–65
Spina, Francis, 34, 35
spousal abuse, 185–86
standardized testing case, 53
Stevens, John Paul, 31, 92–93
Stolichnaya vodka protest, 134
Stone, Brad Elliott, 68
Stonewall Uprising (1969), 101, 107
Stopbullying.gov, 124
straight identity (term), 217n9
Strauss v. Horton, 224n4
*Stringfellows of New York Ltd. v. City of
New York*, 244n87
substantive vs. formal equality, 45–51,
222n73, 226n74
Sullivan, Andrew, 103, 104, 163
Sunday labor laws, 41
Supplemental Nutrition Assistance Pro-
gram (SNAP), 98, 110, 116, 120, 175–76
Supreme Court. *See* U.S. Supreme Court
survivorship rights, 116
Sweden, 201
Sylvia Rivera Law Project, 122

Take Back Boystown, 126
Taylor, Charles, 158–59, 238n69
"tearoom trade," 68
teleological narrative, 12, 103, 105, 131,
133, 138
Temporary Assistance to Needy Families
(TANF), 120
tender years doctrine, 187–88
Tennessee, 145
Terrorist Assemblages (Puar), 83
Texas, 32, 38, 220n27
Third Branch (term), 24, 218n8
Thomas, Clarence, 31, 32–33, 38, 219n13
Tikkun (magazine), 132
Title VII, Civil Rights Act (1964), 46–48,
50, 63, 81, 90
Title VIII, Civil Rights Act (1968), 156
Title IX, Civil Rights Act (1964), 50, 90
tolerance: Gates on, 126–27; in *Goodridge v.
Department of Public Health*, 86; Taylor
on, 158–59; training in, 123, 135; Walters
on, 223n111
transgender equality: and bathroom access,
48–50, 89–91; in employment, 46–49,

81–83, 89–91; and federal marriage equality, 146; and identification, 82, 197–98,
227n82; police abuse, 204; and rights of
survivorship, 116; in sex industry, 130,
132, 201; in South Asia, 147; in temporary shelters, 194; women's rights claims
as competing with, 90–92. *See also* sex
discrimination; *and under* LGBT *entries
and specific cases*
Transgender Law Center, 130
Transgender Legal Defense and Education
Fund (TLDEF), 116
transgender sex workers, 130, 132, 201
Trump, Donald, 50
Turner v. Safley, 106–7
Twilight of Equality (Duggan), 111

Uganda, 147
Ulane, Karen, 46
Ulane v. Eastern Airlines, Inc., 46
union activism, 153–54. *See also* labor laws
United States v. Windsor, 87–88, 110, 163
universalizing conception, 71
University of California, Los Angeles, 11
Urban Peak (shelter), 193
U.S. Agency for International Develop-
ment, 135, 147
U.S. Constitution: First Amendment, 92,
94, 191, 228n109; Second Amendment,
92–93; Fourteenth Amendment, 27;
Constitution in Exile, 219n13; marriage
equality under, 23, 35; relative stability of,
30–31, 220n26
U.S. Department of Education, 50, 124
U.S. Department of Health and Human
Services, 194
U.S. Department of Housing and Urban
Development (HUD), 178
U.S. Department of Justice, 50, 110–11
U.S. Department of Labor, 47
U.S. Supreme Court: basics of constitu-
tional interpretation, 24, 27–31; and
G.G. v. Gloucester County School Board,
50; *Lochner* era, 25–27, 37, 180; Warren
Court era, 27. *See also* federal judiciary;
and specific cases
usury laws, 41
utilitarianism, 243n67